The Night Chant

A NAVAHO CEREMONY

AMS PRESS, INC.

NEW YORK, N.Y.

WHOLE SERIES, VOL. VI.   ANTHROPOLOGY, VOL. V.

MEMOIRS

OF THE

American Museum of Natural History.

VOLUME VI.

———————

PUBLICATIONS OF

THE HYDE SOUTHWESTERN EXPEDITION.

———————

The Night Chant, a Navaho Ceremony.

By WASHINGTON MATTHEWS.

———————

May, 1902.

Library of Congress Cataloging in Publication Data

Matthews, Washington, 1843–1905.
  The night chant, a Navaho ceremony.

  Reprint of the 1902 ed. published by
Knickerbocker Press, New York, which was issued
as v. 6 of Memoirs of the American Museum of
Natural History, v. 5 of Anthropology, and v. 6
of Whole series, Publications of the Hyde
Southwestern Expedition.
  Includes index.
  1.   Navaho Indians—Rites and ceremonies.
2.   Indians of North America—Southwest, New
—Rites and ceremonies.   I.   Title.   II.   Series:
American Museum of Natural History, New York;
Memoirs; v. 6.
E99.N3M43   1978   299.7   74-7991
ISBN 0-404-11880-1

Reprinted by

AMS PRESS, INC.
56 East 13th Street
New York, NY 10003

from the edition of 1902, New York. Original trim size:
26.5×33.4 cm. Original text area, however, has been
maintained, with the exception of the plates at the end
of the volume, which have been slightly reduced to fit
this format.

First AMS edition published in 1978.

MANUFACTURED IN THE UNITED STATES
OF AMERICA

INTRODUCTORY NOTE.

For several years past the Department of Anthropology of the Museum has been so fortunate as to have the co-operation of Messrs. B. Talbot B. Hyde, and Frederick E. Hyde, Jr., in its special researches in the southwestern portion of the United States. An expedition was organized six years ago for the purpose of making a comparative study of the ancient sites and ruins of the Pueblo region. Much general work has been done relating to the archæology of the region ; and important collections have been added to the Museum, furnishing material for a comparison of the culture of the former inhabitants with that of the several tribes now living in the area under investigation.

In the prosecution of this research a large number of Navaho Indians have been regular employés of the expedition in New Mexico. Gradually there has been brought about a permanent settlement in the Chaco Cañon, where a number of Navahos are constantly employed as workmen, teamsters, herders, and blanket makers, thus affording opportunities for the study of the life and customs of this interesting and industrious people.

The work planned for the expedition includes a study of the tribes in the southwestern portion of the United States and in Northern and Central Mexico. The physical characteristics of the people are being recorded by observations, measurements, photographs, and life masks ; and comparative researches are being made on the crania and skeletons found in the extensive region under exploration. From the results of this carefully planned and extensive research the data will be obtained by which the grouping of the peoples by their physical characteristics will be made, and further light will be thrown on the origin and migrations of the ancient and present inhabitants of the region.

It is well known that Dr. Washington Matthews has for a long time given his attention to a study of the Navaho myths and ceremonies, and about two years ago in a conversation with him on the subject I was greatly pleased to find that he had a large mass of material carefully prepared and nearly ready for publication. Acting in behalf of Mr. F. E. Hyde, Jr., I offered to publish the great ceremony of the Night Chant as a Memoir of the Hyde Expedition in connection with the Museum. Dr. Matthews was delighted with the prospect of seeing the results of his many years of labor made useful to others, and arrangements were made for the completion of the manuscript and for the preparation of the illustrations. This instructive and interesting volume is the result.

Students of American ethnology are thus indebted not only to the indefatigable labors of an ardent and most painstaking investigator, but also to the generosity of an enthusiastic and generous patron of American research.

F. W. PUTNAM,
Curator of Anthropology.

AMERICAN MUSEUM OF NATURAL HISTORY,
NEW YORK,
January 8th, 1902.

[iii]

PREFACE.

During nearly eight years' residence in the Navaho country, in New Mexico and Arizona, I witnessed many celebrations, in whole or in part, of the Night Chant—the ceremony described in the following pages—and I received instructions in its observances, myths, prayers and songs from its priests, whom I employed to come to me and instruct me, often for periods of a month or more at a time. The data obtained were largely studied and arranged while I was absent from the Navaho country. I first witnessed the naakhaí, a rite of the last night of this ceremony, on December 19th, 1880. Since then, the study of the ceremony and the elaboration of the material collected has occupied much of my spare time for this period of 21 years.

Nevertheless, I do not pretend to give a complete account of the ceremony, with all that pertains to it. Could I gather the whole of this lore, it would probably fill two more volumes as large as the present. Not every one of its priests, even, knows all that is to be known about it; there are different degrees of excellence in their education; one may know some particular song, prayer or observance of which another is ignorant. There are auxiliary rites, not known to all shamans, which are supposed to increase the efficacy of the ceremony according to different indications of Indian mythic etiology. One shaman told me that he studied six years before he was considered competent to conduct his first ceremony; but that he was not perfect then and had learned much afterwards.

In many cases, I indicate where my knowledge is imperfect. In many other cases, I am not aware of my own ignorance or only suspect it and do not know its extent. I merely claim to have done my best to search carefully for the truth.

Previous to the publication, in 1897, of my book entitled Navaho Legends[3], I spelled the name Navaho according to the Spanish system, *Navajo ;* but in that and subsequent works, I have spelled it, according to English orthography, Navaho (pronounced Năv′-ă-hō), with an English plural, Navahoes. I have done this because I found that the Spanish spelling is misleading to a great majority of English readers even among the well educated. Although this new spelling has been unfavorably criticised by eminent scholars it has been promptly adopted by scholars no less eminent, and I was not the first to employ it.

Yet I feel that some reason for my action is due to the readers of the present work. If the name Navaho were found anywhere outside of our borders, if it were of undoubted Spanish origin, or if it had been from the first and invariably spelled in one way by Spanish authorities, I should have hesitated to make a change; but the name is found only within our territory, its derivation is questionable, and early Spanish writers spell it in many different ways. There is no reason why we should treat our Spanish predecessors in America with more respect than we have treated our French. We write Wabash instead of the earlier *Ouabache*, Wisconsin instead of *Ouisconsin*, Iowa instead of *Ayouez*, and we have made many such changes in names that were not originally of French origin. Why then not Navaho instead of *Navajo?*

The Navahoes themselves do not use this name; all do not even know it and scarcely any of them pronounce it correctly. They call themselves *Dĭné*, which may be anglicized Dinnay′ and means, simply, People.

Washington Matthews.

1262 New Hampshire Avenue,
    Washington, D. C.,
        December 19th, 1901.

CONTENTS.

PART II. RITES IN DETAIL.

PART III. MYTHS.

CONTENTS.

PART IV. TEXTS AND TRANSLATIONS.

LIST OF ILLUSTRATIONS.

FIGURES, IN THE TEXT.

PLATES, AT END OF VOLUME.

[xiii]

ALPHABET.

The characters used in this work, in spelling Navaho words, are given below, with the value assigned to each character.

VOWELS.

a has the sound of English a in father.
ă has the sound of English a in hat.
ạ has the sound of English a in what.

The sound of English a in hall is often heard ; but it is not constant with all speakers — a as in father often takes its place. It is frequently heard in the word ke*t*án which is here Englished, kethawn. Other sounds of a are heard ; but they are not constant and may be interchanged with those given above.

e has the sound of English e in they. In some connections it varies to the sound of English e in their.

ĕ has the sound of English e in then.
i has the sound of English i in marine.
ĭ has the sound of English i in tin.
o has the sound of English o in bone.
u has the sound of English u in rude.

ai unmarked, or accented on the i (aí), is a diphthong having the sound of English i in bind. When it is accented on the a (ái), or has a diæresis (aï), it is pronounced as two vowels.

ow has the sound of English ow in how. It is heard mostly in meaningless syllables.

A vowel followed by an inverted comma (') is aspirated, or pronounced with a peculiar force which cannot be well represented by adding the letter h.

CONSONANTS.

b has the sound of English b in bat.
d has the sound of English d in day.
d has the sound of English th in that. It is often interchanged with d.
g has the sound of English g in go, or, in some connections, the sound of English g in gay.
g has a sound unknown in English. It is the velar g, like the Arabic *ghain*, or the Dakota ġ.
h has the sound of English h in hat.
h has the sound of German ch in *machen*. It is sometimes interchanged with h.
k has usually the sound of English k in koran ; but sometimes the sound of English k in king.

l has the sound of English l in lay.

l has a sound unknown in English.   It is an aspirated l, made with the side rather than with the tip of the tongue.   It is often interchanged with l.

m has the sound of English m in man.

n has the sound of English n in name.

n has the sound of French n in *bon*.   It has no equivalent in English.

p has the sound of English p in pan.

s has the sound of English s in sand.

s has the sound of English sh in shad.   It is often interchanged with s.

t has the sound of English t in tan.

t has the sound of English th in think.   It is often interchanged with t.

w has the sound of English w in war.

y has the sound of English y in yarn.

z has the sound of English z in zone.

z has the sound of English z in azure.   It is often interchanged with z.

c, f, j, q, r, v, and x are not used.   The sound of English ch in chance is represented by t*s*; that of English j in jug by d*z*.

PART I.

General Observations and Elements of the Ceremony.

General Observations and Elements of the Ceremony.

NAVAHO CEREMONIES IN GENERAL.

1.—A great number of ceremonies are practiced by the Navahoes. The more important last for nine nights and portions of ten days; but there are minor ceremonies which may occupy but a single day, or night, or a few hours. As far as has been learned, the great ceremonies are conducted primarily for the curing of disease; although in the accompanying prayers the gods are invoked for happiness, abundant rains, good crops, and other blessings for all the people. The great ceremonies have, too, their social aspect. They are occasions when people gather not only to witness the dances and dramas, but to gamble, practice games, race horses, feast, and otherwise have a merry time.

2.—Many of the minor ceremonies are also for the healing of disease; but there are others for various occasions, such as the planting and harvesting of crops, the building of houses, war, nubility, marriage, travel, the bringing of rain, etc.

3.—The great ceremonies vary much in popularity. Some are going quite out of fashion and may have but one or two priests surviving. We have accounts, in the legends, of ceremonies that have become altogether obsolete, and of some that are known only by name. There are others in great demand and increasing in popularity.

CEREMONY AND RITE.

4.—Throughout this book, we shall use the noun ceremony, and the adjective ceremonial when speaking of the whole work of the night chant or of any other of the worshipful performances of the Navahoes; and we shall use the noun rite and the adjective ritual in speaking of the minor divisions or acts of the ceremony. These applications of the words in question are, of course, quite arbitrary; but it has been found convenient to adopt them.

PRIESTS.

5.—A priest of one of the great ceremonies is called *hatáli*, which means literally a singer of sacred songs, and is usually translated chanter in this work. Shaman, priest, and medicine-man are used as synonyms. A chanter usually knows but one great ceremony perfectly; for the learning of such demands the arduous study of many years; but he may also know some of the minor ceremonies, and usually, if he is old, he has a knowledge of other great ceremonies sufficient to relate their myths and assist in their performance. He may possess property; but he often makes his living largely by the practice of his ceremonies, for which he obtains liberal fees.

6.—The man who knows only how to conduct one of the minor ceremonies is not called *hatáli*, receives small fees, and devotes his time largely to the care of his flocks or to some other occupation.

THE NIGHT CHANT IN PARTICULAR.

7.—The most popular ceremony, at the present time, is that which is described in this work. The writer has had more opportunities of witnessing it than any other. Nearly all the important characters of the Navaho pantheon are named in its myths, depicted in its paintings, or represented by its masqueraders. Many myths must be told to account for the origin or introduction of different parts of its work among the Navahoes,—myths that indicate the ceremony to be of composite origin. To one who would understand the spirit of Navaho religion, it is most instructive. For these reasons it has been selected for extended treatment.

NAME OF THE CEREMONY.

8.—The name of the ceremony is kléd*z*e *hatál*. This is here translated night chant. The majority of informants have told the writer that the name is derived from kle, meaning night, the postposition d*z*e, meaning toward or pertaining to, and *hatál*, which signifies a sacred song or a collection of sacred songs, a hymnody. One informant averred that the name is derived from a place called Klé*h*alt*s*i or Red Earth Valley, somewhere near the San Juan River, where, it is said, the principal prophet of the ceremony first saw it performed. Although other great ceremonies have nocturnal performances, I know of none but this that enjoins continuous and uninterrupted song, from dark until daylight, such as is heard on the ninth night of kléd*z*e *hatál*, hence the name is peculiarly appropriate.

9.—White men often witness the dance of the last night, or a portion of it, and they usually call it the Yébĭt*s*ai dance, from the most conspicuous character of the night, the Yébĭt*s*ai or maternal grandfather of the gods.

SEASON.

10.—This ceremony must be performed only during the frosty weather, in the late autumn and the winter months,—at the season when the snakes are hibernating. This is the case with all the great nine-days' ceremonies of the Navahoes of which we have learned.

EXPENSES.

11.—The expenses of a healing ceremony are defrayed by the patient, assisted usually by his most intimate relations. The cost of a nine-days' ceremony often amounts to the sum of two hundred or three hundred dollars, not all in cash, but mostly in horses, sheep, and goods of various kinds.   Besides giving a large fee to the principal shaman, lesser fees to assistant shamans, and paying for cotton, blankets, and other articles used in the rites, the patient and his people must feed all those who assist in the ceremony and sleep in the medicine-lodge while work is in progress.   During the last day or two, when visitors gather in great crowds, the patient is not expected to feed these ; they must provide their own food.   On the last night, many who come from the near neighborhood of the lodge bring no food.   After the ceremony they expect to get home in time for breakfast.

ORIGIN.

12.—The ceremonies of the Navahoes have many elements in common with those of the Mokis, Zuñis, and other Pueblo Indians.   The resemblances between Moki and Navaho ceremonies have been pointed out to the writer by the late Mr. A. M. Stephen, who had long studied the cults of both tribes, and held the opinion that the Navahoes learned from the Mokis.   With regard to the night chant at least, this theory is to be doubted.   Some reliance must be placed on the myths, fanciful as they are, and they all indicate that the ancient Cliff Dwellers, and not the inhabitants of the great pueblos, were the principal instructors of the Navahoes.   It is more probable that Navahoes and Mokis derived the rites from a common source, than that one was master and the other pupil.   Apart from the teaching of the myths, there are many reasons for believing that the Cliff Dwellers still flourished when the first small bands of Athapascan wanderers strayed into New Mexico and Arizona from the north.   It is not unlikely, too, that these poor immigrants, ignorant of agriculture, subsisting on small mammals and the spontaneous productions of the soil, may have regarded the more advanced Cliff Dwellers as divine beings, and as such, transmitted their memory in legends.

SYMBOLISM OF COLOR.

13.—In the myths and rites of the night chant, and in other healing ceremonies, the cardinal points of the compass are usually thus symbolized and take precedence in the following order : east, white ; south, blue ; west, yellow ; north, black.   Sometimes the north is represented by a mixture of these four colors.   The zenith is associated with blue in the myths of this ceremony, but not in the acts or sacrifices.

14.—In legends that refer to the underground world, or place of danger (and, it is said, in the rites of witchcraft), the east is black and the north white ; the south and west remain unchanged.

15.—In making the dry-paintings, in decorating the implements and sacrifices, we often see what we may call the law of contrasting colors.   It appears where other requirements of symbolism do not intervene.   According to this, a blue surface is bordered or tipped with yellow, a yellow surface with blue ; a white surface with black, and a black surface with white.   Par. 401.

SYMBOLISM OF SEX.

16.—Of two things which are nearly alike, or otherwise comparable, it is common among the Navahoes to speak of or symbolize the one which is the coarser, rougher, stronger, or more violent as the male, and that which is the finer, weaker, or more gentle as the female. Thus: a shower accompanied by thunder and lightning is called nǐ′ltsabaka or he-rain, while a shower without electric display is called nǐ′ltsabaad or she-rain; the turbulent San Juan River is called *Tó‘baka* or Male Water, while the more placid Rio Grande is known as *Tó‘baad* or Female Water. Other instances of this kind might be cited from the vegetable kingdom and from other sources. As an instance of this principle the south, and the color of the south, blue, belong to the female; the north, and the color of the north, black, belong to the male. The north is assigned to the male because it is to the Navahoes a rough and rigorous land. Not only do inclement and violent winds come from the north, but the country north of the Navaho land is rugged and mountainous—within it rise the great snow-covered peaks of Colorado. The south is assigned to the female because gentle and warm breezes come from there, and because the landscape south of the Navaho country is tame compared to that of the north. See pars. 91, 248.

17.—Another mode of symbolizing sex, shown in wooden kethawns (par. 173) and plumed wands (par. 282), is this: a facet is cut at the tip end of each one designed to represent the female, while no such facet is cut in that of the male. The facets are designed to represent the square dominoes or masks (par. 267) worn by female characters who take part in the rites. The round ends of the other sticks sufficiently represent the round, cap-like masks worn by the male characters. Similar features are to be observed among the sacrificial sticks of the Moquis and other Pueblo tribes. See plate II. E.

THE LAWS OF BUTTS AND TIPS.

18.—Among all the Navaho priests and in all the Navaho ceremonies which the author has seen, a careful distinction is made between the butts and tips of all objects, where there are butts and tips to be considered, and between the analogous basal and terminal, central and peripheral, ends. The central or basal has always preference over the peripheral or terminal. Butt must always correspond with butt and tip with tip. Numerous instances of these laws may be found in the rites: in making and depositing the kethawns (pars. 166, 315); in the skinning of a deer for a sacred buckskin (par. 257); in the making of baskets, plumed wands, and other implements (pars. 281, 288), and in numerous other ways (par. 135).

THE ELEMENT OF LIFE.

19.—In this and other healing ceremonies, since the object is to guard against death and prolong life, it is important that a life element, or what appears to the

Indian mind to be such, should be preserved as much as possible in all articles used. Feathers should be obtained from living birds, or, at least, from birds that have been captured alive and killed without wounding. Eagles are caught in earth-traps in a manner similar to that witnessed by the writer among the Indians of the Upper Missouri over thirty years ago. To get living bluebirds, yellow-birds, and other small birds, the Indian observes them nesting during the day; at night he steals noiselessly to the nest and captures bird, nest and all. Sometimes fledglings are run down before they are able to fly. Many different kinds of pollen are prepared by putting live birds and other animals into corn pollen (par. 186). These must be released alive after being used. If you kill the bird that has entered the pollen, your pollen will be dead medicine, they say. In procuring sacred buckskin (par. 257), they do not choose to flay the deer alive, but think that if they do not wound it, and close the exit of its breath with pollen, a certain vital element remains even though the animal dies; one of its souls may depart, but not all. The stone knife used in the rites must be perfect; if it is broken it is like a dead man, and will ruin the efficacy of the whole work.

GODS OF THE NIGHT CHANT.

20.—The gods of the Navahoes are so numerous that we shall not here endeavor to describe them all; or even all that are mentioned in the myths belonging to this ceremony, or are represented in its rites. Attention will be confined to those mentioned in the Waking Song (par. 470). Such may be regarded as the principal gods of the ceremony.

21.—On the fourth night of the night chant, during the vigil of the gods, twenty masks are displayed on the floor of the medicine lodge; but as five of these, all alike, belong to undifferentiated Yébaad, or goddesses, and two to *H*ast*s*ébaka, or gods, there remain but sixteen different masks, and sixteen different deities to be described on the basis of masquerade.

22.—In the Waking Song, which belongs to the vigil of the gods (par. 470), there are sixteen characters mentioned. All of these are represented by masks, except Estsánatlehi, and one of the masks, that of *H*ast*s*éel*t*odi, has no stanza in its honor at least in the version of the song recorded in this work. The order in which the masks are arranged is different from the order in which the gods are mentioned in the song. In neither list are the gods named in the order of their general importance in Navaho mythology. Below is presented a list of these gods in the order of the song, with numbers indicating the order on which they stand on the list of displayed masks. It is not claimed that the order of stanzas in the song, or of masks in the display, is constant and alike with all shamans.

LIST OF GODS.

23.—The order in which the gods are mentioned in the song, is arbitrarily taken as the order in which to describe them.

(Column A in the order of the song.   Column B in the order of the masks.)

A.	B.
1. *H*ats*s*éyal*t*i.	1.
2. *H*ats*s*é*h*og*an.	2.
3. Dsaha*d*oldz*á.	13.
4. Gá*n*aski*d*i.	9.
5. *H*at*d*asts*ĭ'si.	3.
6. *H*ats*s*ébaka.	4 and 5.
7. *H*ats*s*ébaad.	15 to 20.
8. Nayénĕzg̣ani.	11.
9. *T*o'badz*ĭsts*íni.	12.
10. *H*ats*s*éol*t*oi (same as 7).	16.
11. *H*ats*s*é*lts*i.	6.
12. *H*ats*s*éz*ĭ*ni.	14.
13. *T*ó'nen*ĭ*li.	10.
14. Ts*s*óhanoai.	7.
15. Kléhanoai.	8.
16. Estsánatlehi.	*H*ats*s*éel*t*odi 5 ?

"*H*ATS*S*É," YÉI, YE.

24.—The names of eight gods in the above lists begin with the syllables *h*ats*s*é. This is believed to be a corruption of *h*ast and yéi. *H*ast denotes worthy age or dignity. We have it in the word *h*ast*i'n* (*h*ast-*d*íné), which means a worthy or respected old man, senex,—term sometimes applied to a chief. Yéi, or, in compounds, ye, is a name applied to many Navaho divinities, but not to all. Perhaps we should translate the word as demi-god or genius; but it is not well, with our present knowledge, to try to distinguish by name as a class the yéi from other divine personages. We shall call them all gods. The Zuñi Indians have also an order of gods called by them yéyi. The yéi seem more numerous than those which may be regarded as higher gods. Thus, while there is but one Est-sánatlehi, and but one Nayénĕzg̣ani, there are several *H*ats*s*éyal*t*i and several *H*ats*s*é*h*og̣an, who are chiefs among the yéi. They are said to dwell in different localities, and in prayers to them (par. 613) the home is mentioned of the god to whom appeal is specially made. Ts*s*ĕ'na*h*altsi or Ts*s*ĕ'n*ĭ*tsi (par. 568) Tse'gi'hi,[1] the White House (par. 390) in the Chelly Cañon, and the sacred mountains of the Navaho land are important homes of the yéi.

25.—For etymological reasons it is believed that the word should be written *h*astyé, but it is not so pronounced. The combinations of dy and ty (y consonant) present difficulties to the human tongue even among civilized people, as is well known. There are many among us who say " Don't choo," for " Don't you." Such is the difficulty, it is thought, that makes the Navaho say "*h*ats*s*é." In reducing to writing an oral language, it is often difficult to decide how far we shall be guided by our grammatical surmises, or knowledge even, and how far by our ears.

*H*ASTSÉYAL*T*I OR YÉB*Ĭ*T*S*AI.

26.—The name of this divinity comes from *h*ast*s*é and yal*t*í, to speak, he speaks, and is translated Talking God, Talking Elder or Chief of the Gods. He is also known as Yéb*ĭ*t*s*ai or Maternal Grandfather of the Gods. He is the most important character of this ceremony, and as he is the leader of the public dance on the last night, white men who often witness this dance speak of it as the Yéb*ĭ*t*s*ai dance (par. 9).

27.—Although called Talking God, the man who personates him in the rites never speaks while masked ; but makes signs and utters a peculiar whoop or call, which we attempt to represent by the spelling " Wu'hu'hu'hú." But in the myths the god is represented as speaking, and as being usually the chief spokesman of the yéi, although he always announces his approach by his characteristic call four times uttered. He is often mentioned in story and addressed in prayer as if there were but one ; but it is evident from the myths, prayers, and songs that the Navahoes believe in many gods of this name, since they often distinctly specify which god is meant by naming his home in connection with him.

28.—*H*ast*s*éyal*t*i is a god of dawn and of the eastern sky. He is also a god of animals of the chase, although he is not supposed to have created them. In various myths, as well as in the rites, he is always associated with *H*ast*s*é*h*o*g*an and is apparently about equal in importance with the latter, like the peace-chief and the war-chief of some Indian tribes. In some tales and songs the one appears the more important, in some the other. There are people who say that *H*ast*s*éyal*t*i is the more beneficent of the two, and would more frequently help men in distress, if his associate would let him ; yet both are constantly represented as benevolent deities who take a deep interest in human affairs. According to some shamans he is a god of corn, but there are certainly other corn gods.

29.—The personator of *H*ast*s*éyal*t*i has his whole body clothed, while most of the representatives of the other gods go nearly naked. The proper covering of his torso is a number of finely dressed deerskins, placed one over another and tied together in front by the skins of the legs ; his leggings and moccasins are of white deerskin ; but of late years the masquerader often appears with calico shirt and pantaloons cut in Navaho fashion, or even in a white man's suit.

30.—The mask of *H*ast*s*éyal*t*i is the only white one seen in the ceremony. It is the caplike or baglike mask common to all male characters (par. 266). The circular holes for mouth and eyes are each surrounded with a peculiar symbol. This is said to represent a mist arising from the ground and a rain-cloud hanging above. Ascending from the mouth toward the top of the mask is the symbol of a corn-stalk with two ears on it. At the bottom of the mask is a transverse band of yellow, to represent the yellow evening light, crossed by eight vertical black strokes to represent rain. When worn in the dance, it has a fringe of hair from side to side over the top ; two tails of the black-tailed deer hanging over the forehead ; at the back a fanlike ornament of many (6 to 12) eagle-plumes, and, at the base of this, a bunch of owl-feathers.   A large collar of spruce conceals the yellow band under the chin.   (Plate III, A.)

31.—*Hastséyalti* appears in three of the dry-paintings reproduced in this work.   In plate II, D, he is shown in the north bearing his healing talisman or alíli (par. 285).   In plate VI, he is depicted in the east with a bag made of the skin of Abert's squirrel (*Sciurus aberti*), which is his special property.   In plate VII, he is drawn in the northwest corner and again with his bag of squirrel-skin. In plates VI and VII, his mask is shown ornamented with a number of erect eagle-plumes such as are borne on the mask of the Yébĭtsai in the dance ; but in plate II his mask is shown without these plumes, for in the scene of succor here represented, the plumes are rarely worn.   In all the pictures he is painted as dressed in white and " His white robe of buckskin " is the distinctive part of his attire mentioned in the Waking Song (par. 470).   The general dress and adorn-ments of the personator are shown in all the figures to which reference is made ; but the deer-tails and corn-symbol on the mask are omitted, while ornate skirt-fringes and pouch are added.   The red margin around the head represents the fringe of hair and furthermore sunlight.   The red margin on the body also rep-resents sunlight.   The Navaho artist does not confine the halo to the head of his holy one.   The triangular object in three colors, yellow, blue, and black, at one side of the neck, denotes the fox-skin collar which the personator wears sometimes, but never in the dance of the last night.

HASTSÉHOGAN.

32.—The name of *Hastséhogan* is derived from *Hastsé* and *hogan*, a house ; it may be translated Elder or Chief House God or simply House God.   Along with *Hastséyalti* he is one of the leading characters in each of the local groups of divinities who dwell in caves, deserted cliff-houses, and other sacred places of the Navaho land.   The House Gods of Tse'gíhi, Tsĕ'nitsihogan, Kininaékai, and the seven sacred mountains [2] are those chiefly worshipped in this ceremony.   He is often mentioned as if there were only one ; but a careful examination of the myths reveals that the Navahoes believe in many of these gods.   In our earlier studies of their mythology it was thought that *Hastséhogan* as well as other yéi mentioned as having many dwellings, might be only one god with many local manifestations, like the tutelary divinities of the heathen Aryans ; but our present interpretations of the myths and rites lead us to think that the Navahoes believe in many different individuals of this name, and of other names, among the yéi. In many of the myths it is indicated that he is inferior to *Hastséyalti* ; but in others he is represented as equal or even superior to the latter.   Being directly ques-tioned some shamans declare the equality of these gods, while some declare the superiority of one or the other.   Like *Hastséyalti*, this god is a beneficent char-acter, a friend to man, and a healer of disease ; yet the prayers indicate that all the beneficent gods are supposed to cast evil spells on men.   He is a farm god as well as a house god and is said to have orginated the Farm Songs of the night chant.   In the songs of pars. 320 and 333, *Hastséhogan* is alluded to as the superior.   See also par. 818.

33.—*Hastséhogan* appears in acts of succor, and he is usually one of the gods who go on begging tours; but he is rarely seen in the naak*h*ái or dance of the last night.   His call may be approximately represented thus: "Hahuwá, Hahuwá."

34.—*Hastséyalti* is a god of dawn, and of the east; his companion, *Hastséhogan*, is a god of the west and of the sunset sky.   In the myths, the two gods come often together and so they do in the acts of succor, where *Hastséyalti* usually takes precedence.

35.—In the rites, the personator wears a collar of spruce or one of fox-skin, a blue mask decorated with many eagle-plumes and owl-feathers, moccasins, black shirt, leggings and sometimes stockings of Navaho make.   The shirt and leggings should be of buckskin, but of late years, they are not often of this material. His proper implement is a staff; but he does not always carry it.

36.—The mask is the blue mask of the *Hastsébaka* (par. 61) but it is trimmed differently.   Its blue face represents the sky.   Below the mouth is the broad horizontal band of yellow (seen in all male masks), crossed by four pairs of vertical black streaks.   At the back of the mask there is a fanlike bunch of eagle-plumes of some even number, from 6 to 12, and a bunch of owl-feathers, both similar to those that deck the mask of *Hastséyalti*.

37.—The staff, or gĭs, is of cherry, a natural yard in length, blackened with sacred charcoal (par. 214) streaked transversely with white, adorned with a whorl of turkey-feathers and two downy eagle-feathers.   Attached below the whorl is a miniature gaming-ring of yucca and two skins of bluebirds.

38.—*Hastséhogan* is represented only once in the dry-paintings copied in this work,—in the picture of Whirling Logs, shown in plate VI.   In this he is depicted in the west, staff in hand, punching the cross of logs to make it whirl. The various points in dress and accoutrement, mentioned above, are symbolized in the picture.   Instead of the symbol of a fox-skin collar, which drawings of other gods have, he is depicted as having at the neck an otter-skin from which depend six deerskin strings with colored porcupine-quills wrapped around them. The starlike figures on the shirt indicate quill embroideries with which the buckskin shirt was embroidered in former days; they also symbolize sunlight.   The red margins symbolize sunlight also.   No pouch is painted.

DSAHA*D*OLD*Z*Á.

39.—The name of Dsaha*d*old*z*á is said to signify Fringe Mouth, and although there are many gods of this name, it is considered advisable often to use it as a proper noun.   There are two kinds of these divinities: Tsĕ′nitsi Dsaha*d*old*z*á or Fringe Mouths who dwell at Tsĕ′nitsi*h*ogan (par. 568), designated sometimes as

Fringe Mouths of the Land, and *Tha*'tládze Dsaha*d*oldzá or Fringe Mouths of the Water. These gods are mentioned in the myths, are represented in one of the dry-paintings, and are named in the Waking Song; but are never seen in the dance of the last night. One appears occasionally in an act of succor.

40.—The man who personates the Fringe Mouth of Tsĕ'nit*s*i has his body and limbs painted, on the right side red, on the left side black. He who enacts the Fringe Mouth of the Water is yellow on the right side and blue on the left. In other respects, the two personators are alike and only one need be described. His trunk and limbs are naked but painted as aforesaid. In addition to the parti-colored painting, he is marked on each side of the chest, on the back over each shoulder-blade, on each arm and each leg, with a zigzag white line to represent lightning. The mark on the arm has always five salient angles, two of which are below the elbow. The mark on the leg is similar to this, but does not extend above the knee. The designs on breast and back are similar to those on the arms. The hands are painted white. There is a white streak on the median line, both behind and before, separating the lateral colorings. In the myths, the gods are said to carry on their persons strings of real lightning which they use as ropes.

41.—The dress, if such it may be called, of the personator, consists of mask with attached collar and crown, a kilt or loin-cloth, moccasins, necklaces, ear-pendants, and bracelets. He carries in his left hand a bow and in his right hand a gourd rattle.

42.—The mask for both kinds of Fringe Mouths is red on the right and blue on the left — a compromise between the colors of both kinds of Fringe Mouths. Down the centre, from top to mouth, is a line, about half an inch wide, usually in black (but once seen in yellow) bordered with white and crossed with several transverse lines in white. There is a tubular leather mouth-piece or bill about three inches long and one inch wide, around the base of which is a circle of coyote fur, which gives name to these gods, although the masks of other gods have a similar fringe. The black triangles that surround the eyes are fringed with white radiating marks. The usual yellow streak appears at the chin, crossed with black lines, to symbolize rain and the evening sky. On top of the mask is a head-dress or crown, made by cutting the bottom out of a basket; it is fastened by thongs to the mask. This crown is, on its lower surface, painted black to represent a storm-cloud, and encircled with a zigzag line to represent chain lightning; it is painted on the upper or concave surface, not shown in the illustration, red to indicate the sunlight on the back of the cloud; it is bordered with ten tail-feathers of the red-tailed woodpecker to represent rays of sunlight streaming out at the edge of the cloud. Ascending from the basket crown is a tripod of twigs of aromatic sumac, painted white; between the limbs of the tripod, finely-combed red wool is laid, and a downy feather tips each stick. See plate III, F.

43.—The bow, painted red and black or yellow and blue according to the colors of the bearer, is ornamented with lightning symbols in white, with three eagle-plumes, and with two whorls of turkey-feathers, one at each end. The rattle is painted white and is usually trimmed with two whorls of turkey-feathers.

44.—All the dress and adornment, above described, are symbolized in the dry-painting; but the zigzag marks in the picture are more numerous than on the body of the personator and they appear on the thigh. A highly embroidered pouch, elaborate fringes to the skirt, and arm-pendants, are shown in the picture which are not on the person of the actor. It is in the picture of the eighth day that the Dsahaᵭoldzá are delineated. Two of the Fringe Mouths of Tsě'nitsi appear immediately to the north of the corn-stalk in the centre; and two of the Fringe Mouths of the Water appear immediately south of the corn-stalk. (Plate VIII.)

45.—The collar of fox-skin is symbolized, as in pictures of other gods, by a triangular figure in three colors, below the mask, to the right, but the neck is also painted blue, which may designate a collar of spruce (par. 524).

GÁ*N*ASKĬ*D*I.

46.—Gá*n*askĭ*d*i signifies a heap or hump on the back, or, freely translated, Humpback. The name may refer to the black bag on the back which looks like a deformity, or to the fact that the actor always walks with his back bent. In this work Gá*n*askĭ*d*i is often used in the singular, and as a proper name, as if there were but one; yet the Humpbacks are a numerous race of divine ones.

47.—Their chief home is at a place called *D*epé*h*a*h*ati*l* (Tries to Shoot Sheep) near Tse'gíhi, a cañon where there are many ruined cliff-dwellings, north of the San Juan; but they may appear anywhere, and according to the myths, are often found in company with the other yéi, and visiting at the homes of the latter. They belong to the Rocky Mountain Sheep People; they may be considered as apotheosized bighorns. In the myth of the Visionary, it was they who captured the prophet and took him to the divine dwellings where he was taught the mysteries of the night chant. Although playing an important part in the myths, Gá*n*askĭ*d*i appears in the rites only on one occasion—the scene of succor on the afternoon of the ninth day, when he comes in company with *H*ast*s*éyal*t*i and Dsaha*d*oldzá. But he does not always appear, even in this scene. Gá*n*askĭ*d*i is a god of the harvest, a god of plenty, and a god of mist.

48.—The personator of Gá*n*askĭ*d*i has his trunk and limbs naked but painted white. His hands are whitened. He wears a mask with crown and spruce collar attached, a cloth around the loins, moccasins, ear-pendants, necklaces, and bracelets. He carries a bag on his back and a staff in his hands.

49.—The mask is the ordinary blue mask of the Yébaka with the fringe of hair removed. The crown, like that of Dsaha*d*oldzá, consists of a Navaho basket from which the bottom has been removed. On the lower surface, it is painted black to represent a storm-cloud and encircled with a zigzag line to depict lightning on the face of the cloud. Ten quills of the red-shafted woodpecker, radiating from the edge of the crown, symbolize sunbeams streaming out at the edge of the cloud. The god is crowned with the storm-cloud. Arising from the crown are two objects intended to represent the horns of the bighorn. These objects are made of dressed bighorn skin, sewed with yucca fibre and stuffed with bighorn hair or the wool of the domestic sheep. They are painted for the most part blue ; but at the base they are black, striped longitudinally with white, and they are encircled with white rings at tip and butt. They are tipped with eagle-feathers tied on with white strings. (Plate III, H.)

50.—The long slender bag made of dressed deerskin which the actor carries on his back is empty ; but it appears full, being distended with a light frame of twigs of aromatic sumac. The bag is painted black, marked on the sides with short parallel white lines, 12 or 16 in number, arranged in three or four rows (to indicate the contents of the bag) ; and at the back, longitudinally with lines of four different colors emblematic of a rainbow. It is adorned on the back with five eagle-plumes and sometimes with five plumes of the red-tailed wood-pecker. The bag represents a bag of black cloud which the god is supposed to carry, filled with fruits and the products of the field. It is the Navaho equivalent for the horn of plenty. The original bag which the god bears is so heavy, it is said, that he is obliged to lean on a staff, bend his back, and walk as one who bears a heavy burden. So the personator does the same.

51.—The staff or gǐs is made of cherry, newly for each ceremony, a natural yard in length. It is blackened with the sacred charcoal (par. 214), painted with white zigzag lines for lightning, and decorated with two whorls of turkey-feathers and with one eagle-feather.

52.—Gánaskǐdi figures are represented in two of the dry-paintings ; in that of the sixth day, where there are two figures, and in that of the eighth day, where there are four. In each painting the figures are in the extreme north and south within the rainbow. All the dress and adornment of the personator, as described above, are shown in these pictures. The fox-skin collar is shown by a triangular figure under the right ear. In addition to all symbols described, the red borders on the body are said to represent sunlight ; a many-colored border at the butt of the wand represents a rainbow ; strings of rainbow are shown securing the bag to the body, and pollen is typified by red powder, thinly sprinkled over the plumes on the back of the bag. See plates VI and VIII.

HÁTDASTSĪSI.

53.—This god does not appear in the ceremony of the night chant proper, but in the variant of it called to'nastsihégo hatál, where the dance of the last night is omitted. Nevertheless his name is mentioned in the Waking Song (par. 473), and a mask is shaken for him on the night of vigil. His home is at Tsásitsozsakád (*Yucca Angustifolia Standing*), a place near Tse'gíhi.[1]

54.—His personator wears the ordinary mask of the Yébaka, devoid of eagle-plumes, but having many owl-feathers attached. He has a collar of spruce twigs. He is usually clothed in ordinary Navaho dress. In old days he wore white buckskin leggings, and "His white leggings" are the special property assigned to the god in the Waking Song ; but they are rarely worn of late years. He carries on his back a ring about 12 inches in diameter made of yucca leaves and, suspended from this by the roots, a complete plant of *Yucca baccata*. He holds in his hands scourges made of yucca leaves. The ring is like that used in the game of nánzoz and indicates that the god is a great gambler in nánzoz. The yucca scourges are made from leaves taken from the east and west sides of the plants. For the yucca which hangs at the back, they select one whose root sticks well out of the ground and they kick this out of the ground with the foot.

55.—If *Hátd*asts*ĭ*si is to be represented in the ceremony, a kethawn is sacrificed to him. This is of reed, three finger-widths in length, painted black with a design representing a ring in white and a yucca plant in blue. It is buried east of the lodge at the foot of a yucca. Before the kethawn is taken out, a dialogue prayer is said, which begins thus : "*Hátd*asts*ĭ*si, I have made your sacrifice, I have prepared a smoke for you" ; and then it proceeds much in the same form as other prayers that pertain to kethawns. Ten songs belong to the kethawns but the god has no "song of his own," that is, none which he is represented as singing himself. He is never depicted in the dry-paintings.

56.—The representative of this god appears on the ninth day of the ceremony in the afternoon. He goes around among the crowd of visitors to cure disease ; but he never essays to treat the patient who is the patron of the ceremony. He treats simply by flagellating the diseased part. For instance, if a man has lumbago and wishes treatment, he bends over to the west and presents his back. The actor whips him on the back, holding the scourge in his right hand. First he whips with one scourge holding its point toward the north ; then he changes the wands in his hands and strikes again, holding the point toward the south. After he performs these acts, he turns around, sunwise, from the patient, bends low, and utters his call, which is a low hoarse moan something like the lowing of a cow. Anyone who desires may have his services. When he has whipped all the applicants he can find, he returns to the medicine-lodge and removes his divine belongings.

*H*ASTSÉBAKA OR YÉBAKA.

57.—*H*astsébaka means a male *hast*sé (par. 24), a male chief or elder of the gods. It refers to many, but it is also used in the sense of a proper noun. In the list of gods given in paragraph 23, at least eight are regarded as *H*astsébaka and perhaps there are others. All male characters bearing the title *H*astsé in their names belong to this class, also all those who wear the *H*astsébaka mask. The following is a list of such in the order of the song : 1, *H*astséyal*t*i ; 2, *H*astséhogan ; 3, Hátdastsïsi ; 4, Hastsébaka ; 5, Hastséltsi ; 6, Hastsézïni ; 7, Tsó-hanoai ; 8, Kléhanoai.   Of these all but 1 and 6 wear the mask of Hastsébaka. But the list may be more extensive.   In the prayers, the name is applied to the Atsálei and other gods.

58.—Of these it will be seen that one is known by no other name than Hast-sébaka.   He is the undifferentiated chief of the gods, and is the one referred to in song and story under this name when some special definition is not given. Yébaka, which may be translated male divinity or god, is often used as a synonym of Hastsébaka.   Men in the guise of Hastsébaka take part in many acts of succor.   They appear in the dance of the last night most conspicuously.   Then four of them perform as Atsálei or First Dancers, in the beginning of the rites, and six are constantly seen in the naakhai throughout the night.

59.—The dress of the personator, as he appears in the naakhai,— his typical costume we may call it,—is this :   His naked trunk, upper extremities, and thighs are whitened.   He wears a mask ; a collar of spruce ; a loin-cloth of scarlet baize or any rich, showy material ; a leather belt adorned with large plates of silver ; a fox-skin, tail downwards, hanging from the belt behind ; dark woolen stockings of Navaho make ; red garters of Navaho make ; moccasins ; ear-pendants ; bracelets, and as many necklaces of coral, shell, and turquoise, mostly borrowed, as he cares to wear.   He carries in his right hand a gourd rattle, painted white and sometimes decorated with spruce twigs, and in his left hand a bunch of spruce twigs as a wand, which for security is attached to his mask with a string of yucca fibres.

60.—In scenes of succor he often wears a collar of fox-skin instead of spruce and he carries implements other than the gourd rattle and bunch of spruce twigs.

61.—The mask is a cap or helmet of sacred buckskin, painted blue to represent sky, with a horizontal yellow streak at the bottom to symbolize the evening sky ; this is crossed by four pairs of perpendicular black lines to represent rain. A fringe of hair, usually horsehair or wool, crosses the mask from side to side over the crown of the head.   This fringe is constructed on a neatly braided base, is attached to the mask with thongs, and is easily removed.   It may be of long flowing hair, or of short bristly hair or yarn about two inches long.   Sometimes it is seen of a dull red or yellow color and sometimes of black.   The small eye-holes are surrounded by black triangles.   At the mouth a leather tube, with longitudinal slits, projects four finger-widths, or about two inches, from the face ; it is two finger-widths in breadth (pars. 138, 140).   In two of the six Yébaka masks, this tube is terete or pointed, somewhat in the shape of a bird's bill, and in four it is truncated.   Its base is surrounded by a fringe of fur.   When dressed anew for the rites, two eagle-plumes are added and a bunch of owl-feathers below the plumes.   There is a special way of affixing the eagle-plumes ; they are securely tied with yucca fibre to a peeled forked twig of aromatic sumac, so as to stand erect, separate, and in a constant position ; the sumac twig is tied to the mask by thongs which are permanently joined to the mask for this purpose.   A downy eagle-feather is attached to the top of the mask.   In one mask measured, the following dimensions were found : size of painted face, 10 x 12 in. ; from eyes to crown of head, 4 in. ; from eyes to mouth, 2 in. ; between eyes, 4 in. ; length of mouth-tube, 2 in. ; eye-holes, ½ in. ; black triangles around eyes, 1 in.

62.—The *Hast*ʂ́ebaka, thus dressed and adorned, are shown best in the dry picture of the seventh day (plate VII), which represents the naak*h*aí dance, as it is said to have occurred among the gods.   But some slight differences between picture and description may be observed : brilliant pouches and skirt-fringes are added ; the legs are yellow to indicate that the gods dance knee-deep in pollen ; the forearms are also yellow ; pendants of fox-skin hang from the arms.   The red border around the mask shows not only the red hair, but sunshine.   The red border on the body indicates sunshine also.

63.—In the dry-painting of the sixth day (plate VI) four Yébaka are indicated, one at each extremity of the cross.   They differ from the characters of the pictures of the seventh day in these particulars : they have black shirts, no kilts or loin-cloths, and their legs are not shown,—this is to indicate that they are sitting, not dancing.   In the picture that belongs to the scene of succor of the fifth day (plate II, C), if the patient be a male, a Yébaka is drawn in the centre of the picture, devoid of arm-pendants and of the spruce wands and rattles which are implements of the dance.

*H*AST*S*ÉBAAD OR YÉBAAD.

64.—*H*ast*s*ébaad, or *H*ast*s*ébaadi, means a female *h*ast*s*é or chief of the divinities.   The word Yébaad, meaning a female yéi or god, is often used as a synonym. Both words may properly be translated goddess.

65.—Every Navaho god is supposed to have a wife—there are no celibates on the Navaho Olympus—and, although the Navahoes are polygamists, their divinities, with the exception of the Sun Bearer, seem satisfied with one wife each.

66.—Among the Navahoes, the position of the woman is one of much independence and power, and, as might be expected, among their divinities, the female is potent and conspicuous.   The goddesses appear in rites of succor or exorcism. On the last night of the night chant they do not take any part in the performance of the Atsá*l*ei or First Dancers ; but in the dance of the naak*h*aí, which occupies most of the night, provisions are made for the appearance of six, though that number is not always present.

67.—Six masks, all alike, are provided for these goddesses.   In the Waking Song, one of these masks is shaken for *H*ast*s*éol*t*oi, the goddess of the chase, and one for an indefinite *H*ast*s*ébaad ; but the other four are not shaken and there is no song for them.

68.—In most cases, the character of the goddess is taken by a boy, or a man of low stature.   This male personator is mostly naked, the exposed parts of his body being painted white.   He wears an ornate skirt or scarf around the hips, a belt ornamented with silver from which a fox-skin depends behind, dark woolen stockings of Navaho make, moccasins, ear-pendants, necklaces, bracelets, and the mask of the Yébaad, with a collar of spruce twigs. In the dance, he carries a tuft of spruce twigs in each hand and he sings in falsetto.

69.—In the dance of the last night the character is sometimes assumed by women. The female personator is fully clothed in an ordinary Navaho woman's dress—either old- or new-fashioned ; she wears the collar of spruce, but no fox-skin behind, and no blanket. She dances with a step different from that of the male personator and holds her hands in a different position (par. 631). Other-wise she performs all acts in a manner similar to that of the male actor.

70.—The mask differs much from the male mask. While the latter, like a bag inverted, covers the entire head and neck, and completely conceals the hair of the wearer, the former conceals only the face and throat and allows the hair to flow out freely over the shoulders. The Yébaad actor never wears the hair bound up in a queue. While the male mask is soft and pliable, the female mask is stiff and hard, being made of untanned skin. It is nearly square in shape ; the top is always slightly rounded and in some cases the base is a little broader than the top. There is a flap or wing, called the ear, on each side about two inches broad, as long as the margin of the mask proper, and indented or crenated on the outer margin. The margins are all alike in each set of masks but not in any two sets. The hole for the mouth is square. The holes for the eyes are triangular,—the apices pointing outwards. The mask is painted blue, the ears white, a square field around the mouth-hole and a triangular field around each eye-hole are black. The kethawns and the dry-paintings repre-sent the female mask as having a yellow horizontal stripe at the bottom, like the male masks ; but this has not been observed on any mask ; instead there is sometimes a horizontal line of bead-work, about two inches broad, not uniform in design on all masks. From the bottom of the mask proper, i. e., the piece of raw-hide, a curtain of red flannel or red baize, or other material, usually hangs. Sometimes this curtain is covered with beads, or adorned with fragments of shell. No definite rules seem to prevail with regard to this curtain. There is always a piece of abalone (haliotis) shell secured with thongs in the centre at the top, behind which feathers of turkey and eagle, or of red-shafted wood-pecker, are stuck. The mask is tied to the head by means of long buckskin strings. Sometimes there is a fringe of short hair at the upper margin. (Plate III, D).

71.—The Yébaad may be represented in four dry paintings, in a celebration of this ceremony, but they always are shown in three. If the patient be a female, then on the fifth day, in the act of succor, the small picture appropriate to that occasion (plate II, D) has a Yébaad figure in the centre. In the picture of the sixth day, that of the Whirling Logs (plate VI), the four most central figures are those of Yébaad, shown in a sitting posture and carrying in each hand a wand of spruce twigs such as the goddess carries in the dance. In the great painting of the seventh day, which represents the naak*h*aí dance (plate VII), six Yébaad are depicted, in the east, dancing in a row and holding up their hands with a bunch of spruce in each.   In the great painting of the eighth day (plate VIII) there are four yébaad figures, one in the centre of each group of three divinities.   Here each goddess is represented with a bunch of spruce twigs in one hand and a sacred jeweled basket in the other.

72.—The most important distinction presented in the pictures between male and female characters is that the former are shown with round masks and the latter with quadrangular masks.   The quadrangular mask always indicates the female and it appears not only on the figures of the Yébaad but on those of the rainbow as shown in the plates.   The four-cornered mask, and with it the female sex, is symbolized on kethawns and plumed wands by a square facet cut at the tip end.   See plate II, E.

NAYÉNĔZGANI.

73.—This name is derived from aná or na, an alien or enemy; yéi or ye, a god; nezgá, to kill with blows of a heavy weapon, to club to death; and the suffix ni which denotes personality.   The Anáye are the alien or inimical gods mentioned in the Origin Legend; they are the equivalent of the giants of Aryan and Semitic mythology; hence Nayénĕzgani, or Nagénĕzgani as some pronounce it, may be translated Slayer of the Alien Gods, or Giant Killer.

74.—Nayénĕzgani seems, after his mother, Estsánatlehi, and perhaps after his father, T*s*óhanoai, the sun god, to be regarded by the Navahoes as their most potent divinity.   He is the first and most powerful of the war-gods.   The third section of the Navaho Origin Legend[3] is largely devoted to telling of his deeds of prowess by which he destroyed the Alien Gods or giants, who had nearly exterminated the human inhabitants of the world.

75.—It is not stated in the legend what name was given to him in infancy. When his father, the Sun Bearer, sent him down from the sky to the top of Tsótsïl[4] he received the name of Bï*l*naznolklï′*s*i, which means, Descended with the Lightning.   It was not until after he had killed his first enemy—" counted his first *coup*," as the northern Indians say—that he received the name of Nayénĕzgani.

76.—Some of the numerous songs about the war-gods give, in addition to Náyénĕzgani and *T*o'bad*z*ïst*s*íni, two other names: *L*éyaneyani, or Reared beneath the Earth, and Tsówenatlehi, or the Changing Grandchild.   Some say that *L*éyaneyani is but another name for Nayénĕzgani and that Tsówenatlehi is but another name for *T*o'bad*z*ïst*s*íni; but the author inclines to agree with those who think otherwise.   If the former have the better version, then *L*éyaneyani is the infant name of the Giant Killer.   Those who hold that Nayénĕzgani and *L*éyaneyani are one and the same person, say that when the child was little his mother hid him under the ground to save him from the clutches of Yéitso[5] and other giants.   In the Navaho Origin Legend, a long account is given of a hero named *L*éyaneyani who slew his witch sister, but did not otherwise greatly distinguish himself.   This is probably the *Léyaneyani* referred to in the songs, as the third war-god.   Of Changing Grandchild, or the fourth war-god, nothing has been learned. Nayénĕzgạni and *To'*badẕĭstsíni are the principal gods of war and have their counterparts in the myths of many races both of the Old and of the New World.   It is probable that the other two gods are placed in the rank of the war-gods more for completing the sacred number four and allowing the formation of four stanzas to a song, than for any other reason.   See par. 761.

Fig. 1. Medicine-lodge viewed from the south.

77.—Nayénĕzgạni is a beneficent god, a divine knight errant, always ready to help men in distress.   When properly propitiated he is prompt to cure disease, particularly such as is produced by witchcraft. Men in danger, and warriors going to battle, pray and sing to him.   No god is more frequently referred to in the song and story of the Navaho.   Prayers and sacrifices may be offered to him at any place, but his home is at *To'*yétli, the junction of two rivers somewhere in the valley of the San Juan, and warriors who desire his greatest favor, before setting out on the war-path, go there to offer their prayers and deposit their sacrifices.   He is represented in the Navaho Origin Legend[3] as a changer or transformer who changes creatures that were once injurious to man, into others which will be of benefit to our race in the days to come.

78.—The personator of Nayénĕzgạni appears in the night chant, in two acts of succor; one on the second night (par. 349 *et seq.*), the other on the afternoon of the ninth day (par. 594). His body is nearly naked. He wears a mask; a collar of fox-skin; a cloth of crimson silk, scarlet bayeta, or some other brilliant material around the hips; a belt ornamented with plates of silver; moccasins which are usually but not always of black buckskin; ear-pendants; numerous necklaces of turquoise, shell, and coral, most of which are borrowed from friends; and bracelets. He carries in his right hand a large stone knife or pe*sh*ál, which is his special weapon or charm, although in the Waking Song, "His stone necklace" is the property mentioned. His trunk and limbs are painted with sacred charcoal; his hands are whitened with gle*s* (white clay), and on his body eight peculiar marks, symbols of bows, are drawn in gle*s*. These symbols are placed as follows: one on each side of the chest; one on each side of the back, partly over the shoulder-blade; one on each arm extending both above and below the elbow; one on each leg, below the knee, on the outer aspect. The bows are all shown as bent in one direction—to the right of the man who executes the painting as he stands at work. The symbols are painted one at a time, that on the left leg first, that on the left side of the back last. The five lines of

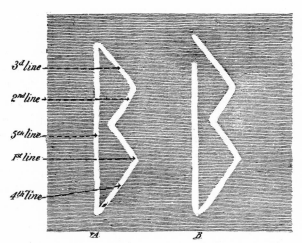

Fig. 2.   Bow symbols on body of Nayénĕzgạni.   *A*, closed or complete symbol.   *B*, open or incomplete symbol.

which the symbol is composed are always drawn from above downwards, and in an established order as shown in the diagram, fig. 2, A. All the bows are represented as strung, except those first and last painted and these are represented as unstrung, (fig. 2, B.)

79.—The mask is the usual inverted buckskin bag of the male character. It is painted black with sacred charcoal and has a lightning symbol on one cheek, either right or left, consisting of five white, narrow, zigzag parallel lines which present, each, four obtuse angles. To each of the holes for eyes and mouth is affixed a brilliant white sea-shell. The shells are said to typify, on the eyes, the way in which the god's orbs glared when he killed Yéitso [5]; but why the shell is put on the mouth is not obvious unless it be for symmetry. A fringe of hair is secured to the seam of the mask, from side to side; this is usually red or yellow and may be either flowing or stiff. A turkey-plume and a downy eagle-feather are attached at the top of the mask, at one side of the centre. See plate III, C.

80.—No picture of Nayénĕzgạni has ever been seen by the writer and he has been assured that none is ever made in the dry-paintings. The kethawn sacred to him is described and figured elsewhere (par. 590).

TO‘BADŽĬSTSÍNI.

81.—To‘badžĭstsíni signifies Child of the Water.   The name is derived from to‘, water ; ba, for him ; džĭstsín, born ; and the personal suffix ni, i. e., Born for the Water.   But the expression bádžĭstsin designates the relation between father and child (Sádžĭstsin = born for me, or my child.   Nádžĭstsin = born for you, or your child).   The reason for the name is explained in the Origin Legend [3] where it is related that his mother conceived of a waterfall.   This was apparently his first name and he continues still to be known by it.   At the scalp-dance, or victory ceremony, held after he first scalped an enemy (Yéitso [5]) he received the name Naídikĭsi, He Cuts Around, i. e., Scalper ; but this name is now rarely applied to him in song or story.

82.—In the version of the legend to which reference is made, he is represented as the son of Yoɫkaí Estsán or White Shell Woman, a sister, by mythic relationship, to Estsánatlehi ; but some versions say he is the son of Estsánatlehi. Some aver that he is a twin brother of Nayénĕzgạni, but later born ; others that some time elapsed between the birth of the two children.   Notwithstanding that the water is his father, the sun-god speaks of him throughout the myths as his child.

83.—Whether he is cousin or brother to the chief war-god, he is called his brother, according to Navaho custom, and he is always represented as the younger and inferior.   In the legends we are told : that when Nayénĕzgạni kills Yéitso, the giant of Tsóɫsiɫ, To‘badžĭstsíni only lifts the scalp ; that when the former goes forth to fight other giants, the latter remains at home to guard the mothers.   In the Song of the Approach (par. 368) the former is spoken of as striding on the mountain peaks, while the other walks among the foot-hills. In the scene of succor where both divinities are represented, the personator of Nayénĕzgạni leads ; while he who enacts To‘badžĭstsíni follows.

84.—There is distinctly but one To‘badžĭstsíni in Navaho mythology.   His home is with his brother at To‘yĕ‘tli ; but according to the myths he is on very friendly terms with the yéi and other gods, frequently visits them, and is often found in their company.

85.—To‘badžĭstsíni is represented in the same scenes of succor with Nayénĕz- gạni on the second and ninth days.   His personator wears the same scanty attire as does the personator of the elder god, viz : sash or kilt, pendant fox-skin, belt, moccasins (red), jewels, collar, and mask ; but the mask is different ; he carries in his right hand a cylinder of piñon one span long, painted black ; and in his left hand a cylinder of cedar, of the same length, painted red.   These are his special implements or talismans and represent thunderbolts.

86.—His body and limbs are painted with a native red ochre.   His hands are whitened.   Eight marks, which will be called queue-symbols, are painted on his person in the same places as the bow-symbols on Nayénĕzgạni, namely : two on the chest, two on the back, one on each arm, and one on each leg.   As with Nayénĕzgạni, the symbol on the left leg is painted first and that on the left side of the back is painted last. The first and last symbols are incomplete or open at one point as shown in fig. 3, C, the other symbols are complete or closed as shown in fig. 3, A. These symbols are said to represent the scalps of enemies taken by the god. The Navahoes and many other tribes of the southwest wear the hair done up in a queue, which is not allowed to hang low like the Chinese queue, but is tied up close to the occiput; hence the symbol of a queue is also that for a scalp. The symbols left open, indicate that the labors of the god are not yet completed. Each symbol is painted according to an established rule as shown in the accompanying diagram, fig. 3, A.

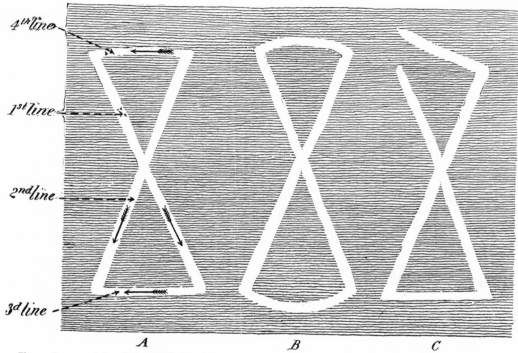

Fig. 3. Queue symbols on body of *To'badzístsíni*. *A*, closed or complete symbol. *B*, a variant of the symbol. *C*, an incomplete symbol. The arrows show direction in which each line is drawn.

87.—The mask is the usual inverted bag made of sacred buckskin. It is painted with red ochre all except a space over the face, triangular in form, with rounded corners. This space is black, bordered with white and large enough to include eye-holes and mouth-hole. On the ground of red ochre, both on the front and on the back of the mask, are painted a number of queue-symbols in white. These vary in number, position, and arrangement on different masks and at each new painting of the same mask; but the number is always a multiple of four. To an angle of each mouth-hole and eye-hole — all diamond-shaped — is attached a white shell. A fringe of red or yellow hair or wool, either stiff or flowing, is attached to the seam across the crown from side to side. A turkey-feather and a downy eagle-feather are fixed to the top of the mask, to one side of the centre. The attached collar is of fox-skin. See plate III, E.

88.—No picture of *To'badz̆ĭstsíni* has ever been seen in the dry-paintings and it is said that none is ever made.

HASTSÉOLTOI.

89.—The name *Hastséoltoi* signifies the Shooting *Hastsé* or Shooting Divinity. Nothing in the name indicates the sex; but we know from the mask and dress worn by the personator, and from the accounts of the medicine-men, that this divinity, although usually personated by a man, is a female. Feminine pronouns will be used in speaking of her and of her personator.

90.—She is the goddess of the chase and of its mysteries. She is the Navaho Artemis. Some speak of her as if there were but one and these say she is the wife of Nayénĕzgạni, the chief war-god; but others speak as if they thought there were many goddesses of the chase and that one dwelt at each one of the sacred places where the yéi have homes.

91.—We can only conjecture why the deity of the chase is a female among the Navahoes as well as among the Greeks and Romans. The reasons given by mythologists for the sex of Diana and Artemis will not apply in the case of *Hastséoltoi*. We may perhaps find an explanation in the Navaho symbolism of sex, described elsewhere (par. 16). Hunting is allied to war, but is a milder and less dangerous occupation; probably the Navahoes regard it as the feminine of war, and have therefore called a goddess to preside over its mysteries, while the "war-medicine" is placed in the keeping of a god.

92.—She appears only once during the ceremony of the night chant and then in company with two war-gods in the act of succor or exorcism on the afternoon of the ninth day (par. 594). The personator is dressed in the old-fashioned costume of the Navaho woman, the textile articles being usually new and of fine quality. She wears the ordinary mask of the Yébaad, which is described elsewhere, and a collar of fox-skin. She is adorned with the usual profusion of Navaho jewelry. She carries on her back a quiver and bow-case of puma-skin, with a bow in the case. She carries two arrows, one in each hand, and these are her special talismans or charms although it is her puma quiver that is mentioned in her stanza of the Waking Song (par. 470).

93.—Each arrow is made of the common reed, and is at least two spans and a hand's breadth long; but the end must be trimmed off three finger-widths beyond a node and, to comply with this rule, the shaft must often be longer than the length mentioned. The arrow has no head. The tip of the shaft is wrapped with fibrous tissue, the so-called sinew, to keep it from splitting; it is covered with moistened pollen, then with moistened white clay or *gles*, and again with moistened pollen. The rules for feathering the shaft are intricate. The feathers must be those of the red-tailed buzzard (*Buteo borealis*) and for both arrows they must be plucked from one bird. Two tail-feathers and one wing-feather, or two wing-feathers and one tail-feather may be used. Each feather is split in two, making six arrow-feathers. If the fletcher selects the former combination of feathers he must put two halves of a tail-feather and one half of a wing-feather to each arrow ; if he selects the latter combination he must attach two halves of wing-feathers and one half of a tail-feather to each arrow. The feathers are secured to the shaft by means of fibrous tissue.

94.—The functions of *Hastséoltoi* in the rite of exorcism are described elsewhere (par. 595). Her cry is a single whoop.

95.—No picture of this goddess is made in the dry-paintings.

HASTSÉLTSI.

96.—The name *Hastséltsi* or *Hastséĭltsi*, is derived from *Hastsé*, a chief or elder of gods, and *litsí*, red ; it may be translated Red God. His body is painted red. This divinity has his principal home at *Litsíthaa'*, or Tsĕ'nahaltsi, Place of Red Horizontal Rock ; but he, or others like him, are spoken of as dwelling at White House, in Chelly Cañon, and at other places where the yéi have their homes. See par. 806.

97.—He is a god of racing. His personator takes no part in the dance or in any act of succor ; he never helps the patient. He appears only on the last afternoon of this ceremony, in that form known as *to'nastsihégo hatál*, where there is no public dance on the last night ; but he does not always appear even then. His function is to get up foot-races ; hence a good runner is selected to enact this character. He goes around among the assembled crowd challenging others, who are known to be good racers, to run with him. He does not speak. He approaches the person whom he wishes to challenge, dancing meanwhile, gives his peculiar squeaking call, which may be spelt " ooh ooh ooh'—ooh ooh'," beckons to him, and makes the sign for racing, which is to place the two extended forefingers together and project them rapidly forward. If he wins in the race, he whips his competitor across the back with his yucca scourges ; if he loses, his competitor may do nothing to him. If the losing competitor asks him to whip gently, he whips violently, and *vice versa* ; but the flagellation is never severe, for the scourges of yucca leaves are light weapons. He races thus some six or seven times or until he is tired ; then he disappears. Each race is only about 200 yards. The people fear him, yet a man when challenged may refuse to race with him. He often resorts to jockeying tricks with his opponent, such as making a false start. He may enter the medicine-lodge to get up a race, but for no other purpose. *Hastséltsi* is a very particular god and likes not to touch anything unclean.

98.—The mask is in shape like that of the yébaad, being a simple domino that only covers the face and throat ; but it is painted differently from the yébaad mask. It is colored red with native ochre ; white circular marks surround the holes for the eyes and mouth ; black semi-circles extend from eyes to mouth on each side. A white shell is attached to each eye-hole and to the mouth-hole, and there is a piece of abalone shell at the top behind which feathers are stuck. See fig. 4.

99.—The two scourges are made of leaves of *Yucca baccata* or *Yucca elata*. They are formed from two leaves ; one taken from the east, the other from the west

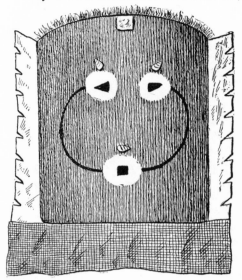

Fig. 4. Mask of *Hastséltsi*.

of the selected plant. These leaves are split in two and interchanged halves are bound together to form a scourge. The personator carries one in each hand. He strikes with the scourge in the right hand, changes the implements from one hand to the other, and strikes again with the other weapon in the right hand. These implements are called béitsis.

100.—If the god is to be represented in the ceremony, he has a cigarette made for him on the morning of the fourth day. It is somewhat like the cigarette of *To'badzĭstsíni*. It is three finger-widths in length. It is painted red, with a representation of the mask on the front and queue-symbols in white on the back. These symbols may be either two or four in number ; if four, two of them are left open or incomplete (See fig. 3, C). There are songs for these cigarettes ; but the songs which the god sung himself are not told. A prayer in the usual form is said for the cigarette ; it begins, " *Hastséltsi*, I have made your sacrifice, I have prepared a smoke for you " ; but the personator is not present when this is repeated. The kethawn is deposited on red ground.

101.—Neither personator, mask, nor cigarette has been seen by the author. The information given above is gathered from different shamans. The accompanying picture of the mask is made from descriptions and rude drawings by Indians ; hence it is not included among the colored illustrations in plate III, which are carefully drawn from the actual objects.

HASTSÉZĬNI.

102.—*Hastsézĭni* signifies Black *Hastsé*, Black Elder of the Gods, or Black God. There are several of these gods ; but unlike the other *hastsé*, they do not abide in different places. Most of them dwell together in one locality called Tsĕ'ni*h*oaïl*y*ĭl (Rock-with-dark-place in-middle), near Tse'gíhi, north of the San Juan River. The myth of the Whirling Logs gives them another home at Tse'zĭ'ni (par. 811). Although there are many of these gods, it is found convenient to speak of *Hastsézĭni* in the singular number.

103.—He is a reserved and exclusive god, not associating freely with other divinities and rarely visited by the latter. This characteristic is often mentioned in the myths. He is the owner of fire—a fire-god. Other gods may possess other things, but all fire is his. He was the inventor of the fire-drill and the first one who produced fire.

104.—His personator is dressed mostly in black — shirt, blanket, breech-cloth, and old-fashioned moccasins. He wears a collar of fox-skin, but has no fox-skin pendant behind. He wears necklaces, which, according to the Waking Song, should be of white shell ; but which in these days may contain coral, turquoise, and other material. He has no cloth or skirt around the loins. His naked lower extremities are painted black, and marked each with a line of white, at the back, extending from the top of the heel to the top of the thigh. He wears a mask. He carries a fire-drill, with the necessary wood and tinder, a fagot, and a bundle of corn-cakes.

105.—The mask is painted black with sacred charcoal (par. 214), marked with white circular spots around the eye-holes and mouth-hole, and a white figure of the shape shown in the illustration, extending in the median line from the circle around the mouth-hole to the level of the eye-holes. It has a fringe of red hair extending over the crown from side to side. See fig. 5.

Fig. 5.   Mask of *H*asts*é*z*ĭ*ni.

106.—The two parts of the fire-drill—the shaft and the stick in which the shaft works—must come from a cedar-tree which has been struck by lightning. Some light bark from the same tree is used as tinder to catch the spark from the fire-drill.

107.—The fagot, called *hanolyél*, is made from the bark of the same stricken cedar-tree that furnished material for the fire-drill. The bark must be shredded from tip end to butt end. The fagot is a span long and of such diameter that it may be completely encircled by the thumb and forefinger of one hand ; it is tied by four strings of yucca fibre at equal distances from one another and from the ends.

108.—The corn-cakes, four in number, are made of blue corn, naněská*d*i,[11] mixed with meal made from corn which a thieving crow has dropped in its flight. Each is a contracted finger-circle in diameter. (See par. 152.) Each has a hole in the middle, perforated with an owl-quill, through which hole yucca fibres are passed and tied so as to form a handle or grip, by which the cakes are carried suspended in one hand.   The yucca fibres used for the fagot and for the corn-cakes must come from one plant and from two leaves, one culled from the east side of the plant and one from the west.

109.—The personator of *H*ast*s*éz*ĭ*ni never appears when the public dance of the naak*h*aí is to occur on the last night ; but only when the variety of the ceremony known as *to*'nast*si*h*é*go hat*á*l is to be celebrated. Then his labors occupy the whole day from sunrise to sunset and he receives a liberal reward for the arduous work, which must be accurately performed.

110.—While the personator of the *H*ast*s*éz*ĭ*ni is gone on his strange journey, the people inside the lodge busy themselves executing a large dry-painting called *Hastsézĭni* beyikál (par. 880).   This picture has a figure of a corn-stalk in the centre and figures of 16 *Hastsézĭni* with their fagots and bundles of corn-cakes ; it remains on the floor of the lodge until the arrival of the personator of the Black God in the evening.

111.—The personator comes to the medicine-lodge early in the morning on the ninth day of the ceremony.   He has himself clothed and painted.   Before he leaves the lodge his fagot is lighted and immediately extinguished with kĕ′tlo (par. 215).   He hides his mask and other properties under his blanket, and proceeds to a point some distance east of the lodge.   Here he puts on his mask and at sunrise begins his slow journey back to the lodge.   He spends all day, until sunset, in re-turning.   He walks a few paces, stops, lights his fagot with his fire-drill, lies down with his back to the fire—a favorite attitude of his according to the myths—and pretends to sleep and make camp.   But he does not lie long ; he rises in a moment and extinguishes his fire, for his little fagot must be husbanded.   He must make it last all day and have some left, when he gets through with his journey in the evening, to deposit as a sacrifice.   Thus he makes a number of symbolic journeys and camps, so timing his labors, that he arrives in front of the lodge and in the presence of the patient when the sun is a hand's breadth above the horizon.

112.—As the personator approaches, a buffalo robe is spread on the ground, near the lodge to the east, the patient is led out to it and places himself on it in the genu-pectoral position with his head to the east.   The personator walks astraddle over the patient from east to west and from west to east uttering as he does so his low, hoarse call, " Waaah."   In the same position, the patient places himself in turn, with his head to the south, to the west, and to the north, while the actor walks over him astraddle back and forth once for each direction.   He helps the patient to his feet and both enter the lodge, the patient leading.

113.—Having entered the lodge, the patient sprinkles the picture with meal, and disrobes to the breech-cloth.   The actor sprinkles it with kĕ′tlo (par. 215) in ceremonial form.   The patient sits on the corn-symbol, facing east.   The per-sonator administers to him a medicinal infusion in four draughts.   He gives a fifth draught to an attendant who squirts it on the palms of the actor in order that the latter may take up the dust from the picture on his moist hands, and apply it to the body of the patient.   The patient then assumes on the pic-ture the position he had on the buffalo robe, before entering the lodge, and the actor walks again astraddle over him back and forth in four different directions.   The patient sits up.   In general all the acts performed on the other great pic-tures (par. 556) are performed in this rite.   The fagot is lighted once more and it is extinguished by the patient, who applies kĕ′tlo with his finger tips, four times, to the flame, while the actor holds the fagot.

114.—When the fagot is thus for the last time extinguished, the actor gives his cakes to the officiating shaman, who keeps a portion for himself and divides the remainder with visiting priests.   The cakes are not eaten ; but are reserved for future magic uses.

115.—The actor goes out of the lodge with the remnant of his fagot, carries it to the west, and hides it under the roots of a cedar-tree where cattle cannot trample on it.   Here he puts on an ordinary blanket, which an accomplice has brought for him, hides under this his mask, and returns to the medicine-lodge, to wash himself and change his dress.

116.—As in the case of the Red God, the above items concerning the Black God are compiled from information given by the priests.   The author has never witnessed the rites or seen the personator.   The war-gods appear with *Hast-sézïni* in his act of succor, but their part in the act has not been satisfactorily noted.

TÓ‘NENILI.

117.—Water-Sprinkler is the literal translation of the name of *Tó‘nenïli*,— the rain-god,— the Navaho Tlaloc.   We speak of him in the singular although there are thought to be many gods of this name.   It seems that the home of the most important rain-god is at Tse‘gíhí, yet one is represented as dwelling at each place where there is a community of yéi.   He is the lord of waters ; but particularly of celestial waters, of precipitated waters.   The ocean, rivers, and lakes seem more under the control of Tiéholtsodi.   When *Tó‘nenïli* wishes to produce rain, he scatters his sacred waters to the four cardinal points and immediately the storm-clouds begin to gather.   He is a water-carrier for the other gods.

118.—His personator appears only on the last night of the ceremony in the dance of the naak*h*ai' (par. 621).   He wears the mask and dress of the ordinary yébaka (pars. 59–61) ; but all the articles of his apparel are of inferior quality.   "Why should he (the god proper) dress well, when he may get his clothes wet with water ?" ask the priests.   The actor has no special implement ; he does not carry a rattle, like the other dancers ; he may bear the bunch of spruce, or the skin of a wild animal, usually a fox-skin, with which he plays his pranks.   In the myths, the god is represented as carrying a wicker water-bottle, or two water-bottles, one black and one blue (par. 708) ; but the personator never carries such a bottle.   The strings of the divine bottles were rainbows.   His clownish actions at the dance are described elsewhere (par. 636).   We attempt to represent his peculiar cry thus : "Yuw yuw yuw yuw."

119.—*Tó‘nenïli* is represented in one of the dry-paintings — that of the naak*h*ai', on the seventh day (plate VII).   He is shown standing at the head of the line of female dancers, in the northwest corner of the picture, dressed and masked like a yébaka, but without a skirt ; his shirt spotted with pollen of all colors.   His hands appear empty to show that he carries no special property.   Rarely he is represented with a wicker water-jar which may be black or blue. See pars. 713, 720.

TSÓHANOAI OR TSÍNHANOAI.

120.—The name Tsóhanoai is said to mean Day Bearer, He Who Carries during the Day. Sometimes the name is given as Tsínhanoai, which seems more modern, as the present ordinary word for day is tsín or dzin. In various previous works the writer speaks of Tsóhanoai as the Sun, in deference to the usual way of denominating sun-gods among other peoples ; but more correctly speaking he should be called a sun-god or sun-bearer, or, as above, Day Bearer ; for the orb of day is to the Navaho, only the luminous shield of the god, behind which the bearer walks or rides, invisible to those on earth.

121.—The name of the solar orb is sa'. According to the Navaho Origin Legend,[3] it was made by the primeval people when they emerged from the fourth lower world to this world. The legend says they made the disk of a clear stone called tsé'tsagi ; around the edge of this they set turquoises, and outside of these they put rays of red rain, lightning, and serpents of many kinds. They selected one of their own number to carry it, and he is now Tsóhanoai.

122.—Much is said about the sun-god in the Origin Legend and in other legends of the tribe. In these tales he appears as a god of the greatest power ; yet his cultus, to-day, is not so important as that of other gods. He is not appealed to as frequently as some others are. Certainly his wife Estsánatlehi and his son Nayénězgani receive more reverence. To him is attributed the creation of all the great game animals ; but he did not create other beings on the Earth. He is not a supreme god and there seems to be no supreme god in the Navaho mythology. He has two wives, one living in the east and one in the west. According to some informants, he walks on a holy trail of sunbeam or rainbow across the sky ; according to others he rides on a blue steed. The latter version is probably modern.

123.—Tsóhanoai is never personated in any of the rites of the night chant and never represented in the dry-paintings. There is a stanza for him in the Waking Song, which alludes to a pendant of haliotis or abalone shell as his ornament, and when this stanza is sung, an ordinary yébaka mask is shaken.

124.—There is so much to be said about this divinity that we shall not devote more space to him here. The reader who desires further information about him, is referred to a previous work of the writer, entitled " Navaho Legends."[3]

KLÉHANOAI OR TLÉHANOAI.

125.—The Navaho word for night is kle or tle. Kléhanoai is said to mean Night Bearer, or He Who Carries during the Night. Such is the name of the Navaho moon-god. He is often referred to by the writer as the Moon ; but moon-bearer, moon-god, or Night Bearer are more accurate terms. To these Indians, the orb of night is only a shield that the god carries.

126.—The moon, according to their legends, was made, immediately after, or at the same time with, the sun, by the primeval people, when they first came up to this world through the Place of Emergence.[6] They made the disk of the moon of tsé‘tso*n*, star-stone, a kind of crystal; bordered it with white shells, and covered its face with sheet lightning and the sacred mixed water, tó‘*l*anats*s*i (par. 209). The one selected to carry the moon was an old and gray-haired person, who had joined them in one of the lower worlds. The tale speaks of him as a man; but he is now the immortal moon-bearer and receives the homage due to a god. There are some reasons for believing that the moon-god is identical with Békots*i d*i, the creator of domestic animals. He receives much less honor than the sun-god and is considered less potent, although in all songs to the Day Bearer, the Night Bearer is mentioned.

127.—The Origin Legend tells us that when Day Bearer and Night Bearer were about to leave the primeval people and ascend to the heavens to begin their labors, the people were sorry, for they loved the twain. But First Man consoled the sorrowers, saying: "Mourn not for them for you will see them in the heavens and all that die will be theirs in return for their labors." Since those days the sun-god demands the life of a Navaho for every day that he passes over the earth and the moon-god demands the life of a Pueblo Indian for every night that he passes.

128.—Kléhanoai, like T*s*óhanoai, is never personated in the night chant or depicted in its dry-paintings. He has a stanza appropriate to him in the Waking Song (par. 470), in which a pendant of white shell is mentioned as his attribute. When this stanza is sung one of the six yébaka masks is shaken.

ESTSÁNATLEHI.

129.—The name of Estsánatlehi is derived by syncopation from estsán, woman, and natléhi, to change or transform. It may be translated Woman that Changes, or Woman that Rejuvenates Herself. This name is given because, it is said, she never remains in one state of development; that she grows to be an old woman, returns at will to the condition of a young girl again, and so passes through an endless course of lives, changing but never dying.

130.—Usually, if you ask a Navaho, who is his most powerful and revered deity, you will be told that it is Estsánatlehi. To those who are accustomed to believe that the position of the female among Indians is a degraded one, it may seem strange that a goddess should hold the highest rank in their pantheon; but a careful study of Navaho sociology shows us that the position of the Navaho woman is one of respect and influence, and that a man owes his chief allegiance to his mother. The myths also make clear the latter fact. As the mother of their greatest war-god, she deserves special honor; but this is not her only claim to worship: she is beneficient, she loves mankind, she dwells in the west and sends from there the plentiful rains of the summer and the thawing breezes of the spring. She created several of the Navaho gentes from her own epidermis and hence is called their mother, and she assisted in the creation of others from ears of corn.

131.—The version of the Origin Legend[8] which the writer most favors tells us that she was created from a small turquoise image into which life was infused by means of an elaborate ceremonial act of the gods ; that she conceived of the Sun and bore the great war-god Nayénĕzgạni ; that *Hast.séyal.ti* was her accoucheur ; that, when her son had slain all the Alien Gods and the children of men began to increase on the earth, she went at the bidding of the sun-god to the western ocean and that she dwells there now on an island which floats on the bosom of the Pacific. She is regarded as the sister of a goddess called Yo.lkai' Estsán or White Shell Woman whom the gods created by ceremonially giving life to a white shell image; who conceived of a waterfall, and became the mother of *To'bad.zïst.síni*, the second war-god. Another version of the Origin Legend says that Estsánatlehi was born of the sky father and the earth mother, and was found as an infant by First Woman on the summit of the mountain of T.solíhi. [2]

132.—Much is said of both of these goddesses in the Origin Legend, to which the reader, who desires to know more about them, is referred. [3] Many songs are sung in their honor. But in song and story Estsánatlehi is always represented as the greater. The cult of White Shell Woman is insignificant compared with that of her sister.

133.—It is conjectured by the writer that Estsánatlehi is a deification of fruitful nature, a goddess of the changing year, and that as such she is properly represented as the wife of the Sun to whom nature owes her fertility : yet there are relations concerning her in the myths which seem to indicate that she has some of the attributes of a moon-deity.

134.—She is never, we are assured, personated in any of the rites or depicted in any of the dry-paintings. When *Hast.séol.toi*, the goddess of the hunt, appears by proxy, in the scene of succor on the ninth day, some Navaho laymen think it is Est.sánatlehi, and so told the writer in the earlier years of his investigations ; but all the shamans questioned declare that such informants are mistaken and that Estsánatlehi is never personated. In the Waking Song she has a stanza in her honor, where " Her plants of all kinds " are mentioned as her special attribute. This is further evidence that she is an apotheosis of Mother Nature. When her stanza is sung one of the six yébaad, or female, masks is shaken.

ESSENTIAL OR SACRED PARTS.

135.—There are certain parts of the body of the patient to which kethawns or other sacred articles are always applied. These parts, which are called, for convenience, sacred or essential parts, are as follows : (1) the soles of the feet ; (2) the knees just below the knee-caps ; (3) the palms, outstretched on the knees ; (4) the chest ; (5) the back between the scapulæ ; (6) the right shoulder ; (7) the left shoulder ; (8) the top of the head ; (9) the right cheek ; (10) the left cheek ; (11) the middle of the mouth. The sacred objects are always applied in the order in which the parts are named (from butt to tip ; see par. 18). Sometimes other parts of the body receive the application—those which are supposed to be the special seat of the disease. Sometimes the article is applied twice in succession at each place—once with the point to the right of the operator and once with the point to the left. After each application (often) a motion is made as if throwing some invisible evil influence out at the smoke-hole.

MEASUREMENTS.

136.—The various properties of this and other ceremonies are made not only according to rigid rules of work ; but according to established standards of measurement.   Of course this rude people have not accurate scales of dimension such as ours ; but they have the natural standards from which most civilized measurements were derived previous to the introduction of the metric system.   It will save much repetition and encourage a more extended and accurate description, if these standards of measure are defined in this section, than if they are left to the section on Rites.   All the measurements here described may perhaps not be employed in the night chant ; but it is deemed best to make here a list of Navaho measurements as complete as our knowledge will permit.   The names of the measures are mostly devices of the author.

137.—I. One finger-width :—the width of the last joint of the index finger, taken on the palmar aspect over the centre or most prominent point.

138.—II. Two finger-widths :—the width of the terminal joints of the first and second fingers on the palmar aspect over the centres ; the fingers being pressed closely together and their tips brought to the same level.

139.—III. Three finger-widths :—width of the terminal joints of the first, second, and third fingers taken under conditions similar to those of measurement II.   On the writer's hand this is equal to $1\frac{3}{4}$ inches.   The majority of kethawns are made of this length.

140.—IV. Four finger-widths:—width of terminal joints of all four fingers of one hand taken under conditions similar to those of measurement II.

141.—V. Six finger-widths:—is found by doubling the measure of three finger-widths.   This is also often applied to kethawns.

142.—VI. The joint :—the length of a single digital phalanx, usually the middle phalanx of the little finger.

143.—VII. The palm:—the width of the open palm including the adducted thumb.

144.—VIII. The finger-stretch :—from the tip of the first to the tip of the fourth finger ; both fingers being extended and abducted while the second and third are flexed.

145.—IX. The span :—the same as our span, from the tip of the thumb to the tip of the index finger, these digits being stretched as far apart as possible.

146.—X. The great span :—from the tip of the thumb to the tip of the little finger, all the digits being extended, while the thumb and little finger are strongly abducted.

147.—XI. The cubit :—from the point of the elbow to the tip of the extended middle finger, the arm being bent.

148.—XII. The natural yard :—from the middle of the chest to the end of the middle finger, the arm being outstretched laterally at right angles with the body ; this on a tall Indian equals about three feet.

149.—XIII. The natural fathom :—measured on the laterally outstretched arms, across the chest from the tip of one middle finger to the tip of the other. This is, of course, twice the natural yard, or about six feet.　Among white men the height usually equals or exceeds this measure.　Among the Navahoes the contrary is the rule.

150.—XIV. The arm-circle :—the arms held in front as if embracing a tree-trunk, the tips of the fingers just meeting.

151.—XV. The finger-circle :—the fingers of both hands held so as to enclose a nearly circular space, the tips of the index fingers and the tips of the thumbs just touching.

152.—XVI.　The contracted finger-circle :—like the finger-circle ; but diminished by making the first and second joints of one index finger overlap those of the other.

153.—XVII. The grasp :—a circle formed by the thumb and index finger of one hand.

154.—In addition to the above measurements, which are used for sacred articles, the story tellers often resort to the expressions, " so big," with explanatory signs, and " as far as."　But such are only temporary makeshifts of the narrator and not accepted standards of measurement.

155.—Of course these measurements vary on different individuals ; hence, where several men work on a numerous series of sacrifices, as in the ke*t*án *l*áni (pars. 399–403), each gauging on his own person, we find objects measured according to the same rule, of different lengths.　In making a series of uniform objects, such as kethawns and plumed wands, it is customary for the operator to measure only one object on his person and then to use this object as a standard for the others.

DRY-PAINTINGS.

156.—An important factor in the greater, and in many of the minor, ceremonies of the Navahoes is the dry-paintings.　Thus the author has always called them. Others, writing later, and describing them among other tribes, speak of them as sand-altars and sand-paintings.　Objections to these terms are : (1) that the pictures are not always painted on sand, neither are the colors all sand ; and (2) that they are not always drawn in places which can be regarded as altars, as, for instance, the tops of sweat-houses.　No doubt objections may be found to the term dry-paintings.

157.—The excellence to which the Navahoes have carried the art of dry-painting is as remarkable as that to which they have brought the art of weaving. Unlike the neighboring Pueblos, they make no graven images of their divinities. They do not decorate robes and skins with moist colors as do the Indians of the plains. They make little pottery and this little is neither artistically nor symbolically decorated. Their petroglyphs are rare and crude ; the best rock inscriptions, which abound in the southwest, are believed to be the work of Cliff Dwellers and Pueblo Indians, or their ancestors. Seeing no evidence of symbolic art among them, one might readily suppose they had none. Such was the opinion of white men (some of whom had lived fifteen years or more among the Navahoes) with whom the author conversed when first he went to the Navaho country, and such was the opinion of all ethnographers before his time. The symbolic art of the Navahoes is to be studied in the medicine-lodge. The Pueblo Indians — those of Zuñi and Moki — and some of the wilder tribes — Apaches and Cheyennes—understand the art of dry-painting ; but none seem to have such numerous and elaborate designs as the Navahoes.

158.—The pigments are five in number ; they are : white, made of white sandstone ; yellow, of yellow sandstone ; red, of red sandstone ; black, of charcoal, mixed with a small proportion of powdered red sandstone to give it weight and stability ; "blue" made of black and white mixed. These are ground into fine powder, between two stones as the Indians grind corn. The so-called blue is, of course, gray ; but it is the only inexpensive representative of the blue tint they can obtain and, combined with other colors, on the sandy floor, it looks like a real blue. These colored powders, prepared before the picture is begun, are kept on improvised trays of pine-bark. To apply them, the artist picks up a little between his first and second finger, and his opposed thumb, and allows it to flow out slowly as he moves his hand. When he takes up his pinch of powder he blows on his fingers to remove aberrant particles and keep them from falling on the picture, out of place. When he makes a mistake he does not brush away the color ; he obliterates it by pouring sand on it and then draws the corrected design on the new surface.

159.—The dry-paintings of the largest size, which are drawn on the floor of the medicine-lodge, are often 10 or 12 feet in diameter. They are sometimes so large that the fire in the centre of the lodge must be moved to one side to accommodate them. They are made as nearly to the west side of the lodge as practicable. The lodge is poorly lighted, and on a short winter day the artists must often begin their work before sunrise if they would finish before nightfall, which it is essential they should do.

160.—To prepare the groundwork for a picture in the lodge, several young men go forth and bring in a quantity of dry sand in blankets ; this is thrown on the floor and spread out over a surface of sufficient size, to the depth of about three inches ; it is leveled and made smooth by means of the broad oaken battens used in weaving.

161.—The drawings are begun as much toward the centre as the design will permit, due regard being paid to the precedence of the points of the compass ; the figure in the east being begun first, that in the south second, that in the west third, and that in the north fourth. The figures in the periphery come after these.   The reason for thus working from within, outward is practical ; it is that the operators may not have to step over and thus risk the safety of their finished work.

162.—The pictures are drawn according to an exact system, except in certain well-defined cases, where the limner is allowed to indulge his fancy.   This is the case with the embroidered pouches the gods carry at the waist.   Within reasonable limits the artist may give his god as handsome a pouch as he wishes. On the other hand some parts are measured by palms and spans and not a line of the sacred design may be varied in them.   Straight and parallel lines are drawn with the aid of a tightened cord.   The naked bodies of the mythical figures are first drawn and then the clothing is put on.

163.—While the work is in progress the chanter does little more than direct and criticise ; a number of young men perform the labor, each working on a different part.   These must be men who have taken the rite of initiation ; but they need not be priests or even aspirants to the priesthood.   It is usually, but not always, the task of the shaman, when the painting is completed, to apply pollen or meal to the divine figures, and to set up the plumed wands around the picture when the rite requires.   When all is done the picture is obliterated, by different methods in different rites.   When no semblance of the picture remains, the sand of which it was made is gathered in blankets, carried to a distance from the lodge, and thrown away, leaving no trace of the work.

164.—The shamans declare that these pictures are transmitted unaltered from year to year and from generation to generation.   It may be doubted if such is strictly the case.   No permanent design is anywhere preserved by them and there is no final authority in the tribe.   The pictures are carried from winter to winter in the fallible memories of men.   They may not be drawn in the summer. The custom of destroying these pictures at the close of the ceremonies and preserving no permanent copies of them arose, no doubt, largely from a desire to preserve the secrets of the lodge from the uninitiated ; but it had also perhaps a more practical reason for its existence.   The Navahoes had no way of drawing permanent designs in color.   When it became known to the shamans (and no attempt was ever made to hide the fact from them) that the author kept water-color drawings of the sacred pictures in his possession, these men, at the proper season, when about to perform a ceremony, often brought their assistants to look at the drawings, and then and there would lecture the young men and call their attention to special features in the pictures, thus, no doubt, saving themselves much trouble afterwards, in the medicine-lodge.   These water-colors were never shown to the uninitiated among the Indians and never to any Indian during the forbidden season.

SACRIFICES, KETHAWNS.

165.—The principal objects of sacrifice are the ke*t*án, whose name is here Englished kethawn and pluralized kethawns.   They are not only sacrifices, but they are messages to the gods. They are very various in character and each one embodies one or more ideas which are usually easily explained. Sacrifices of this character are widely diffused. Most of the Indians of the Southwest use them, or have used them, and the writer has known them to be employed by tribes of the Upper Missouri. The inahos of Japan seem closely allied to the kethawns. Many of them are sacrificed with feathers either attached or enclosed in the same bundle with them, and such are to be classed with the plumesticks of the Zuñi Indians. Much as these sacrifices differ from one another in size, material, painting, accessories and modes of sacrifice or deposit, there are certain rules of general application which will be described here to avoid frequent repetition hereafter. Special rules for special kethawns will be reserved for the part on Rites in Detail. There are two principal kinds of kethawns used in this ceremony, cigarettes made of hollow reed, and sticks made of various exogenous woods.

CIGARETTES.

166.—The cigarettes are usually made of the common reed or *Phragmites communis*. The reed is first rubbed well with a piece of sandstone for the purpose of removing the glossy silicious surface in order to make the paint adhere well. It is next rubbed, for metaphysical reasons, with tsïldïlgï'si or scareweed (*Gutierrezia euthamiæ*) a composite plant growing abundantly in the Navaho country. The reed is cut with a stone knife or arrow head which must be unbroken (par. 19). The law of butts and tips (par. 18) is observed with great pains in making these objects. In cutting up a reed for a series of cigarettes the operator facing east, holds the butt end toward his body, the tip end toward the east, and cuts off that section which comes next to the root. This he marks near its base, on what he calls its front (par. 171) with a single transverse notch, made also with a stone knife. The severed section he lays on a clean stone, buckskin, or cloth, front down, and proceeds to cut off another section from the butt end of the remaining part of the cane. If it is the same length as the preceding piece he marks it with two transverse notches in the manner described. A third section he would mark with three, and a fourth with four notches. These notches are cut in order that throughout all subsequent manipulations the butt may be distinguished from the tip, the front from the back, and that the order of precedence in which they were cut may not be disregarded. But in making the notches the sacred number four must never be exceeded. If there are more than four cigarettes of the same size in one set, the fifth must be the beginning of a new series, to be marked with one notch, while the operator must depend on his memory and on his care in handling to keep the sets separate. The nodes and the adjoining portions of the culm must not be used. They are carefully excluded and split into fragments with the point of a stone knife before being thrown away, lest the gods, coming for their sacrifices, might mistake empty segments for cigarettes and, meeting with disappointment, withhold their succor from the patient. The god, it is said, examines and smells the cigarette to see if it is made for him ; if he is pleased with it he takes it away and rewards the giver.

167.—The second section is laid south of the first and parallel to it, the last section is placed farthest to the south, the order of precedence being from north to south (left to right), when sacrifices are laid out in a straight line in the east. In the subsequent operations to be described, such as painting, inserting feathers and tobacco, pollenizing, "lighting," and sacrificing, the cigarettes are always handled in the order of from left to right. If there is an order of precedence among the gods to whom they belong, the higher god owns the more northern sacrifice, the one that comes from nearest the butt.

168.—The cut ends of the section are next ground smooth on a stone, and a splinter of fresh yucca leaf, long enough to protrude at both ends is inserted to serve as a handle and support while the cigarette is being painted. A thin slice of yucca leaf is also used as a brush, and curved sections of the leaf are commonly used as saucers to hold the paints. The gummy juice of yucca leaf is mixed with the paints to make them adhere when dry. Fig. 14 shows how they are arranged when the paint is drying.

169.—When the painting is completed a small pledget of feathers is inserted into the hollow of each section, at the tip end, and shoved down toward the opposite extremity, to keep the tobacco from falling out. The pledget consists usually of feathers of bluebird and yellow warbler and an owl-quill is, in most cases, the implement with which the wad is shoved in. The sections are then filled with some kind of tobacco,[7] native to the southwest—in the night chant, usually with *Nicotiana attenuata.*

170.—After the tobacco is inserted, pollen is placed on the tip end of the cigarette and moistened with a drop of sacred water ; thus the cigarette is sealed. The next act is to light it symbolically. To do this a piece of rock crystal is held up in the direction of the smoke-hole or in the beams of the sun, should they enter the lodge ; it is then swept down and touched to the tip of the cigarette. On one occasion (par. 484) it is so arranged that the cigarettes are prepared early in the morning, and "lighted" just as the rays of the rising sun shine in through the doorway of the lodge, over the curtain.

171.—The front or face of the cigarette has been mentioned (par. 166). This corresponds with the side of the internode on which the alternate leaf grows, and is marked at the base of the internode, on the dry culm, by the axillary pit or scar which the Navahoes call the eye ; this is the side which is notched and which lies next to the ground when the cigarette is sacrificed or planted.

WOODEN KETHAWNS.

172.—Wooden kethawns are made of various kinds of wood selected in each case for symbolic reasons. Sex is symbolized by form and color (pars. 16, 17) ; direction of sacrifice, as regards the points of the compass, is symbolized by color only. The distinction between butt and tip is as carefully observed as with cigarettes; but in most species of wood this may be determined without making notches at the butt, hence these may be omitted. As handles of yucca cannot be applied to them they are sometimes in danger of being smeared when painted. In general they are prepared with less care than the cigarettes.

PREPARATION OF KETHAWNS.

173.—The kethawns are always prepared in the western quarter of the lodge. One or more blankets are first laid on the floor; or sheepskins may first be laid down and blankets put on top of these. The blankets, nowadays, are usually ordinary American goods and not those of Navaho make. Sometimes several folds of new calico are laid next to the blankets. The last covering of all is new white cotton sheeting, usually unbleached, and it is on this that the kethawns and other sacred articles must rest. In old days, they say, finely dressed, new deerskins were used for the top covering. All these coverings, skins and textiles, are laid with their longer dimensions extending from north to south.

174.—Upon these cloths are placed the kethawns, during the various stages of their manufacture, when they are not in the hands of the operators; the rock crystal with which the cigarettes are symbolically lighted; the pollen bag of the shaman; the wild tobacco used for filling the cigarettes; the owl-feather employed in forcing the tobacco in; and the corn-husks, or small pieces of cotton sheeting in which the kethawns are folded. The husks are grouped in a row from north to south with their tips to the east and parallel to one another. Often the shaman displays, in similar groups, the plumes and the jewels which accompany the cigarettes; but sometimes he transfers these directly from their receptacles to the husk or cloth envelopes. The stone on which the paints are mixed is sometimes placed on the blankets at the edge of the sheeting and the paints are taken directly from it to be applied to the kethawns; but at other times it may be placed in some other part of the lodge and the paints may be put on little trays or palettes of concave yucca leaves. The one or more receptacles that contain the shaman's supply of feathers may be laid on the blankets.

175.—There is no special place on the covers assigned to each of these articles or groups of articles and an attempt to illustrate their varying positions would be useless, or worse than useless as it might lead the reader to place an undue value on the arrangement. One picture will suffice to give an idea of how the shaman sets his workshop in order, for the preparation of the kethawns. Plate I, fig. A, shows how all appeared once, on the morning of the third day when the kethawns of the White House were made. In this the kethawns are represented as first painted and put to dry, before they are filled with tobacco and placed in the husks. Fig. 14 also shows sections of reed (unfinished kethawns) as they appear when painted and left to dry.

176.—During the work the shaman sits west of the white cloth with his face to the east, while his assistants sit near him in any convenient place or attitude.

PAINTS FOR KETHAWNS.

177.—In decorating kethawns of both kinds, Navahoes usually employ paints found in their own country, of five different colors, viz. : white, blue, yellow, black and red. The white is an infusorial earth called gle*s*; the blue is a carbonate of copper; the yellow, a yellow ocher; the black, "a ferruginous deposit (clay) containing manganese and some organic matter"; and the red, a red ocher. What is called sacred charcoal is sometimes used for the black. Indigo, a substance long known to the Navahoes, and traded in old days from the Mexicans, is often used in place of carbonate of copper.

SONGS FOR KETHAWNS.

178.—During work on the kethawns songs appropriate to different occasions are sung. There are songs for painting, songs when the tobacco is inserted, songs for the symbolic lighting, songs for their application to the patient, and songs of sacrifice when the kethawns are taken out to their hiding-places (pars. 320, 330, 333).

DEPOSITING KETHAWNS.

179.—The modes of sacrificing or depositing the kethawns are so various that only a few general rules can be given. In describing special rites hereafter, it will be said that a certain set of cigarettes or sticks is sacrificed in the east, or in an easterly direction, another in the south or in a southerly direction, etc. Such expressions must not be understood as meaning east or south even approximately. The local conditions required for the sacrifice, such as a certain kind of rock or tree, are not always to be found in the required directions and a wide territory must be allowed the bearers. Hence, all the world that lies east of the meridian of the lodge is considered east, and all that is west of it is considered west; all the world that lies north of the degree of latitude that bisects the lodge answers for north, and all that lies south of it answers for south; yet, the nearer they can come to the true point the better. Sometimes when the proper place is many miles away, the sacrifice is merely pointed toward it and then laid down in some nearer place. The general conditions are that the sacrifices should be put in a safe place where cattle cannot trample on them.

180.—In returning from the place of sacrifice the bearer of the kethawns must never cross his own outgoing trail and never turn to his left. He must always go sunwise. After he deposits his sacrifice he must face around " by the right flank " before starting on his return journey. He must run all the way both going and coming, no matter how far he has to go. He must never pass through an ant-hill.

MEDICINES.

181.—There are administered to the patient and otherwise used during the ceremony, a variety of substances and compounds for which we can find no better name than medicine although they may have no remedial power and are not supposed, even by the shamans, to exert any influence on the body except in a supernatural way. The Navahoes have a knowledge of the physical effects of many plants and employ them in the treatment of disease with a view to their physical effects; but the medicines of the klédze *hatál* do not belong to this class. As the ceremony is supposed to drive away disease by spiritual or supernatural means, so the medicines are supposed to act in a similar way.

POLLEN.

182.—The most important medicine, in all Navaho ceremonies yet studied, is pollen. What we may call the pollen cult is very elaborate; all of its mysteries have not been unraveled, but many facts have been gathered, which are here submitted.

183.—It is not certain why the Navahoes ascribe remedial virtues to this substance; but it is probably largely because they understand its fructifying and life-giving powers. That such is their understanding is learned from a conversation with them and is indicated in an agricultural song of this ceremony.

184.—In old days, tradition says, the pollen of the cat-tail was most used by the Navahoes as it now is by the Apaches; but of late years, pollen of corn is the kind commonly employed; it is the pollen of general use; but many other kinds are collected for special purposes.

185.—The ceremonial uses to which pollen is applied are very various: it is scattered on dancing grounds, along trails of ceremonial processions, on keth-awns when they are deposited, on the masks and sacred properties in various rites, on the dry-paintings, and is applied in other ways which will not be mentioned here, but which may be learned by consulting the text with the aid of the index. But here is the most suitable place to describe the mode in which the shaman administers it to the patient and to himself and the way in which others take it, for sometimes every person in the lodge is expected to partake: A pinch is taken from the bag and dropped on the extended tongue; another pinch (or the remains of the first pinch) is held a couple of inches above the crown of the head, and, as the hand is raised upward, the pollen is allowed to fall on the head. The substance is sometimes applied to the essential parts of the patient's person.

186.—Much of the corn-pollen is used just as it is collected, being subjected to no manipulation or rite; but the shamans have a system of vivifying the medicine, whereby several varieties are produced, which, after all are simple pollen and nothing more. This vivifying consists in putting a live animal into a bag of the substance, allowing it to remain there for some time and then liberating it. The more it struggles in its dusty prison, the better. It is supposed to impart some of its character or spirit to the medicine while imprisoned. If it dies while captive, the pollen, they say, is dead and must not be used. Perhaps any animal may be subjected to this or some pollenizing treatment but the following are those most frequently used for the klédze *hatál*: bluebird, yellow warbler, *Pipilo chlorurus*, humming-bird and grasshopper. Pollen of the lizard is used as an oxytocic.   In a version of the Origin Legend it is said that at the time of the Emergence, when the people were threatened with a third flood, they restored to Tiéholtsodi,[10] the water monster, his young; but before they did so they put pollen on the bodies of these creatures, took it off again and preserved it; it brought the Navahoes rain and game and much good fortune.   See par. 263.

187.—A mixture of two or more of these life pollens is much used under the name of i'yi*dezná*.   It is often moistened and applied as a paint to kethawns or to feathers that accompany kethawns.   It is daubed on, by means of a splinter of yucca leaf, from butt to tip.   This may be made by putting different animals, consecutively into the same bag of pollen.

188.—The shaman collects pollen from different plants, in pursuance of different mytho-therapeutic theories.   Pollen of pine and cedar are gathered. Pollen of larkspur is sometimes employed, on account of color, as a sacrifice to gods of the south; but as this plant yields very little pollen, the dried and powdered corolla is added to give bulk to the collection.   During the summer rains, in the Navaho land, a fine yellow powder collects on the surface of pools; it is probably the pollen of pine; but the Navahoes seem to think it is a product of the water, call it water-pollen, and collect it for use on special occasions.

189.—In the autumn of 1884, the writer had with him in Washington the Navaho shaman, *Hatáli* Nĕz or Tall Chanter.   While in the city he made, under the author's observation a number of kethawns.   Although he understood they were not to be sacrificed to the gods, but to be used only as exhibits, he insisted on having all the materials genuine.   It was possible to comply with his demands in most cases: but true pollen was not to be obtained at that time of the year. In this dilemma lycopodium was offered to him under the name of pollen.   He tasted it and said: " This tastes like no pollen of my country.   From what plant does it come?"   Being frankly told he replied that it would do.   He took a good supply of it home with him to New Mexico, to show his brother priests as a sample of the kind of pollen that white doctors used.

190.—In telling *Hatáli* Nĕz that the lycopodium was pollen, no real deception was practised.   Many fine impalpable powders which are not pollen are considered such by the Indians.   Perhaps I would have had difficulty in explaining to him the difference between spores and pollen.   In sacred song and speech the Navahoes talk of haze and of the smoky dimness of the horizon due in desert lands perhaps usually to dust in the air, as pollen; thus we have references to the pollen of the morning sky and the pollen of the evening sky.

191.—Pollen is an emblem of peace, of happiness, of prosperity, and it is supposed to bring these blessings.   When, in the Origin Legend, one of the war-gods bids his enemy to put his feet down in pollen he constrains him to peace.   When in prayer the devotee says " May my trail be in pollen," he pleads for a happy and peaceful life.   See Origin Legend p. 109.   See par. 472.

192.—When needed in large quantities, pollen is put in fawnskin bags ; but ordinarily it is kept in small buckskin bags, which are carried on the person, not only by the priests but by many of the laymen. A rock crystal or other precious stone may be kept in the pollen, or the stone fetish of a horse which at times is "fed" with pollen to bring good luck to the herds.

CORN-MEAL.

193.—Corn-meal is used in larger quantities than pollen, perhaps because more easily obtained ; but not on so many occasions. It seems to be considered less sacred than pollen. It is employed in many ways the same as pollen and in connection with the latter. Some shamans too occasionally use meal where others employ pollen. It is scattered on dance-grounds, on the trails of cere-monial processions, on sacrifices, on dry-paintings, on succoring gods and in vari-ous acts described in the part on Rites in Detail. Mixed with water it forms the food with which the masks are symbolically fed and which is used for the sacramental feast on the fourth night. See par. 463 *et seq.*

194.—One important purpose which it serves is to dry the patient after he has bathed. In this case, it answers a practical as well as a religious purpose. It is a substitute for towels — articles of which the Navahoes know very little. When they take the hot air sweat-bath, for purposes of comfort or cleanliness, they roll themselves in sand after they leave the sweat-house and brush the sand off when it has sufficiently absorbed the moisture. This resembles the system of sanding letters which was in vogue before blotting paper became common. Corn-meal is a refined substitute for sand.

195.—For most purposes, plain meal, ground on a metate, is used, and it has not been learned that any special rites are observed when it is prepared to answer a sacred purpose. The meal used in the communal supper of the fourth night is of corn called nĭs*ts*áiakan which is baked in the ground.

196.—If the ceremony is for the benefit of a male patient, white meal must be used ; if it is for the benefit of a female, yellow meal is required. It is said that this custom arises because, according to the Origin Legend, the ancestors of the first Navaho gens were created out of corn — the man of white, the woman of yellow corn. But it is probable that myth and custom are alike derived from something antecedent to both.

INCENSE, YÁ*DIDĪNIL*.

197.—All of the most important rites, such as the making and applying of kethawns, the painting of the great pictures, and the singing of long series of songs of sequence, are closed by the act of fumigating the patient. Sometimes others besides the patient are fumigated. At the close of the initiation into the mystery of the Yébĭ*t*sai, all the candidates receive fumigation. See par. 510.

198.—The usual mode of administering it is this : Two hot coals are taken from the fire and placed in front of the kneeling patient. On these a powder called yád̓id̓inil is sprinkled ; from this, dense, whitish pungent fumes arise which fill the whole lodge with their odor. The devotee leans over the coals and strongly inhales the fumes, sometimes drawing them in toward the face with the hand or holding his blanket out over his forehead like a hood so as to get the full benefit of the fumigation. Sometimes he bathes his hands in the smoke.

199.—When the fumes have died down, sacred water is thrown on the coals to cool them. When cooled, they are, in some rites, carried from the lodge to be deposited in the north along with other refuse of the ceremony ; in other rites they are cast out through the smoke-hole of the lodge.

200.—The ingredients of the yád̓id̓inil or incense are these : The complete teguments of five different birds, including head, bill, feathers, and feet, namely— bluebird, yellow warbler, *Pipilo chlorurus* and birds called tsïdisási and tsolgáli ; a gummy, inflammable earthy substance called ke'atíd̓itlis ; dry piñon gum, and a plant called tihid̓iaí. This mixture must be made while a ceremony is in progress.

201.—As feathers constitute a part of this mixture, it might be supposed that the odor would be offensive ; but it is not ; though pungent, it is rather fragrant. The smell of the other ingredients obscures that of the feathers.

202.—Incense is used in other Navaho ceremonies as well as in klédze *hatál* and, judging from the odor, it is believed to be the same in all ceremonies witnessed.

KLÉDZE AZÉ, NIGHT MEDICINE.

203.—Of the many medicines used in the night chant, only one has received the name of the ceremony. It is called klédze azé which may be freely translated night medicine or night chant medicine. It is administered with ritual observances every day, after the sweat bath, for four days. It is an elaborate compound in mythic medicine which reminds one of the old polypharmacy of civilized medicine. Only a part of its composition has been determined. It consists of three series or collections each of which is gathered on a different occasion and kept in a separate bag or bundle until used.

204.—The first series is vegetable. The collector enters a field at night, in the rainy season, during a violent thunder storm. He culls in the east of the field a leaf from a stalk that produces white corn. Passing sunwise he culls in the south a leaf from a stalk of blue corn ; in the west, a leaf from a stalk of yellow corn ; in the north, a leaf from a stalk of variegated corn. Passing around the field again, he culls squash leaves in the southeast, bean leaves in the southwest, watermelon leaves in the northwest and muskmelon leaves in the northeast. Going sunwise around the field a third time, he gathers tobacco at each of the cardinal points. Going around a fourth time he collects wild plants at the cardinal points. Each of these things must be collected at the instant that it is illuminated by a flash of lightning. To these is added a mixture called azé *dotli'z* or blue medicine the ingredients of which are not known, but they need not be collected by lightning's glare.

205.—The second collection consists chiefly of pásgles, *i. e.*, gles or dried white paint taken from the bodies of men who personate gods, immediately after they have returned from the act of personation to the medicine-lodge, to clean their bodies.   The gods whose personators furnish this paint or white earth are the following :   Neyénĕzgạni, Dsaha*d*old*z*á, *T*o'bad*z*ĭst*s*íni, Gá*n*askĭ*d*i, *T*ó'nenĭli, *H*ast*s*éol*t*o*d*i, Hat*s*é*l*tsi, *H*ast*s*éz*i*ni, *H*ast*s*éol*t*oi, *H*ast*s*é*h*ogan, *H*ast*s*éyal*t*i and *H*a*t*d*d*ast*s*ĭ'si.   The pásgle*s* of Nayénĕzgạni must come from his head and his bow symbols ; that of Dsaha*d*old*z*á, from the lightning symbols on his arms ; that of *T*o'bad*z*ĭst*s*íni from his head and queue symbols ; that of Gá*n*askĭ*d*i from his hump.   It is not specified from what parts of the person the other actors must yield their gle*s*.   Spruce leaves from the collars of the actors are added to this mixture.

206.—The third collection consists of pollen of pine (*Pinus ponderosa*), piñon (*Pinus edulis*), cedar (*Juniperus virginiana*) and juniper (*J. occidentalis*) mixed together.

207.—To form the night medicine, these three collections are mixed together in a wicker bowl—water-tight basket—with sacred water (par. 209).

208.—If the patient has fever, dá‘tsos, or frost medicine, is added to the above (par. 213).

*TO‘LANAST*SÍ, MIXED WATER, SACRED WATER.

209.—In various parts of the description of the ceremony which follows, the use of water is mentioned.   In many cases mixed or sacred water is specified, but in many other cases, where it is not specified, it must be understood.   The name *t*o‘*l*anast*s*í may be freely translated mixed water ; but the fluid may also properly be called sacred water.

210.—It is used in mixing all lotions and draughts of the ceremony, in sealing cigarettes, in moistening life pollen, in painting kethawns, in washing the patient, in preparing the cold gruel for the communal supper, in short, on all ceremonial occasions where water is required.   It is not used in cooking food, not even for the ancient dishes served in the banquet of the fourth night.

211.—According to the myths, four kinds of water were originally required for this mixture : spring or stream water from the east, hail water from the south, rain water from the west, and snow water from the north.   At present they only approximate this mixture as best they can and usually content themselves with two different kinds, namely : spring or stream water — flowing water, earth water — obtained from a point east of the meridian of the medicine-lodge and the water of precipitation—pool water, sky water—from a point west of the meridian of the lodge.   As the ceremony takes place in the winter, after the beginning of a season of precipitation, it is usually not difficult, even in arid New Mexico, to get water of both kinds.

212.—The proper receptacles of the sacred water are wicker water-jars and gourd cups ; but of late years the Navahoes are getting careless in this matter and are coming to use Zuñi pots and cups and even vessels procured from the whites.

AZÉ *DÁ'*TSOS OR *DÁ'*TSOS, FROST MEDICINE.

213—*Dá*'tsos means simply hoar frost, but it is also a name of a preparation used for fevers, which is supposed to contain all the virtues and cooling properties of frost.   Often this is called azé *dá*'tsos or frost medicine.   It must be prepared by a virgin.   She grinds meal and puts it in a sacred basket.   She takes this out before sunrise on a frosty morning, places it under one or more plants and shakes frost crystals into it until it is moist enough for her purpose.   She works the moistened meal into a dough, which she carries home before the sun rises and puts away where the sun cannot shine on it.   See par. 726.

SACRED CHARCOAL.

214.—On many occasions, where a surface is to be blackened, particularly if it is a large surface, charcoal is employed.   The ordinary charcoal of wood does not usually answer, although it is used exclusively as the black in making the dry-paintings.   On most occasions they employ what is here called sacred charcoal, which is prepared by burning together four plants, viz. : (1) A composite flower, *Gutierrezia euthamiæ*, which grows abundantly in the Navaho land through a wide range of altitude.   It is called by the Navahoes tsïld′ïlgése (meaning scare-weed or dodge-weed) because frightened reptiles and small animals seek its cover.   (2) *Bouteloua hirsuta*, a species of that genus to which the name grama grass is most commonly applied.   Perhaps other species of *Bouteloua* are used.   (3) *Eurotia lanata*, called winter-fat and white sage by the whites, and kátso*t*a, or jack-rabbits corn by the Navahoes.   (4) An undetermined herb called tsé'*z*i.   This mixture, though scarcely to be considered a medicine, is most conveniently described in this connection.

KĔ′TLO.

215.—All lotions for external use applied in healing ceremonies are called kĕ′tlo.   Frequent reference is made to kĕ′tlo in the descriptions of the rites. The lotion chiefly used in the ceremony of klédze *hatál* is the cold infusion, in sacred water, of an undetermined umbelliferous plant called tsóltsïn or tsóztsïn, mixed with spruce leaves.   It is usually brewed in a water-tight basket in which a couple of ears of corn are first laid.   The plant must be freshly gathered.   The writer has seen a rite delayed awaiting the arrival of fresh tsóltsïn.   The mode of adding the water is described in par. 461 and elsewhere.

216.—There are other medicines used in the ceremony but they do not require special description.

FOODS.

217.—During this ceremony there are served many dishes of the ancient food on which the Navahoes subsisted before they adopted, to any extent, the food of the Europeans. Most of these messes are served during the vigil of the fourth night, when they form an element of the rite. See par. 459. The following are brief descriptions of some of them.

218.—I. K̤at ĕ′ƚ́in, literally, no cedar, a white corn-meal mush from which the usual ingredient of cedar ashes has been omitted.

219.—II. Wa, the leaves and branchlets of bee-weed, *Cleome pungens;* cooked as we cook greens, but boiled in several waters to remove the pungent taste.

220.—III. Wa bĕltsé, a watery stew or gravy made of wa, or bee-weed.

221.—IV. Alkán, or sweet bread. This is made in part of chewed meal, which the saliva converts into glucose and in part of the meal of parched corn. Sometimes roots and herbs are added. It is baked in a hole in the ground in which a fire has been kept burning for hours. The ashes are removed; the hole is lined with corn-husks; the mixture is poured in and covered with husks and earth; a fire is built on top and maintained for many hours more. This forms a large soft loaf, which is the principal dish of the fourth evening. The Navaho alkan is similar to the Zuñi hépalokiya; but the people of Zuñi have permanent stone ovens in which to bake their dish.

222.—V. *Thá*‘bĭtsaï, literally, three ears, cake or dumpling made of the pulp of green corn, wrapped in corn-husks and boiled in water. Three cones are made of one complete husk, whose leaves are not removed from the stem; thus the dish has the appearance of three deer's ears fastened together, whence the name.

223.—VI. Tsé‘as*t*é, literally, stone-baked. This is the same as the paper bread of the Pueblo Indians, the héwe of Zuñi. It is a thin, broad, flexible, cake having the appearance of paper. It is made by spreading, with the hand, a very thin corn-meal batter over a large flat, polished, stone slab, under which is a fire. Corn of different colors is commonly selected to make different batches; thus they have: tsé‘as*t*é *l*akaí, or white stone-baked; tsé‘as*t*é *dotl*í′z, or blue stone-baked; tsé‘as*t*é *l*ĭtsói, or yellow stone-baked, and tsé‘as*t*é lĭts*í*, or red stone-baked.

224.—VII. Klesán, or *d*ĭtlógi klesán. To make this dish, the Navahoes cut grains from the unripe ears of corn and grind them to a pulp on a metate; they spread out hot embers and lay on them a covering of green corn-leaves; on this covering they lay the pulp in small masses to form cakes; over these they place more corn-leaves; then they rake glowing embers over all and leave the cakes to bake.

225.—VIII. *T*anaskĭ′z, a very thin mush.

226.—IX. *L*éilzoz or kléilzoz, literally, side by side in earth, consists of cakes made partly of chewed meal and partly of the meal of baked corn, formed into a stiff dough. Pieces of the dough are rolled into oblong shape, encased in corn-husks which are tied with yucca fibre and laid side by side, in rows, in hot ashes, to bake.

227.—X. Na*d*ínogési, or spread bread, a thin corn batter poured on hot coals.

228.—XI. *D*ïtlógïn tsï*d*ïkói, or ïntsï*d*ïkói, is made of dried green corn which is ground with water, to a pulp, on a metate. The pulp is encased in corn-husks which are folded at the ends and placed between corn-leaves and hot coals to bake.

229.—XII. Ba*d*ahastlóni, corn-meal dumplings, enveloped in husks and boiled.

230.—XIII. Kïnïspï'*z*i, boiled corn-meal dumplings without husk covers.

231.—XIV. *Th*á'nil, gray mush made of corn-meal mixed with cedar ashes.

232.—XV. No'ká*z*i or *d*okó*z*i. The former name means, tracked, and refers to the traces of the fingers of the cook, left in the stiff dough; the latter name refers to the salty taste. Thick flat cakes of salted meal baked on a hot stone which serves as a griddle.

233.—XVI. *H*azáale', boiled greens made from the leaves of an early-flowered umbelliferous plant not determined.

234.—Other dishes of ancient food, which require no special description, are prepared. These are mentioned in the account of the rites of the fourth night. [11]

SACRED ARTICLES—THE DEMANDS OF THE GODS.

235.—In the accompanying myths, particularly in that of *To*'nast*si*/*é*go *Hatál*, there are frequent allusions to certain articles demanded by the gods as rewards for their labors in curing disease. The story-tellers rarely repeat the whole list at once but usually the greater part of it, and at one repetition they mention names which, at another time they omit. These numerous repetitions are tedious and the reader will be spared them. Once for all we give the complete list here and refer to it later on. This list is compiled from the various lists of the narrators. All these articles are now used in the ceremony except the five jeweled baskets, or baskets made of jewels, which are probably mythical.

236.— List.

1. Wrought beads of all kinds.
2. A white shell basket.
3. A turquoise basket.
4. A haliotis basket.
5. A cannel-coal basket.
6. A rock crystal basket.
7. White shell (fragments).
8. Turquoise.
9. Haliotis.
10. Cannel-coal.
11. Rock crystal.
12. Sacred buckskins.
13. Wild tobacco.

List.

14. Eagle feathers.
15. Bluebird feathers.
16. Yellow warbler feathers.
17. Turkey-feathers.
18. Turkey "beard."
19. Cotton string.
20. Specular iron-ore.
21. Corn-pollen.
22. Pollen of larkspur.
23. Life pollen.
24. A special life pollen made of bluebird pollen, yellow warbler pollen and grasshopper pollen.

MEDICINE-LODGES.

237.—Buildings of two different forms are constructed to serve as medicine-lodges in this ceremony : the first is conical in form, the second is flat-topped.

238.—The conical or conoidal lodge is by far the more common.   It is constructed on the same principles as the ordinary conical dwelling or *hogan* of the Navaho ; but it is much larger and requires the use of heavier beams.   Fig. 1 shows a lodge built for the ceremony of the mountain chant[12]; but that built for the night chant is quite similar except in one slight particular, which the casual observer might never detect and which does not show in the illustration : in the lodge of the mountain chant, a recess is made in the north, where a character clad in evergreens is hidden during the rites of the fifth night ; in the lodge of the night chant, a small recess is made in the west to contain the masks and other ceremonial properties.   Plate I, fig. B, is from a photograph taken on the morning after the last night's performance of the night chant.   It shows the form of the lodge less perfectly than fig. 1.   The piñon branches over the smoke-hole were placed there to protect the pictures on the floor from rain or snow.

239.—In a paper on " Navaho Houses "[13] by Cosmos Mindeleff, p. 509, there is an excellent description of the flat-topped medicine-lodge and of its mode of construction.   Mr. Mindeleff calls it " Hogán of the Yébĭtcai dance " and " Yébĭtcai house."   He says :   " For the observance of this ceremony it is usual to construct a flat-roof hut called *iyádaskuni*, meaning, literally, ' under the flat.' " We might easily draw the inference from the quoted remark that the flat-topped lodge is almost the only form of lodge used in the night chant ; but the experience of the writer leads him to declare to the contrary.   He has observed in wide travel over the Navaho country more than a score of night chant lodges, some in process of construction, others completed and ready for use, others in use during the ceremony, and many more abandoned and in various stages of decay.   In all, he has seen but one of the flat-topped variety.   This was observed at a ceremony which he attended at the ranch of Thomas Torlino near the Chusca Mountains. Not only is the flat-topped lodge not the usual form used for this ceremony, but it is a rare form.

240.—It is for no mythic or religious reason, that the flat-topped lodge is constructed.   It is preferred to the other form solely for economic reasons. Torlino is a graduate of the Carlisle school and speaks English.   He is a full-blooded Navaho and was the patron of this ceremony, which he had performed for the benefit of an invalid brother.   Being asked why he built a flat-topped lodge instead of a conical one, as was usual, he said that it was because in the neighborhood of his house the trees were of low size ; that he could not find, without going to a distance, logs long enough for the conical house.   Under favorable conditions the conical house is the more easily built.   Torlino's ranch is at an altitude of about 5000 feet, where piñon and cedar are stunted ; at higher altitudes in New Mexico they grow to greater height.

241.—The lodge is never destroyed after the conclusion of the ceremony, neither is the arbor or greenroom. They are left to decay. Sometimes, but rarely, a lodge is used a second time for a ceremony, and it may be used as a workroom or a temporary shelter; but it is not used as a regular residence. Lodges, falling to ruins, may be seen all over the Navaho country. It is easy to distinguish an old lodge of the night chant from one of another ceremony, by the remains of the arbor in the east.

ARBOR OR GREENROOM.

242.—The above names are applied to a rude structure erected on the afternoon of the ninth day of the ceremony about one hundred paces east of the medicine-lodge. The arbor consists of a circle of evergreen saplings and branches, stuck firmly in the ground and closely set. It is about twenty feet in diameter, about twelve feet high and has an opening in the south. A fire is made in the centre at night. Often it is built so that living trees may form a part of the circle. It is used as a dressing-room for the dancers of the last night. Here the relays that have finished their work take off their masks and properties, and wash the paint from their persons; and here the new relays paint themselves and assume the properties which their predecessors take off. Men not performing in the rite often loiter here to assist the actors in their toilets, to smoke and to gossip. See plate I, figure D.

SUDORIFIC TREATMENT.

243.—The patient receives sudorific treatment during four days of the ceremony—second, third, fourth, and fifth,—and always in the forenoon. Diaphoresis is usually produced by means of a hot-air bath given in a sweat-house; but there is another method of producing it, called kónnike (par. 255). The sweat-house system will be first described.

SWEAT-HOUSES AND SWEAT-HOUSE TREATMENT.

244.—In the mythic days, the legends tell us, four sweat-houses were built in this ceremony, each on a separate day, and this is still often done, but the custom of building only one sweat-house and using it four times is now becoming common. The sweat-house is ordinarily called *tha'dzéhogán* or *hogán tha'dzé*, water-house, or simply *tha'dzé*, but in the songs it is referred to as tsa*lyél* biázi, or the little darkness. It is erected at a variable distance from the medicine-lodge—east on the first day— of from 100 to 200 paces.

245.—Whether one or four houses are built, the method of construction is always the same. A round hole three feet or more in diameter and nearly a foot deep is dug. Over this, four small forked sticks are planted at an angle of about 45°, the forked ends interlocking above, in the middle. Two of these sticks are of piñon, placed one in the east and one in the south; two are of cedar, placed one in the west and one in the north.   Other sticks are laid around, leaning on the first four sticks, so as to form a conical structure, with an opening or doorway in the east through which the patient enters.   Over the frame thus constructed, is placed a vegetal covering so thick that none of the sand or clay, afterwards piled on, may fall through it.   This covering is preferably made of spruce twigs ; but if spruce is scarce, artemisia or any other plant may be added to the spruce or altogether substituted for it.   The last covering is of earth or sand, taken from the ground immediately around the house ; this is lightly beaten down and smoothed with the oaken battens used by the weavers.   The little hut thus made, which takes an hour or more to build, measures externally from five to six feet in diameter and about three feet high above the general surface of the ground.   The doorway is usually two feet or a little more in height, is about a foot and a half wide at the bottom, and tapers toward the top, where it is edged with a cross-piece or lintel (plate I, C).   Spruce twigs, or other material in default of spruce, are strewn on the floor, for the patient to sit on.   A portion of the top of the sweat-house is smoothed with extra care and may be extended or built up at the edges to form the groundwork for the pictorial decoration, which is next applied.

DECORATIONS OF THE SWEAT-HOUSE.

246.--The decorations are not always the same.   The reasons for varying them have not been fully investigated. The houses of the first and third days are usually decorated alike ; so also are those of the second and fourth days.   The decorations of the latter two are usually simpler than those of the former, and are sometimes omitted.   Plate II, figs. A and B, represents two forms of decoration of the first and third sweat-houses.   Other variants of rainbow and lightning designs may be used.   These decorations are dry-paintings, executed by a method elsewhere described (pars. 156–164).   Fig. 6 shows the decorations done in corn-meal of the second and fourth days in the same rites.

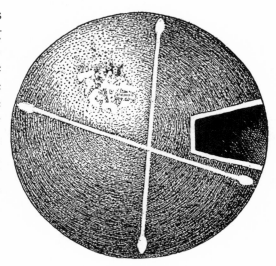

Fig. 6.   Akán tsïsenîl ; decoration in meal of the sudatory on the second and fourth days of the sweat-bath.   Diagram.   See par. 396.

DESCRIPTION OF PLATE.

247.--Fig. A.   The red and blue lines running from north to south (or rather in a northerly and southerly direction, for the orientation is rarely perfect) represent the plumed rainbow, or flying rainbow—not the anthropomorphic god.   The symbol at the northern extremity of the rainbow represents five quills of the tail of a magpie (*Pica hudsonica*), they are black tipped with white; the blue sprinkled on the surface, imperfectly shown in the illustration, represents the changing sheen of the feathers. The symbol at the southern extremity of the rainbow is that of the tail of the chicken-hawk (*Accipiter cooperi*), the gíni of the Navahoes. The zigzag white and black lines running approximately from east to west represent the white and "black" lightning. The figure terminating the lightning in the west represents the tail of the red-tailed buzzard (*Buteo borealis*), called by the Navahoes atsé*l*ĭtsoi, or yellow-tail. They regard the indistinct color of the tail as yellow, and so depict it, while we regard it as red. The figure at the eastern end of the lightning symbolizes the tail of a war-eagle (*Aquila chrysaëtus*), the atsá of the Navahoes.

248.—Fig. B. In this decoration we have also the designs of rainbow and lightning; but they appear as men, not birds; they are anthropomorphic deities. The rainbow is here shown, not as one individual, the usual way, but as two; each color of the rainbow represents a separate individual.[14] The lightning is also represented as two individuals, the black and the white lightnings being regarded as separate divinities. The lightnings are supplied with the masks of male dancers; the rainbows with those of female dancers. Here we have again an illustration of a law of symbolism of sex, elsewhere described (par. 16). Lightning and rainbow are regarded as allied phenomena; but the lightning, being active, noisy, and destructive, is considered as the male, while the rainbow, being gentle, silent, and harmless, is considered as the female.

PLANTING OF PLUMED WANDS.

249.—The eight plumed wands or ĭn*d*iá' of the shaman are stuck vertically in the ground around the sweat-house when the decoration is completed. The four black wands are placed north of the lodge and the four blue south. He who plants them moves sunwise.

FIRE AND HOT STONES.

250.—While the building is in progress a fire is lighted about two paces east of the sweat-house. The sticks used in the fire are piñon and cedar and must have their butts towards the house. Four large stones, of a kind that will not easily disintegrate when heated, are placed in the fire. When the stones are hot they are taken from the fire and transferred to the sweat-house to the north of where the patient sits, with two sticks which are used as tongs. New fire is built every day and the material of the old fire removed and ceremonially deposited. No water is thrown on the stones as is the custom among other Indian tribes. The Navaho sweat-bath is a hot-air bath, not a steam bath.

CURTAINS OF THE DOOR.

251.—The door of the lodge is covered with four coverings. In former days sacred buckskins were used for this purpose, now blankets and cotton sheeting are largely substituted for buckskin. In the myths it is related that the gods covered their sweat-houses with four coverings: first, a sheet of darkness; second, a sheet of blue sky; third, a sheet of yellow sky; fourth, a sheet of white sky. For this reason it is a common practice now to spread over the door of the sweat-house a black blanket first and a sheet of white cotton last; but little consideration is given to the colors of the second and third covers. These coverings are among the many perquisites of the shaman.

WHERE ONE SWEAT-HOUSE IS BUILT.

252.—If only one sudatory is built, it is erected east of the medicine-lodge. Each day the picture is erased, the bed of spruce and the stones taken out; but otherwise the structure is not in any way despoiled or injured until the last day's rite is done.

WHERE FOUR SWEAT-HOUSES ARE BUILT.

253.—If four sweat-houses are erected, the first is built east of the medicine-lodge; the second, south; the third, west; the fourth, north; but in each case the door faces east and the fire is built east of the sudatory. Each day when the rites are done, the house is torn down, the hole filled up, the debris of the fire removed, and all traces of the house and rite are obliterated. Some shamans use the material, or at least the four principal sticks, of the first house in building the others; but usually the material of each house is ceremonially deposited or sacrificed when the house is demolished, and new material collected for the next house.

254.—The material of the first sweat-house is deposited east of the site of the house; the material of the second, south of the site of the house; the material of the third, west of the site of the house; and the material of the fourth, north of the site of the house to which it belonged — approximately, at least, in each case. They are usually placed in the branches or under the shade of trees, piñon being preferred. It is customary to place the material which formed the sweat-house in a spot different but adjacent to that in which the heated stones, the spruce carpeting, and the remains of the fire are laid. Thus, the different collections may be laid in different trees, or one may be laid in the branches and the other at the base of the tree. Some shamans deposit, with the refuse of each lodge, a kethawn three finger-widths in length, colored according to the direction in which it is sacrificed — white, blue, yellow, or black. The tips of the sticks from the sweat-house and of the kethawns must point away from the medicine-lodge. Each kethawn is laid on a trail of meal. Pollen is sprinkled on the sacrificial heap and a benediction uttered in the usual manner. See pars. 968 and 985–989.

KÓɴNIKE, OR OUT-DOOR SUDORIFIC.

255.—Sometimes the patient gets a form of sudorific treatment called kóɴnike instead of the sweat-house. In the kóɴnike there is no lodge built; but instead four open fires are made, each at a different point of the compass, from the medicine-lodge, on a different day. The fire is made of juniper and piñon and is kept up until the ground underneath is well heated. When the fire has burned down, the ashes are cleared away and the hot ground is covered with seven layers of different woods and herbs, spread from below upward in the following order: juniper, piñon, spruce, *Gutierrezia euthamiæ*, a plant called tsé'aze or rock medicine, *Bouteloua* grass, and *Eurotia lanata* or winter fat. The patient is laid on this bed, his head toward the medicine-lodge; he is covered with blankets; a few leaves are put under his head for a pillow; there he remains until certain songs are sung and he perspires freely.

256.—In all other respects the rites and medicines are the same for kónnike as for the sweat-house. In the myths (pars. 775, 867), a trench is mentioned in which the fire was made, and various acts connected with the fire are described. The writer has never witnessed the application of kónnike; but has obtained descriptions of it from different medicine-men.

SACRED DEERSKIN.

257.—Before telling how masks are made, it is well to speak of the principal material used in their construction—a material used, too, for many other purposes besides the fabrication of masks—*i. e.*, *t*okakéhi or unwounded buckskin. The deer which supplies the skin must not be wounded in any way. It is surrounded by men, mounted or on foot, and chased around in a circle, from which it cannot escape, until it is overcome by exhaustion and falls. A bag containing pollen is put over the nostrils and mouth and held there until the deer is smothered. The carcass is laid on its back. Lines are marked with pollen along the median line and along the insides of the limbs, in both cases from the centre outward. Incisions are made with a stone knife from centre toward periphery along the lines of pollen until the skin is fully opened. The skinning may, of late years, be completed with a steel knife. After the skin is removed it is laid east of the carcass with its head to the east and its hairy side down. The ulnæ and fibulæ are cut out and put in the places where they belong; i. e. the right ulna is put in the skin of the right fore leg, the left ulna in that of the left fore leg, the right fibula in that of the right hind leg, and the left fibula in that of the left hind leg. The skin may then be rolled up and carried away to be dressed at leisure elsewhere. Both ulnæ are used as scrapers for the skin, one for the right side, the other for the left. If the skin is used in making masks the fibulæ are employed as awls— the right fibula in sewing the right sides of the masks, the left fibula in sewing the left sides.

258.—As there are thus many other requirements for these skins besides the mere fact of their being unwounded, they are often spoken of in this work as sacred buckskins or sacred deerskins although the Navahoes do not so call them.

259.—Such skins are used for many other purposes in the rites, as will be seen in the following pages.

MASKS.

260.—The majority of masks worn during the ceremony may be called permanent masks. They are the property of the chanter, are easily portable, are stored in a bag. One set of them may last the priest through his professional career.

261.—There are two masks of an ephemeral character, made for the occasion of a particular act, and destroyed as soon as they have served their purpose. Such masks are best considered in connection with the acts to which they belong (pars. 357–361).

262.—As the chanters are comparatively few in number, the work of making permanent masks and the ceremonies connected therewith rarely occur. The writer has never witnessed them and gives the following information on the authority of several shamans.

263.—The unwounded buckskin and all other material for the manufacture must be provided in advance by the shaman and he must cause the construction of the special lodge in which the work is done. Pollen vitalized by a bird called nikéni, is used. This bird, would seem, from the description to be a species of owl. The reason it is used for the masks is that its face looks somewhat like a human face. With pollen in which the whole bird has been immersed they mark off the pattern of the mask on the buckskin; with pollen which has been applied to the eyes of the bird they mark the location of the eyes on the mask, and with pollen which has been applied to the mouth of the bird they mark the position of the mouth.

264.—A full set of twenty masks must all be made in one day and a sufficient number of men must be assembled to accomplish this. The masks thus made are: one for Nayénĕzgạni, one for *To*'bad*z*ĭst*s*íni, one for *Tŏ*'nen*i*li, one for *H*ast*s*éyal*t*i, one for *H*ast*s*é*l*tsi, one for *H*ast*s*é*z*ĭni, one for Dsaha*d*old*z*á, one for Gá*n*askĭ*d*i, six for the other yébaka and six for the yébaad or goddesses. Seven bunches of owl feathers and the wreaths of hair to adorn the masks are also then prepared and so are the fourteen fox-skins used as collars to these masks. The spruce collars are not made on this occasion. The shaman begins to sing when work begins. When the masks are all done they have a ceremonious vigil of the masks much like that which now occurs in the ordinary night chant, on the fourth night (pars. 454 *et seq.*). In this they sing, with occasional rests, all night.

265.—It is allowable to make two sets, or forty masks in one day. In this case two contiguous lodges are built and occupied simultaneously, and a separate set is made in each lodge. The singers in both lodges do not sing at the same time; when the song is taken up in one lodge there is silence in the other, and *vice versa*. Thus they sing alternately in one lodge or the other during the night.

266.—Fourteen of the masks, those representing males, are caps of buckskin that completely cover the head and face; each is made of two pieces of skin shaped like an inverted U. These are sewed together with 12 interrupted sutures, six on each side. At the seam, from about the level of the eyes, upward there is a fringe of hair which may be black, red, or yellow. Buckskin thongs are attached to the mask for the purpose of securing plumes, collars, and other temporary appendages. See fig. 7.

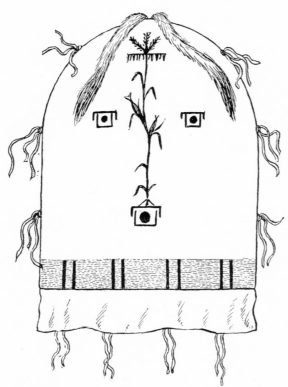

267.—The six yébaad or female masks, are simply dominoes that cover the face only and allow the natural hair to flow out over the shoulders. They have fringes of hair on top. They are made of soft deerskin secured to a backing of rawhide by means of an adhesive substance. While the male masks are very flexible these are quite stiff.

268.—The special decorations of the different masks will be described when we come to speak of the divine characters that wear them.

269.—Eight masks of the more important characters of the ceremony are illustrated in plate III. All these have been seen, handled, and sketched at leisure by the writer when a ceremony was not in progress. Three other masks, of less important characters, are illustrated by engravings in the text. Two of these, belonging to a variant of the ceremony called *to‘nastsiহégo hatál*, have not been seen by the writer. The sketches are made from descriptions and rude drawings by the Indians. See figs. 4 and 5.

Fig. 7. Mask of *Hastséyalti*, untrimmed, showing arrangement of buckskin thongs.

DESCRIPTION OF PLATE.

270.—The hair on the masks may be either stiff or flowing. Six of the masks are here shown with stiff hair in order that the figures on the faces may not be obscured. In this description of the plate, brief references only, will be given.

271.—Fig. A. Mask of *Hastséyalti* as it appears in the dance of the last night, with collar of spruce-twigs.

272.—Fig. B. Mask of *Hastséhogan*, as worn when he appears in the guise of a begging god on the ninth day of the ceremony, with collar of spruce.

273.—Fig. C. Mask of Nayénĕzgani, with collar of skin of kit-fox (*Vulpes velox*) as worn in the act of succor of the ninth day.

274.—Fig. D. Mask of *Hastsébaad*, shown without any collar, so as to display ornamentation at bottom of mask.

275.—Fig. E. Mask of *To'badzĭstsíni* as worn by the personator in the scene of succor on the afternoon of the ninth day.

276.—Fig. F. Mask of Dsaha*d*oldzá with head-dress and fox-skin collar complete. The collar with this, as with other masks, hides the yellow streak at the bottom which symbolizes the evening sky.

277.—Fig. G. Mask of *H*asts*é*baka with flowing hair and without collar so as to display, at the bottom, the symbol of the evening sky, which is a horizontal band of yellow crossed with eight perpendicular black lines to represent rain. The mouth-tube is cylindrical.

278.—Fig. H. Mask of Gá*n*askĭ*d*i with head-dress complete and collar of fox-skin.

THE PLUMED WANDS.

279.—Among the important properties of the night chant are eight plumed wands or ĭn*d*iá' as they are called. They are set around the great pictures and around the sudatories (par. 337). They are used in symbolic massage (par. 340) and in other ways. See plate IV, fig. A.

280.—They represent Navahoes of the mythic days (see Navaho Legends, pp. 71 *et seq.*), when the people dwelt on the banks of the central stream, the prototype of the San Juan in the fourth world, before they emerged to this, the fifth world.

281.—They are made of willows which must be obtained only on the banks of the San Juan River, the most sacred stream of the Navahoes. In procuring them the shaman begins on the south bank of the river, faces west and cuts a stick from a willow of suitable size and of the proper description, as hereafter specified : this he marks with one notch near its butt end to show, until it is finished, its butt end (par. 18), and to indicate its order of precedence. From the point where this is done he proceeds westward until he finds a second suitable stick, which he cuts and marks with two notches near the butt. In like manner, moving westward, he cuts a third stick which he marks with three notches, and a fourth stick which he marks with four notches. He wraps these four sticks in a bundle by themselves. He scatters pollen before him, to the north, in the way he intends to go and crosses the San Juan River to its north bank. Here he cuts and appropriately marks (with one to four notches), four more sticks, proceeding, as he does this, from west to east or in a direction opposite to that which he took on the south side. In his whole journey he follows the sunwise ceremonial circuit. The four northern sticks are wrapped in a separate bundle. As each willow is cut, it is trimmed to the proper length at the top and the discarded part is placed upright among the growing willows, as close as possible to the stump from which it was cut. Pollen is rubbed to the cut surface of the stump and scattered in the air by the ascending hand from the stump upward in the place where the stick was, apparently as a sacrifice to the spirit of the stick. They say this makes the willow grow again.

282.—The proper length of the sticks is either two spans or the natural cubit (par. 147), measures which the Navahoes declare always coincide on the same individual. Throughout this distance the stick must be free from branch, knot or blemish of any kind. One stick, duly measured, is taken as a standard for the other sticks. They are carefully denuded of bark and each is whittled to a point at the butt end in order that it may be easily stuck in the ground. Each of the four sticks cut on the south side of the river has a facet cut near its tip end (par. 17) to represent the square domino or mask worn by the female dancers in the rites. The sticks cut on the north side of the river have no such facets; their round ends sufficiently represent the round cap-like masks worn by the male dancers. After this is done the sticks are painted; those of the south blue, the color of the female in Navaho symbolism (par. 16); those of the north, black, the color of the male. According to the Origin Legend, when the sexes were separated in the fourth world, the women dwelt on the south bank, the men on the north bank of the river. The black sticks are painted white at the upper extremity in accordance with a law of Navaho hieratic art elsewhere explained (par. 15). The facet on each blue stick is marked with small black spots, to represent the eyes and mouth of the female mask and, at the bottom, is the yellow horizontal streak which represents the naʰotsói, or yellow evening sky. The upper end of each blue stick is painted black to represent the hair of the female characters which flows freely out, not being confined by the domino, while the hair of the male dancer is hidden by his mask. The points of all the wands are painted white.

283.—When the painting is finished each stick is decked with two whorls of turkey- and eagle-feathers. Each whorl is secured by one continuous cotton string which is terminated by a downy feather plucked from a live eagle — a breath feather. The string must be twilled from raw cotton on an old-fashioned spindle. Cotton string obtained from the whites is never used. The Indians prefer, too, the aboriginal cotton of New Mexico and Arizona. When the wands are finished the debris of manufacture is carried to the north and thrown away among a cluster of willows on the north bank of a stream or arroyo. Song and ceremony, which have not been obtained, accompany the making of the wands.

284.—The ĭnᵈiá‘ are expected to last a shaman throughout his professional career and may be, by him, bequeathed to a pupil.

TALISMAN OF THE YÉBĬTSAI.

285.—The talisman of the Yébĭtsai or Yébĭtsai baalíli consists of four sticks of peeled willow each three spans long, culled with much care and many ceremonial observances. They are so attached to one another with woolen strings that they may be spread into an open quadrangle and folded up again into what seems a simple cluster of parallel sticks, and again formed into a quadrangle and again folded, instantaneously and repeatedly by a simple motion of the arms. To each of the four strings is attached a downy eagle-feather. The talisman is not sacrificed. The chanter usually receives it from his preceptor, may retain it all his life and transmit it, in turn, to a pupil.   See plate IV, figs. B and C.   It is whitened with gles, which is applied anew at each ceremony.

CEREMONIAL BASKETS.

286.—The writer has observed but two forms of baskets made by the Navaho women and these are for ceremonial purposes.   Perhaps other forms are woven but he has not seen them in process of construction and, on inquiry, has not heard of them.   In developing their blanket-making to a high point of art the women of this tribe have neglected other labors.   The ruder but allied Apaches, who weave no woolen fabrics, make more baskets than the Navahoes and make them in greater variety of form, color, and quality.   The Navahoes buy most of their baskets from other tribes ; but, having greatly neglected the art of basketry, they still continue to make these two forms, because such are essential to the sacred rites and must be supplied by women of the tribe who know what is required.   The baskets are skilfully fabricated of twigs of aromatic sumac wound in the form of a helix.

BASKET-DRUM.

287.—The most important variety of sacred basket is that which is here called the basket-drum (plate IV, fig. D) because in this ceremony it is used (inverted) chiefly as a drum, although it is also used in other ways.   In none of the ancient Navaho rites is a regular drum or tom-tom employed.

288.—A colored band, red in the middle, with black serrated edges, is the sole decoration.   This band is not continuous but is intersected at one point by a narrow line of uncolored wood.   Although this resembles the line of life observed in ancient and modern Pueblo pottery, its presence is explained by reasons more practical than those which the Pueblos attribute to their line of life.   The Navaho line is formed to assist in the orientation of the basket, at night, in the medicine-lodge, when the fire burns low and the light is dim.   The law of butts and tips (par. 18) applies to this basket as well as to other sacred articles.   In making the basket the fabricator must always put the butt end of the twig toward the centre, and the tip end toward the periphery.   The butt of the first twig placed in the centre, and the tip of the last twig in the edge, must lie in the same radial line, and this line is marked by the hiatus in the ornamental band. The rim of the basket is usually so neatly finished that the medicine-man could not easily tell where the helix ended were not the pale line there to guide him.   It must lie due east and west when the basket is ceremonially employed.

289.—The border of this, as of other Navaho baskets, is finished in a diagonally woven or plaited pattern.   These Indians say that the Apaches and other neighboring tribes finish the margins of their baskets with simple circular turns of the investing fibre like that in the rest of the basket.   The Navaho basket, they believe, may always be known by the peculiar finish described, and they say that if among other tribes a woman is found who makes the Navaho finish she is of Navaho descent or has learned her art from a Navaho. They account for this by a legend which is perhaps not wholly mythical. In the ancient days a Navaho woman was seated under a juniper tree finishing a basket in the style of the other tribes, as was then the Navaho custom, and while so engaged she was intently thinking if some stronger and more beautiful margin could not be devised. As she thus sat in thought, the god *Hastséyalti* tore from the overhanging juniper tree a small spray and cast it into her basket. It immediately occurred to her to imitate in her work the peculiar fold of the juniper leaves and she soon devised a way of doing so. If this margin is worn through or torn in any way the basket is unfit for sacred use.

290.—The basket is given to the shaman when the rites are done. He must not keep it, but must give it away, and he must be careful never to eat out of it, for, notwithstanding its sacred use, it is no desecration to serve food in it.

291.—It seems best to describe in this place some of the general observances connected with the use of the basket-drum in the night chant. During the first four nights song is accompanied only by the rattle. During the last five nights noises are elicited from the basket-drum by means of the yucca drumstick. This drum is beaten only in the western side of the lodge. For four of these five nights the following methods are pursued: A small Navaho blanket is laid on the ground, its longer dimension extending east and west. An incomplete circle of meal, open in the east, of the diameter of the basket, is traced on the blanket near its eastern end. A cross in meal, its ends touching the circle near the cardinal points, is then described within the circle. In making this cross a line is first drawn from east to west, and then a line is drawn from south to north. Meal is then applied sunwise to the rim of the upturned basket so as to form an incomplete circle with its opening in the east. A cross similar to that on the blanket is drawn in meal on the concavity of the basket, the east-and-west line of which cross must pass directly through the hiatus in the ornamental band. The basket is then inverted on the blanket in such a manner that the figures in meal on the one shall correspond in position to those on the other. The western half of the blanket is then folded over the convexity of the basket and the musicians are ready to begin ; but before they begin to beat time to a song they tap the basket with the drumstick at the four cardinal points in the order of east, south, west, and north. The Navahoes say, "We turn down the basket" when they refer to the commencement of songs in which the basket-drum is used, and "We turn up the basket" when they refer to the ending of the songs for the night. On the last night the basket is turned down with much the same observances as on the previous nights, but the openings in the ornamental band and in the circles of meal are turned to the west instead of to the east, and the eastern half of the blanket is folded over the concavity of the basket. There are songs for turning up and for turning down the basket, and there are certain words in these songs at which the shaman prepares to turn up the basket by putting his hand under its eastern rim, and other words at which he does the turning. For four nights, when the basket is turned down, the eastern part is laid on the outstretched blanket first and it is inverted toward the west.   On the fifth night it is inverted in the opposite direction.   When it is turned up, it is always lifted first at the eastern edge. As it is raised an imaginary something is blown toward the east, in the direction of the smoke-hole of the lodge, and when it is completely turned up hands are waved in the same direction, to drive out the evil influences which the sacred songs have collected and imprisoned under the basket.

MEAL-BASKET.

292.—The other form of sacred basket is also used for various purposes; but as its chief use is for holding meal, it is called the meal-basket.   It is made on the same general principles as the basket-drum.   Its decorations consist of four crosses and four zigzag lines as shown in plate IV, fig. E.   The crosses are said to represent clouds, and the zigzag lines, lightning.   Usually the crosses are in red and the body of the basket in uncolored wood; but I have seen a few samples in which the crosses were in uncolored wood and the body of the basket in red. The crosses have a margin of brown and usually at each salient angle is a small square of brown.   The lightning symbols are generally brown, red, or part brown and part red.

DRUMSTICK.

293.—The next thing to be examined is the drumstick with which the drum is beaten.   The task of making this stick does not necessarily belong to the shaman; any assistant may make it; but so intricate are the rules pertaining to its construction that one shaman has told that he never found any one who could form it merely from verbal instructions.   Practical instructions are necessary.   The drumstick is made anew for each ceremony, and destroyed, in a manner to be described, when the ceremony is over.   It is formed from the stout leaves of *Yucca baccata*, a species of Spanish bayonet, but not every plant of this kind is worthy to furnish the material.   We have seen an hour spent in search for the proper plant on a hillside bristling with *Yucca baccata*.   Four leaves only may be used, and they must all come from the same plant, one from each of the cardinal points of the stem.   All must be of the proper length and absolutely free from wound, stain, withered point, or blemish of any kind.   These conditions are not fulfilled on every yucca.   The leaves may not be cut off, but must be torn off downward at their articulations.   The collector first pulls the selected leaf from the east side of the plant, making a mark with his thumb nail on the east or dorsal side of the leaf near its root, in order that he may know this leaf thereafter.   He walks sunwise around the plant to the west side, marks the selected leaf near the tip on its palmar (east) surface, and culls it.   He then retreats to the south side of the plant and collects his leaf there, but does not mark it,   Lastly, he proceeds sunwise to the north and culls his last leaf, also without marking it.   When the leaves are all obtained the sharp, flinty points and the curling marginal cilia are torn off and stuck, points upward, in among the remaining leaves of the plant from which they were culled. The four leaves are then taken to the medicine-lodge to be made up. The leaves from the east and west are used for the center or core of the stick and are left whole. The leaves from the north and south are torn into long shreds and used for the wrapper.

294.—In plate IV, fig. F, which represents the drumstick, it will be observed that the core of the stick is divided by a suture of yucca-shred into five compartments, one for each night during which the stick is used. Into each of these sections are usually put one or more grains of corn, which, during the five nights that the implement is in use, are supposed to imbibe some sacred properties. When the ceremony is all over these grains are divided among the visiting medicine-men, to be ground up and put in their medicine-bags.

295.—On the last morning of the ceremony, at dawn, when the last song of sequence has been sung and the basket turned up, this drumstick is pulled to pieces in an order the reverse of that in which it was put together. This work may only be done by the shaman who conducted the rites, and, as he proceeds with his work, he sings the song of the unraveling. As each piece is unwrapped it is straightened out and laid down with its point to the east. The debris which accumulated in the manufacture of the drumstick and which has been carefully laid away for five days is now brought forth and one fascicle is made of all. This is taken out of the lodge by an assistant, carried in an easterly direction, and laid in the forks of a cedar tree (or in the branches of some large plant, if a cedar tree is not at hand), where it will be safe from the trampling feet of cattle. There it is left until destroyed or scattered by the forces of nature. The man who sacrifices these fragments takes out with him in the hollow of his left hand some corn-meal, which he sprinkles with the same hand on the shreds from butt to tip. He takes out also, in a bag, some pollen, which he sprinkles on them in the same direction with his right hand. As he does this he repeats in a low voice the prayer or benediction, given in par. 988.

296.—The drumstick soon loses its freshness and becomes withered, shriveled, and loose. A few taps of one in this condition on the basket would knock it all to pieces. Even during the short time that the stick is in use for its sacred purpose it would shrivel and become worthless were it not buried in moist earth all day and taken forth from its hiding place only when needed for the ceremonies of the night.

297.—It has been said that the drumstick, when the ceremonies are done, must be pulled apart while a song is sung, and that its fragments must be deposited, with prayer and ceremony, in the fork of a cedar tree or other secure place. How, then, it may be asked, have I come into possession of a drumstick which is now on exhibition at the National Museum? It was made for my instruction by a sha-man, not in the medicine-lodge, but in my own study. Such it is his privilege to do for any recognized student of the rites. I have had several drumsticks made and pulled apart for my instruction, and I have made them myself, under the observation and criticism of the shaman.   This one I was allowed to retain intact. No one had ever sung or prayed over it.   It had never been used in the rites. It was therefore unnecessary to tear it apart, to release its soul and sacrifice its substance to the gods.

YÉ*DA*DĔSTSANI.

298.—The name yé*da*dĕstsani is applied to the two wands or implements used in the initiation of females into the mysteries of the Yébĭtsai.   Each consists of an ear of corn, one white and one yellow, to which is bound, by means of yucca fibres, four fresh sprays of spruce.   The sprays are but little longer than the ears of corn ; they are fastened about equal distances apart, around the circumference of the ear, with their axes parallel to that of the latter and their tips approximate to the tip of the ear.   The corn is of a kind so rare that the shaman always carries the necessary ears with him.   Each ear must have at its tip four grains of corn fitting closely together and completely concealing the cob at this point.   This kind of corn is called bohoni*t*i'ni.

PART II.

Rites in Detail.

Rites in Detail.

FIRST DAY.

299.—The work usually begins at nightfall (about 6 P.M.) of the day on which the chanter arrives. This first evening's ceremonies consist principally (1) in applying to the patient the talisman of the yébĭtsai (par. 285) and (2) in making and applying the circle kethawns. Shortly before the work proper is begun men collect twigs of aromatic sumac to make the kethawns.

CIRCLE KETHAWNS.

300.—These objects, called by the various but nearly synonymous names of Yébĭtsai-tsápas, yétsĭda-ĭ'lpas, yébapas and tsápasiazi-ol*tál*, are twelve in number. Each circle is made of a twig of tsĭ'ltsĭn or aromatic sumac (*Rhus aromatica var. trilobata*) two spans long. The diameter of the kethawn must correspond with a circle formed by the thumbs and forefingers of both hands touching at the tips. It is usually about five inches, depending of course on the size of the constructor's hand. In bringing the ends of the twig together, to form the circle, the butt end goes the nearer to the centre; the overlapping tip end is placed on the circumference. The ends are tied together by means of a yucca fiber exactly two spans long. The butt end of the fiber is applied to the butt end of the twig, underneath it, and at first parallel to it, the fiber is then wound around the spliced extremities of the twig, so that its tip end shall approximate the tip end of the twig. The fiber is secured by passing the end under the last turn and drawing it tight, in such a manner that its free extremity shall lie parallel with the extremity of the twig. Some shamans cause the twigs of sumac to be peeled, others do not. Great care must be exercised in bending the twigs; should a break or even a greenstick fracture occur, the twig must be discarded.

301.—When the circles are completed a woolen string called wol*thád* is firmly tied to each and then secured in three or four places, to the circle (so as to form an irregular square or triangle on it) with a sort of loose crochet knot which opens easily when the free extremity is pulled. Each woolen string is of a length measured from the centre of the left breast to the end of the right thumb, the arm being fully extended laterally. At the end of each string is a white downy eagle-plume or breath-feather. These strings, like the talisman of the yébĭtsai, are not sacrificed; they are permanent properties of the chanter. They are made for him on the occasion of conducting his first ceremony, after he has left the tutelage of his instructor. If the first patient is a woman, it is she who spins the strings; if it is a married man it is his wife who spins them; if it is an unmarried male it is his nearest female relative who does the work. The completed kethawn is emblematic of the rings on which the wind-gods ride.

302.—Like other sacred articles these kethawns must not touch the ground, while being prepared. They must be laid on clean cloths or buckskins which must, in turn, be laid on blankets. When a finished kethawn is placed in the basket, the point must be in the east and the breath-feather must hang over the edge of the basket.

Fig. 8. Kethawn of the first day. Circle kethawn.

303.—It takes about an hour to prepare the kethawns, several men working on them at the same time. When done they are placed one on top of another in one or more sacred baskets (I have seen them once divided into three groups, each group in a separate basket) to await the preparation of the actors who are to handle them.

304.—The debris produced in their manufacture is taken out to be deposited on the ground, north of the medicine-lodge. After they are laid in the basket, the chanter chews a plant called azénaol*tháde* (*Townsendia sericea*, Hook.) or unwinding medicine, and spits the juice on them. This is supposed to facilitate the disentanglement of the string. The juice is spat also on the talisman of the Yébïtsai (par. 285).

CONSECRATION OF LODGE.

305.—The shaman, or an assistant, moving sunwise, now applies meal to the inside of the lodge. If the lodge is conical (par. 238) he rubs it on the five principal posts or rafters beginning with the pole immediately south and ending with that immediately north of the doorway. In a flat-topped lodge (par. 239) he applies meal to the stringers. In both cases he makes a second circuit of the lodge scattering meal around the edge of the apartment. If the patient is a male, white meal is used, if a female, yellow meal is employed. On one occasion I have seen the meal applied by the shaman immediately after his arrival, before any other work or ceremony had begun. It is applied thus again to the lodge on the night of the vigil.

RITES OF TALISMAN AND KETHAWNS.

306.—While the kethawns are being prepared the talisman of Yébïtsai is freshly painted with white earth and the toilet of those who are to personate the mythic characters progresses; but this is usually not finished until after the kethawns are completed. The four following characters are usually arrayed in the paint, masks and other properties described elsewhere (par. 260). *Hastsé-*yal*i, *Hastsé*l*pahi and two *Hast*ébaad or goddesses. When they are ready, the shaman gives them careful instructions how they are to act on their return. Then they leave the lodge, carrying their masks hidden under their blankets, and proceed a short distance to the east, to a place free from observation, where they put on their masks and await the arrival of the patient at the lodge. Sometimes the talisman is not painted till after the kethawns are finished.

307.—While the actors are gone, the floor is swept; a crier goes to the door; calls aloud " Biké *hat*á*l*i *h*akú ", " Come on the trail of song "; the patient enters, sits down on a blanket to the northwest or west of the fire, facing east, with legs extended, and the shaman, accompanied by his assistants, begins to sing.

308.—Soon after the song begins *Hast*séyal*i enters, approaches the patient, opens his talisman (par. 285) to its quadrangular form and places it around the patient four times, accompanying each motion with his peculiar cry of " Wu‘ hu‘ hu‘ hú ". The first time he places it around the waist; the second time around the chest; the third time around the shoulders; the fourth time around the head; taking it completely away from the body and folding it up in his hands after each application.

309.—He leaves the lodge and the moment he has disappeared a Yébaad enters. A circle kethawn is given to him (or to her, we might figuratively say, since the Yébaad is a man, personating a female divinity). He applies this in silence to the sacred or essential parts (par. 135) of the patient, holding it by both hands until he comes to the mouth. While the kethawn is held in the last position, at the mouth, by one hand, he, with the other hand takes hold of the free end of the string and ravels it out with a single pull. He then lets the wooden ring drop. Holding fast to the end of the string he drags the attached ring after him, through the dust, along the floor of the lodge, and departs.

310.—When the first *Hast*ébaad leaves, *Hast*sé*l*pahi enters and, taking a circle kethawn, goes through with all the motions of his immediate predecessor; and besides utters a cry while so doing. When he has disappeared, dragging his kethawn after him, the second *Hast*ébaad enters and repeats exactly all the acts performed by the first *Hast*ébaad, or Yébaad (par. 64).

311.—Four times these four characters enter in the order and manner described, and on each occasion they go through exactly the same performances, with this exception : on the second and fourth occasions, when *Hast*séyal*i enters, instead of surrounding his patient with the open talisman he applies it folded to the sacred parts. As each one of three of these characters carries out with him at each exit one of the circle kethawns, it is evident that, when the last actor has departed for the fourth time, all the kethawns have been taken out of the lodge.

312.—The characters that enact this scene are not always the same. I have known *Hast*sé*l*pahi to be omitted, on which occasion *Hast*séyal*i performed the service usually assigned to the former, in addition to his own, making separate exits and entrances for each function; and I have known *Hast*sé*h*og*an to be added, applying plumed wands to the patient, after *Hastséyalti* had applied his talisman, and in an analogous manner.

313.—When the actors leave the lodge in costume, for the fourth time, they take off their masks, outside, and in a few moments return to the lodge, unmasked. *Hastséyalti* delivers up his talisman to the shaman, assistants proceed to take off the paraphernalia from the actors and to wash the coating of white earth from their bodies. When this is done, the actors array themselves in their ordinary clothes and the work of the evening is completed. This usually occurs a little after 9 P. M.

314.—I have it noted, from observation, that *Hastséyalti* returns the talisman to the shaman, who lays it away in the mask recess in the west of the lodge, but I have been informed by one shaman that according to his custom it is laid on the roof, over the doorway on top of the circle kethawns, remains there all night, is brought in at sunrise, wrapped in buckskin and put away in the chanter's bag.

315.—The circle kethawns are thus disposed of: According as they are taken out by the masked actors, the strings are wound simply around them and they are laid on top of one another, on the roof of the vestibule of the lodge, where they remain all night. Next morning at sunrise they are taken into the lodge and turned over to the shaman. He unties the woolen strings and puts these back in his bag. He unwinds the yucca fibers which hold the ends of the twigs, to form the circles, and straightens out both twigs and fibers (always holding the butts next to his body and the tips to the east). He arranges them all in a single bundle with all the butts at one end and all the tips at the other. The bundle is carried some distance to the north of the lodge and tied securely (tips pointing north), in the forks of a tree which may be of any species. The bundle is sprinkled from butt to tip with meal by the left hand, and pollen by the right, while a benediction is muttered (par. 988). If there is no tree convenient it may be laid on the top of a stout weed and need not be tied if it will stay on without tying.

SONGS OF THE EVENING.

316.—The songs sung on this evening, called Aga'hoágĭsĭn or Summit Songs, are 26 in number; but not all are sung on this occasion; more of them are heard later during the nine-days' ceremony. The whole set is sung on the third night. When there is no dance of the naak*h*aí to be held on the last night, only three songs of the set are repeated.

SECOND DAY.

317.—The second day of the ceremony is a busy one. (1) In the forenoon sacrifices (kethawns) are prepared, (2) a sudatory is built (if one is to be used), and the first sweat-bath administered. (3) In the afternoon a small dry-painting is made and various properties are prepared to be used in the performances of the night.   (4) The evening is occupied in dressing the patient in garlands of spruce and removing them.   Songs, prayers, and elaborate ceremonials accompany these acts.

KETHAWNS.

318.—The preparation of the sacrificial kethawns for this morning begins about 7.30 A. M., the patient being present while the work is in progress.   The general rules, previously described (pars. 165, *et seq.*) are observed.   According as the pieces are cut from the reed they are laid on a broad flat stone which rests on a large piece of white cotton cloth, or they may be laid directly on the cotton cloth.   Each piece is three finger-widths in length.   The reeds are usually procured in the Chelly Cañon.   While one assistant is engaged in cutting off the pieces another is mixing the paints on the flat stone, and the chanter busies himself with taking various properties out of his medicine-bag and preparing the accessories of the sacrifice.   He takes out four corn-husks and lays them in a row with their tips to the east on the white cotton cloth, south of the flat stone.

319.—He puts into the first and third husks (counting from north to south) beads, or fragments of the material from which beads are made, of three different kinds, in this order: white, blue, black, (shell, turquoise, cannel-coal).   He puts into the second and fourth husks, white, haliotis (for yellow), and black.   South or east of the corn-husks, on the cotton cloth, he arranges four piles of objects laid down in the following order for each pile: three bluebird feathers, three yellow warbler feathers (either of these two kinds may be omitted at times, but not both), one feather of the cedar-bird, one downy eagle-feather,[15] one turkey-feather, one hair from a turkey's beard, and one cotton string, about an inch long, rubbed in meal.   When these piles are completed he transfers one to each husk, next he puts in each husk in the following order: specular iron-ore, blue pollen, and corn-pollen.   Then he moistens a brush made of bluebird feathers, and applies with it, on each feather bundle, from butt to tip the i'yi*d*ezná or life pollen.

320.—The painting of the cigarettes is next in order, and when this begins, so do the songs.   These are usually sung by three persons: the chanter, the shaker of the rattle, and another.   They sit in the west of the lodge and in the order mentioned, from north to south.

FIRST SONG OF THE PAINTING.

I.

A little one now is prepared.   A little one now is prepared.
For *Hastséhogan*, it now is prepared.
A little message now is prepared,
Toward the trail of the he-rain, now is prepared,
As the rain will hang downward, now is prepared.

II.

A little one now is prepared.   A little one now is prepared.
For *Hastséyalti*, it now is prepared.
A little kethawn now is prepared,
Toward the trail of the she-rain, now is prepared,
As the rain will hang downward, now is prepared.   See pars. 900, 901.

The other songs are similar except that for " little message " and " little kethawn,"
it says : in the second song, " holy message " and " holy kethawn "; in the third,
" beautiful message " and " beautiful kethawn " ; in the fourth, " happy message "
and " happy kethawn."

321.—The first cigarette, that which comes from the butt end of the reed, and
is placed in the north of the row, is painted yellow and marked with four rows
of black dots, six dots in each row ; this is to represent an owl and is called naestsá
biketán or the kethawn of the owl.   The second cigarette is painted blue, is sacred
to a god called *Hastséayuhi*, and is known as *Hastséayuhi* biketán.   The third
cigarette is painted black and is known as *Hastséeltlihi* biketán ; it belongs to a
god called *Hastséeltlihi* who dwells in old ruins.   The fourth cigarette, that from
nearest the tip of the reed, is painted blue and is called Tse'yaltí biketán or kethawn
of the Talking Stone.   All are sprinkled with specular iron-ore before they are
dry so that it may stick and cause them to glisten.   When the paint is dry, the
cigarettes are filled, sealed, and symbolically lighted (par. 170).   The remainder
of the water used in preparing the kethawns is poured on the ground to the east
of the blankets.

TOBACCO SONG (SUNG WHILE FILLING CIGARETTES).

322.—Now the yellow tobacco am I.
Now the broad leaf am I.
Now the blue flower am I.
With a trail to walk on, that am I.   See pars. 902, 903.

Another stanza speaks of a " narrow leaf " and a " white mountain flower."   There
are four stanzas, each referring to a different kind of native tobacco.[7]

323.—The finished cigarettes are laid in the husks on top of the other articles,
in the order in which they have been named,—the first cigarette, that of the owl,
being laid in the husk furthest north ; the second, that of *Hastséayuhi*, in the next
husk, to the south, and so on.   This done, the chanter sprinkles pollen from butt
to tip, in each husk, taking it in its regular order.   He folds the husk around its
contents by turning down first the northern edge (about one third) of the leaf and
then turning down, over this, the southern edge.

324.—He collects the bundles from north to south, placing one on top of
another in his left hand.   He applies pollen to the essential parts of the patient,
making a motion as if bringing it from the sun, and takes pollen on his own tongue
and head.   Then he transfers the sacrificial bundles, without disarranging them,
to the hands of the patient.   While the latter holds them, the chanter sits squatting

by his side and repeats a long prayer, sentence by sentence, and the patient repeats it after him in like manner.

PRAYER.

FIRST PART. TO THE OWL GOD.

325.——1. Owl !
    2. I have made your sacrifice.
    3. I have prepared a smoke for you.
    4. My feet restore for me.
    5. My legs restore for me.
    6. My body restore for me.
    7. My mind restore for me.
    8. My voice restore for me.
    9. To-day take out your spell for me.
    10. To-day your spell for me is removed.
    11. Away from me you have taken it.
    12. Far off from me it is taken.
    13. Far off you have done it.
    14. To-day I shall recover.
    15. To-day for me it is taken off.
    16. To-day my interior shall become cool.
    17. My interior feeling cold, I shall go forth.
    18. My interior feeling cold, may I walk.
    19. No longer sore, may I walk.
    20. Impervious to pain, may I walk.
    21. Feeling light within, may I walk.
    22. With lively feelings, may I walk.
    23. Happily may I walk.
    24. Happily abundant dark clouds I desire.
    25. Happily abundant showers I desire.
    26. Happily abundant vegetation I desire.
    27. Happily abundant pollen I desire.
    28. Happily abundant dew I desire.
    29. Happily (in earthly beauty) may I walk.
    30. (Not translated).
    31. May it be happy before me.
    32. May it be happy behind me.
    33. May it be happy below me.
    34. May it be happy above me.
    35. With it happy all around me, may I walk.
    36. It is finished in beauty (or happily restored).
    37. It is finished in beauty.

SECOND PART. TO *H*AST*S*ÉAYUHI.

326.——This is the same as the first part except in the following lines :

    0. High on top,
    1. *H*ast*s*éayuhi.
    24. Happily abundant dark mist I desire.
    31 and 32 transposed.

THIRD PART. TO *HAST*SÉELTLIHI.

327.—This is the same as the first part except in the following lines :

> o. Beneath,
> 1. *H*ast*s*éeltlihi.

FOURTH PART. TO TSE'YAL*T*Í, THE TALKING (OR ECHOING) STONE, CALLED TSE'ETLÍHI IN THE PRAYER.

328.—This is the same as the first part except in the following lines :

> 1. Tse'etlíhi.
> 24. Happily abundant dark mist I desire.
> 31 and 32 same as in second part.

The final words " It is finished in beauty " are repeated four times, instead of twice as in the previous parts. (Texts, pars. 971–974.)

329.—When the prayer is finished, the chanter takes the four bundles in his hands and applies them to the essential parts of the patient's person. An assistant receives them from the chanter and takes them out of the lodge to dispose of them. Usually the chanter instructs the assistant in his duties before he starts.

330.—The following is sung immediately after the kethawns are applied to the body of the patient :

SEVENTH KE*T*ÁN BIGĬ'N.

I.

> Across the Chelly Cañon from the other side he crosses,
> On a slender horizontal string of blue he crosses,
> For his kethawn of blue, upon the string he crosses.

II.

> Across the Chelly Cañon from the other side he crosses,
> On a slender horizontal string of white he crosses,
> For his kethawn of black, upon the string he crosses. See pars. 904, 905.

331.—The first kethawn, that of the Owl, is laid at the root of a large piñon tree. The second kethawn, that of *H*ast*s*éayuhi, is put on top of a small natural hillock, because he is a mountain god. The third, that of *H*ast*s*éeltlihi, is put in a deserted house or old ruin, or, if such is not near, among rocks that look like a ruin, because he is a god of ruins. The fourth kethawn, that of Tse'yal*t*í, is placed at the base of a perpendicular rock that is found to give forth an echo. Through all the manipulations to which they are subjected these sacrifices are, as already described, maintained in a certain order. As before stated, when the shaman takes up the bundles, he takes that of the north, with the owl kethawn, first and puts one on top of another in his hand. When they come to be sacrificed therefore the owl kethawn is at the bottom of the heap and is sacrificed first. The kethawn of the Talking Rock is at the top and is sacrificed last. They may be taken in any direction from the lodge except north.

332.—These sacrifices for the morning of the second day are, it is said, never omitted and no change is made in them in consequence of differences in sex of the patients; but slight changes are made for other reasons. At a ceremony witnessed in 1890, two kethawns were added for the gods of Tsé'ĭntyel or Broad Rock in the Chelly Cañon. These were double the length of those already described. Each was painted half black and half white. In one it was the butt, in the other the tip end that was blackened. These kethawns were sealed by the patient, not by the shaman. In the myth of the Stricken Twins (par. 866) a different arrangement of kethawns is described and it is not improbable that this arrangement is sometimes practiced by modern shamans in the *to'nastsiḥégo ḥatál.*

333.—The patient retains his seat for a while after the cigarettes have been taken out, and the chanter, joined by one who rattles, sings the Tenth Keṭán Bigĭ'n, or Song of the Kethawn. When this song is done, the ceremonies in the lodge, connected with the kethawns, come to an end. This usually occurs about 9 A.M.

TENTH KEṬÁN BIGĬ'N.

I.

1. In a beautiful manner now he bears,
2. For *Ḥastséḥogan*, now he bears,
3. A little message now he bears,
4. Toward the trail of the he-rain, now he bears.

II.

1. In a beautiful manner now he bears,
2. For *Ḥastséyalṭi*, now he bears,
3. A little message now he bears,
4. Toward the trail of the she-rain, now he bears. See pars. 906, 907.

SUDATORY.

334.—As soon as the ceremonies of the kethawns are done, the work of preparing the sudatory begins. Here will be described that form of sudatory in which the sweat-house is built. The work of constructing the house may begin before sunrise; but the ceremonies do not begin till after the kethawns are disposed of.

335.—Inside the medicine-lodge, one or two men grind, between stones, the dry pigments to be used in decorating the sweat-house, and put them on the inner surface of curved pieces of bark to be kept till used; another twills, with a spindle, short strings to be used later in the work; another puts in order the eight plumed wands which are to be planted around the sweat-house, and two Indians dress themselves to represent *Ḥastséyalṭi* and *Ḥastsébaad*. Outside the lodge, other assistants finish and decorate the sweat-house, make the fire,—the coal for starting which is taken from the medicine-lodge,—and get everything ready for the sweat-bath. Before the masqueraders dress, the foxskins they are to wear are often taken out and buried for a while in moist soil to freshen them. The construction and decoration of the sweat-house is described elsewhere (pars. 243 *et seq.*).

336.—When the workmen, having finished the sudatory, return to the medicine-lodge to report, a crier goes to the door and shouts the usual call, "Biké *hatáli haku.*" Those who assist in singing enter and begin to sing, and the procession, in single file, starts for the sweat-house. The shaman sprinkles pollen on the ground in the direction they are to take. The patient leads, the chanter immediately follows him, and the assistant singers and relatives of the patient come after. One member of the procession, often the shaman, bears a sacred basket (plate IV, E) containing meal and the plumed wands. The following is a free translation of the song sung on the march and continued at the sudatory, if need be, until it is finished:

I.

This I walk with, this I walk with.
1. Now *Hastséyalti*, I walk with.
2. These are his feet I walk with.
3. These are his limbs I walk with.
4. This is his body I walk with.
5. This is his mind I walk with.
6. This is his voice I walk with.
7. These are his twelve white plumes I walk with.
8. Beauty before me, I walk with.
9. Beauty behind me, I walk with.
10. Beauty above me, I walk with.
11. Beauty below me, I walk with.
12. Beauty all around me, I walk with.
13. In old age, the beautiful trail, I walk with.
14. It is I, I walk with.

II.

The same as stanza I. except as follows:

1. Now *Hastséhogan*, I walk with.
8 and 9 transposed.
10 and 11 transposed.   See pars. 908, 909.

337.—Arrived at his destination the patient sits to the south of the sweat-house door and disrobes. If the patient be a woman, a blanket, held by women, is raised as a screen, under cover of which she takes off all her clothes except a short skirt reaching below the knees, and she retains the blanket until she enters the door of the sweat-house so that there is no exposure of the person above the middle of the legs. If the patient be a man, he strips to the breech-cloth and on screen is raised.   In the sweat-house he sits on spruce twigs which have been spread on the ground before he enters.   I have seen " sage " (*Artemisia*) used here instead of spruce when the spruce gatherers did not arrive in time and I have heard of other plants being used ; but spruce is the material preferred for carpeting the sweat-house.   The hot stones are taken from the fire and put in the sudatory to the north of the occupant, the curtains of the door are let fall, and the patient is left to take his hot-air bath.   Before the patient enters, the plumed wands are set up ; the black sticks north, the blue south ; their faces turned toward the sweat-house.

338.—While the patient is undressing and, afterwards, while sitting in the sweat-house, the chanter busies himself in mixing two cold infusions.   One of these, called tsóɬtsĭn, or kĕ'tlo, is for external application (par 215).   The other infusion is for internal administration, is called klédʑe aʑé, is prepared in a large gourd, and is a very elaborate compound described elsewhere (pars. 203–208).   When the two infusions are ready the chanter dips his fingers four times into the bowl of kétlo, transferring, each time, some of the liquid to his mouth ; he spits twice on the sweat-house and twice on his rattler ; sits south of the house facing north, and, joined by two or more men, begins, to the accompaniment of the rattle, to sing the *Tʜa'dʑé* Bigĭ'n or Sweat-house Song, the first of which is the

TSĔ'NI GISĬ'N, OR SONG IN THE ROCK.

I.

1. In the House of the Red Rock,
2. There I enter ;
3. Half way in, I am come.
4. The corn-plants shake.

II.

1. In the House of Blue Water,
2. There I enter ;
3. Half way in, I am come.
4. The plants shake.   See pars. 910, 911.

339.—After the lapse of 15 or 20 minutes, the men who enact the part of the yéi, *H*astséyal*ʇ*i and *H*ast*s*ébaad, leave the medicine-lodge and approach the sweat-house.   They take their cue from the song ; but if they are tardy a messenger is sent for them.   They are so draped in heavy blankets that all their paint and sacred paraphernalia are hidden from view ; their masks are held concealed under their blankets and to the casual observer they seem to be a pair of Indians out for a stroll.   They approach the sweat-house as if on no special errand bent.   Each of them drops a piece of white string into a basket containing meal which the shaman has before him ; the shaman rubs the string with meal and hands it back.   If they are inexperienced in their work, the shaman may coach the actors on their duties, particularly on the mode of massage.   Their interview with the chanter ended, they pass to a spot some 50 paces to the east of the sweat-house,

—in sight of those sitting at the sweat-house, if the woods are not dense,—lay down their blankets, and adjust their masks.   All this is done in silence until the masks are adjusted : then *H*ast*s*éyal*t*i whoops.

340.—They return to the sweat-house as full-fledged gods approaching from the east, after the patient has been in the bath some 20 or 25 minutes. Song is resumed, *H*ast*s*éyal*t*i throws the blankets off from the entrance to the sweat-house and by giving his characteristic call, sometimes by beckoning also, signals to the patient to come out.   The two gods (as it is now convenient to call them) walk around the patient four times.   The chanter pulls up the plumed wands ; hands to *H*ast*s*éyal*t*i the four black sticks that stood north of the lodge and to *H*ast*s*ébaad the four blue sticks that stood south.   (Once it was noted that the gods pulled up the wands.)   Holding them two in each hand, the butts approximated, each god, in turn, applies his wands, with strong pressure, to the essential parts of the patient's body.   One does not wait for the other to get entirely through ; but *H*ast*s*éyal*t*i applies his implements to one part at a time and steps aside to allow *H*ast*s*ébaad to follow his example.   Besides this there is application of the wands to parts specially diseased.   On one occasion the gods were seen to perform all this application or massage four times.   When the massage is done, *H*ast*s*éyal*t*i (sometimes taking a preliminary drink himself) administers to the patient, in four separate draughts, the infusion of kléd*z*e azé in the gourd and gives to the chanter, to drink, the residue, if any is left. After this both gods in turn howl hideously into both the patient's ears and deliver the wands to the shaman.

341.—They run back to the place east of the sweat-house where they left their blankets.   Here they take off their masks, again conceal under their blankets their divine trappings, and rejoin, in the guise of ordinary Indians, the group at the sweat-house.   Before they return, they sacrifice the strings which, when they first came to the sweat-house, they threw into the vessel of meal.   To do this, they lay them in any little channel or gully cut by the rains, saying, " *H*ozógo na*s*ádo."

342.—While the two yéi have gone to resume the garb of ordinary mortals, the patient (screened with a blanket if a woman, not screened and nearly naked if a man) washes himself all over with the kétlo which the chanter has prepared in the wicker bowl.   The patient also drinks some of this lotion.   While the washing is in progress the chanter, joined usually by four others, sings a song.

LAST TSĚ'NI GISI'N, OR SONG IN THE ROCK.

I.

1. At the Red Rock House it grows,
2. There the giant corn-plant grows,
3. With ears on either side it grows,
4. With its ruddy silk it grows,
5. Ripening in one day it grows,
6. Greatly multiplying grows.

II.

1. At Blue Water House it grows,
2. There the giant squash-vine grows,
3. With fruit on either side it grows,
4. With its yellow blossom grows,
5. Ripening in one night it grows,
6. Greatly multiplying grows. See pars. 912, 913.

343.—The pictures on the sweat-house are obliterated by being scraped from one end to another,—foot to head in anthropomorphic figures,—and the dust of which they were constructed is gathered in a blanket and thrown away a few paces to the north of the sweat-house. The stones used to heat the house are taken out; so are the spruce twigs and other materials with which the floor was covered; the stones are laid on the twigs; both are thrown on the ground north of the sweat-house and meal is sprinkled on them while a benediction is uttered, by the man who throws them away.

344.—The bath occupies in all about thirty minutes. The strictest silence is required of the patient while he is in the sweat-house. This is a lesson forcibly inculcated in the myth of the Stricken Twins (par. 835).

345.—When the treatment is for disease of the eye, massage is also performed with a strip of skin cut lengthwise from the middle of the nose of a big-horn and the tip of the horn of the same animal, each piece being held in a different hand and transferred from hand to hand like the plumed wands. When the treatment is for paralysis or stiffness of the limbs, the tendones Achillis of this animal is used. All these articles may be applied at the same time with the wands, as stated in the myth (par. 866), or separately. A mixture containing water from the eye of a big-horn is, at this time, applied to the eye in a case of eye-disease. One medicine-man has told me that he also uses the contused root of a plant called nakéʰin, which he places between the lids for ophthalmia (par. 866).

346.—While the party is at the sweat-house, the unburned wood around the fire is thrown into the flames so that it may be all burned up. When the unmasked personators of the gods return to the sweat-house, the party there forms a line in the following order: patient, chanter, personator of god, personator of goddess, friends of patient including singers. The chanter sprinkles pollen on the ground indicating the line of march and all return in single file to the medicine-lodge. The chanter carries the wands in the meal-basket; while unassisted and without a rattle he sings all the way on his return and continues to sing after his return until certain songs of sequence are concluded. These are *Hastséyalti Bigïn* or Songs of the Talking God. They are sung after each one of the four sweats, but not on the last night of the ceremony.

347.—When the party returns to the medicine-lodge the patient sits in the west, for he has still further treatment to undergo, and the whilom yéi proceed to divest themselves of their divine toggery and to scrape the paint from their bodies. The chanter applies pollen to the essential parts of the patient, puts some into his or her mouth, takes a pinch of it on his own tongue, and applies a little to the top of his own head. These applications of pollen are all timed so as to coincide with certain words of the accompanying song. In placing the pollen in the mouth of the patient, a motion is sometimes made as if bringing the pollen from the sky.

348.—This concludes, for the day, the rites of the sweat-house, which are brought to a close about midday. The patient leaves the lodge; the chanter puts away his properties; the inmates of the lodge engage in laughing, joking, general conversation and comments of the events of the morning until food is brought in, when all proceed to refreshment.

RITE OF SUCCOR.

349.—When the midday meal is over, or while some may still be eating, assistants begin to prepare for the rites of the afternoon and night: the floor of the lodge is swept, sand for the groundwork of the dry-painting is brought in, spruce twigs and yucca leaves are provided, and the work is begun of preparing the masks of the gods who appear later in the afternoon and the evergreen dress which the patient is to wear at night. Then work on the dry-painting is begun. As this is comparatively small it does not require more than half an hour to paint.

DESCRIPTION OF THE DRY-PAINTING.

350.—The picture is about a yard in diameter. The circular colored figures in the periphery represent the four principal sacred mountains of the Navahoes, (or, more properly speaking, perhaps, the counterparts of these in the Fourth World. See par. 14). The black mountain in the east is Tsĭsnadzĭ′ni or Pelado Peak; the blue one in the south is Tsótsĭl or San Mateo; the yellow one in the west is Dokoslíd or San Francisco Mountain, the white one in the north is Depĕ′ntsa or the San Juan Mountains.[2] These mountains are supposed to be divine houses, the doors of which are represented by double lines in contrasting colors on the sides of the mountains. The four single colored lines leading from the mountains toward the central figure indicate the trails of succoring gods—although only one divine character appears in the real act of succor. Proceeding from the south, at a point beyond the blue mountain and reaching the heart of the central figure, is a line made in corn-meal (white for a male, yellow for a female patient) and in its course are figures of four shod foot-prints; it makes the trail of Hastséyalti and of the patient, who, it is said, must walk exactly in the footsteps of the god if he would recover. The figure in the centre is that of Anĭltáni Atét, or the Grasshopper Girl, drawn in pollen. This figure is made if the patient is a female; but if the patient is a male, they substitute for the form of the Grasshopper Girl that of Thadĭtín Asiké or the Pollen Boy, her mythic brother, shown in fig. C′, plate II. The east and west mountains are said to be two homes of Hastséyalti (probably Hastséyalti and his wife Hastsébaad);

the north and south mountains are said to be homes of *Hastséhogan* (or of him and his wife). In the original sand-painting the mountains were in relief—little hemispheres of sand. At one ceremony which the writer attended, this picture was omitted, for the reason, it was said, that no sacred buckskin could be procured for *Hastséyalti* to wear, when he came to the act of succor. See fig. C, plate II.

351.—While the picture is being made, the mask of *Hastséyalti*, the Yébĭtsai, is dressed and the débris accumulated in the dressing is carried away. When the picture and mask are done, the chanter instructs his assistants, in the work before them. The man who is to enact the part of the Yébĭtsai dresses all but putting on his mask. He is covered with a large blanket which conceals all his paraphernalia and, hiding his mask under his blanket, he leaves the lodge. He proceeds to a retired spot, east of the lodge, where, secure from casual observation, he drops his blanket and puts on his mask.

352.—As soon as he is gone a crier goes to the door and announces in the usual way that song and rite are to be resumed. The patient enters, walks along the line of meal, stepping carefully on the pictured foot-prints, and sits down on the central figure of the picture, facing east. The moment he is seated, the singers commence a

DSĬ*L* BIGĬ'N OR MOUNTAIN SONG.

1. In a holy place with a god I walk,
2. In a holy place with a god I walk,
3. On Tsĭsnadzĭ'ni with a god I walk,
4. On a chief of mountains with a god I walk,
5. In old age wandering with a god I walk,
6. On a trail of beauty with a god I walk. See pars. 914, 915.

353.—The other three stanzas are the same as this except that in the third line the names of other mountains are substituted for Tsĭsnadzĭ'ni or Pelado Peak, thus: II, Tsótsĭ*l* or San Mateo ; III, *D*okoslí*d* or San Francisco ; IV, *D*epĕ'ntsa or San Juan. *Hatáli* Natlói has told the writer that this is a favorite song of his and that he feels peculiarly happy while singing it.

354.—Song is continued for about 20 minutes. Soon after it begins the Yébĭtsai enters, walks along the trail of meal, stepping carefully in the pictured foot-prints, and stands before the patient. As he advances an attendant obliterates the trail of meal behind him, until he reaches the fourth foot-print. This is not erased until later, when the entire picture is destroyed. Arriving at the middle of the picture the Yébĭtsai howls wildly into each of the patient's ears, and takes his seat to the north of the patient, facing east.

355.—When the singing is done, the chanter puts pollen on the sacred or essential parts of the patient and on some of his own sacred parts ; he administers some to the patient and to himself *per orem*, and passes the bag around that others may partake of the sacred substance. Then follows a long prayer of 298 sentences or verses given out as usual, sentence by sentence, by the squatting priest and repeated after him, in like manner, by the patient.

356.—When the prayer is finished the Yébĭtsai goes around the patient sunwise and always facing west.   As he progresses, he kneels at each of the four miniature mountains, takes sand from the mountain, and applies it to the patient, into whose ears he utters, at the same time, his peculiar cry.   This done, the Yébĭtsai leaves the lodge, goes to the place in the east where he laid his blanket ; this he resumes, hides his mask under it, and returns in ordinary guise, to the lodge, where he re-moves his paint and trappings.   The patient leaves the picture and sits in another part of the lodge where the shaman administers the fumigation (par. 198).   The picture is obliterated, and the sand carried out.   The rites of the afternoon are completed usually between three and four o'clock.

OOHAÍ OR RITES OF THE EVERGREEN DRESS.

357.—Soon after the rites of the dry-painting are over, the work of prepar-ing for the evening rites is resumed : the chanter washes himself all over with a solution of yucca root, giving special attention to his hair ; assistants make the long garlands of spruce twigs, tied with yucca fibre, with which the patient is to be festooned at night, and the mask which the patient is to wear is made.   If the patient be a woman, the mask is made of yucca leaves ; if the patient be a man, it should be made of dressed antelope skin.   Other assistants prepare the masks of the gods, a cigarette, and·other properties.

358.—The garlands which compose the *th*aokĭ's or evergreen dress are made of the smallest sprays of spruce, which are collected in bunches and placed butt to butt.   Each little bunch is of such a size as to be conveniently clasped between the thumb and forefinger.   The bunches are tied together with strings of yucca fibre in a running series of simple knots.   Four bunches are placed close together forming a group ; then a space is left and another group of four is formed.

359.—The mask for the female is called nikéhe.   It is about ten inches square, depending on the size of the patient's face, and consists of yucca leaves woven together in a simple woof and warp.   In preparing a leaf for the mask the dorsal part at the midrib is cut off to facilitate weaving.   A fringe of spruce is put on around the mask to represent hair ; small holes are cut to represent eyes and mouth ; under the mouth a horizontal streak of black, a horizontal streak of yellow, and eight vertical streaks of black are painted as shown in plate IV., figs. G and H.   The vertical streaks are called nĭ'ltsa natsí and symbolize rain. The holes for the eyes are triangular and one finger-stretch apart (par. 144). The square hole for the mouth must be a similar distance from each eye.   These orifices are surrounded by black painted spots of their own shape.   Strings of yucca fibre are used to secure the mask to the head of the patient.   The pieces cut out for the eyes and mouth are tied in a strip of yucca fibre and secured to the back of a projecting end of yucca leaf at the bottom of the mask ; this is done in order that they may not be separated from the mask and may be sacrificed with it.

360.—Figs. G and H, plate IV, are taken from photographs of the female mask, or nikéhe. One shows the incomplete mask, before the fringe of spruce is added; the other represents the finished mask. As the reader will readily surmise, it is not practicable to get a photograph of this during the ceremony. The object here depicted was, in the presence of the author, during the daytime, at Fort Wingate, made, unmade, and its material sacrificed, by a learned shaman, with all the observances employed in the rites. He consented to the photographing; but would not consent to the preservation of the mask.

361.—As has been said, when the patient is a male, the mask—called *th*adĭlkaí, —is made of dressed antelope skin, and it must be of the kind known as sacred or unwounded skin (par. 257). The piece cut out for the mask must be the size of two outstretched hands. It is painted blue; holes like those of the female mask are cut for eyes and mouth; it is marked below the mouth with lines, and it is trimmed with a fringe of spruce, like the female mask. Of late this is rarely used, owing to the scarcity of antelope in the Navaho country, and the face of the male patient is usually hidden only with the evergreen dress in this particular rite.

362.—The cigarette kethawn which goes with the mask is one span long. For a male patient it is painted black, for a female patient blue; but no design is painted on it. Tobacco only is put in it—no feathers or other materials. It is sealed with moistened pollen.

363.—About half-past five or six o'clock the workers in the lodge are served with supper and labor is suspended. When the meal is over, there is usually a season of gossiping and smoking until dark or about seven o'clock, when they go to work again.

364.—The first thing is to paint and dress two men to represent the Navaho war-gods Nayénĕzgạni and *T*o'bad*z*ĭst*s*íni, which characters are described and depicted elsewhere (pars. 73–88). Their preparation occupies about half an hour. When they are ready the chanter instructs them as to their duties and they go forth blanketed and with masks concealed as did previous personators of the divine—although it is now dark—to a secluded place in the east, where they don their masks preparatory to their return to the lodge as succoring gods. Blankets covered with a white cotton cloth are spread in the west of the lodge for the patient to sit on.

365.—As soon as the actors have departed, the crier goes to the door and utters aloud the usual call (par. 336). The floor is swept. The spruce garlands made during the afternoon are brought forth and laid half to the south and half to the north on the white cotton sheeting. Presently the patient enters and sits on the middle of the sheeting. He takes off his moccasins and shirt and extends his legs toward the east. He may wear for the occasion, besides his own, a number of borrowed necklaces of shell and coral. Two or three comrades, of the same sex as the patient, may enter with him or her and sit down at the door of the lodge. A female patient bares her feet and legs only.

366.—The following is the order in which the body is dressed: 1, right ankle ; 2, right leg ; 3, right thigh ; 4, left ankle ; 5, left leg ; 6, left thigh ; 7, waist ; 8, chest with wreath passing diagonally over left shoulder and under right axilla ; 9, chest with wreath passing over right shoulder and under left axilla ; 10, right arm ; 11, right forearm ; 12, right wrist ; 13, left arm ; 14, left forearm ; 15, left wrist ; 16, neck ; 17, head.

367.—When the work is finished the patient looks like a great formless pile of evergreen twigs on which the mask appears as a patch. It has not been discovered that this sylvan costume represents any special mythic character. It is inferred that it symbolizes the bonds of disease.

368.—When the dress of green is completed, song is resumed. At its sound the war-gods, fully caparisoned, enter the lodge and approach the patient. Here is a free translation of the song sung as they advance.

SONG OF THE APPROACH.

I.

In a land divine he strides,
In a land divine he strides,
Now Nayénĕzgạni strides,
Above on the summits high he strides,
In a land divine he strides.

II.

In a land divine he strides,
In a land divine he strides,
Now *To'badzĭstsíni* strides,
Below on the lesser hills he strides,
In a land divine he strides. See pars. 916,917.

369.—The gods walk around the patient sunwise, making toward him, at each of the cardinal points, a downward sweep of the right hand, armed with its proper implement (pars. 78, 85). They halt in front of him when they get back to the east and Nayénĕzgạni, who holds the knife, assisted by his brother god proceeds to divest the patient of the evergreen dress. This is done by cutting with the stone knife and is a tedious task. The mask, if of yucca, is first cut in two down the centre and the halves are cut into smaller pieces. The garlands are cut down the centre in front and back and as exactly as practicable down both sides of the body. The right side, in each region, is cut before the left. The wreaths are cut in pieces after they come off. They are cut over the patient's head and allowed to fall on it until every fascicle is freed. The pile of débris is carefully examined to see that the work is complete. All this time, song is continued. The work of cutting is called *th*aokï's. Each god then takes a bundle of spruce in hand and applies it to the usual parts. They do this in turn, i. e., one does not wait for the other to get completely through ; but Nayénĕzgạni applies his bundle to the soles ; *To'badzĭstsíni* follows immediately, doing the same, and so on for other parts. Each god utters, with each motion, his peculiar sub-vocal call: Nayénězgạni says "*Ha*‘a‘a‘á"; *To*‘bad*ʑ*ĭst*s*íni says, "*H*áaaá." The gods then give the patient a vigorous massage, in different parts of the body, and retire from the lodge (about 8.30 P.M.). Song and work end together.

370.—When the gods have departed the chanter stands for a while facing the patient and dropping fragments of the evergreen dress on the patient's head. Afterwards, while still thus standing, he begins to sing and to beat time with a grass brush on a bunch of the spruce twigs. Continuing to sing he wanders all around the patient, sunwise, and makes motions with his grass brush as if he were brushing away some evil influence which, at length, he pretends to brush out at the smoke hole. Another shaman may join in the songs.

*TH*AOKĪ'*S* BE*H*AKINÁLD*Z*O. A SONG TO SWEEP OFF WITH.

I.

The corn grows up ; the rain descends.
I sweep it off, I sweep it off.

II.

The rain descends ; the corn grows up.
I sweep it off, I sweep it off.   See pars. 923, 924.

In all, twelve songs belong to the oo*h*aí; ten precede the brushing and two accompany it.

371.—After song and brushing are finished, the fumes of yá*d*i*d*ĭnil are administered to the patient in a manner elsewhere described (par. 198). When the fumes have died down and the coals are extinguished the chanter says "Kạ*l*" (now) to the patient, whereat the latter arises and dresses himself. Thus end the rites of the night in the lodge, usually about 9 P.M.

372.—About the time the brushing is completed the personators of the war-gods return unmasked, divest themselves of their trappings, and wash off their paint. The debris of the evergreen dress is carried out of the lodge, to be deposited on the ground a short distance to the north of the lodge, preferably under a tree. The fragments of the dress are laid down first, tips to the north, then the fragments of the mask on top of the dress, and lastly the kethawn on top of all. Pollen is sprinkled on the heap and a benediction is uttered in low tones.

THIRD DAY.

373.—The work of the third day consists in the preparation of two sets of kethawns,—one in the morning, the other at night,—in the sacrifice of the first set, in the application of the second set, and in the administration of a second sudorific treatment, which occurs in the forenoon.

KETHAWNS OF THE MORNING.

374.—The kethawns usually prepared on the third morning will first be described. These vary in number from six to twelve and are cigarettes, made of reed, preferably culled in the Chelly Cañon. A chanter never makes the same number twice in succession, although he always makes an even number. Thus, if he makes six at one ceremony, he must make eight or ten at the next that he conducts. So, too, the number of accompanying songs are changed; some will purposely be omitted one day, to be sung another day. The larger kethawns to be described are always a pair. It is among the smaller kethawns that the number is varied.

375.—The two larger kethawns, each half a span or six finger-widths long, are called Kĭninaekaígi ke*t*án, or kethawns of the White House. The first in order is painted yellow on its western half and white on its eastern half; the second is white on its western and yellow on its eastern half. A white cotton string is attached to each kethawn at its centre by means of a peculiar knot[76]. Included in the circles of this knot are three feathers of the bluebird and three of the yellow warbler. One of these feathers is taken from each wing of the bird and one from the tail. Feathers of *Pipilo chlorurus*, called by the Navahoes, *d*a*t*óinogá*l*i, or he-shakes-the-dew, may be substituted for those of the yellow warbler. Five beads are strung along each string; one of white shell, one of turquoise, one of haliotis, one of cannel-coal, and one again of white shell. Beyond, east of these, a bunch of plumage is secured by means of the peculiar knot mentioned above; the bunch consists of a downy eagle feather, the breast feather of a turkey, and a hair from the beard of a turkey-cock. The positions of the five beads on the string are determined by stretching out the digits of one hand on the string as nearly equidistant as possible from one another as shown in fig. 9, e; an attachment is made where the centre of each digit falls. The string is originally two spans long; but when it is tied to the cigarette and all objects are attached the end is cut off three finger-widths beyond the most extreme eastern attachment — that of the bunch of plumage. See fig. 9. Each end of the string, when tied, must lie parallel and close to its enclosed feathers. Sometimes the beads are drilled in the medicine-lodge, just before they are applied. When the kethawns are finished they are laid on the cotton sheet, in proper order, butts aligned.

376.—The four, or more, smaller kethawns are called naak*h*aígi ke*t*án, or kethawns of the naak*h*aí dance (par. 621). Each one is three finger-widths long. One half of the number are painted black and are marked each near its eastern extremity with a design representing the two eagle-plumes and the bunch of owl-feathers worn in the dance by the male yéi or yébaka (par. 61). The eagle-plumes are drawn in white with a black spot near the tip; the owl-feathers, are done in yellow. The other half, in number, of the smaller otherwise kethawns are simply painted blue to symbolize the female yéi or yébaad and not decorated.

377.—In preparing this whole set of kethawns, the general rules already given (par. 165) are observed. They are plugged first with a small wad of feathers of the yellow warbler, next with a wad of feathers of the arctic bluebird, and then with native tobacco; all of which are rammed down with an owl's feather. They are symbolically lighted and sealed. They are placed each in a separate corn-husk into which are put the following articles in the order named: white shell, turquoise, haliotis shell (or cannel-coal), specular iron-ore, blue pollen, corn-pollen, feather of yellow warbler, feather of bluebird, eagle-feather, turkey-feather, hair of turkey's beard, cotton string. The shells, turquoise, and cannel-coal are put with the large kethawns as finished beads, while with the small kethawns they go as small fragments or powder.

378.—Fig. 9 is a representation of these kethawns, drawn by Dr. McConnell from a set now in the author's possession. The owl-feathers are not so perfectly formed in the original decorations.

379.—Songs are sung during the painting of the kethawns, some of which are the same as those sung while painting the cigarettes of the second morning.

380.—It takes over an hour to get the kethawns ready; they are usually done before 9 A.M. Then the patient, who has been in the lodge all the time, sits in the

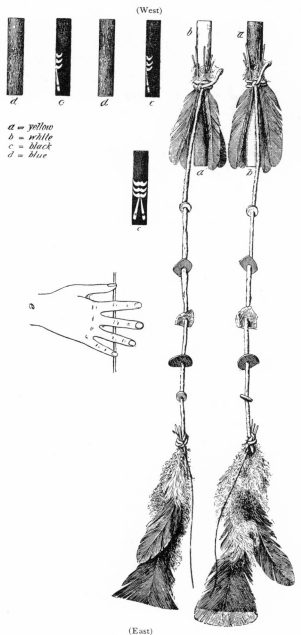

Fig. 9. Kethawns of the third morning.

west, on the blankets and cotton, facing the east, with lower extremities extended and hands open, resting, palms upward, on the knees. The shaman first puts the bundles containing the two long kethawns, those of the White House, with their tips to the right, in both hands of the patient, who grasps them.   While the kethawns are thus held, the shaman repeats a long prayer which the patient repeats after him, sentence by sentence, in the usual manner.

381.—After the prayer, the shaman takes the kethawns, applies them to the essential parts (par. 135) of the patient's body and with special force to any part which is supposed to be the particular seat of disease.   Then pollen is applied as elsewhere described (par. 185), but on one occasion it was observed that this was done also before the kethawns were lifted from the cotton sheet. The patient must still retain his seat on the blankets and cotton until all the kethawns have been applied, and must not put his feet on the ground.   The shaman gives the kethawns to the assistant who is to take them out of the lodge. The assistant stands and waits for the rest of the cigarettes.

382.—The chanter then collects, proceeding from north to south, the bundles containing the smaller kethawns ; applies them to the body of the patient ; places them in the hands of the latter, as he did before ; prays again ; again applies pollen, and gives the bundles to the assistant.

PRAYER.

PRAYER OF THE FIRST LONG KETHAWN.

383.—1. In the house of Horizontal White,
2. He who rises with the morning light,
3. He who moves with the morning light ;
4. Oh Talking God !   (*Hast s éyal t i*).
5. I have prepared your sacrifice,
6. I have made a smoke for you.
7. His feet restore for him.
8. His limbs restore for him.
9. His body restore for him.
10. His mind restore for him.
11. His voice restore for him.
12. To-day your spell take out for him.
13. This very day your spell is taken out.
14. Away from him you took it.
15. Far away from him it has been taken.
16. Far away from him you have done it.
17. Happily he will recover.
18. Happily he has recovered.
19. Happily his interior will become cool.
20. Happily, feeling cold may he walk around.
21. It is finished again in beauty.
22. It is finished again in beauty.
23. In beauty may you walk, my grandchild.
24. Thus will it be beautiful.

PRAYER OF THE SECOND LONG KETHAWN.

384.—1. In the House of Horizontal White,
2. He who rises with the evening light,
3. He who moves with the evening light,
4. Oh House God !   (*Hast sého g an*).

The rest is as in the previous prayer.

PRAYER OF THE FIRST SHORT KETHAWN.

385.—1. With the blue face,
    2. Oh Male Divinity ! (*H*ast*s*ébaka).

The rest as in the previous prayers.

PRAYER OF THE SECOND SHORT KETHAWN.

386.—1. With yellow streak,
    2. Oh Female Divinity ! (*H*ast*s*ébaad).

The rest as in the previous prayers.

387.—The prayer of the third small kethawn is the same as that of the first The prayer of the fourth small kethawn is the same as that of the second except that the words " It is finished again in beauty " are repeated four times.

388.—When the prayer is done the kethawns are taken out to be sacrificed in the east. The assistant finds a steep rock with its declivity to the west. He makes a faint furrow on the ground with the outer edge of the right moccasin, from east to west, near the base of the rock. He lays down a bunch of *Gutier-rezia*, usually collected en route, in the furrow. He takes the kethawn out of its husk and places it on the *Gutierrezia*, at such a distance from the rock that the attached feathers on the end of the string, fully strung out eastward, just touch the base of the rock. He puts on a pinch of the sacred powders and other sacred articles and then empties, by turning over, the entire contents of the husk on the kethawn. He says a short prayer while crouching to do all this, and rises when it is finished. He covers the kethawn and its accompaniments with *Gutierrezia* and earth. He measures off a foot's length southward from the first kethawn, makes a furrow with his foot at this distance, and deposits the second kethawn with exactly the same observances as were used on the first kethawn.

389.—When all this is done he proceeds again in an easterly direction to find a place for the smaller kethawns. A small piece of clear level ground, devoid of vegetation, is selected. The kethawns are laid, tips to the east, a foot's length apart, in a row extending from north to south ; the north kethawn being planted first as is the invariable rule. In placing each of these kethawns the same rites are observed as with the first two or K*ĭ*ninaeka*í*gi ke*t*án. When the objects are laid, face down (par. 171), the pictures of the eagle-plumes do not appear on top, but to the south side, for thus the plumes of the living dancers come in the dance of the last night, when they face the east. The sacrifice completed, the assistant returns to the lodge in the prescribed manner (par. 180).

390.—In the Chelly Cañon, Arizona, there still stands, in an excellent state of preservation, a remarkable ruined cliff-house built of yellow sandstone, two stories high, which has often been sketched, photographed, and described. Its upper portion is painted white, horizontally ; its lower unpainted portion is yellow.

As it lies in a deep rock-shelter, well overshadowed by a towering cliff, the white paint has been protected from rain and snow and looks almost as fresh now as when first applied, many centuries ago perhaps.   The Navahoes call this structure Kĭninaékai, which signifies a stone house with a white horizontal streak.   This name, in the present work, is often translated House of the Horizontal White or House of the White Horizontal Streak ; but the Americans in Arizona apply the brief free translation White House, a name which is also used in this work. Here, according to the myths, dwelt certain gods who practiced the rites of the klédᴢe haʈál and taught them to the Navahoes.   It is to the gods of this house that these sacrifices are offered.   See plate V, fig. C.

391.—The colors of the long kethawns, white and yellow, typify the White House in an obvious manner ; but they also typify the morning and the evening light—the east and the west.   One of the kethawns is sacred, as the prayers show, to the *H*astséyalʈi of the White House, its god of the east and of the dawn ; the other is sacred to its *H*astsé*h*ogan, its god of the west and of the evening, and it is for this reason that the colors on one cigarette are placed in a reverse order to those on the other cigarette.   At the White House the patient is supposed to stand in the centre of the world ; for this reason the string is attached to the middle of the kethawn.   The white cotton string represents the biké *h*oᴢóni, the beautiful or happy trail of life so often mentioned in the songs and prayers, which the devotee hopes, with the aid of the gods, to travel.   "With all around me beautiful, may I walk," say the prayers, and for this reason the string passes through beautiful beads, which, by their colors, symbolize the four cardinal points of the compass.   "With beauty above me, may I walk," "With beauty below me may I walk," are again the words of the prayers ; so the string includes feather and hair of the turkey, a bird of the earth, and of the eagle, a bird of the sky. "My voice restore for me," "Make beautiful my voice," are expressions of the prayers and to typify these sentiments the string includes feathers of warbling birds whose voices "flow in gladness" as the Navaho song says.   The steep-faced rock, at which the long kethawns are sacrificed, some say, represents the White House ; others, the cliff in which the White House stands.

392.—The smaller cigarettes, as has been said, represent the dancers of the naak*h*aí in the last night of the ceremony of klédᴢe *h*aʈál.   As this dance first became known to the Navahoes at the White House, in the mythic days, these kethawns go with those of the White House.   As the dancers at a certain part of the dance appear alternately, male and female, so the male and female objects are made to alternate.   As the ground on which the dance takes place is carefully levelled, smoothed, and cleared of obstructions, so the ground selected for sacrifice must be clear and level.   The plumes on the masks of the male dancers are placed on the right side and when they dance, as they usually do, facing the east the plumes are seen to the south ; so the kethawns, when placed in proper order, tip ends east, and faces downward, show the plumes in the south. The articles sacrificed with the small kethawns have the same symbolism as similar articles that go with the large kethawns, though many are less carefully arranged.

393.—On one occasion when ten kethawns were made, four were observed which were sacred to the Bighorn (gods) or Rocky Mountain Sheep. They were of the same length as the smaller or dance kethawns just described, were accompanied with the same materials, and were arranged in a row with the latter, south of them, on the cotton cloth. They were colored, in order from north to south thus: white, blue, yellow, black. The first and third were sacred to males and were deposited on top of a steep-sided rock. The second and fourth were sacred to females and were deposited on a ledge on the face of such a rock. They were applied to the patient after the other kethawns had been taken out and were sacrificed by a different assistant.

394.—Such are the usual kethawns for this morning; but occasionally other forms may be employed. A set called yebĭ*l*naiskági ke*t*án deserves especial mention. A man who personates a divine character in the rites is charged to observe continence while thus personating and afterwards while a particle of sacred paint remains upon his body. If he transgresses this rule, disease of the eyes and ultimate blindness is the penalty. But the proper and timely application of the ceremony of klédze *h*atál may save him. In treating such cases these cigarettes are prepared on the morning of the third day. They are twenty in number and are made according to the usual rules. Two are four finger-widths in length; the rest are three finger-widths long (pars. 139, 140). Ten are painted black to symbolize the male; ten blue, to symbolize the female. Before they are placed in the corn-husks and applied to the body of the patient they are arranged as shown in fig. 10. Those marked 1 stand for the feet; those marked 2, the knees; those marked 3, the palms; those marked 4, the shoulders; those marked 5 (the longest cigarettes), the trunk; and those marked 6, the head. The parts mentioned are the sacred parts to which the kethawns are applied. In manipulating the objects, the order of precedence is according to the numbers given in fig. 10, but in addition,

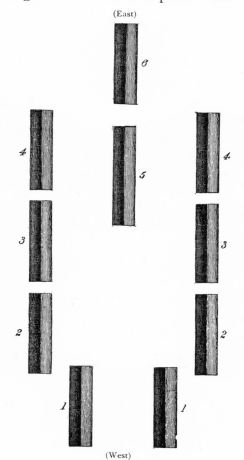

Fig. 10. Kethawns of third morning. Yebĭ*l*naiskági ketan.

the black cigarette always precedes the blue, and the right side always precedes the left. The cigarettes are wrapped in two husks—all the black in one, all the blue in another—with white shell, haliotis, turquoise, cannel-coal, and pollen.

When the rites are done the kethawns are deposited north of the medicine-lodge, preferably at the base of a tree.

395.—No matter which set of kethawns is made, while the bearers are absent, the chanter and others continue to sing and the patient receives the fumigation of yádidínil (par. 198). The bearers return in ten minutes or more, the length of their absence depending on the number of kethawns and the distance they have to travel in order to find suitable places for deposit. They bring back with them the corn-husks in which the sacrifices were enveloped. These husks they return to the shaman, who either puts them in his bag or stores them among the rafters in the west of the lodge, for they have been culled with care and may be used again. They must be clean white husks, free from red spots, mould, rents, or traces of worms. They must not be used for smoking. They are finally deposited to the east of the lodge, in the forks of a cedar-tree if one can conveniently be found.

SUDORIFIC.

396.—After a pause of about an hour, some men go out to make the final preparations of the second sweat-house. If a new house has not been built, but the house of the previous day used, a new fire at least is made, fresh spruce twigs are strewn on the floor, fresh stones are heated, and fresh infusions made,—this last may be done in the medicine-lodge. The only design seen drawn on the top of the second sweat-house is shown in fig. 6 ; it is done in corn-meal, and is called akán tsïseníl. The songs of the second sudatory are only twelve in number and although alike in character and sentiment to those sung the day before, they are differently worded. If a new sweat-house is built in the south the masqueraders go to the south to assume their masks, and there are other slight changes made in the work, which are noted elsewhere (par. 253). In all other respects the rites, medicines, etc., of the sudatory of this day are exactly the same as those of the day before, and need not again be described ; but the work is usually begun and finished at an earlier hour.

KETHAWNS OF THE EVENING.

397.—The only work done in the lodge on the afternoon of the third day is the preparation of the numerous kethawns to be sacrificed at night. The four or more men who do the work, seem not particularly impressed with the sacred character of their labors ; they smoke, tell stories, laugh, joke, and banter one another—the hour of song and prayer has not yet arrived. The labor begins at 1 P.M. or soon after—when the mid-day meal is finished in the lodge—and continues for about an hour and a half.

398.—The kethawns are fifty-two in number ; four are sections of reed for cigarettes, and forty-eight are little sticks of solid wood.

399.—Of these forty-eight there are twelve belonging to the east, made of mountain mahogany (*Cercocarpus parvifolius*) ; twelve belonging to the south, made of a shrub called mai*tá* or coyote-corn by the Navahoes (*Forestiera neo-mexicana*); twelve belonging to the west, made of juniper (*Juniperus occidentalis*), and twelve belonging to the north, made of cherry (*Prunus demissa*). The four pieces of reed are each three finger-widths in length. The forty-eight sticks are each four finger-widths in length. All these are not just the same length, for the measurements are taken on the hands of different men. Each workman measures one stick on his fingers and takes this as a standard for the others. Mountain mahogany is probably selected for the east, because its abundant plumose white styles give the shrub a whitish aspect and white is the color of the east. *Forestiera* may be chosen for the south because its small olive-shaped fruit is blue, the color of the south. Juniper is perhaps taken for the west because its outer branchlets and leaves have, in the arid region, a tone of yellow, which is the color of the west. Cherry seems to be adopted for the north because the fruit of *Prunus demissa*, the common wild cherry of New Mexico, ripens black, and black is the color of the north. In the myth of The Visionary (par. 660) certain mythic reasons are given for selecting these trees for the kethawns; yet it is probable that the custom does not follow the myth, but that both follow the primary law of symbolism. See par. 659.

400.—The four cigarettes are cut from a single cane and prepared with the usual observances. The first is painted white; the second, blue; the third, yellow; the fourth, black; the colors of the cardinal points. There are no devices painted on them.

401.—The bark is left on the wooden kethawns except at the butt ends where they are sharpened to a point one finger-width long, and here they are not painted. The bark of the sticks of mountain mahogany is painted white; that of the sticks of coyote-corn, blue; that of the juniper, yellow, and that of the cherry, black. The flat outer or tip end of each male kethawn is painted in a contrasting color (par. 15), i. e., the ends of the white kethawns are painted black; the ends of the blue kethawns, yellow; the ends of the yellow kethawns, blue; the ends of the black kethawns, white. The flat ends of the female sticks are all painted black; this is to indicate that the female mask does not cover the entire head, but allows the hair to be seen. Sex is also shown by cutting facets, one finger-width long, on alternate sticks, to represent the female masks. The naturally circular ends of the other sticks sufficiently represent the cap-like male mask (par. 17). Each facet is painted blue, and has a yellow streak at the chin (pars. 61, 267); usually eyes and mouth are indicated by black spots.

402.—A sacred basket of the kind described as a basket-drum (par. 287) duly oriented, is used to receive these kethawns according as they are finished. The four cigarettes are placed in the centre on a little pile of corn-meal, in the usual order, tips east. The wooden kethawns are arranged in four groups, side by side around the centre, tip ends outward, radiating slightly as the form of the basket compels. The twelve white kethawns are put in the eastern quarter of the basket; the twelve blue, in the southern quarter; the twelve yellow, in the western quarter; and the twelve black, in the northern quarter. In laying them down, male and female kethawns are made to alternate and the male takes the precedence, in order, of the female. Fig. E, plate II, shows a sample of each kind of wooden kethawn, and fig. A, plate V, from a photograph, shows the completed sacrifice.

403.—The objects are called ke*l*án *l*áni, or the many kethawns. They are said to belong to a numerous divine company called *H*ast*s*éayuhi. The wooden pieces are for the minor deities of the group; the cigarettes for the superior ones. The white cigarette is for a *H*ast*s*éyal*t*i; the blue for a *H*ast*s*ébaad; the yellow for a *H*ast*s*ébaka; the black for a *H*ast*s*éol*t*oi.

404.—The basket containing the finished kethawns is put to one side, in the mask recess or other secure place, where it is kept until needed at night.

405.—While the work of preparing the kethawns progresses inside, and after it is done, men are engaged outside the lodge in cleaning the ground around it, cutting down bushes, grubbing sage-brush, removing sticks and other obstructions,—in short, in clearing the ground for the rites of the last night and the practice dances which precede them.

406.—Soon after dark, about 7 o'clock, four men begin to dress themselves as yéi. One of these is always *H*ast*s*éyal*t*i; another is usually *H*ast*s*é*h*og*a*n, but occasionally *H*ast*s*él*p*ahi takes his place; the other two are *H*ast*s*ébaad, or goddesses. They are ready in about half an hour and leave the lodge. Blankets and cotton sheeting are spread for the patient in the west of the lodge; the usual call is cried at the door; the patient enters and, having first divested himself of his necklace and all clothing except his breechcloth, takes the seat prepared for him in the west; the kethawns in the basket are brought forth, and song is begun, in which many join the chanter. The series of songs now sung is that of the Aga'hoá Gisĭ'n, or Summit Songs (par. 897). The singers begin with No. 1, and finish the set before they stop.

407.—They have not been singing long when *H*ast*s*éyal*t*i enters, runs toward the patient, and applies his quadrangular talisman four times in the same manner as he did on the first night (par. 308).

408.—He runs out of the lodge; returns instantly without his talisman; again approaches the patient at a run, and, being handed one of the kethawns, applies it to the usual parts of the patient, giving his characteristic whoop with each application. He also applies it to parts most diseased. The patient draws in breath when the kethawn is at his mouth. When all this is done the god runs with the kethawn out of the lodge.

409.—The moment he disappears, one of the *H*ast*s*ébaad rushes in, takes a kethawn from the hand of the chanter and repeats all the acts of *H*ast*s*éyal*t*i with the first kethawn, but utters no sound.

410.—As the *H*ast*s*ébaad, or goddess, rushes out *H*ast*s*é*h*og*a*n (or *H*ast*s*él*h*pahi) runs in and, taking a kethawn, repeats the operations of his predecessors, giving his own peculiar howl or whoop with each application.

411.—When this god leaves, the second *Hastsébaad* enters, running, and does exactly as the others did, but utters no sound.

412.—In this order they follow one another and repeat over and over again these acts, until all the kethawns are taken out. Then *Hastséyalti* runs in once more and applies his talisman as he did in the beginning.

413.—As there are fifty-two kethawns to be disposed of, each one of the gods must have thirteen entrances and thirteen exits, besides those made by *Hastséyalti* to apply his talisman. It has once been noted that this particular rite occupied just one hour, ending at 8 P.M. During all the work song never ceases.

414.—In taking the kethawns, they begin with the four cigarettes in the centre and of these, with the white one belonging to the east. They take the rest in their proper order,—blue, yellow, black (south, west, north). When the cigarettes are gone, they take of the wooden kethawns; first the most northerly white one—in the eastern quarter of the basket—and proceed thence around the basket, sunwise, taking the most easterly black one in the north last. All is so arranged that the male divinities take male kethawns, and the goddesses, female kethawns.

415.—The kethawns, according as they are taken out, may be laid on the flat roof of the entry to the lodge, to be left there all night and sacrificed early in the morning in the following manner: The white kethawns are put away in the east, the blue in the south, the yellow in the west, the black in the north, at a little distance from the medicine-lodge. Each cigarette is placed with some care, stuck in an upright position in the ground, under a ledge of rock, or other protecting object, safe from the tramping of cattle. The wooden kethawns are scattered, one by one, on the ground in the neighborhood of the cigarettes. There is a special method of throwing them away: Standing with his back to the lodge, the bearer holds under his thumb the point of his flexed index finger; he places the stick, pointed end forward (face upward if a female), on the back of the flexed finger; suddenly and forcibly he extends the finger, releasing it from the thumb like a spring, and thereby throwing the stick some distance away. Such is the usual way of disposing of them; but one chanter related that he directs his assistants to sacrifice the kethawns at night. According to his method, as each bearer goes with his kethawn out of the lodge, he runs a little distance away—east, south, west, or north, according to the color of the stick; throws the object away in the manner described, and runs back in time to take his place when next it becomes his turn to enter the lodge. A description of this latter method has already been published by the author.[16]

416.—In a few moments after the last kethawn is taken out the actors return, unmasked, and proceed to wash off the paint and divest themselves of their trappings. The shaman receives back from the actor the talisman of the yébitsai and puts it in his bag. Lastly, he administers the fumigation to the patient in the usual form.

OCCASIONAL RITES.

417.—Thus—usually between 8 and 9 P.M.—the rites of the third day come to an end.   But, in addition, the following was once witnessed : After a lapse of about a quarter of an hour from the return of the masqueraders, the chanter mixes some paints on a stone and touches with them the essential parts of the patient and of himself.   He then sings a song and utters a long prayer which the patient repeats after him, in the manner that other prayers are repeated.   This, it is said, is a rite rarely performed, and the chanter must have for it an additional fee of a new buckskin, on which he draws a picture of the Pollen Boy if his patient is a male and a picture of the Grasshopper Girl if his patient is a female.   (Plate II, C.)

418.—When the work is done, supper is brought in and all persons in the lodge, who desire, may partake.

419.—In the ceremony of *to'nastsihégo hatál*, or that form of the night-chant, where there is no dance on the last night (par. 648), it is related that the ke*t*án *l*áni are not made ; but that, instead, twelve hoops or circles large enough to encircle the body are formed out of the trees used in the kó*nn*ike (par. 255) tied at the joinings with yucca fibre.   *H*astséyal*t*i, *H*astséel-*t*odi, and two *H*astsébaad are the actors.   The hoops are made outside, wheeled into the lodge, one by one, by the divinities, and placed around the patient, one on top of another, till all are placed and he is concealed.   This arrangement is called i*l*yá*d*itli*n*.   The gods return, remove the hoops, one by one, and as they roll them out the patient blows after the hoops.   As each circle is taken out it is pressed from east to west and from north to south.   The bond is loosed and the stick straightened.   The débris lies outside until morning, then it is laid under a tree and sprinkled with meal while a benediction is spoken.   This is, of course, a very meagre description of this rite of the ïlyá*d*itli*n*.   Par. 867.

420.—The third day is the day of the south, and when the work is done it is said that the patient finds everything clear and beautiful in the south, where before all was dark and unlovely.

FOURTH DAY. (UNTIL NIGHTFALL).

421.—The rites proper of the fourth day consist of : 1st, the preparation and sacrifice of kethawns in the morning ; 2nd, the administration of the sudorific, later in the forenoon ; 3rd, the ablution with amole early in the afternoon, and 4th, the rite of the tree and mask in the evening.   But there is some work done before the kethawns are made.   If a new sweat-house is to be built, the labor of construction is begun early—usually before sunrise—and at this time also two men go out to select the sapling which is to be used in the evening rites.   They mark this by tying an eagle-plume to its top.   As already told (par. 415), very early on the morning of this day the sacrifices of the previous night may be deposited ; but this is to be regarded only as a consummation of yesterday's ceremonies.

422.—After nightfall, about 8 P.M., the vigil of the gods begins; but as the rites connected with this are continued all night until dawn of the fifth day and form a separate and peculiar feature of the whole work, they will be described under a separate heading: Fourth Night.

KETHAWNS OF THE MORNING.

423.—The work of the fourth day in the medicine-lodge begins about 7 A.M. with the preparation, by assistants, of sacrificial cigarettes, which take about an hour to make. Breakfast is brought in and eaten, sometimes immediately before this particular task is begun, sometimes immediately after it is finished. The cigarettes for this occasion vary, the variation depending on the nature of the disease treated, on the kind of cigarettes used by the presiding shaman in preceding ceremonies, and perhaps, on other conditions.

424.—The following is a description of eight cigarettes, the making and application of which have been noted on three different occasions. They are prepared in accordance with general rules already described. Eagle- and owl-feathers, mixed with pollen, are used for the plugs, which are laid out in a row on the white cotton sheeting before being inserted. When painted and finished the cigarettes are arranged in the following order: 1st, red; 2nd, red; 3rd, blue; 4th red, decorated with the queue-symbol of To'badẓïstsíni; 5th, blue; 6th, black; 7th, blue; 8th, white. Each is placed in a separate corn-husk with the following materials: beads or bead material of four kinds, specular iron-ore, corn-pollen, blue pollen, life pollen, moistened pollen, bluebird feathers, yellow-warbler feathers, eagle breath-feather,[15] turkey-feather, hair of turkey's beard, cotton string.

425.—Songs are repeated at various times during the progress of the work, the finishing song being one whose refrain is, Kạt hadanïsté, Now it is finished (par. 900).

426.—After the cigarettes are made the patient takes his, or her, seat in the usual place in the west. The priest applies pollen to the essential parts, administers pollen to himself, and throws a pinch of it toward the sky (smoke-hole). He then collects the sacrificial bundles, proceeding from north to south, as usual, places them in the hands of the devotee, squats beside him, and utters a long prayer in his usual hasty manner, which the patient repeats after him, sentence by sentence. This prayer begins: " House made of the dawn in Tse'gíhi," and is addressed to gods of that place. It consists of four parts, three of which contain forty-six verses, and one, the last, forty-eight verses. Of the forty-six verses, thirty-eight have their counterparts in the prayer of the First Dancers (par. 613).

427.—When the prayer is done, the kethawns are applied by the shaman to the patient's essential parts and handed to an assistant who takes them out to sacrifice them.

428.—Four of these kethawns belong to the Atsá'lei, or First Dancers of the ninth night, and four to *Hast*sébaka. They are sacrificed or planted south of the lodge, with their tips pointing south. A small space of ground is smoothed off with the foot; furrows a hand's breadth apart, are marked on this space with the foot; one cigarette with its accompaniments is laid in each furrow. The corn-husks, only, are returned to the shaman.

429.—Another set of eight cigarettes, sometimes substituted for those just described, is shown in the diagram, fig. 11, laid out, in regular order from north

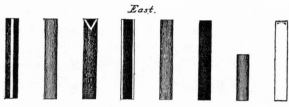

East.

Fig. 11.   Kethawns of the fourth day.

to south, as seen before being placed in the corn-husks. Each of these is three finger-widths in length, except No. 7, which is as long as the middle joint of the little finger. The patient performs the symbolic act of lighting with the crystal. After each cigarette is laid in its proper corn-husk, beads of the usual four kinds are added, then the usual feathers and hair of a turkey's beard, and lastly four sacred powders in the following order: specular iron-ore, blue pollen, corn pollen, life pollen. The patient presents a rock crystal to the bundles as if reflecting light into them. The chanter again puts pollen on the kethawns, with a low muttered blessing, but without song. He administers pollen to the patient and to himself with another muttered blessing. The bundles are folded in the prescribed manner (par. 323). The first four bundles are given to the patient, who grasps them with both hands. One of the usual long prayers is said. The assistant (once observed to be a brother of the patient) who is to sacrifice, applies pollen to himself in the usual way, and again to the bundles, and departs to deposit the cigarettes and their accompaniments. The chanter then takes up the remaining four bundles and repeats, with them, all the acts performed with the former four. He hands them to another assistant who repeats the acts of the previous assistant and, after receiving instructions from the shaman, carries the cigarettes away to sacrifice them. The débris of manufacture is collected. Song is resumed. The patient sits until the first assistant returns from the act of sacrifice. Once it was observed, on this occasion, that the waiting patient smoked something in an ancient terra-cotta pipe. This was the only time the writer ever saw a pipe used in the Navaho rites.

430.—In addition to the kethawns last described, the writer once saw a large kethawn sacred to the sun, made from a thick section of some kind of grass or sedge (possibly tule) which, it was said, does not grow in the Navaho country; but is obtained usually from the people of Moki, who cull it far west of their villages. Often this plant cannot be procured; then, of course, this cigarette must be omitted.

SUDATORY.

431.—The sweat-house, on the third day of its use — the fourth day of the whole work—is decorated exactly as on the first day, and all the rites are repeated exactly as on that occasion. All the properties used are the same and the same medicines are employed. The songs only are different. The rites of the sweat-house on this day have been noted on one occasion as lasting from 10.15 to 10.45 A.M.

432.—When the patient returns to the medicine-lodge, after the sweat, he sits in the west and a song is begun whose burden is Naniʻsóye. The chanter approaches him still singing and proceeds to apply pollen to his essential parts in the manner elsewhere described. The pollen is applied to each part at an appropriate passage in the song. The chanter, ceasing to sing, takes pollen himself and passes the bag to those who enacted the part of the yéi; they in turn pass the bag to others; it goes the rounds of the lodge until all partake of it in the usual way (par. 185). On this occasion visiting chanters have been observed to pass their pollen bags among the crowd either to save time or the pollen of the presiding chanter.

433.—The usual fumigation of the patient closes the rites of the forenoon, generally about thirty minutes before the noon hour.

PREPARATIONS FOR THE VIGIL.

434.—This is a day of general cleaning. Not only the patient gets his bath, which is ceremonial; but all others connected with the rites, clean themselves. In addition to the regular sudatory for the patient, a sweat-house for general use is built. After taking the hot-air bath, the shaman and his assistants clean their hair and bodies with amole suds and dry themselves with corn-meal. This is in anticipation of the vigil at night, when the gods are supposed to visit the medicine-lodge and feast with men. Often in the myths, the necessity is inculcated for men to cleanse themselves when expecting a visit from the gods.

435. — Outside the lodge on this day, visitors and friends of the patient are engaged in clearing the ground around the medicine-lodge; while at the camp of the patient's relations, women are preparing the great corn-meal cake or aⳑkán which is baked in the earth and they are busy preparing other special dishes which are eaten in the feast at night. See par. 221 and plate V, fig. B.

THE AMOLE BATH OF THE PATIENT.

436.—Some time previous to the beginning of the rites, connected with the amole bath in the lodge, a near relation, the brother or father of the patient, goes out to collect the soap-root. He takes it from four different species of yucca if these can conveniently be found [17]. He cuts of each of these only a small piece, the size of a finger, from the shady side of the plant, with a stone knife, and applies corn pollen to the wounds. He goes then to *Yucca baccata* or *Yucca elata*, for the large pieces which form the chief ingredient of the lather. When he severs one of these from its deep attachments, he must begin the cutting with a stone knife, but may finish with an instrument of steel. Again he must apply pollen.   The roots must be mashed on a hard boulder or some kind of stone not easily broken, and not on the soft sandstone so common in the Navaho country. When the mashing is over, the stone is laid away, in the shade of a tree or some other umbrageous object.   One or two men collect for the "platter" the necessary mud, which must come from the centre of a cultivated field or alkali flat. Naturally moist earth must be sought.   This earth is called *thaꞎahatáan*, which signifies mud taken from the centre of water, as from a drying pond.   There are, no doubt, other observances connected with these preparatory acts, but they have not been witnessed by the writer.   Much of the information in this paragraph is derived from numerous descriptions.

437.—The rites within the lodge, connected with the bath of soap-root or amole, are usually begun about noon, but they have been seen delayed as late as 3 P.M.   When all is ready, the patient enters the lodge and sits, in the south or southwest, facing the east, while the chanter forms on the ground, to the west of the fire, a circular object, about two feet in diameter, called by the Navahoes *thaákïs*; which might here be called, in order to be graphic, a "mud pie," but, to be more elegant, will be called a mud platter, or simply a platter.   He spreads on the floor a layer of mud of the size mentioned, and nearly encircles it with a mud rim about three inches high, leaving an opening in the east.   He lays on the platter thus formed, from centre to circumference, four spreading spruce branches, which almost conceal it.   At the first ceremony he ever performs he makes these branches point to the four cardinal points; at the next ceremony he directs them to the intermediate points, and thus he continues to alternate them through his professional career.   Some shamans use five spruce branches, putting one in the centre.   See par. 778.

438.—Having completed the platter, the chanter takes a Navaho basket of the kind known as the basket-drum, puts pollen on its margin, leaving a hiatus in the east, and lays it to the south of the platter with its line of orientation pointing to the east.   Into the basket he puts spruce twigs, and then the ingredients for making kĕ'tlo, or tsóꞎtsïn (par. 215).   A young boy, or girl, assistant pours water into the basket; he waves one cupful from the east, another from the south, another from the west, a fourth from the north, a fifth from the zenith, and after this he puts in the required amount without ceremony. An adult assistant of the same sex as the patient now stirs the mixture.   This infusion is for application to the body after the yucca suds; but it is not always made on this occasion—the suds is sometimes washed off with water only.

439.—At this time, too, the cold detergent solution of amole, or soap-root, is prepared.   A Navaho water-tight basket-drum is laid down near the middle of the lodge, duly oriented; meal is sprinkled on its margin in the usual way; the four small pieces of yucca first cut from the plants are laid in the bottom of the basket; the rest of the yucca root, or amole, is put in; water is added in the same manner as with the mixture of tsóꞎtsïn, and an assistant, sitting south of the basket bowl and facing north, begins to work up the lather.   A high, stiff, lasting lather is produced by whirling in the solution a beater of spruce twigs between the hands, as a hand-drill is twirled. The moment the assistant begins to make the foam the shaman begins to sing. The song and the work cease simultaneously. The songs sung on this occasion are the first and second of the *Tsalyél* Bigï'n, or Darkness Songs. The refrain of these is, E samós, which has reference to the lather. When the suds is ready, the chanter sprinkles pollen on the rim of the platter, sunwise, leaving a hiatus in the east, and places the basket of suds (or an assistant may do this) in the centre of the platter, on top of the butts of the spruce twigs. Pollen is applied to the rim of the oriented basket, leaving an opening in the east. Three superimposed circles of pollen are made around the edge of the suds and three superimposed crosses of pollen are drawn on it from edge to edge. The first line of each cross is drawn from east to west through the centre of the bowl; the second line from south to north. The first circle and cross are made of *tó'bithadítin*, or water pollen (par. 188), the second of tyélbi*thadítin*, or cat-tail pollen, and the third of corn pollen.

440.—Four crosses in pollen are now made around the mud platter, as shown in the diagram (fig. 12) and in the order as numbered in the diagram. The patient kneels beside the basket of suds, south of it facing north (or west of it facing east, as once observed). He puts to the ground: first, his right knee on cross 1 ; second, his left knee on cross 2 ; third, his right hand on cross 3 ; fourth, his left hand on cross 4 ; this brings over the suds his head, which he holds low down. An assistant, who must not be of the same gens as the patient, takes a little suds from the tips and centre of the pollen cross and applies it to the pa-tient's head. He next

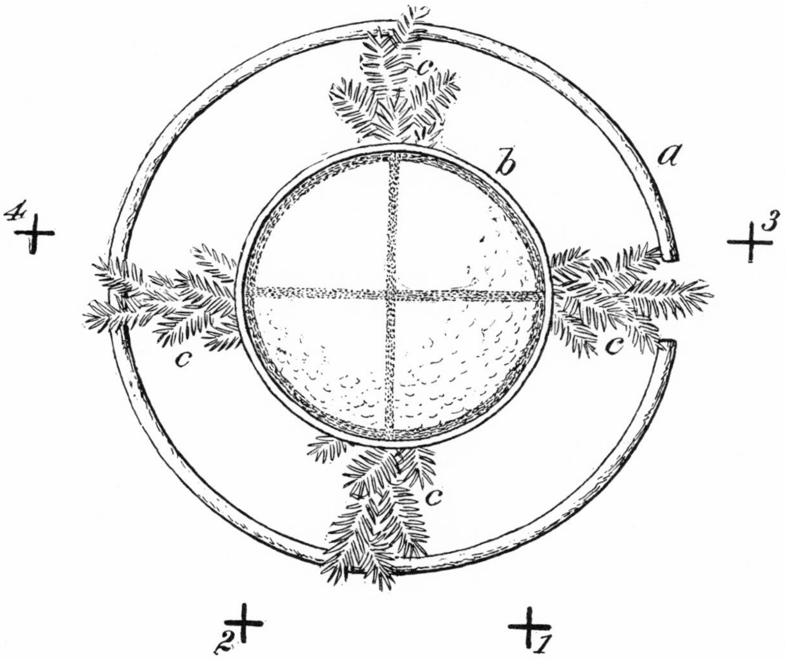

Fig. 12. Diagram of mud platter and basket of soap-root solution ; *a*, rim of platter, open in the east ; *b*, basket containing solution ; *c*, spruce twigs ; 1, 2, 3, 4, crosses of meal in the order in which they are made and occupied.

washes well the patient's hair in the suds. The necklace and jewels of the patient may now be washed and rinsed. The patient washes his own face, feet, lower limbs, trunk (in front), and arms. An assistant washes his back. The suds is emptied into the platter, sometimes over the patient's head, and the basket is rinsed into the platter. The body and head of the patient are rinsed. If kĕ'tlo has been made it is now applied to the body, which it covers with wet spruce leaves. The patient turns around sunwise and, without touching the earth, gets on a blanket north and west of the mud platter.

441.—The platter is broken up; the debris, with the spruce twigs is collected in a blanket and deposited in a shady place. It may be thrown into the edge of the lodge, or it may be taken out and deposited to the north of the lodge at the shady side of a spreading tree of any species.

442.—A basket (par. 292) containing a goodly quantity of corn-meal is placed before the patient, who sits on a rug. To the accompaniment of song, his essential parts are touched with a little of the meal, each application being made at a designated passage in the song. The patient then rubs meal all over his own body—except the back, where a friend rubs it—while a special song to Estsánatlehi is sung. This song, which is sung at no other part of the ceremony and is not one of the regular series of Estsánatlehi songs, is called:

AKÁN BÉNASA BIGĬ'N.—MEAL-RUBBING SONG.

1. From his body, it is rubbed away.
2. By Estsánatlehi, it is rubbed away.
3. With the white corn, it is rubbed away.
4. Made of the corn-root, it is rubbed away.
5. Made of the corn-leaf, it is rubbed away.
6. Made of the corn-dew, it is rubbed away.
7. Made of the tassel, it is rubbed away.
8. Made of the pollen, it is rubbed away.
9. Made of the corn-grain, it is rubbed away.
10. In old age wandering, it is rubbed away.
11. On the trail of beauty, it is rubbed away.

There are three other stanzas, in which they name corn of other colors.

443.—When the application of the meal is completed and its song finished, the chanter begins a special song to *Hastséyalti* the burden or refrain of which is Bénasoie. At certain parts of this song, he applies pollen to the appropriate parts of the patient. He ceases to sing; takes pollen on his own tongue and head and scatters it in the air above his head. The chanter must be very particular in singing this song. Visiting chanters listen to him carefully and notify him of his mistake if he makes one. This completes the ceremony of the amole bath, which usually occupies something less than two hours.

444.—Not the jewels of the invalid only, but those of the shaman and assistants are washed on this occasion. In addition to an ordinary washing with suds and a rinsing with water, they are sometimes allowed to lie for a while in the bowl of sacred suds, before the circles and crosses of pollen are applied, and sometimes in the bowl of spruce and tsóltsĭn.

445.—If the patient be a female, three or four female relations accompany her and sit in the north of the lodge, until their turn comes to make themselves useful. One of these may mix the amole; another may wash the patient's head and necklace with the suds. When the body is being washed, two of the women raise a blanket for a screen, while a third assists the patient to bathe the body and a fourth carries the water or cold infusion behind the screen. After a brief interruption, song is resumed, the screen is lowered and the patient is seen standing, clothed. Afterwards, when the woman rubs meal to her person, the screen is again raised by two of her companions and a third rubs the meal on the patient's back. During all this time, there is no exposure of the patient's person to the men in the lodge.

DOG KETHAWNS.

446.—On one occasion, in the afternoon, certain sacrifices called dog kethawns were observed, but the description of them has been mislaid. Soon after sunset they were applied in the usual manner and were taken out to be sacrificed by the brothers of the patient. The prayer on this occasion was uttered in voices scarcely audible and all instructions, questions and conversations were conducted in whispers.

TREE AND MASK.

447.—The rite of the tree and mask, within the lodge, begins at nightfall. Two men paint and decorate themselves to represent divinities. The usual characters are *Hastséyalti* and a *Hastsébaad*, or goddess, his wife; but sometimes *Hastséhogan* takes the place of the *Hastsébaad*, and sometimes another male divinity takes the place of *Hastséyalti*. Once the female character was seen represented by *Hastséoltoi*, the Navaho Diana. The rites shall be described as conducted by the first pair mentioned. It has not been discovered why the characters are changed.

448.—While these men are preparing themselves, a hole about four inches in diameter and six inches deep is dug in the ground to the west of the fire; the mask to be worn by the patient and those of the yéi are laid out, and a blanket covered with white sheeting is spread to the west of the hole for the patient to sit on. The actors, hiding their masks under their blankets, leave the lodge. The call to song is shouted from outside the door.

449.—The patient enters and disrobes on a blanket north of his prepared seat. He sits then on the blankets and sheeting in the west, facing the east. The domino-like mask of a yébaad is put over the patient's face and rather loosely tied behind the head with its attached strings. While the mask is being tied on, one song is sung. It is the third of the Aga‘hoá Gisǐ'n or Summit Songs; but is especially called I*lyáilthad* Bigǐ'n. The yéi now enter dressed and masked. *Hastséyalti* bears a small sapling—piñon, if the patient is a male; cedar, if the patient is a female (par. 731)—almost entirely stripped of its branches. *Hastsébaad* carries a bag made of a single fawnskin, containing some meal and grains of corn.

Four grains of corn are dropped into the hole and then the sapling is planted in it ; earth being packed in to keep the sapling erect.   Before planting it *H*ast*s*éyal*t*i points the top of the sapling to each of the four cardinal points in their usual order. Alternately with each motion *H*ast*s*ébaad sprinkles meal to the cardinal points. The sapling is then lifted toward the zenith above the hole and brought down vertically into the latter to be planted.

450.—The sapling is then bent over to the west by *H*ast*s*éyal*t*i ; being steadied, if necessary, by *H*ast*s*ébaad.   Its top is tied to the top of the mask by means of a long string, and it is held a moment in the bent position.   An assistant unties from behind the strings that hold the mask on the patient's head.   The sapling, released, flies backward to an upright position, carries the mask with it, exposes the face of the patient, and draws away, it is said, all disease from the patient's head.

451.—The yéi run out carrying tree and mask with them and the hole is filled up.   A few minutes later the yéi return, unmasked, give back their masks to the shaman and divest themselves of paint and finery.   Fumigation of the patient, in the usual form, follows (par. 198).

452.—This completes the rites of the tree and mask within the lodge ; but, in addition, some observances occur outside the lodge which must be described. The work, in the morning, of selecting and marking the sapling has already been mentioned.   The sapling is trimmed at the place where it is cut, being deprived of all its branches except a small tuft at the top.   In carrying it to the lodge, the bearer lays it down four times.   Arrived at the lodge, he lays it on the level roof over the entry, where it remains until the yéi require it.   When the work in the lodge is done, the sapling and mask are laid on the roof over the entry.   The mask is returned to the chanter later.   The sapling is left on the roof until morning, when it is taken to the north or northeast of the lodge, laid in the branches of a tree and sprinkled with meal while a benediction is spoken.

453.—After the rite of the tree and mask is done, the men in the lodge gossip, smoke, sleep and eat the plentiful supper which is provided for them, before the work of the night begins.

FOURTH NIGHT.

YÉBĬKE *T*OIL*H*ÁS, VIGIL OF THE GODS.

454.—From about nine o'clock on the fourth night, until nearly dawn on the fifth day, a vigil is kept over the masks and other properties of the rites.   This is called yébĭke *t*oil*h*ás, which means literally, no sleep on the trail of the gods, but is here freely translated, vigil of the gods.   The patient and a virgin girl and boy who accompany him into the lodge, or enter after the masks have been pollened, are expected to stay awake all night ; yet on one occasion the patient was seen to drop his weary lids for a little while after 2 A.M.   At any moment of the night it may be seen that the great majority of the numerous occupants of the lodge are awake; wakefulness is the order of the night; still there are few, the shaman not excepted, who do not take an occasional doze during the watch; while a limited number, who take no part in the singing, may be observed, stretched on the ground in slumber, for an hour or more at a time.

455.—There are some rites which will be described; but the time is mostly spent in song which, with occasional short intervals of rest, is kept up all night. The shaman often leads in the songs which belong to the occasion, but not always. Among the visitors in the lodge there are many middle-aged and old men who know some particular set of songs and take the lead to the relief of the tired shaman. The rattle is the only instrument used, and this not always.

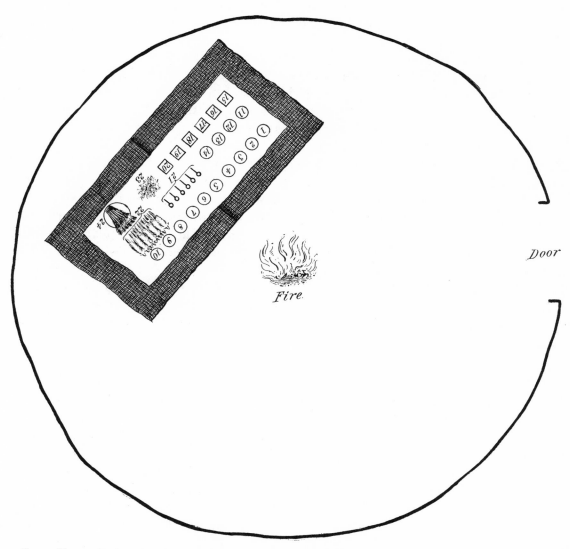

Fig. 13. Diagram showing arrangement of masks and other properties during the vigil of the gods. 1, (mask of) *Hastséyalti*; 2, *Hastséhogan*; 3, *Hátdastsisi*; 4 and 5, *Hastsébaka*; 6, *Hastséltsi*; 7, Tsóhanoai; 8, Kléhanoai; 9, Gánaskïdi; 10, *Tó'nenili*; 11, Nayénez-gani; 12, To'badzīstsíni; 13, Dsahadoldzá; 14, *Hastsézini*; 15 to 20 are for *Hastsébaad* or goddesses, one of which, 16, is for *Hastséoltoi*; 21; rattles; 22, fox-skins; 23, miscellaneous, fringes, etc.; 24, plumed wands in basket.

LAYING OUT MASKS, ETC.

456.—Between 8.30 and 9 P.M. usually, blankets are spread on the ground to the northwest of the fire. If a buffalo robe can be obtained, it is laid over these with its head to the northeast. These are in turn covered with many folds of new calico. Over all is spread a covering of new white cotton sheeting and sometimes a fine white buckskin. In former days, it is said, only buffalo robes and buckskins were used; but owing to the modern scarcity of these articles, the white man's goods are now employed. These goods are retained by the shaman as a special fee. On the white sheeting, the masks, fox-skins, rattles, meal-bags, medicine-bags, and other permanent properties of the night chant are laid out in two rows, usually in the order shown in the diagram, fig. 13. The masks have their faces up and their tops toward the fire.

APPLICATION OF POLLEN.

457.—The patient now applies pollen to the masks in the following manner. Standing by the tops of the masks, with his back to the fire, he sprinkles pollen in a straight line — letting it drop from between his thumb and first two fingers — thinly, down the centre of the mask from top to mouth. He sprinkles it in a similar manner on the right cheek or edge from bottom to top and then on the left cheek in the same direction. This is the common method of applying the votive pollen to the masks; it is followed in other rites and will be mentioned again (par. 509). He then sprinkles pollen from right to left along both rows of sacred objects and scatters it widely on the ground in front of him. When this is done, the shaman and, after him, his principal assistants follow and repeat these acts. Sometimes the shaman precedes the patient. Then others who desire may follow and apply pollen in the same manner to the sacred objects. These acts are of a worshipful nature and are accompanied by silent or low-muttered prayers; but there is no loud prayer, song or conversation at this time. Afterwards pollen-bags are passed around among the audience, for any one who chooses to partake — praying in silence in the meantime.

FOOD FOR THE BANQUET.

458.—When the sprinkling of the pollen is done, there is a silent and expectant pause which is broken by the cry "Biké *hatáli hakú*," just outside the door of the lodge. The curtain is thrown aside and a number of women enter bearing bowls and dishes of food in great variety. The women walk in single file around the fire, sunwise, until the one who heads the procession gets back to the east, or just north of the eastern extremity of the fire. The women form a ring around the fire with a hiatus in the east. The woman at the head lays down a dish of food called ka*tĕ'tí*n; the woman at the end of the procession lays down a dish called na*dí*nogési, followed by another called *h*azáale‘, and the woman, at the head lays down a dish called wa. These four ancient Navaho dishes are essential; their positions in the circle and the order in which they are deposited is established ; not so with the other dishes. When these women have placed the four dishes mentioned, the others lay theirs down, one after another, in the order in which they entered the lodge. They make a circle of dishes around the fire with an opening in the east, which is defined by the two first dishes laid down. The vessels are usually from twenty to thirty; but the exact number is not material. Some women carry several vessels.

459.—The following is a list of those dishes whose names and character have been discovered : 1, Ḳaṭĕ′ṭïn ; 2, naḍïnogési ; 3, ḥazáale‘ ; 4, wa ; 5, wa bĕltsé ; 6, alkán ; 7, ṭhá‘bïtsaï ; 8, tsé‘asṭe ; tsé‘asṭe ḷakaí ; 9, tsé‘asṭe doṭlï′z ; 10, tsé‘asṭe ḷïtsói ; 11, tsé‘asṭe ḷïtsí ; 12, klesán ; 13, ṭanaskï′z ; 14, ḷéilzoz ; 15, ḍïtlógïn tsïḍïkói ; 16, baḍahastlóni ; 17, kïnïspï′zi ; 18, ṭhá‘nil ; 19, no‘kázi or ḍokózi ; 20, nanĕskáḍi ; 21, dumplings of tloṭáhi and other wild seeds. These are ancient aboriginal dishes, the nature and preparation of which has been described (par. 217 *et seq.*) The aboriginal dishes of boiled beans and squashes, dried melons, yucca and other wild fruits, dried or preserved, are also commonly served. In addition to all this ancient food, there are dishes of European origin, such as wheaten cakes, mutton cooked in various ways, stewed peaches, etc. Of the rarer old-fashioned foods there is usually one dish of each ; but there may be many dishes of mutton, wheaten cakes, boiled pumpkin and such substantial articles. The culinary art of the Navaho woman is taxed for this occasion. The ancient forms of food are usually served in Indian baskets and pottery ; but the modern foods may be presented in any sort of tin or crockeryware.

AN INTERVAL OF SONG.

460.—The women who brought the food sit down in the lodge. The boy and girl before mentioned often enter with these women ; when the children come, they sit southeast of the line of masks beside the patient. The one must be of a different gens to the invalid ; hence, in the case of a male patient, it may be his son. The other must be of the same gens as the invalid and hence is often his niece. But they need not be intimate relations of the patient. After a pause in which many indulge in cigarette smoking, song accompanied by rattling is begun and it is continued for about an hour before the next important rite, that of the sprinkling begins. The songs now sung are the Ïnḍiá‘ Bigï′n or Wand Songs, thirty-two in number, all of which must be repeated with perfect exactness. The last is sung when the sacred mush is mixed. During one of the songs, which is very spirited, the women and children take pollen.

SPRINKLING MASKS AND OTHER SACRED OBJECTS.

461.—In the meantime the shaman makes, in a water-tight basket, the cold infusion of tsóltsïn. He takes sacred water from a wicker bottle and pours it into the basket in five gourd cupfuls, waving each cupful from a different direction toward the basket ; on the surface of the water he may sprinkle ḍátsos, thus forming what is called ḍá‘tsos kĕ′tlo (par. 213). At the proper time, as indicated by the songs, he bids the boy and girl approach and instructs them in their duties.   To the former he gives a black plumed wand, or ĭn*d*iá', in each hand ; to the other he gives a blue plumed wand in each hand.   These wands are taken from a basket at the south-western extremity of the row of masks, etc. The boy, dipping his right-hand wand into the solution, sprinkles the masks and other sacred objects, each row separately, from right to left, the nearer row first. He steps aside and gives way to the girl, who sprinkles exactly in the same manner, except that she waves her wand from left to right.   The boy changes his wands from one hand to another, dips and sprinkles as before with the right hand, but with a different wand.   Thus the boy and girl continue alternately to dip the wands and sprinkle the sacred objects until each has sprinkled four times.   The masks, etc., having been properly asperged, the boy sprinkles the spectators in the north half of the lodge ; the girl those in the south half.   They sprinkle themselves. The boy sprinkles the bottom of the lodge in the north ; the girl does the same in the south.   Lastly they sprinkle the roof of the lodge continuing until the infusion is exhausted.   They return their wands to the chanter and resume their seats.

COMMUNAL SUPPER.

462.—After an interval of a few minutes, the girl puts into a sacred basket or earthen bowl four handfuls of meal made of unripe corn baked in the earth ; on this she pours sacred water and stirs the mixture into a thin mush or gruel.   In adding the water she advances one cupful toward the bowl with a sweep of the arm from the east ; another similarly, from the south ; a third from the west ; a fourth from the north ; a fifth from the zenith; she adds more water, if needed, unceremoniously.   On one occasion she was observed to enact the ceremonious pouring of water four times, making twenty cupfuls in all, and to add no more. Sometimes the boy pours the water while the girl stirs the mixture.   He always fills for her the gourd cup from the wicker bottle.

463.—Now comes a communal feast or love feast, a sacramental feast or communion it might be called, of gods and men.   To begin with, the gods are honored ; in other words food is given to the masks.   The boy puts a small portion of the gruel on the mouth of each mask, beginning at the right end and with the row nearest to him ; he sprinkles gruel over the other properties ; the girl follows his example, and thus, alternately, each four times they apply food to the masks and other properties.   The boy then, by dipping the tips of all the digits of the right hand into the gruel, secures a morsel, carries it to his lips, and sucks it audibly into his mouth ; this he does four times.   His example is followed in turn by the girl, the patient, the shaman, the principal assistants and, after these, by every one in the lodge.   In passing the bowl to the multitude they begin with those who sit south of the door, in the east, and pass it sunwise.   If any of the gruel is left after all have partaken once, some help themselves a second time until all is gone.   Each devotee, as he takes the gruel, prays in silence for whatever blessing he desires. The feast occupies about twenty minutes and is finished between 10 and 11 P.M.

464.—There are some variations allowed in feeding the masks. It has once been noted that the shaman did this, instead of the boy and girl. A myth says the children made only a motion as if feeding the masks, and that the girl did not begin until the boy had done it the required four times. It is also stated in a myth that after the feast *Hastsézĭni* started the *Hozóni* song and all followed him in singing. It is not now the practice to sing just after this feast; but all partake of pollen. Two bags are passed; one to those who sit in the north of the lodge and one to those in the south. As each guest partakes, he prays in silence—grace after meals.

BANQUET AFTER COMMUNAL SUPPER.

465.—After the pollen is passed, the shaman or some one directed by him, takes a small morsel from each of the bowls which contain the ancient Indian foods, and puts it in a separate bowl which is laid away in the west of the lodge. This material is, later, dried and used in certain healing rites. One such collection, at least, is always made; but sometimes two or three are made. The extra ones, which are for the benefit of visiting shamans, are put in other parts of the lodge, close to the edge.

466.—Then the dishes, which have been standing around the fire for over an hour, are passed from hand to hand and laid in different parts of the lodge, where each is soon surrounded by a small group of persons. All who wish to eat now do so. The patient and the two children only may not partake; their sole food during the night being the morsels which each took of the sacred gruel. Moreover, they have not eaten since breakfast, their fast is of about twenty-four hours' duration. The shaman eats only of the sacred gruel between breakfast and this ritual banquet. It is said if they broke this fast they would soon die. When the banquet is finished, two pollen bags are passed and all who have eaten partake of pollen in the usual manner, making meanwhile a silent prayer. One pollen bag is passed from the shaman in the west, by the north, to the east; the other bag is passed from one sitting at the door, by the south, to the west.

AN INTERVAL OF SONG.

467.—Song, without drum, rattle or other accompaniment, is resumed after this meal and continued until near midnight. The first songs sung are *Hastséhogan Bigĭ'n*. These the myth declares were sung by *Hastséyalti* and *Hastséhogan* when they built the first lodge; there are twelve short songs and one long song, making thirteen in all; the last describes how the house was built. After this series, come other songs of sequence. There is sometimes a pause between the ending of one set and the beginning of another, during which people may pass in and out of the lodge.

SMOKING THE MASKS.

468.—It is usually when these songs are done, that the chanter or an assistant smokes the masks.   He takes a long piece of reed filled with wild tobacco, lights it and, inhaling the smoke, puffs toward the heavens and the earth, each alternately, four times.   He puffs the smoke on each mask separately and at last puffs it, with less particularity, over the other sacred objects.   This rite is called dzĭʻsbáʻ *tiłayáʻ*, or a smoke for the masks.   Sometimes the cigarette is made with a piece of corn-husk for a cover instead of a piece of reed.   Sometimes this rite is deferred until after the rite of shaking the masks.

SHAKING THE MASKS.

469.—At midnight or wonderfully near that hour for a people who use no time-pieces, the shaman starts the waking song, the refrain of which is hyĭ*d*ĕzná or hĭ*d*ĕzná, which means, he moves, he stirs, and proceeds to "waken" or shake the masks.   As he begins each stanza, putting one hand under and the other over the selected mask, he lifts it two or three inches from the ground, holding it horizontally ; when he comes to the refrain he shakes the mask, horizontally, and when he ends the refrain he lays the mask down.   He does not proceed in the order in which the masks are laid on the cotton sheeting ; but in the different order in which they are mentioned in the song.   When the masks are all shaken he begins a song somewhat different from the first in words, but similar in tune, and proceeds to shake the other properties.   Some shamans carry a rock crystal in the right hand, which is put under the mask in shaking.

WAKING SONG.

470.—The song of waking, or shaking, begins thus :

I.

He stirs, he stirs, he stirs, he stirs.
Among the lands of dawning, he stirs, he stirs ;
The pollen of the dawning, he stirs, he stirs ;
Now in old age wandering, he stirs, he stirs ;
Now on the trail of beauty, he stirs, he stirs.
He stirs (four times).

II.

He stirs (four times).
Among the lands of evening, he stirs, he stirs ;
The pollen of the evening, he stirs, he stirs ;
Now in old age wandering, he stirs, he stirs ;
Now on the trail of beauty, he stirs, he stirs.
He stirs (four times).

III.

He stirs (four times).
Now *H*astseyal*t*íhi, he stirs, he stirs ;

> Now his white robe of buckskin, he stirs, he stirs ;
> Now in old age wandering, he stirs, he stirs ;
> Now on the trail of beauty, he stirs, he stirs.
> He stirs (four times).

Then follow fifteen more stanzas framed like the third ; but substituting in each for "*H*astséyal*t*i" the name of a different god and for "his white robe of buckskin," the name of a different property. It is unnecessary to repeat all the words. The name of each god and the special property associated with him will suffice. The numbers that follow are those of the stanzas.

IV.	*H*astsé*h*ogan.	His white kilt, or loin-cloth.
V.	Dsaha*d*oldzá.	His bow of darkness.
VI.	Gá*n*askï*d*i.	His white tobacco-pouch.
VII.	*H*á*t*dastsï′si.	His white leggings.
VIII.	*H*astsébaka.	His soft goods of all kinds.
IX.	*H*astsébaad.	Her jewels of all kinds.
X.	Nayénĕzgani.	His stone necklace.
XI.	*T*ó‘badzïstsíni.	His ear pendants.
XII.	*H*astséol*t*oi.	Her puma quiver.
XIII.	*H*astsé*l*tsi.	His coral beads.
XIV.	*H*astsézïni.	His white beads.
XV.	*T*ó‘nenïli.	His jar of mixed waters.
XVI.	Tsóhanoai.	His haliotis pendant.
XVII.	Kléhanoai.	His white shell pendant.
XVIII.	Estsánatlehi.	Her plants of all kinds.

471.—Some of the gods named may not be represented by masks. When the singer repeats the stanza appropriate to such, his hands are empty, and no shaking motion is made.

MONOLOGUE PRAYER.

472.—After he finishes the rite and songs of shaking the masks, the chanter repeats, for his own benefit, in a low tone, the following monologue prayer, in which the patient takes no part :

1. In beauty (happiness) may I dwell.
2. In beauty may I walk.
3. In beauty may my male kindred dwell.
4. In beauty may my female kindred dwell.
5. In beauty may it rain on my young men.
6. In beauty may it rain on my young women.
7. In beauty may it rain on my chiefs.
8. In beauty may it rain on us.
9. In beauty may our corn grow.
10. In the trail of pollen may it rain.
11. In beauty before us, may it rain.
12. In beauty behind us, may it rain.
13. In beauty below us, may it rain.
14. In beauty above us, may it rain.
15. In beauty all around us, may it rain
16. In beauty may I walk.

17. Goods, may I acquire.[18]
18. Jewels, may I acquire.[19]
19. Horses, may I acquire.
20. Sheep, may I acquire.
21. Beeves, may I acquire.
22. In old age,
23. The beautiful trail,
24. May I walk.

SINGING.

473.—The rest of the night is spent in song which continues with brief interruptions, until the concluding rites in the morning. It is at this time that any sacred songs of sequence may be sung (pars. 889 *et seq.*) and that songs belonging to other rites may be introduced.

A SPECIAL RITE.

474.—On one occasion a rite was witnessed which it was said was not a constant feature of the ceremony, but was desired by the patient, who paid extra for it. It may be briefly described as follows : About 4 A.M. the masks are collected, the chanter takes that of *Hastséyalti* and another ; an assistant or the patient takes all the rest. The chanter, the assistant and the patient stand in the west, in the order named, from north to south. While they stand, holding the masks in their hands, the chanter repeats one of his long prayers and the assistant — not the patient — repeats it sentence by sentence after him. If the patient be a man, he holds the masks ; if the patient be a woman, some male relation holds them. Women are not allowed to hold the masks. When the prayer is done, the masks are laid down — those which the chanter held, by themselves, the rest in one pile, one on top of another.

CONCLUDING ACTS.

475.—As dawn approaches an assistant squats before the masks and sings a very long song. He puts pollen on two of the masks and takes pollen himself.

476.—After this there is a brief pause, when the shaman may go out to look at the sky. Singing is resumed and is continued until a crier, shouting "*Hayilkáli* !" outside the door, announces the first streak of dawn. Then the *Hozóni* Yikaígĭn or Songs of the Beautiful Dawn are begun. These form a special series of six of the *Hastséyalti Hozóni* Songs, but are not a part of the *Hastséyalti* Songs sung to the drum on the last night. They have no instrumental accompaniment. When they are done the shaman utters another monologue prayer, applies pollen to the boy and girl, takes it himself and passes the bag around for all to help themselves. The boy and girl leave the lodge. The patient is now allowed a brief absence from the lodge. On one occasion a female patient was seen who started to go out by walking to the south of the pile of masks, but was recalled by the shaman and made to pass north of the pile.

477.—There now follows a period of gossiping and smoking in the lodge.

After a while, the masks and other sacred articles are laid away in the recess, in the edge of the lodge in the west, and the ground is cleared to make ready for the work of the fifth day.

FIFTH DAY.

478.—The rites of the fifth day consist always, (1) in the preparation and sacrifice of a kethawn early in the morning, (2) the administration of the fourth sweat, soon after, and (3) the initiation of candidates into the mystery of the Yébĭtsai at night, (4). Sometimes, but not always, a small picture is drawn on the floor of the lodge in the afternoon and a rite of succor from hypnotism, connected with the picture, occurs after sunset. The ground for the last night's dance is further prepared in the afternoon, but this is done informally.

KETHAWN.

479.—Shortly before sunrise a buffalo-robe or blanket—preferably the former —is spread on the ground in the west of the lodge, covered with white sheeting for the reception of the kethawn, and the work of making the kethawn is begun. The singers now raise their voices and continue their incantations until five songs are sung. The kethawn and the song are usually finished together. The songs for this sacrifice are ten in number called Tsĕnidzenétyĭn Gisĭ'n ; five of these are sung before the prayer and five after.

480.—In the meantime an attendant prepares yucca suds in a wicker bowl and the man who is to bear the kethawn—a brother or near relation of the patient— strips himself to the breech-cloth. With the help of the attendant he washes his hair in the suds and the assistant rinses it by pouring sacred water over it from a wicker jar. He washes his whole body and the assistant rinses him by pouring water all over him. The bath concluded, he daubs his own face and hands with gles or white earth until they are completely covered. He is clothed in new white cotton shirt, pantaloons, and shawl ; his hair is combed out loose over his back ; he dons numerous necklaces, but discards other ornament, and he carries a leather pouch at his side. Thus equipped he represents a divinity called Tsĕnidzenétyĭn, He-who-carries-toward-a-rock-shelter, who lives in the Tóïntsa (the Tunicha Mountains) and there fulfills the office of the Hastséhogan of other places.

481.—The kethawn is a span long and is properly made of a great reed, or similar plant, which does not grow in the Navaho country and has not been identified. It is painted black if the patient be a male and blue, if a female. Like other kethawns, it is stuffed at its butt end with feathers, filled with wild tobacco, lighted with rock crystal and sealed with moistened corn-pollen. To its center is attached a string with feathers, beads, etc., just like those belonging to the Kĭninaekaígi ketán previously described (par. 375). The description of one will do for the other. The same number of beads (5) have been seen attached ; but it is said, the number may be varied. The sacrificial accompaniments are similar to those of the Kĭninaekaígi ketan. It is folded in a corn-husk.

482.—The sacred bundle containing the kethawn and its accompaniments, is placed in the patient's hands by the chanter; pollen is administered, a motion being made as if carrying it from the sky; a dialogue prayer to six gods (*H*ast*s*éyal*t*i, *H*ast*s*é*h*o*g*an, Dsaha*d*old*z*á, Gá*n*aski*a*i, *H*ast*s*ébaka, *H*ast*s*ébaad) is repeated and at its conclusion the bundle is given to the character in white who, having applied it to the essential parts of the patient, takes it out of the lodge to sacrifice it.

483.—The kethawn is placed near a high echoing rock where it is secure from the feet of cattle, in such a position that the tip of its terminal bunch of feathers, with the string outstretched, may touch the rock. The general rules for depositing are similar to those of the K*ĭ*ninaeka*í*gi ke*t*án. It must not be laid away to the north of the lodge. When the bearer deposits it he prays to the same six gods who were invoked before, asking for many blessings for himself and his people.

484.—When the bearer of the kethawn departs, song is resumed and the five remaining songs of the Ts*ĕ*nid*z*ené*t*y*ĭ*n Gis*í*'n are sung. All the work connected with the kethawn occupies about an hour and a half. At the symbolic lighting of the cigarette it was observed that the patient caught the first beams of the rising sun on his crystal as they streamed into the lodge over the top of the curtain, which had been purposely lowered a little to allow of this — a desirable but not essential feature of the work. Usually it is considered sufficient to point the crystal toward the smoke-hole.

SUDATORY.

485.—This is the fourth and last day of the sweat-house. The house is decorated with a cross in meal as on the second day (fig. 6), and the rites are the same as on that occasion. The songs are different. They are I*d*ní' Big*ĭ*'n or Thunder Songs, 15 in number, and are the same as the Thunder Songs sung on the last night. "If you are lazy you may leave one out, but no more" said Smiling Chanter, with a smile. The patient usually enters the sweat-house about 9 a. m. and returns to the medicine-lodge about half an hour later.

486.—When the party from the sweat-house returns to the lodge there is singing, without rattling for about ten minutes; then pollen is applied to the patient and the song ceases. The patient is fumigated and so are those who enacted the part of the succoring gods at the sweat-house. The latter not only inhale the fragrant smoke of the powder which is cast on the hot coal, but rub the fumes into their hands and faces. When the coal is quenched with water and taken out, song is resumed and the patient applies pollen to his own tongue and head in the usual manner. Song is continued for a few minutes longer until the series is done. When it ceases the shaman repeats a monologue prayer, in a low murmuring tone with downcast face and closed eyes. This finishes the work of the morning.

*HO D*ITLÁ*T* YIKÁ*L*, PICTURE OF THE TREMBLING PLACE.

487.—The picture, which is sometimes painted in the afternoon, is prepared according to the rules for dry-paintings already given (par. 156 *et seq.*) It is about four feet in diameter and is made near the center of the lodge. Plate II, D, shows one form of it, drawn, as usual, in five different colors. It is called *hod*itlá*t* yiká*l*, picture of the trembling or shaking place, the reason for which name will presently appear.

DESCRIPTION OF PICTURE (PLATE II, FIG. D).

488.—The picture represents the rite which takes place over it. The figure in the north is that of *H*ast*s*éyal*t*i, with his talisman extended; but without the plumes and squirrel bag, which are his properties, in the last night's dance, as shown in plate VII. The figure in the center is that of a male divinity, or yébaka, but it also stands for the patient in the accompanying rite. This character is shown also in plate VII. The figure in the south is that of a yébaad or goddess, carrying two plumed wands. Plate VIII. shows this character without the plumed wands, but with other properties. Fuller descriptions of these figures may be found in the descriptions of the gods.

489.—Changes may be made in this picture depending on changes in the ceremony. For instance, if the patient be a female the central figure is that of a yébaad or goddess, and if the divinity who assists *H*ast*s*éyal*t*i in the acts of succor be *H*ast*s*é*h*o*g*an, or other male divinity, the figure of such a god is drawn in the south.

490.—When the picture proper is finished, a line is drawn in corn-meal from a little distance east of the picture into the bed of sand on which the picture is drawn and figures of four shod footprints are made in meal on this trail. Then plumed wands are set up—the four black wands in the north; the four blue, in the south (par. 282).

RITES OF THE PICTURE.

491.—When the picture is partly done, two personators of the gods begin to prepare themselves, and when they are ready they depart—their bodies and masks hidden under blankets—to complete their toilet outside the lodge, in the dark, for night has now come. When the picture is done, the singers seat themselves in the west of the lodge and hide behind them an inverted basket for a drum. The usual announcement is shouted at the door of the lodge and, soon after, the patient enters. The moment he enters the shaman leads in song, accompanied by rattle, and begins to sing the *Hod*itlá*t* Gisï'n, or Songs in the Trembling Place, seven in number. If the patient be a man, he is stripped to the breech-cloth (a female patient retains her clothes). He has a single breath-feather, taken from the shoulder of an eagle, tied to his hair. As soon as it is tied on he begins to tremble violently (or should tremble) as if under the influence of a hypnotic spasm. He walks, trembling, along the track of meal, placing his feet exactly in the figured footprints, and on reaching the picture he sits down on the skirt of the central figure, his face turned to the east and his limbs flexed. As he advances along the line of meal the trail is erased, all except the fourth painted footprint, which is allowed to remain.

492.—The song continues; at a particular part of it a singer reaches behind him and gives four loud taps on the hidden drum; this is a signal to the gods who wait outside. The moment they hear it they rush into the lodge, *H*astséyal*t*i giving his appropriate call. Every one in the lodge acts as if alarmed; some, who have the power, imitating the voices of various alarmed animals. *H*astséyal*t*i approaches the patient from the east and, opening his talisman (par. 285), places it horizontally around the head of the patient, giving his call. He steps back and makes way for *H*ast*s*ébaad, who places, horizontally, a plumed wand on each side of the patient's head and then places one before and the other behind the patient's head. The gods rush out of the lodge, *H*astséyal*t*i leading. Song continues and again, at certain words, the hidden drum is loudly beaten and the gods again enter. All the acts of the gods are performed altogether four times; but with these differences: when the gods enter the second time the talisman and wands are put around the shoulders of the patient; the third time they are put around the chest, and the fourth time around the waist. When the gods leave for the last time the patient ceases to be convulsed, rises, and leaves the lodge.

493.—Those who desire to apply sacred dust from the picture to their bodies, now do so (par. 540). When they are done, the wands are pulled up and the picture is erased by scraping the sand from circumference to centre into a pile. All this sand is put into blankets and carried out of the lodge to be deposited in the north. The singing is continued until the series of songs, appropriate to this occasion, is all sung.

494.—This rite is not only therapeutic but diagnostic, in a mythic sense. If the patient is seized with trembling, which is usually the case, the shamans say they know the malady is caused by the gods casting a spell on the patient; but if he is not thus seized they must seek some other cause.

INITIATION.

495.—On the fifth night of the night chant, an hour or two after sunset, "the basket is turned down," as the Navahoes express it; in other words, a basket is inverted to serve as a drum; this is done with many mystic observances. A crier at the door of the medicine-lodge cries "Biké *h*at*á l*i *h*akú!" "Come on the trail of song," a moment later the singers begin to sing, and the drummer to pound on his basket-drum. At the same time the two men who are to enact the part of yéi, or divine ones, at the ceremony begin to dress, adorn, and paint themselves. At last they put on their masks. While they are dressing an assistant prepares the two yé*dad*ĕstsani, or implements used in the initiation of the females. A buffalo-robe is spread on a blanket west of the fire and, after a special series of ten songs have been sung, the divine masqueraders leave the lodge.

496.—These two implements for initiating the female consist each of an ear of yellow corn which must be tipped with four grains arranged compactly together ; to the ear, four branchlets of yucca are tied (par. 298).

497.—After the masqueraders (yéi let us call them) are gone, the singing stops and there is an expectant silence in the lodge. The yéi have gone to conduct, or drive before them, rather, the candidates to the lodge. Soon the procession enters—the patient first, a number of candidates for initiation following, and the yéi bringing up the rear.

498.—The divinities represented on this occasion are *Hastséyalti* or the Talking God and *Hastsébaad*, or Yébaad, a goddess. *Hastséyalti* is also called Yébĭtsai or maternal grandfather of the gods or genii. The person who enacts the goddess is a man, but feminine pronouns will be used in speaking of him. When these gods now enter the lodge Hastséyalti carries in his hands two large leaves of *Yucca baccata*, while Hastsébaad carries a spotted fawnskin containing pollen.

499.—On entering, the patient sits in the south of the lodge ; the candidates sit west of the central fire and buffalo robe, facing the east, in a curved row. The males sit in a squatting position in the north ; the females sit to the south with lower limbs extended towards the east ; the mothers sit south of the girls. The candidates enter the lodge with their heads bowed and faces hidden in the folds of their blankets and they remain thus after sitting until they are otherwise bidden. The males disrobe under their screening blankets, taking off everything but their breech-cloths. Meanwhile the yéi keep up an occasional hooting and stand facing the group of candidates. When the males are all ready, the yéi stand facing that one who sits farthest north. The goddess whoops as a signal. The candidate throws off his blanket, rises and takes one step forward. The goddess applies meal transversely to the shins of the candidate from south to north. The Talking God advances and strikes the candidate in the same place with a yucca leaf. He carries a leaf in each hand ; he strikes with one leaf holding its point to the north ; changes the leaves in his hand and strikes with the other leaf holding its point to the south. The goddess then applies meal from below upward to the right side of the chest and to the left side, from nipple to collar-bone in the order mentioned. The god follows, striking in the same places and in the same order, once on each side, with his yucca leaf held upright and changing, as before, the leaves from hand to hand between strokes. The candidate turns sunwise around with his back to the yéi, is sprinkled with meal and struck on the shoulder-blades in a manner similar to that in which he was struck on the breast. He turns round again, facing the yéi and extends his forearms, hands clinched, palms up. Meal is applied transversely across the forearms from south to north and from north to south and they are struck with the yucca leaves, pointing alternately in these directions, in a manner similar to that in which the shins were treated. The Yébaad or goddess always applies the meal and *H*ast*s*éyal*t*i, the Talking God, always applies the yucca wands and always changes them in his hands between the strokes.

500.—The candidate returns to his place in the line, sits down, bows his head and covers it with his blanket. The youth sitting next him in the south then rises, and submits himself to similar operations at the hands of the yéi ; and so on down the line, until all the males have been powdered and flagellated.

501.—As the leaf of this yucca, which is often called Spanish bayonet, is two feet or more in length, very stout and much like a large bayonet in size and shape it might be supposed that the stroke is painful, but I did not find it so in my own case, and I have questioned Indians who were initiated at a tender age and have been told that they did not suffer from the stroke. The punishment is symbolic only.

502.—The females are not compelled to rise while the yéi are operating on them, nor to remove any of their clothing except that portion of the blanket which covers the head and shoulders. Neither are they flagellated ; but they must still keep their heads bowed. Instead of the yucca wands, the implements of corn and spruce called yé*d*a*d*ĕstsani are used and merely pressed against their persons. The parts of the females alternately sprinkled with meal and pressed with the implements are the following, in the order mentioned : the soles of the feet ; the palms and forearms (which lie extended on the thighs) ; the upper parts of the chest, to the collar-bones ; the scapular regions ; the top of the head on both sides of the parting of the hair. The Yébaad sprinkles the meal from below upward— for example, on the feet she sprinkles from heel to toe, and always first on the south or right side of the body and then on the north side. *H*ast*s*éyal*t*i presses his instruments simultaneously on both sides, and between applications, while his companion applies the meal, he changes the implements in his hands. Throughout the work, on all the candidates, each yéi gives his own peculiar cry, with the performance of each act. Each candidate covers his (or her) head with the blanket when the yéi are done with him.

503.—The difference between the treatment of the male and the female candidates in this rite is worthy of consideration, in view of the wide-spread opinion that the savage has no consideration or respect for his females.

504.—Now while the candidates are all seated again in a row, with heads bowed and faces covered, the yéi take off their masks and lay them side by side, on the buffalo-robe, faces up, and tops to the east. The female mask—that of *H*ast*s*ébaad—lies south of the male mask — that of *H*ast*s*éyal*t*i. The men who personated the gods then stand with uncovered faces turned toward the row of candidates. The latter are bidden to throw back their blankets and look up. They do so, and the secret of the Yébĭt*s*ai is revealed !

505.—And the secret of the Yébĭt*s*ai is this : The yéi are the bugaboos of the Navaho children. These Indians rarely inflict corporal punishment on the young ; but instead threaten them with the vengeance of these masked characters, if they are unruly.   Up to the time of their initiation they are taught to believe,—and, in most cases, probably do believe,—that the yéi are genuine abnormal creatures whose function it is to chastise bad children.   When the children are old enough to understand the value of obedience without resort to threats they are allowed to undergo this initiation and learn that the dreaded yéi is only some intimate friend or relation in disguise.   After this initiation they are privileged to enter the medicine-lodge during the performance of a rite.

506.—Some Navahoes neglect this initiation until they have reached mature years, and though it is, of course, well known that they no longer believe in the bugbear, they are not admitted into the lodges while esoteric work is in progress. On the other hand they are not anxious to intrude themselves, for the oldest among the tribe profess to believe that if they were to witness the secret ceremonies without having been duly initiated, they would sooner or later be stricken blind, or would catch the disease which is being driven out of the patient.

507.—To attain the highest privileges in these rites one must go through this rite four times—twice at night and twice in the day.   I have seen many adult men and women and some even past middle life going through their second, third, or fourth ordeals.   It is not until one has submitted himself for the fourth time to the flagellation that he is permitted to wear the masks and personate the gods.

508.—The next part of the ceremony is the application of the mask.   He who masquerades as a goddess takes the female mask and applies it in turn to the face of each of the candidates—proceeding along the row from north to south—and adjusts the mask carefully to the face so that the candidate can look out through the eye-holes and understand fully the mechanism of the mask.   The mask is then laid in its former position, south of the other mask on the buffalo-robe.   The actor takes good care that the eyes of the candidate are seen clearly through the eye-holes in the mask.   If they are not, it is thought, blindness would result.

509.—The next part of the performance is the act of sprinkling or sacrificing to the masks.   Each candidate, in turn, beginning as usual in the north, rises and walks to the east of the recumbent masks, passing by way of the west and north.   Standing facing the west he (or she) takes a pinch of pollen from the fawn-skin bag, which now lies west of the masks in charge of an assistant.   He sprinkles it in a line downwards on each mask from the tip of the forehead to the mouth, then upwards on the right cheek or margin, and lastly upwards on the left (south) cheek or margin.   He powders first the mask of *Hastséyalti* in the north and then that of *Hastsébaad* in the south.   Any pollen that may adhere to his fingers is brushed off so that it may fall on the mask (but not on the eye-holes, for this would endanger the sight of the devotee).   This done, he returns to his seat and resumes his clothing.   When the candidates have finished sprinkling, others in the lodge may follow their example.   Each person should pray in silence for what he most desires while sprinkling.   Great care is observed in sprinkling the masks, for this part of the ceremony is of the gravest import.   Before they begin the children are told carefully how to proceed and the younger ones have their hands guided by the actors.   If one sprinkles upwards on the nose of the mask it is supposed the act may hinder the fall of rain and occasion drought; if he sprinkles downwards on the divine cheeks, the act may injure the growth of crops and even the growth of the sprinkler himself.

510.—The last act is the fumigation.   Hot coals, taken directly from the fire, are placed at intervals in front of the line of candidates; around these coals they gather in groups of three or four.   The powder called yádid'ínil is sprinkled on the coals and the dense odorous fumes arising therefrom are inhaled by the candidates for a few seconds.   This completes the initiation.   They now sit around the lodge wherever it suits their convenience and listen to the songs of sequence, which, beginning while the candidates were sacrificing to the masks, continue for about fifteen minutes after the services are completed.   The last two of the Atsá'lei songs and the song for turning up the basket are sung.   Then "the basket is turned up" (par. 291) and put in the west edge of the lodge and the work of the night is done.

511.—Usually the nightly initiation is conducted only on the fifth night of the klédze hatál, but on one occasion I have seen candidates admitted also on the sixth night.   The next repetition of the rite occurs out of doors and in the day time.   No one initiated may tell the secret of initiation to an outsider.   "What would happen to one if he did reveal?" I asked a shaman.   "I know not," he answered, "but it has never been done."   Benjamin Damon had a Navaho mother and was reared on the Navaho reservation until nearly grown.   Then he went to school at Carlisle, was five years in the east, and returned to New Mexico, where I met him.   He took his first initiation only after I advised him to do so.   He told me that in his boyhood he had often tried to get children of his own age to tell him what was done to them in the medicine-lodge but always met with refusal.

SIXTH DAY.

512.—The principal events of the sixth day are (1) the making of a great dry-painting, and the rites connected therewith, and (2) the preparation and journey of the begging gods.   These acts occupy the forenoon and often, also, the early hours of the afternoon.   When they are concluded, there is no more work save a few songs of sequence and the fumigation of the patient early in the evening.   At night there is an informal practice dance outside the lodge, an undress rehearsal of the last night's performance.

SĬLNÉOLE YIKÁL, PICTURE OF THE WHIRLING LOGS.

513.—The painting for this day is that of the Sĭlnéole, which may be called that of the Whirling Sticks or the Whirlpool, depicted in plate VI.   It is painted according to general rules previously laid down (par. 156 et seq.).   After the sand for the groundwork has been brought in and leveled, usually the first act is the burying or setting of a small hemispherical earthen bowl in the center. It is set carefully, so that its margin shall be exactly even with the surface of the surrounding sand. It is filled with water to the brim; the surface of the water is thickly sprinkled, first with pollen and then with finely-powdered charcoal, so that it appears like a mere black circular mark about four inches in diameter on the surface of the ground. The painting, when completed, is usually about ten feet in its largest diameter.

514.—The work, from the commencement of the picture until it is obliterated, takes from five to seven-and-a-half hours. The task of painting the picture, alone, takes from half an hour to an hour less. The time occupied depends much on the number of men engaged, and the elaborateness of the work. When the four cornstalks are omitted the work is accomplished in the shorter time mentioned. The painters usually begin before 8 A. M., sometimes as soon as there is sufficient light to work.

DESCRIPTION OF THE PICTURE. (PLATE VI.)

515.—This picture represents the vision of Bĭtáhatíni at the lake of Tŏ'nihilin, as related in the myth of the Whirling Logs, paragraphs 724 *et seq.* The bowl of water in the center, sprinkled with charcoal, symbolizes the lake. The black cross represents the spruce logs crossing one another. The colors edging the cross show the white foam on the waters, the yellow water-pollen, the blue and red rainbow tints.

516.—Four stalks of corn are depicted as growing on the shores of the lake; each has three roots and two ears. The white stalk of corn, according to its color, belongs to the east; the blue, to the south; the yellow, to the west, and the black to the north; but the conditions of the picture require that these stalks should be directed to intermediate points. Each stalk is bordered with a contrasting color (par. 15).

517.—Eight yéi or divine characters — four male and four female — are shown seated on the floating logs. The legs of the four gods in the periphery of the picture are depicted; this is to indicate that they are standing; but the legs of the eight gods on the cross are not depicted; this is done to indicate that they are sitting; the feet seem hanging below the logs. The four outer yéi, on the cross, dressed in black, are males. The sex is indicated: (1) by the round head representing the cap-like or helmet-like mask which a personator of a male divinity wears; (2) by showing attached to the mask the two eagle-plumes and the tuft of owl-feathers worn by each male dancer in the dance of the last night; (3) by the symbol of a spruce twig in the left hand and of a gourd rattle painted white in the right — such implements are carried by the male dancers. The four inner yéi, dressed in white, are females. The sex is indicated: (1) by the rectangular mask or domino (par. 622); (2) by the yellow arms and chests,—females were created of yellow corn and males of white corn according to the myths,—

and (3) by a symbol of a spruce wand in each hand, for such wands does the female dancer carry in the dance of the last night.

518.—The figures in the north and south represent Gánaskĭdi or humpbacks as they appear in the rites. These are Mountain Sheep or Bighorn Gods, which figure so prominently in the myth of the Visionary. The blue male mask, the headdress with its zigzag line for white lightning, the radiating scarlet feathers to represent sunbeams, the blue imitation horns of the mountain sheep, the black sack of plenty on the back, and the gĭs or staff on which the laden god leans, are all symbolized or depicted in the picture (pars. 48–53).

519.—The white figure in the east is that of Hastséyalti, the Talking God. He is thus represented : He wears the white mask which the personator of this character always wears in the ceremonies (par. 30), with its eagle-plumes tipped with breath-feathers, its tuft of yellow owl-feathers, its ornament of fox-skin under the right ear, and its peculiar mouth-symbol and eye-symbols, but without the corn-symbol on the nose. He carries a pouch made of the gray skin of Abert's squirrel (*Sciurus aberti*), which is depicted with care. The general gray color of the squirrel is shown by the gray or so-called blue color of the body. The fact that the hairs of the animal are tipped with white is indicated by making a white margin and by sprinkling white powder lightly over the blue — the latter device is very imperfectly shown in the illustration. The black tips on ears, nose, and feet, as well as the chestnut spot on the back, are indicated — the latter by a short red marginal line interrupting the white.

520.—The black figure in the west is that of Hastséhogan. He is shown in this manner : He wears a beautifully ornamented black dress and a blue mask decorated with eagle-plumes and owl-feathers. The ornament under his right ear consists of strips of otter-skin tipped with porcupine quills. He carries in his hand a black wand colored with the charcoal of four different plants (par. 214) ; ornamented with a single whorl of turkey-feathers, with two eagle-feathers tied on with cotton string, with a white ring at the base of the whorl, and with the skins of two bluebirds (par. 35).

521.—The two Gánaskĭdi and Hastséhogan are supposed to be punching the logs and causing them to whirl with their staves, while Hastséyalti scatters pollen from his pouch.

522.—Surrounding the picture on three sides, appears the anthropomorphic rainbow, or rainbow goddess (248), wearing the rectangular female mask and carrying at the waist an embroidered pouch, tied on with four strings. The hands of all the other divinities are shown occupied, but the hands of the rainbow are shown empty ; this is that they may be ready to receive the cup of medicine which is placed on them after the picture is finished.

523.—The rainbow and the eight divinities on the cross are represented with breath-feathers tied to the tops of the heads by means of white cotton strings, and the horns of the Gánaskĭdi are similarly decked. All the gods are shown with garnished moccasins, tied with white strings. All of those showing their

legs have rainbow garters.   Five have ornamented fringes on their kilts or loin-
cloths.   The bodies of all are fringed with red to represent sunlight ; the Navaho
artist does not confine the halo to the head of his holy subject.   All have ear-
pendants of turquois and coral.   The eight central figures are represented with
strips of fox-skin — blue and yellow — hanging from elbows and wrists and garnished at their ends.   Such adornments, it is said, were once used in the dance
but are now obsolete ; they, in turn, represented beams of light.   The yellow
horizontal line at the bottom of each pictured mask represents a band at the
bottom of the actual mask worn by the actor, and this band in turn symbolizes
the yellow evening light.

524.—All have the neck depicted in the same manner.   The blue is generally conceded by the shamans to symbolize the collar of spruce twigs ; but
opinion is divided with regard to the meaning of the transverse red lines.   The
original significance of these is perhaps forgotten.   Some say they represent the
rings of the trachea ; but those shamans whose opinion the writer most values
say they represent an obsolete neck ornament called tsĭtsé'yo or cherry-beads,
which was made neither of cherries nor corals.

VARIATIONS OF THE PICTURE.

525.—There are variations of this picture.   It was once seen by the writer
with the corn-stalks and the bowl of water omitted.   The shaman argued : " If
we leave out the corn, there is no use for the water, and if we leave out the water,
the corn cannot grow.   It needs water to live.   It eats the water."   Sometimes
the two eagle-plumes of the four male yéi on the cross are put on the left side of
the head.   It is said that when the plumes and rattle are on the same side of the
figure it calls for rain ; while if they are on opposite sides of the figure, it calls
for corn, since corn-ears sprout from opposite sides of the stalk.

RITES OF THE PICTURE.

526.—While the painting is in progress, the succoring god, a *H*astsébaka
and the begging gods (to be described later) are prepared.   The mask of this
*H*astsébaka is painted and decorated by an assistant.   His body is painted white
and he is otherwise dressed and decked as described in pars. 59–61 ; he wears a
collar of fox-skin instead of one of spruce twigs.

527.—When the picture is finished and before the patient arrives, the shaman
performs on it three, sometimes four, acts in the following order : (1) he applies
meal to the figures ; (2) he sets up plumed wands around the whole picture ; (3)
he makes a cold infusion in a vessel lying on the hands of the rainbow ; (4) he
applies pollen.

528.—In applying the meal, he deposits a heap of about a teaspoonful at each
point.   On the figures of the gods, he places it on the feet, skirt, chest, and mouth
in the order named.   In treating this picture he applies meal to the figures on the

cross, beginning as usual with those in the east ; to the four external divine figures ; to the cross at its extremities ; to the stalks of corn at the base of each ear ; to the squirrel, on the chest, and to the rainbow as to the other gods, all in the order named and going sunwise. This act is done only when the shaman needs meal, thus rendered sacred, for ceremonial purposes. But the three following acts are never omitted.

529.—The eight plumed wands or ĭn*d*iá‘ are set up around the picture on three sides—not in the east. The shaman proceeds sunwise as he sticks them in the ground, placing the blue wands towards the south and the black towards the north.

530. — To prepare the infusion, he places a gourd cup, its tip end pointing east, on the hands of the rainbow ; he pours sacred water into the cup and throws on the surface of the water a powdered vegetable substance. He places a sprig of cedar on top of the cup, its tip pointing east.

531.—This done, he steps in, carefully, among the figures on the picture ; he applies pollen to the pictured masks in the same way that the candidates on the fifth night apply pollen to the real masks (par. 509) ; he applies pollen from below, upward on the bodies of the gods. The gods are pollened in the order in which they are mealed.

532.—Before or during the application of the pollen, the man who is to enact the succoring god departs from the lodge in the guise of an ordinary mortal —his mask hidden under his blanket—and goes to the east of the lodge, with an assistant, to prepare himself. All being now ready for the reception of the patient, he is called in the usual way, by a crier who stands at the door of the lodge. As soon as the patient enters, the singers begin to sing the *Sĭ*/néo/e Bigĭ'n, which are twelve in number. They continue to sing these until the rite of succor is completed and the yéi departs ; then they stop, even if they have not finished the set of songs.

533. — The patient enters, enfolding with his right arm a basket of Navaho make, wrought with designs of crosses (par. 292), and containing corn-meal. On one occasion it was noted that a boy and girl accompanied the patient and on another occasion that a female patient was accompanied by four women who took seats near the door. Standing east of the picture and facing it, the patient with his left hand sprinkles meal on the picture, in the east, in the south, in the west, and in the north, from the center outward, dipping newly from the basket for each quarter. Then he scatters meal all around the periphery of the picture sunwise. As he does this he prays, employing customary prayerful expressions such as these : " In beauty I walk. In beauty it is finished again. In beauty I recover. With beauty before me I walk. With beauty behind me I walk. With beauty below me I walk. With beauty above me I walk. With beauty all around me I walk. Thus will it be beautiful, my grandchild." The singers intone a song whose burden is, Ooni/éna. The patient then sits near the southeast corner of the picture. Here, if a man, he disrobes to his breech-cloth (a woman takes off her moccasins

and leggings only), lays his clothes and the basket on the ground beside him, and awaits the arrival of the succoring god.

534.—The patient has usually but a moment to wait. When the god enters he advances to the picture, whooping; dips the sprinkler into the infusion contained in the gourd cup, on the hands of the rainbow, and sprinkles the picture thus: the cross from east to west and from north to south; the gods on the cross, from foot to head, the male of each pair first; the four gods outside the cross, from foot to head; the corn-stalks from root to tassel; the rainbow from foot to head.

535.—After the sprinkling, an assistant picks up as much as he can, without injuring the picture, of each little heap of meal deposited by the shaman, and puts it in a bag. In doing this he proceeds in an order the reverse of that in which the shaman laid the meal down (par. 528).

536.—The god then dips the cedar twig into the bowl buried in the center of the picture and touches various parts of the picture in the following order: the edge of the bowl at the four cardinal points; the tips of the cross; the figures on the cross—feet, chest, mouth; the four stalks of corn—top of root, base of lower ear, base of tassel; the four outer yéi—feet, chest, mouth; the rainbow in the same places. At the beginning of each part of the work, as mentioned above, he dips the sprinkler in the bowl and then moves sunwise. When he is done he gives the sprinkler to an attendant. If the central bowl of water is omitted there is no substitute for this part of the work.

537.—Next, the patient sits on the western limb of the cross with the center of the picture just between his feet. If the patient be a man, the lower extremities are flexed and the hands clasped around the knees. If the patient be a woman, the lower extremities are extended and the hands lie on the knees. The god takes the gourd cup with its contents from the rainbow's hands; he makes a motion as if offering it to the gods in the eastern quarter of the picture, and administers a sip of the infusion to the patient; he offers it, let us say, to the gods in the south and administers a second sip; he offers it to the gods in the west and administers a third sip; he offers it to the gods in the north and administers a fourth sip to the patient. He utters his peculiar cry, a whoop or yelp, each time he offers the bowl the pictured gods.

538.—An assistant now receives into his mouth the residue of the infusion from the gourd cup; but he does not swallow it; he squirts it out on the hands of the succoring god held open to receive it. The succorer then proceeds to take dust from the figures in the picture by pressing to them his moistened palms, and he applies this dust to the person of the patient. Dust from the feet of the figures he applies to the patient's feet; dust from their hips he applies to his hips; dust from their chests, to his chest; dust from their heads, to his head. He takes it first from the forms on the cross, next from those outside the cross, then from the corn tassels (for the patient's head), and lastly from the rainbow, proceeding sunwise in each case. Each time that he applies dust to the patient's body, he lifts his hands toward the smoke-hole of the lodge. When the application of dust is done, the god yells twice, loudly, into each ear of the patient and leaves the lodge. Song ceases.

539.—As soon as the god departs, the patient leaves his seat on the picture and sits elsewhere in the lodge. A hot coal is placed before him ; the powder, yád id ínil, is scattered on it by the shaman ; the patient inhales the odorous fumes arising from the burning powder, and rubs them into his hands. When he is done, the coal is extinguished with water poured four times on it and is thrown out at the smoke-hole or carried out of the lodge. Others may receive the fumigation at the same time. About the time the coal is cast out, the man who enacted the succoring god returns to the lodge, unmasked and covered with a blanket. He surrenders his mask, divests himself of his properties, and washes off his paint. When the patient leaves the lodge he takes the meal-basket with him.

540.—The next acts of the shaman are to pull up, moving sunwise, the plumed wands which surround the picture, and to take out the bowl buried in the center. As soon as the bowl is taken out, although the picture is by this time badly marred, there is a rush made for the latter by a number of men, headed often by the shaman, who are ill or who fancy themselves ailing. They trample at will over the picture, and take dust on their palms, from the figures, to apply to their own bodies. If one's head aches, he takes dust from the heads of the pictured gods and applies it to his own head ; if his chest aches, he takes dust from the pictured chests, and so on. When every one has all the remedial dust he wishes, the sand is scraped off the floor from center to periphery, by several persons working at the same time ; it is gathered in blankets, carried out of the lodge, and thrown away to the north in a shady place. If the fire has been removed from the center of the lodge, to make way for the picture, it is now put back.

BEGGING GODS.

541.—Reference has been made to certain begging gods. These are first sent out on the sixth day ; but they may also be sent out on any or all of the subsequent days of the ceremony. The same divine characters go out more than once during the ceremony, but rarely the same individual Indians. The characters dispatched are usually *Hastséyalti, Tó'nenïli, Hastsélpahi, Hastsébaka,* and *Hastsébaad.* If they go to a distance they usually form a party of four—two representing male, and two female, characters. If they beg near the lodge, a pair, or even a single individual may go on the errand.

542.—They are dressed and adorned, in the lodge, early in the day, while the painting and other work is in progress, and set forth as soon as they are ready. They are expected to go and return in one day and not to remain away over night. If they have but a short way to go, they are fully masked, dressed, and equipped in the lodge and travel the whole distance on foot. If they have a long journey to make, which requires the use of horses, they have their masks, collars of spruce, and other properties prepared in the lodge, packed in blankets, and loaded on their horses. They depart, dressed in ordinary clothes, and ride to a secure place near the camp they intend to visit; here they tie their horses, paint their bodies, put on their trappings, and enter the camp on foot. The masqueraders never ride in costume on horseback—a survival, no doubt, of the days when neither the Navahoes nor their gods had horses.

543.—When they enter the visited camp they speak to no one; but go dancing around, uttering their appropriate cries and one of the number holding out a fawn-skin bag to receive donations. If some object is offered, the beggar does not always accept it at once, but advances and retreats four times; the fourth time he advances he opens the bag and allows the donor to put the offering in it. The gifts are usually food and tobacco for the use of the lodge; but the gods will not refuse money or any other offering of value.

544.—If a traveler, on his way to the medicine-lodge, meets the divine beggars, he should wait on the trail until they return and pass him. If he overtakes them on their return journey he should not pass them, but follow in their rear. It is not a lucky thing to precede the yéi on the trail or to get into camp before them.

SONGS OF SEQUENCE AT NIGHT.

545.—After the rites connected with the picture are done, there is no work in the lodge until about dusk. Then the patient, called as usual, goes to the lodge and sits in the south while songs of sequence are sung accompanied by the beating of the basket-drum. The singing continues from twenty minutes to an hour, the time depending on the number of songs sung. The songs are selected from the series of Aga‘hoá Gisĭ'n or Summit Songs.

546.—The Summit Songs are followed by the first and second of the Béna *Hatá*li or Finishing Hymns. As the last of these is sung the basket is "turned up" in the manner described, and the invisible evil influences chased out through the smoke-hole of the lodge.

547.—When the singing is done, the patient is fumigated, in the manner previously described (par. 198), and the ceremonial work of the sixth day is finished.

UNDRESS REHEARSAL.

548.—An undress rehearsal of the dance and song of the last night — the naak*h*aí — occupies the rest of the evening, until midnight or later. The performance takes place on the prepared dance-ground east of the lodge. The first to practise are those known as the Atsá‘*h*ei or First Dancers. They practise every night from this to the last. While the dancers are practising outside, those who are to sing within the lodge on the last night practise their songs inside.

PASTIMES OF VISITORS.

549.—On the sixth day the visitors begin to gather and they continue to increase in number until the last night.   Those who are not busy in the medicine-lodge must find pastime.   During the afternoon of this day, Navaho games of various kinds are in progress around the camp, among the men and women, and these continue daily to the end.

SEVENTH DAY.

550.—The ritual work of the seventh day consists in (1) the painting of a picture, with accompanying rites, early in the day, and (2) the acts of singing over the patient and fumigating him in the evening.   Begging gods often may be dressed and set forth as on the sixth day, while at night there is again a practice dance or rehearsal of the naak*h*aí outside, and a rehearsal of song inside the lodge.

PICTURES OF THE DAY.

551.—Either one of two different designs may be painted on the seventh day.   That of the naak*h*aí yiká*l*, or dance picture, is the one usually executed; but sometimes one called *H*astse*h*ogánbe yiká*l* or picture with *H*astsé*h*ogan is made.   There are many variants of these pictures.

NAAK*H*AÍ YIKÁ*L*.   PICTURE OF THE DANCE OF NAAK*H*AÍ.

552.—The dry-painting of this subject as it appears on the floor of the lodge is usually about ten feet broad and twelve feet long.   It is said to depict the naak*h*aí, or dance of the last night as it took place among the gods at Tsĕ'nit*si*h*o*gan, and disregarding such mythic accessories as clouds and rainbow, it represents also the dance as it is now conducted among the Navahoes.

DESCRIPTION OF THE PICTURE.   (PLATE VII.)

553.—As will be learned from the description given elsewhere (par. 621 *et seq.*) the naak*h*aí is a contra-dance in which the personators of males and females stand in two opposite rows; thus they are shown in the picture, six male dancers in the west and six female dancers in the east, besides the two special characters to be described later.   The females are depicted like those shown in plate VI., and described in par. 517; but here the legs are displayed to show they are standing or dancing, not sitting.   Ornamental fringes to the skirts and embroidered pouches are added.   The males are symbolized in most respects as are those sitting on the cross of the *si*lné*ole* yiká*l* (plate VI.) with round heads, eagle-plumes, owl-feathers, rattles, spruce wands, and arm-pendants; but the bodies are white, not black, and again the embroidered pouches and skirt fringes are added.   In our illustration, the female dancers are shown as turned toward the west; but they are often depicted turned toward the east.   The reason for this change has not been noted.   The long straight lines in the west represent a black cloud bestrewn with pollen, on which the gods dance.   The corresponding lines in the east represent blue mist bestrewn with pollen on which the goddesses dance.   The legs of the dancing figures are yellow — not white as in other pictures — to show that they dance knee-deep in pollen. " How can they be knee-deep in pollen?" a shaman was asked. "Walk through a bed of sun-flowers in the summer and you will be knee-deep in pollen," he answered.

554.—The figure which stands at the head of the line of female dancers in the northeast is that of *Tó‘nenĭli*, the Water Sprinkler, who in these days is the clown of the dance (par. 636). He is represented as having his body sprinkled with powders of many colors, and as wearing the same mask as the yébaka or male dancers, but unlike the other dancers, his hands are empty. This is because in the dance he carries neither wand, rattle, nor other regular implement, and if he joins in the dance at all he does so in an erratic manner; his function is to play the buffoon. Occasionally he carries for a while the skin of some animal in the dance, but this is not a regular property of his. In the myths he is spoken of as carrying two water-bottles, one blue and one black (par. 708), and for this reason he is sometimes shown in the picture with a water-bottle of either color; but the personator never carries such a bottle. The figure at the head of the line of male dancers in the northwest is that of *Hastséyalti*, shown as in plate VI. and as described in pars. 29–31.

RITES OF THE PICTURE.

555.—It takes about five or six hours to make the picture. When it is done, the various acts performed on it and the various rites connected with it are much the same as those of the previous day, and are performed in much the same order. Some modifications will be noted later.

556.—Synopsis of the picture-rites, in order of occurrence.

1. Meal applied to divine figures.
2. Plumed wands erected.
3. Cup placed on the rainbow's hands.
4. Cold infusion made. Sprinkler placed on cup.
5. Pollen applied to figures.
6. Succorer departs, unmasked.
7. Patient enters. Song begins.
8. Patient sprinkles picture.
9. Patient sits, southeast, and disrobes.
10. Succorer (god) returns, masked.
11. Succorer sprinkles picture.
12. Assistant takes up meal from picture.
13. Succorer touches moistened sprinkler to figures.
14. Patient sits on picture.
15. Infusion offered to gods and given to patient.
16. Assistant moistens succorer's hands.
17. Sacred dust applied to patient.
18. Succorer yells into patient's ears.
19. Succorer departs, masked.
20. Patient leaves picture.
21. Patient fumigated.
22. Succorer returns, unmasked, and proceeds to divest.
23. Plumed wands pulled out.

24. Picture despoiled.
25. Picture erased.
26. Material taken out and deposited.

557.—As on the sixth day, different gods may come to the succor of the patient : On some occasions *H*ast*sé*h*og*an, the House God, is seen, on others it is *H*ast*sé*lpahi, the Brown God, who appears. Still other gods may perform the rites of succor. Each of the four times that he administers the infusion to the patient, *H*ast*sé*h*og*an utters a cry which may be approximately represented as " Hahuwá Hahuwá " and this is what he shouts into the patient's ears before he departs. *H*ast*sé*lpahi utters a cry somewhat like " Hawú Hawú ".

558.—As the figures on the painting of the seventh day are arranged very differently from those of the painting of the sixth day, the actors must necessarily proceed differently in performing their various offices on the picture, such as the application of pollen, the sprinkling with water, and touching the figures with the wet sprinkler. Each row of figures is treated separately, that of the east first. The actor sometimes proceeds from north to south, and sometimes in the opposite direction. The rainbow is treated last—always from foot to head.

559.—On the sixth day there are usually two vessels of fluid—one in the rainbow's hands and one in the centre of the picture—for the succorer to use in sprinkling and touching ; on the seventh day there is but one, the infusion on the rainbow's hands,—so he uses this both to sprinkle the picture when he enters and to touch the sacred parts of each pictured god afterwards.

560.—Such are some of the differences between the rites of the sixth and seventh days, which are enforced by the different forms of the pictures and the different gods who come to the succor ; but minor differences are often observed which are made in accordance with a certain law of variety which belongs to the Navaho ceremonies. Changes are made merely for the sake of change, or under the impression that some good will result from the change. Such changes may consist in a different order in which the wands are planted and pulled up, a different order in which meal and the infusion are applied to the divine figures, in a different selection of parts of the figures on which to make the application. The gourd cup, on the rainbow's hands, may have its tip pointed to the east on the sixth and to the west on the seventh day. The picture may be erased from circumference to centre one day, and from centre to circumference the next day. Other slight alterations are made.

SONGS OF THE PICTURES.

561.—The songs pertaining to the picture, as on the sixth day, are usually begun when the patient enters ; but they have been seen deferred until he began to sprinkle ; they are concluded when the succoring god departs. If the picture of naak*h*aí yiká*l* is painted, the Aga‘hoá Gisï'n or Summit Songs are sung ; but if *H*ast*sé*h*og*anbe yiká*l* is drawn, the *H*ast*sé*h*og*an Bigï'n are sung. The complete set of these is 40 in number.

WORK OF THE EVENING.

562.—The songs of sequence in the evening, when for the third time "the basket is turned down," or inverted, begin usually between six and seven o'clock and continue for an hour or more.   They are the same songs that are sung in the forenoon, during the rites of the picture ; but while in the morning the series may not be finished, since song ceases when the yéi leaves the lodge, the series is completed at night.   Besides these there are three songs sung at the turning up of the drum (par. 291).   The second of these is sung while the hand is under the edge of the basket ready to turn it up and the last is sung when the basket is turned.

563.—When the songs of sequence are done, the patient is fumigated in the usual manner.

564.—After the ritual work is completed there is, as on the previous night, a rehearsal of the dance and song outside the lodge and a rehearsal of song inside.

EIGHTH DAY.

565.—On the eighth day (1) a picture is painted and rites are performed on it, similar to those of the seventh day.   But between the finishing of the picture and the rites mentioned, some important events occur outside the lodge different from anything that happens on the previous days of painting.   (2) The first of these is a diurnal repetition of the rites of initiation of the Yébĭtsai, for the benefit of those who desire to take their second or fourth degrees.   (3) The second is an elaborate exorcism or succor by three gods.   Again, when night falls, there are (4) songs of sequence and fumigation of the patient.   Later the rehearsals of the dance outside the lodge and of song inside are resumed and continued to a late hour.

DSAHA*D*OLD*Z*ÁBE YIKÁ*L*, PICTURE WITH THE FRINGE MOUTHS.

566.—The picture with the Fringe Mouths, shown in plate VIII, is the only picture which has been seen by the writer painted on the eighth day ; but it is understood that other pictures, or at least variants of this picture, may be produced on this occasion.   When the painting is finished to the satisfaction of the shaman, he places meal on four parts of each figure, sets up the plumed wands, prepares an infusion in the bowl on the hands of the rainbow, and applies pollen to the figures as on the sixth day ; then he and his assistants sit down and await the completion of events which occur outside the lodge.   They usually, too, partake of food about this time, for it is now early in the afternoon.

DESCRIPTION OF THE PICTURE. (PLATE VIII.)

567.—The original dry-painting is about ten feet wide and thirteen feet long. It is said to represent a ceremony which, according to the myth (par. 765), took place among the gods at Tsĕ′nitsi*h*ogán.   Possibly some such ceremony still exists among the Navahoes.   The scenes of succor on the eighth and ninth days are, to some extent, symbolized by it.

568.—Tsĕ'nitsihogán, Rock-red-in-middle-house, is a large cliff-ruin, in a cañon abounding with ruins, somewhere north of the San Juan River, probably in Colorado or Utah. From the people (gods) of this place many rites of the night chant are supposed to be derived. The elements of the name are found in the words : tse‘, rock ; aɫní‘, in the middle ; tsi, red, and hogán, house. The building is said to stand in a long cavern or rock shelter in the face of a whitish cliff through which runs a seam of red. The black line in the west of the picture represents this cave. The small white lines on the black represent the houses within the cave.

569.—The myths say that rainbows illuminated the divine dwellings, hence the bounding rainbow is represented as passing into the cave at one end and coming out at the other. The hands of the rainbow, as before, are left vacant to receive the bowl of medicine.

570.—The terraced figure in blue, called kosistsín, or the shapen cloud, in the west, represents a cloud from which arises, by three roots, a stalk of corn. In the gardens of the gods, say the myths, each stalk bore twelve ears ; but the Navaho cornstalk now bears only two, hence two ears are shown on the stalk.

571.—We are already familiar with eight of the twelve divine figures embraced by the rainbow, and they need not be again described. The four outer figures are the Gánaskĭdi, or Humpbacks (par. 46 et seq.). The four next to these are yébaad, or goddesses : they differ slightly from the goddesses shown in plate VII., for each carries in the right hand a jeweled basket, instead of a bunch of spruce twigs, and there is no pollen on the legs.

572.—The four figures next to the cornstalk are the Dsahadoldzá, or Fringe Mouths (par. 39 et seq.). These characters are mentioned in the myths. Those north of the corn-stalk are Fringe Mouths of Tsĕ'nitsi, or Fringe Mouths of the land ; those south, are Fringe Mouths under the Water, Thalklá‘ Dsahadoldzá. The former have their bodies painted half red and half black, while the latter are half blue and half yellow. The marks on their bodies and limbs are those of the white zigzag lightning. The masks are the same in all, and represent that described in par. 42, and depicted in plate III., fig. F. Each of the Fringe Mouths carries in his right hand a gourd rattle, ornamented with two circles of plumes, and in his left hand a bow ornamented with plumes and breath-feathers. The bow is painted in two colors to correspond with the body of the bearer.

TOILET OF THE GODS.

573.—Before the picture is finished, certain characters, who are to appear later in the outdoor ceremonies, begin to dress themselves. The two who first are ready and go out, and who are to act in the rite of initiation, are Hastséyalti and Hastsébaad, dressed the same as those who appeared in the rite of initiation of the sixth night. Three other characters, whose preparations are completed later, are another Hastséyalti, another Hastsébaad, and Dsahadoldzá. The Hastsébaad of the second group dresses differently from that of the first, and in the manner of a modern Navaho woman, with gown, silver-studded belt, blanket, moccasins, and leggings. The *H*ast*s*éyal*t*i of the second group is usually dressed differently from that of the first—the latter wears an ordinary Navaho cotton shirt; the former has his torso covered with several finely dressed buckskins, tied on by the skin of the legs (par. 29). The masks worn by *H*ast*s*éyal*t*i and by *H*ast*s*ébaad of both groups are not only alike, but identical, as will be explained later (par. 575).

SECOND RITE OF INITIATION.

574.—The first two characters leave the lodge before, or very soon after, the shaman has finished his work on the picture. While they are preparing, the candidates for the second (and fourth) degree have been grouped at a distance from the lodge, usually south of it. When *H*ast*s*éyal*t*i leaves the lodge with his companion, he gives his peculiar call, whereat all the candidates hide their faces in their blankets. *H*ast*s*éyal*t*i calls four times on his way. When he and his comrade reach the waiting group, the candidates, with heads bowed and faces hidden, go, under guidance, to a secluded place east of the lodge, the gods following them. Here the candidates sit in a line—males north, females south—facing east, and go through a rite similar in all respects to that of the first initiation of the fifth night (par. 495 *et seq.*).

575.—The actors, as on the fifth night, take off their masks for the candidates to sacrifice to them (par. 504) and when the rite is over they leave the masks where they took them off, under guard, for the characters of the second group to assume when these come to the east to dress. The candidates, when the rite is over, go where they will. The men who impersonated the yéi, when they have removed their properties, in the lodge, washed off their paint, and resumed their ordinary clothing, also go wherever they wish. The yé*d*a*d*ĕstsani, or implements for initiating the females, are allowed to lie in a basket, beside the masks (par. 298).

RITE OF SUCCOR OR EXORCISM.

576.—Soon after the actors of the initiation return to the lodge, the second group is ready. It consists, as before stated, of three characters: *H*ast*s*éyal*t*i, *H*ast*s*ébaad, and Dsaha*d*old*z*á. They depart from the lodge with their peculiar dress and painting concealed under their blankets. Dsaha*d*old*z*á carries his mask concealed. All have their faces and heads bare and they endeavor to appear like ordinary Indians out for a stroll. They proceed to the east of the lodge, to the locality where the initiation took place and where the guarded masks of two of the characters are lying. Here they drop their blankets, don their masks, and stand, the representatives of the gods. Let us now speak of them as gods. The Dsaha*d*old*z*á may be of either of the two kinds mentioned, either of the land or of the water.

577.—As soon as the personators have left the lodge the patient is called.

He comes bearing on his right arm a basket containing meal. He is placed standing about ten paces to the east of the lodge on a buffalo robe and facing east. When he has stood there a few moments, the succoring gods are seen to approach from the east. *H*ast*s*éyal*t*i comes first, the *H*ast*s*ébaad follows at a distance of about ten paces, both walking. Between them, Dsaha*d*old*z*á comes dancing and, from time to time, turning around and facing *H*ast*s*ébaad. Thus the three advance until they get within a few paces of the patient, when they all halt without changing their relative positions.

578.—It is recorded that the head of the buffalo robe during this rite pointed on different occasions east, west, and north. Barthelmess observed it pointed north and makes the following instructive remark : " In front of it [*i. e.*, the lodge] the snow was cleared away and a buffalo robe spread out, so that its head lay to the north, the tail to the south. I mention this fact because the medicine-man went into a fury because it was laid east and west, and it was hastily turned north and south."[21]   There is little doubt that the direction of the axis of the robe is changed in accordance with different rules, but it has not been discovered what these rules are.

579.—*H*ast*s*éyal*t*i now leaves his two companions standing and advances alone toward the patient. He retreats three times, and advances, in all, four times ; the last time he stops close to the patient, facing him, but does not step on the robe. He takes a pinch of meal from a fawnskin bag which he carries ; sprinkles it upward near the body of the patient from waist to head ; holds it just above the crown ; allows it to drop down upon the person ; gives his peculiar whoop and steps aside to make room for Dsaha*d*old*z*á. The latter approaches the patient dancing (four times) ; he bears in one hand a decorated rattle, in the other a decorated bow (plate VIII.) ; he holds these for a moment near the patient's head, one on each side, uttering at the same time his peculiar call ; he turns sunwise around and dances back to *H*ast*s*ébaad on whom he repeats the acts performed on the patient. The *H*ast*s*ébaad does nothing to the patient, but when Dsaha*d*old*z*á holds his implements near her head, she lifts to a level with his face a basket that she carries, containing the yé*d*a*d*ĕstsani, or implements of female initiation. It is once noted that, when the patient was a woman, Dsaha*d*old*z*á carried one of the two yé*d*a*d*ĕstsani instead of a bow.

580.—The three succorers next pass to the south of the patient and the latter, as they pass, scatters after them meal taken from the basket with his left hand. They arrange themselves in a line in the south in the order which they previously held in the east, and they repeat in the south all the acts which they performed in the east and in the same order. As they pass to the west the patient as before sprinkles meal after them. In the west and in the north all these acts are again repeated. Through all this work the patient never changes his position on the buffalo robe.

581.—These labors accomplished, the three divinities return to the east of the patient and range themselves in a line facing west, as they originally stood before the exorcism began. The patient then turns around sunwise, faces the west, and marches into the lodge, followed by the three succorers.

582.—On returning to the lodge, the patient sprinkles the picture with meal, as on the previous day, disrobes, and sits on the central figure—the cornstalk—in the western half of the picture as on previous occasions. Then all the rites and observances of the seventh day are repeated and in nearly or quite the same order (par. 556). Dsaha*d*oldzá is the divine character who performs the various acts of the succoring god on the picture and on the patient. The picture is erased and the debris thrown to the north of that of the previous day.

SONGS OF SEQUENCE.

583.—When the gods appear in the east, approaching to perform the rite of succor, a herald stationed at the door of the medicine-lodge calls aloud, "A*d*é yéi as!", "There come the gods,"—a cue to the singers inside the lodge, who at once begin to sing, to the accompaniment of the rattle, the Dsaha*d*oldzá Bigï'n or Fringe Mouth Songs. These are continued all through the rite on the picture until the yéi go out, but they are not finished until night.

WORK OF THE EVENING.

584.—At night the basket is turned down and song is accompanied by drum and rattle. When the twelve songs of sequence are finished, one song of the series of *Sïléna*h*otil* is sung, during which the basket is turned up and the evil influences blown out toward the smoke-hole as before. After this the patient is fumigated and the ritual work of the eighth day is done.

REHEARSAL.

585.—Later in the evening, songs are sung for practice inside and there is dancing for practice outside the lodge.

PRACTICE DANCES AND SONGS OF THE NAAK*H*AÍ.

586.—These practice dances, with their accompanying songs, as has been stated, occur on the prepared dancing-ground in front of the medicine-lodge for several hours after sunset, on the sixth, seventh, and eighth days, but these are only final rehearsals. All over the Navaho land during the autumn and early winter, groups of young men practise this dance and rehearse songs to be sung at the naak*h*aí on the ninth night. Several men living in a certain locality will get together and, knowing that a night chant will be celebrated somewhere in their neighborhood during the winter, will make arrangements to form a group or relay for the occasion. They will compose new songs and rehearse these with old ones, to the cadence of the dance, night after night for many weeks, or until they feel themselves proficient.   After the great nine-days' ceremony has begun, men loitering about the camp or plying their various industries, sacred or profane, may be heard in every direction, by day as well as by night, rehearsing words to the tunes that characterize the songs of the last night.

587.—They may practise the song in the daytime, but may practise the dance only after sunset.   For such occasions they use bunches of artemisia or some other plant to represent the spruce wands.   When they practise before the medicine-lodge they use the regular rattles of the shaman, but when they practise at home they extemporize rattles.   They have been known, of late years, to thrust, for a handle, a stick through an old fruit-can, and fill the latter with pebbles to make a rattle.

NINTH DAY, — UNTIL NIGHTFALL.

588.—The early hours of the ninth day, which is called Bitsín or last day of the ceremony, are spent : (1) in making the kethawns to be offered to the succoring gods late in the afternoon, and (2) in preparing the masks and other properties of the succoring gods and of those who dance at night.   This work was once seen by the writer finished before noon, but it is usually not completed till the middle of the afternoon.   Later in the day (3) the greenroom or arbor is erected (par. 242, plate 1, D) and (4) about sunset the succor or exorcism of the patient takes place.   Sometimes (5) a diurnal initiation, similar to that of the eighth day, occurs in the afternoon, if there should be a number of persons present desiring it.   The rite of succor ends the work of the daytime.   The rites of the night will be considered under a separate section, entitled " Last Night."

PREPARATION OF PROPERTIES.

589.—The work of making the kethawns and preparing the masks and other properties requires the labor of several men for three or four hours.   There is no need to describe minutely in this section the way in which the work on these properties is done, for in speaking of the various articles elsewhere the method of work is given.   A few remarks will suffice here.   The masks, as they are carried in the chanter's bag, are not trimmed ; on this occasion they are newly painted ; the eagle-plumes and other plumes are mounted on them, the collars of spruce are fashioned from fresh twigs and attached to them.   When the masks are completed, an assistant chews fruit of a plant called tsé'tsagi and spits the juice on them.   The gourd rattles are painted anew with white and trimmed anew with four spruce twigs on each handle.   The talismans of To'badzïstsíni (par. 85) are made and painted if he is one of the gods of succor, or the special implements of other gods of succor are prepared.

KETHAWNS.

590.—The kethawns for this day are cigarettes and are usually three in number, as there are usually three suc-coring gods and there is one kethawn for each.   The kethawns are not always the same, for the gods are not always the same.   The first to be described are three kethawns (fig. 14), whose empty cases are now in the writer's collection. They are made of the common reed (*Phragmites communis*) and are each three finger-widths in length.   One is sacred to *To'badzĭstsíni*, another to *Dsahadoldzá* of *Tsĕ'nitsi*, and another to *Hastséoltoi*.   The first is painted red and has the emblem of *To'badzĭs-tsíni*, the queue or scalp-lock, done in white, twice on the back or once on each side.   The second is colored lon-gitudinally, black and red on opposite sides, and these colors are separated from one another by narrow lines of white, like the body of *Dsahadoldzá*; there is a lightning symbol in white on

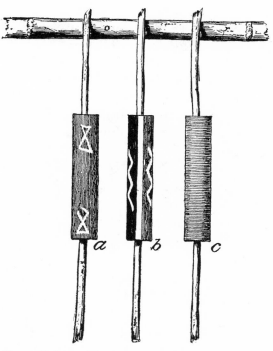

Fig. 14.   Kethawns of the ninth day.   Cases for cigarettes as they appear when painted and left to dry.

each side.   The third is simply painted all blue to indicate the female, for *Has-tséoltoi*, the Navaho deity of the chase, is a goddess.   Sometimes a cigarette for Nayénĕzgani is seen, which is black with a bow-symbol on each side.   There is a cigarette for Fringe Mouth Under Water which is like the second above de-scribed, except that blue and yellow take the place of black and red.

SONGS OF THE MASKS.

591.—The songs of sequence, five in number, which are sung during the painting of the masks, are Anĭltáni Bigĭ'n or Grasshopper Songs.   These are also called Dzĭ'sbehatadĭ'lne Bigĭ'n or Songs with Preparing Masks.   When the masks are all ready and the robe is spread on which these are to be displayed, they begin to sing one song of *Hastséyalti*, a song which is independent of the regular set and may or may not be sung with the *Hastséyalti* Bigĭ'n or the Anĭltáni Bigĭ'n at night.

ARRANGEMENT OF MASKS AND OTHER PROPERTIES.

592.—When the masks and other properties are all finished they are taken up in the hands of the assistants and other spectators and held while the refuse of preparation is swept up and carried out of the lodge to be deposited according to rule ; then they are laid down on blankets and cloths in the north of the lodge. In one group there are the 14 masks used in the dance of the naak*h*aí, *viz.*, one of *H*ast*s*éyal*t*i, one of *T*ó‘nen*ĭ*li, six of yébaka or ordinary male characters, and six of yébaad or female characters.   The eight masks first mentioned—male masks —are laid down first, in a row extending east and west ; to the south of these the six female masks are laid down in a parallel row ; and behind all, in the north, the six great gourd rattles are deposited in a row.   The masks to be used by the personators of the male divinities in the act of succor are laid in a separate group to the east of the larger group of masks.   If the goddess *H*ast*s*éol*t*oi is to appear in the act of succor, a female mask is borrowed for the occasion, from the row of yébaad masks.

RITE OF SUCCOR OR EXORCISM.

593.—Before the preparation of the masks is completed, or very soon after, the actors in the rite of succor or exorcism begin, with assistance, to paint and decorate themselves.   When ready, they cover themselves in the usual way with blankets, under which they carry their hidden masks, and go to a retired place, east of the lodge.   They soon reappear in the full dress and adornment of gods, and approach the patient.   The latter, meanwhile, has been called and placed standing, meal-basket on arm, as on the previous day, on a buffalo robe, a few paces east of the lodge and facing east.

594.—It is not always the same gods that figure in this scene of succor or exorcism ; *H*ast*s*éyal*t*i, Gá*n*askĭ*d*i, Dsaha*d*oldzá, *H*ast*s*éz*ĭ*ni, and others may appear ; but the three which are usually seen, and whose presence from an Aryan point of view seems most appropriate, are the war-gods, Nayénĕzg*a*ni and *T*o‘bad*z*īst*s*íni, and the divine huntress, *H*ast*s*éol*t*oi.   The act shall be described as performed by these.   When other gods figure, the rite is similarly conducted ; the only important difference being in the dress, implements, and cries of the gods. Elsewhere (par. 109 *et seq.*) a description is given of the peculiar circumstances under which the fire-god *H*ast*s*éz*ĭ*ni takes part in the rite.

595.—Nayénĕzg*a*ni comes first, *T*o‘bad*z*īst*s*íni second, *H*ast*s*éol*t*oi third, walking in single file.   When they first appear in the east, Nayénĕzg*a*ni lifts on high and brandishes his great stone knife, whereat all three halt and sing the third Nayénĕzg*a*ni Bigĭ′n.   This finished, they advance until Nayénĕzg*a*ni stands face to face with the patient.   The god makes a motion in the air with his great stone knife, near the patient from head to foot, uttering at the same time a low, hoarse groan.   *T*o‘bad*z*īst*s*íni follows, making a similar motion with his talismans but giving a different call.   *H*ast*s*éol*t*oi comes last, making a like motion with her bow and arrows and uttering a single yelp as she does so.   All these acts are performed to the east, to the south, to the west, and to the north in the order named.   The succoring gods pass from one point to the other as do those of the previous day, and as each one passes, the patient sprinkles meal after him.

596.—When they have done in the north they pass around the patient by

way of the east and the south, and go to the lodge, which they treat at the four
cardinal points with forms quite similar to those used on the patient; for, during
the nine days of ceremony, it is thought that some of the evil influence drawn from
the patient has entered the structure of the lodge so the latter needs exorcism
as well as the patient. Then, as on the previous day, they form a procession of
four, the patient leading, and march into the lodge. No one may follow them.
He who would witness the succeeding rites in the lodge should enter before the
rites of succor begin.

597.—On entering the lodge, the patient sits in the west, facing east, and the
three gods sit facing him, ranged in their previous order of precedence from north
to south. From his basket of meal, the patient takes the kethawn of
Nayénězgạni, presents it to the god and, following the shaman or some one else
who is competent to lead, repeats a dialogue prayer. A kethawn is given and a
similar prayer is made to each of the other gods in turn. The gods leave the
lodge and go to the west to deposit the cigarettes and take off their masks, and
the patient is at liberty to depart. After a while the actors return, remove their
paint and paraphernalia, and resume their ordinary clothing. The dried white
pigment taken from the characteristic marks on their bodies is, by some, carefully
scraped off and preserved in medicine-bags.

598.—Sometimes the shaman takes the cigarette from the hand of the
patient and places it in the hand of the god. Nayénězgạni and To‘badẕïstsíni
deposit their cigarettes in the shade of a tree, preferably a piñon, while
Hastséoltoi lays hers on the ground in a cluster of *Gutierrezia euthamiæ*.

REHEARSALS OF THE FIRST DANCERS.

599.—In the afternoon and early evening, when other work is not in progress,
the men who are to sing the first song of the night and to dance the first dance
— the Atsá‘lei, or First Dancers — enter the medicine-lodge several times, and
rehearse their important part in the rites under the criticisms of the shaman and
other experts. They rehearse this with extra care and attention for reasons which
are explained elsewhere (par. 617).

GATHERING OF SPECTATORS.

600.—On the previous days people have been coming in gradually, in no
great numbers, to witness and participate in the ceremonies. Many of these have
made themselves little huts and enclosures of evergreen boughs, particularly such
as are accompanied by women and children. Men coming alone spend much of
their time in the medicine-lodge and sleep there. But it is on the afternoon and
evening of the last day that the great crowd arrives. Many of them come without impedimenta; some bringing food for one meal; others bringing none and
prepared to stay only one night, during which time they sit by the fires, watch the
dance, and take no sleep. From 300 to 500 persons may be present on the last
night. The writer has made a count, as careful as practicable, of the assembled

spectators, on more than one occasion, not only during the night chant but during the mountain chant, and he has gotten others to count ; as a result he considers 500 as a high estimate of the largest crowd he has ever seen collected to witness these ceremonies.

LAST NIGHT.

601.—In order to give a clear understanding of the work of the last night, it will be necessary to repeat some statements already made.

602.—The medicine-lodge, as has been said (par. 237), was built before the ceremony began and we have noted that, at different times, other preparations were made ; that the ground in front of the lodge was cleared and levelled for the dancers ; that an enclosure of evergreen branches and saplings, which we call the arbor or greenroom (iⅬnásti), was constructed about one hundred paces east of the lodge ; that the ground between the greenroom and the dancing-place was cleared of brush, weeds, and other obstructions in order that the dancers might pass easily back and forth in the dark, and that great piles of dried wood were placed at the edges of the dance-ground, north and south, to serve for fuel and as seats for the spectators.   Four great fires are kindled on each side of the dance-ground at nightfall, and other fires may be made later in the same locality.   The arrangements, when all is ready for the ceremonies of the last night, may be best understood by referring to figure 15.

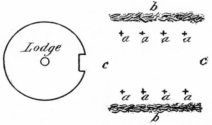

Fig. 15.   Diagram of dancing-ground.   *a*, fires ; *b*, piles of wood ; *c, c*, dancing-ground.

PREPARATION OF THE FIRST DANCERS.

603.—The characters paint themselves in the medicine-lodge, simultaneously, facing the east.   The right hand is the part first painted ; then they whiten from above downward.   While they paint, a song called Atsá'ⅬeiⅬ Yedadiglés is sung without accompaniment of drum or rattle.   The following is offered as an approximate, free translation of this song :

> Now the holy one paints his form,
> The Wind Boy, the holy one, paints his form,
> All over his body, he paints his form,
> With the dark cloud he paints his form,
> With the misty rain he paints his form,
> With the rainy bubbles he paints his form,
> To the ends of his toes he paints his form,
> To fingers and rattle he paints his form,
> To the plume on his head he paints his form.   See par. 929.

604.—After the painting is done, they dress, with assistance, while another song, which has not been recorded, is sung. The masks and rattles which were painted and decorated during the day, the wands of spruce which were prepared, and the fox-skins are carried out, after dark, and laid in a row in the north of the greenroom. When the characters are ready, in the lodge, they go out blanketed to the greenroom to assume their masks.

RITE OF THE ATSÁ‘ℓEI OR FIRST DANCERS.

605.—The public performance of the night begins with the ceremony of the Atsá‘ℓei or First Dancers, and this is usually conducted in the manner to be now described.

606.—The performers consist of four yébaka or ordinary male divinities and *H*ast*s*éyal*t*i, the Talking God or Yébĭtsai. Besides these, the chanter and the patient appear on the scene. The yébaka, like those who appear later in the dance of the naak*h*aí, are nearly naked, their bodies heavily coated with a mixture of white earth and water. Each wears moccasins, long blue stockings of Navaho make, a short kilt or loin-cloth of red baize, crimson silk, or some showy material, a silver-studded belt from which the skin of a kit-fox hangs at the back, numerous rich necklaces borrowed from friends for the occasion, and the blue, plumed mask of the yébaka with its attached collar of spruce twigs. Large plumes are attached to the stockings and small feathers to the wrists. Each carries, in his left hand, a wand of spruce twigs, attached for security to his mask, by means of a string of yucca fibres, and in his right hand a gourd rattle. The fifth character is *H*ast*s*éyal*t*i, who wears the peculiar mask of that god, with a collar of spruce. In one hand he carries a fawnskin bag. Unlike his four companions, he is comfortably clothed in some form of Navaho dress.

607.—Each one of the four yébaka represents a different character. The first is a chief, genius, or god of corn; the second is a chief of the child-rain;[2] the third is a chief of all kinds of plants, of vegetation, and the fourth is a chief of pollen. Such is the order of their precedence in the dance, and in this order they are mentioned in the songs. Besides being chiefs of these four things, they are spoken of as thunder-birds and as having the colors of the four cardinal points.

608.—*H*ast*s*éyal*t*i masks and dresses himself completely in the lodge. Usually about 8 P.M. they all leave the lodge together. *H*ast*s*éyal*t*i whoops as they come out and then clears the dance-ground, motioning intruders away, while the four others precede him to the greenroom to don their masks. Before putting on their masks they chew spruce leaves, bitten off their wands, and spit juice and leaves into the masks in the belief that this act helps the masks to go on. They often have to stretch and pull their masks, finding difficulty in making them fit at first.

609.—When they are all ready, they leave the green-room for the dance-ground in the following order: the chanter, *H*ast*s*éyal*t*i, the four Atsá‘ℓei in the order of their precedence. When they start, the chanter, uttering the benediction, "*H*oz*ó*les kó*t*e sĭtsówe," scatters pollen on the ground, toward the west along the way they are to follow.   They move very quietly, in single file, softly shaking their rattles and singing in a low tone.   Sometimes they stop on the way to readjust their masks.   They enter softly and stealthily on to the dance-ground.

610.—As they enter the ground a watcher at the door of the lodge cries, "Biké *hatál*i *h*akú," and the patient emerges from the lodge bearing meal in a sacred basket, and, on top of the meal, sometimes four kethawns.   While the priest says a prayer over the meal, the four yébaka keep up a constant motion of the feet somewhat similar to that of the dance to be presently described.   The following diagram (fig. 16) shows the position of the whole party at this time :

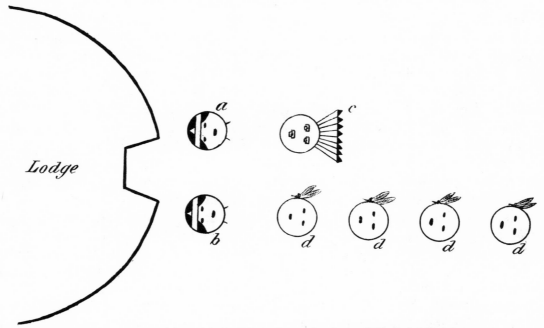

Fig. 16.   Diagram of dance of the Atsá'*l*ei.   *a*, shaman ; *b*, patient ; *c*, Yébïtsai ; *d*, *d*, dancers.

611.—After this prayer, the patient, prompted and assisted by the chanter (or the chanter, if the patient is a child), advances to each of the Atsá'*l*ei in turn, and sprinkles meal on him thus : He picks up a large pinch between the thumb and two fingers, allows the substance to fall on the right hand of the subject, up the right arm, over the top of the forehead, and down the left arm ; he drops what remains into the palm of the left hand.   Immediately after, he may deposit a sacrificial cigarette in the left hand.   Four cigarettes thus given form a set which is sometimes made and sacrificed on the fourth day, and sometimes, according to rules and theories not ascertained, on the last night.   When reserved for the last night they are thus given to the Atsá'*l*ei.   In applying the meal the patient carries the basket on the left arm.

612.—When the application is finished, patient and shaman resume their former position in the west, facing the east, and the priest prays a long prayer to each god, which the patient repeats after him, sentence by sentence, in the usual manner. The four prayers are alike in all respects, except in the mention of certain attributes of the gods. I have collected and translated one of these prayers and have given text, interlinear translation and free translation in " Navaho Legends."[3] To make clearer the description of the rite, I here repeat the free translation of the prayer to the dark bird who is the chief of pollen. While the prayer is being said, the dancers keep up a constant motion, bending and straightening the left knee and swaying the head from side to side.

613.—   FREE TRANSLATION OF PRAYER.

1. In Tse'gíhi,
2. In the house made of the dawn,
3. In the house made of the evening twilight,
4. In the house made of the dark cloud,
5. In the house made of the he-rain,
6. In the house made of the dark mist,
7. In the house made of the she-rain,
8. In the house made of pollen,
9. In the house made of grasshoppers,
10. Where the dark mist curtains the doorway,
11. The path to which is on the rainbow,
12. Where the zigzag lightning stands high on top,
13. Where the he-rain stands high on top,
14. Oh, male divinity !
15. With your moccasins of dark cloud, come to us.
16. With your leggings of dark cloud, come to us.
17. With your shirt of dark cloud, come to us.
18. With your head-dress of dark cloud, come to us.
19. With your mind enveloped in dark cloud, come to us.
20. With the dark thunder above you, come to us soaring.
21. With the shapen cloud at your feet, come to us soaring.
22. With the far darkness made of the dark cloud over your head, come to us soaring.
23. With the far darkness made of the he-rain over your head, come to us soaring.
24. With the far darkness made of the dark mist over your head, come to us soaring.
25. With the far darkness made of the she-rain over your head, come to us soaring.
26. With the zigzag lightning flung out on high over your head, come to us soaring.
27. With the rainbow hanging high over your head, come to us soaring.
28. With the far darkness made of the dark cloud on the ends of your wings, come to us soaring.
29. With the far darkness made of the he-rain on the ends of your wings, come to us soaring.
30. With the far darkness made of the dark mist on the ends of your wings, come to us soaring.
31. With the far darkness made of the she-rain on the ends of your wings, come to us soaring.
32. With the zigzag lightning flung out on high on the ends of your wings, come to us soaring.
33. With the rainbow hanging high on the ends of your wings, come to us soaring.
34. With the near darkness made of the dark cloud, of the he-rain, of the dark mist and of the she-rain, come to us.
35. With the darkness on the earth, come to us.
36. With these I wish the foam floating on the flowing water over the roots of the great corn.
37. I have made your sacrifice.
38. I have prepared a smoke for you.
39. My feet restore for me.

40. My limbs restore for me.
41. My body restore for me.
42. My mind restore for me.
43. My voice restore for me.
44. To-day, take out your spell for me.
45. To-day, take away your spell for me.
46. Away from me you have taken it.
47. Far off from me it is taken.
48. Far off you have done it.
49. Happily I recover.
50. Happily my interior becomes cool.
51. Happily my eyes regain their power.
52. Happily my head becomes cool.
53. Happily my limbs regain their power.
54. Happily I hear again.
55. Happily for me (the spell) is taken off.
56. Happily I walk (or, may I walk).
57. Impervious to pain, I walk.
58. Feeling light within, I walk.
59. With lively feelings, I walk.
60. Happily (or in beauty) abundant dark clouds I desire.
61. Happily abundant dark mists I desire.
62. Happily abundant passing showers I desire.
63. Happily an abundance of vegetation I desire.
64. Happily an abundance of pollen I desire.
65. Happily abundant dew I desire.
66. Happily may fair white corn, to the ends of the earth, come with you.
67. Happily may fair yellow corn, to the ends of the earth, come with you.
68. Happily may fair blue corn, to the ends of the earth, come with you.
69. Happily may fair corn of all kinds, to the ends of the earth, come with you.
70. Happily may fair plants of all kinds, to the ends of the earth, come with you.
71. Happily may fair goods of all kinds, to the ends of the earth, come with you.
72. Happily may fair jewels of all kinds, to the ends of the earth, come with you.
73. With these before you, happily may they come with you.
74. With these behind you, happily may they come with you
75. With these below you, happily may they come with you.
76. With these above you, happily may they come with you.
77. With these all around you, happily may they come with you.
78. Thus happily you accomplish your tasks.
79. Happily the old men will regard you.
80. Happily the old women will regard you.
81. Happily the young men will regard you.
82. Happily the young women will regard you.
83. Happily the boys will regard you.
84. Happily the girls will regard you.
85. Happily the children will regard you.
86. Happily the chiefs will regard you.
87. Happily, as they scatter in different directions, they will regard you.
88. Happily, as they approach their homes, they will regard you.
89. Happily may their roads home be on the trail of pollen (peace).
90. Happily may they all get back.

91. In beauty (happily) I walk.
92. With beauty before me, I walk.
93. With beauty behind me, I walk.
94. With beauty below me, I walk.
95. With beauty above me, I walk.
96. With beauty all around me, I walk.
97. It is finished (again) in beauty,
98. It is finished in beauty,
99. It is finished in beauty,
100. It is finished in beauty.

614.—When these prayers are ended, the patient, followed by the chanter, passes eastward, down the north side of the line and back again. As they pass east, the former scatters meal up the right arm of each dancer from hand to shoulder, and the latter scatters pollen in a similar manner. When they return to the west, the patient lays down his basket and sits beside it near the door of the lodge. The chanter sits to the left of the patient. Both face east, looking at the dancers. All the spectators now become silent and attentive, waiting for the sacred song.

615.—*H*astséyal*t*i, who has been standing north of the line of dancers, facing south, rushes whooping to the east and holds up his bag as a signal to the four Atsá‘*l*ei, who are now facing the west. Immediately the Atsá‘*l*ei advance the left foot, bend bodies to the right, whoop, shake their rattles, dip them with a long sweep of the arm as if dipping water and bring them up close to their mouths. They almost touch the ground in doing this. *H*astséyal*t*i rushes to the west and repeats his acts, while the dancers face east and repeat their acts. They face west again, always turning sunwise.

616.—After a brief pause in the west, *H*astséyal*t*i stamps twice, violently, with his right foot as a signal ; whereat the Atsá‘*l*ei begin a peculiar dancing step in which the right foot, held horizontally, is lifted from the ground. This may be considered marking time rather than dancing. Meanwhile, the right forearm moves up and down, in time with the corresponding foot, and shakes the rattle. The left arm hangs inactive. This step is taken four times in silence before the song begins and continues through the song. At certain parts of each stanza the singers face the east and at other parts they face the west again ; thus there are eight changes of direction during the song. They poise themselves on the toes of the left foot before they turn and slowly shake their rattles at a distance, laterally, from their bodies, as they wheel around.

617.—The song sung on this occasion, although it consists mostly of meaningless syllables, is, perhaps, the most important of the whole ceremony. The singers are drilled long and thoroughly in private before they are allowed to sing in public. It is said that, if a single syllable is omitted or misplaced, the ceremony terminates at once ; all the preceding work of nine days is considered valueless and the participators and spectators may return, at once, to their homes. Visiting chanters, and others who know the song well, having sung it at other celebrations of the rite, listen attentively and, if they note an error, proclaim it. The song consists of two stanzas; here is a free translation:

I.

The corn comes up, the rain descends,
The corn-plant comes therewith.
The rain descends, the corn comes up,
The child-rain comes therewith.

II.

The corn comes up, the rain descends,
Vegetation comes therewith.
The rain descends, the corn comes up,
The pollen comes therewith.   See pars. 931.

618.—*Hastséyalti* takes no part in the song or dance. He may stand still for a while or walk back and forth along the lines of dancers. At the end of each stanza, he utters his peculiar whoop to indicate that he is satisfied with the way in which the song has been sung, that he has detected no error. When the song is finished the four singers are facing the west. Then they turn in the manner already described and face the east. *Hastséyalti* takes his place at the head of the line, and all depart to the greenroom. Just as they leave the dance-ground they whoop and shake rattles, but after that they move in silence.

619.—In the greenroom, the actors take off their masks, with the wands attached, and lay them down, with their rattles, in the north of the bower, for other dancers to take when the time comes. If they have received sacred cigarettes they must now go out and plant them. They return to the greenroom when this is done. When their masks are off they may enter into informal conversation with their friends. After a while they return without formality to the lodge, where they pray (each separately for any special blessings he may desire), wash the paint from their bodies and resume their ordinary dress.

620.—The cigarettes are the male Atsá'*l*ei bike*t*án. They are deposited east of the greenroom in a safe place where cattle cannot trample on them, preferably among the roots of a piñon tree, without the feathers or other belongings which go with them when they are deposited on the fourth day.

DANCE OF NAAK*H*AÍ.

621.—The next rite, which is the longest and most important of all, begins after dark—7 o'clock or later—and lasts incessantly until daylight. It is called naak*h*aí. It consists of a performance out-doors, which is mostly dance and song, and a performance within the medicine-lodge which is mostly song and in which there is no dancing. Let us first consider the performance which occurs outside.

CHARACTERS. DRESS.

622.—The requisite characters are: *Hastséyalti*, the Talking God, or Yébĭtsai, *Tó*'nenĭli, the Water Sprinkler, and a number of dancers, preferably twelve. Of these, six represent Yébaka, or male divinities, and six Yébaad or female divinities. Besides these the chanter and patient participate. The dress of *H*astséyal*t*i and of *T*ó'nen*ï*li are described elsewhere (pars. 29, 30, and 118). The Yébaka have their bodies whitened and are decorated, masked, and equipped, as are those who appear in the dance of the Atsá'*l*ei (par. 606). The Yébaad are usually represented by small men and youths. The males thus acting are nearly naked like the Yébaka; have their bodies daubed with white earth; wear silver-studded belts with pendant fox-skins, showy kilts, long woollen stockings, garters, and moccasins; but, instead of the cap-like masks of the Yébaka, each wears a blue domino, which allows the hair to flow out behind. They have no eagle plumes on head, or on stockings, and no collars of spruce. They carry rattles and wands like those of the Yébaka. Sometimes women and so-called hermaphrodites are found who understand the dance. When such take part, as they sometimes do, in place of small men and youths, they are fully dressed in ordinary female costume and wear the domino of the Yébaad; but they carry no rattles; they have spruce wands in both hands. As has been said, there should be six Yébaad characters; but there is often a deficiency of the small men and youths, and when such is the case arrangements are made to do with a less number.

TYPICAL DANCE.

623.—That which is considered the typical or complete dance will first be described and then the variations will be discussed. The dancers are dressed and painted in the lodge, and then proceed to the greenroom, blanketed, to get their masks, wands, and rattles. When they are fully attired they leave the arbor and proceed to the dance-ground. The chanter leads, observing all the forms he used in conducting the Atsá'*l*ei; *H*astséyal*t*i follows immediately after the chanter; the twelve dancers come next, all in single file, and *T*ó'nen*ï*li brings up the rear. Among the twelve dancers the first is a Yébaka, the second a Yébaad, and thus the male and female characters follow one another alternately. As they march in the darkness they sing in undertones and shake their rattles in a subdued way.

624.—When they reach the dance-ground, between the two lines of fires, the chanter turns and faces them; they halt; the patient, warned by the call, as before,

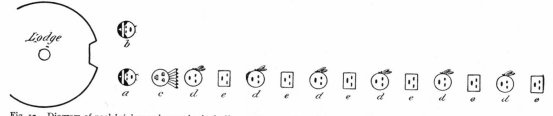

Fig. 17. Diagram of naak*h*aí dance, dancers in single file. *a*, shaman; *b*, patient; *c*, Yébïtsai; *d*, male characters; *e*, female characters.

comes out of the lodge. They all now stand in the order shown in the diagram, fig. 17. The patient and chanter walk down along the line of dancers from west to east. As they pass, the chanter takes meal from the basket carried by the patient and sprinkles it on the right arm of each dancer from below upwards. This done, the patient and chanter turn sunwise and retrace their steps to their original position west of and facing the line of dancers. Meantime the dancers keep up motions such as those made by the Atsá'ʍei when they are sprinkled.

625.—When the patient returns to the west, *Hastséyalʍi* runs to the east, whoops, and holds up his bag as he did with the Atsá'ʍei; the dancers whoop, lean to the right and dip their rattles toward the earth, in the manner already described (par. 615). *Hastséyalʍi* runs to the west, whoops and holds up his bag; the dancers turn toward the east and repeat their motions. They turn toward the west again. *Hastséyalʍi*, now in the west, turns toward the dancers and stamps twice with his right foot as a signal to them; they whoop and begin to dance and sing. Usually now the chanter goes into the lodge to superintend the singing and the patient sits beside the meal-basket, near the door.

626.—For a while they dance in single line, nodding their heads oddly and facing around in different directions, each one apparently according to his own caprice. At a certain part of the song, the Yébaad move, dancing, a couple of paces to the north and form a separate line, leaving the Yébaka dancing in a line to the south. The position of the dancers, at this time is represented by the following diagram, fig. 18 :

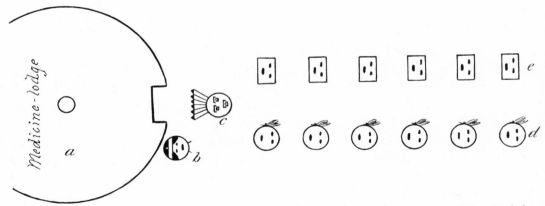

Fig. 18. Diagram showing position of dancers of the naak*h*ai in two lines. *a*, lodge ; *b*, patient ; *c*, Yébītsai ; *d*, line of male dancers ; *e*, line of female dancers.

They dance only for a brief time in this position, when the two lines again intermingle and they form a promiscuous group, the dancers facing in different directions and moving around. After dancing thus for a little while the Yébaad dance again to the north and two lines are formed as before.

627.—They dance thus for a while when, at another part of the song, the single Yébaka and Yébaad who dance furthest west approach one another and face east in the middle. Here the Yébaka, or male, offers his left arm to the Yébaad, or female, much in the manner in which civilized people perform this act; the Yébaad takes the proffered arm, thrusting "hers" through to the elbow; with arms thus interlocked they dance down the middle toward the east.   Before they reach the eastern end of the lines, they are met by *H*astséyal*t*i, who dances up toward them; they retreat backward, facing him; when they reach the west again, *H*astséyal*t*i begins to retreat, dancing backward, and they follow him.   When they reach the eastern end of the lines they separate and take new positions, each at the eastern end of his and "her" appropriate line.   Soon after they have begun to dance "down the middle" the second time, the pair now in the extreme west lock arms and dance east.   As soon as the first couple separate, *H*astséyal*t*i dances up to meet the second couple.   All the evolutions performed by the first couple are now performed by the second.   This is continued by each couple in turn until all have changed their places and those who first danced at the west end of the line dance there again.   White people, witnessing this dance, usually liken it to the well-known American contra-dance, the Virginia reel.

628.—When all the figures of the dance, proper, heretofore described, have been repeated four times, the Yébaad return from their line in the north and a single line is formed of alternate Yébaka and Yébaad facing west.   *H*astséyal*t*i whoops and places himself at the eastern end of the line; all face east and, dancing in a lock-step, as closely packed together as the dancing will allow, they move to the east.   When they get off the dancing-ground they halt, give a prolonged shake of the rattles, whoop and move away at an ordinary walk, in silence, until they get beyond the glare of the fires, about midway between the dance-ground and the arbor.   Here in the darkness they cool off, and breathe themselves for the next dance.   They may take off their masks and chat with one another, or with anyone else.

629.—All the acts described are performed in a most orderly and regular manner, without the slightest hitch, hesitancy, or confusion on the part of any of the participants.   No orders or verbal promptings are given.   The dancers take their cue, partly from the acts and calls of *H*astséyal*t*i; but mostly from the meaningless syllables of the song they are singing.   At certain parts of the song certain changes of the figure are made.

630.—When the dancers have rested for about five minutes, they return to the dance-ground in the same order in which they first came; but the chanter does not accompany them, neither does he sprinkle meal on them when they arrive on the dance-ground, unless the patient be a child.   The chanter only leads, and, as a rule, only sprinkles meal on each group of dancers once, and that is when they make their first appearance.

631.—Except when performing the dipping motion described and when turning around, the veritable male dancer holds the upper arms hanging by the side, the forearms partly flexed, a gourd rattle in the right hand, a wand of spruce in the left.   When a real woman enacts the part of the Yébaad she holds both arms extended outward horizontally, or nearly so, the elbow bent at right angles, the forearms held upwards, and a wand of spruce in each hand.

632.—At those parts of the dance where men remain in one place, they raise the right foot high and hold it horizontally in marking time.   At certain parts of the song they hold the foot raised for a period of two notes.   When moving, also, the men lift the feet well from the ground ; but the women do not do this ; they shuffle along on their toes, lifting the feet but little.

633.—The average duration of a figure such as described is five minutes, and that of the breathing-time is about the same.   But on occasions when many sets of dancers are prepared and the programme for the night is crowded, the periods of rest are greatly shortened or altogether neglected.   The dancers sometimes go but a few paces away from the dance-ground, when their song is done, and return immediately to begin a new song.

634.—There is often no change in the general character of this figure all night. From the beginning, soon after dark, until the ending after daybreak it may be constantly repeated and the accompanying song may be sung to the same time and in the same cadence.

635.—The most desirable number of repetitions for the dance is said to be forty-eight, when four sets of dancers each perform twelve times.   This, it is said, was, in old times, the invariable rule.   On such occasions each set holds the ground about two hours and there is a pause of about half an hour between the final exit of one set and the first appearance of another.   This gives us, with the work of the Atsá'lei, an entertainment of ten hours' duration.   But great variations are made from this standard, depending on the number of groups which have drilled themselves and come to the ground prepared to dance—also on the number of songs which each group may have composed and practised for the occasion.   For the first set we have noted always twelve or thirteen dances ; but for subsequent sets we have sometimes noted higher numbers, up to twenty—not always multiples of four and not always even numbers.   When the night's programme was crowded, we have seen two dances conducted within an hour : then the rests were short or omitted.   There may be six or more relays and they may dance until perilously near sunrise.

BUFFOONERY.

636.—The performances of Tó'nenïli, the clown, next demand our attention. While the others are dancing he performs various acts according to his caprice, such as these : He walks along the line of dancers and gets in their way.   He dances out of order and out of time.   He peers foolishly at different persons. He sits on the ground, his hands clasped across his knees, and rocks his body to and fro.   He joins regularly in the dance toward the close of a figure and when the others have retired he remains going through his steps, pretending to be oblivious of their departure ; then, feigning to discover their absence, he follows them on a full run.   He carries a fox-skin ; drops it on the ground ; walks away as if unconscious of his loss ; pretends to become aware of his loss ; acts as if searching anxiously for the skin, which lies in plain sight ; screens his eyes with his hand and crouches low to look ; imitates in various exaggerated ways the acts of Indian hunters; pretends, at length, to find the lost skin; jumps on it as if it were a live animal he was killing; shoulders it and carries it off as if it were a heavy burden; staggers and falls under it. Sometimes he imitates the acts of *Hastséyalti*; tries to anticipate the latter in giving the signals for the dance; rushes around with wands or skins in his hands in clumsy imitation of *Hastséyalti*; in intervals between the dances goes around soliciting gifts with a fox-skin for a begging-bag, to which no one contributes. Thus with acts of buffoonery does he endeavor to relieve the tedium of the monotonous performance of the night. He does not always come regularly in or depart with the regular dancers. His exits and entrances are often erratic.

VARIATIONS.

637.—There are some variations of the dance which have not been yet described. Sometimes a set of dancers is made up without any Yébaad characters; then, instead of the dance down the middle, two men lock arms to dance along the north side of the line and other changes are made to suit circumstances. Sometimes the number of Yébaad is less than six: in this case some of them dance down the middle more than twice. Portions of the song may be varied in length. If the song is longer than that given (par. 641) *Hastséyalti* may cause the dancers coming down the middle to retreat more than once to the west. On some occasions they are not required to retreat to the west at all, but dance directly down the middle and then separate. There seems to be difficulty often in finding men and boys of suitable size to enact the part of the Yébaad, and even when present they have been seen, as the work approached its conclusion, to become exhausted by the severe exercise, to throw themselves on the ground and refuse to take part.

8.—There is a variety of the dance called béziton, occasionally employed, which has not been carefully noted on the dance-ground, but which has been demonstrated in private to the author. In this, the hands are thrust far downwards and thrown backwards in time to the song. The step is slower and more halting than in the regular form. As compared with the latter it bears somewhat the relation of *deux-temps* to *trois-temps* in our waltz.

OUT-DOOR SONGS.

639.—In the element of music, the songs sung out-doors are much alike. To the ear untrained in music they sound quite alike. Even a musician, Sergeant Barthelmess, says of them: " In all the figures of the dance, the melody of the song remained the same."[21] Yet it is apparent, from a study of phonographic records, that some latitude is allowed the musical composer in framing these melodies. The author is not sufficiently versed in music to declare wherein they must agree and wherein they may differ. In " Navaho Legends "[3] pp. 283, 284, may be found the music of two different naak*h*aí songs noted by Professor Fillmore from phonographic records. The male personators of female divinities sing in falsetto.

640.—In the matter of language, the songs have little significance. They consist mostly of meaningless syllables or of words whose meanings are forgotten. Yet many of these are all-important and must not be changed or omitted.   As before stated, some of them serve as cues to the dancers.   There are changes made in the few significant words of the song ; those of the first song after dark and of the last song in the morning are invariable ; it is in the intervening songs that the modern Navaho poet is allowed to exercise his fancy. All the songs begin with these vocables, Óhohohó, héhehe.   In singing these the dancer in the west sings the first syllables " o " and " he " alone ; in all the subsequent syllables the other singers join.

641.—It is thought better to introduce here the full text of a stanza of the first song than to defer it to the chapter on songs.

FIRST SONG OF THE NAAK*H*AÍ.

I

1. Óhohohó héhehe héya héya
2. Óhohohó héhehe héya héya
3. Éo lá*d*o éo lá*d*o éo lá*d*o nasé
4. Hówani hów owów owé
5. Éo lá*d*o éo lá*d*o éo lá*d*o nasé
6. Hówani how owów owé
7. Hówani hówani how héyeyéye yéyeyáhi
8. Hówowów héya héya héya héya
9. Hówa héhehe héya héya héya
10. Óhohohó howé héya héya
11. Óhohohó héhehe héya héya
12. *H*ábi níye *h*ábi níye
13. *H*á‘huizánaha, *s*íhiwánaha.
14. *H*á‘hayá‘ éaheóo éaheóo
15. *S*íhiwánaha, *H*á‘huizánaha.
16. *H*á‘hayá‘ éaheóo eaheóo éaheóo éaheóo.

The words in this stanza to which any significance is now assigned are those in the 13th and 15th verses, and the meanings of these are only traditional : The rain descends.   The corn comes up.   The other three stanzas are the same as this, except that in the second and fourth the words are placed in inverse order.

BEGGING GODS.

642.—Sometimes, in the intervals that occur between the final disappearance of one set of dancers and the first appearance of the next set, *H*astséyal*t*i or some other of the masked characters go around among the spectators with a begging-bag, soliciting contributions, in the manner already described (par. 543), and receiving tobacco and other articles.   He does not speak, but merely holds out the bag ; when the contribution has been put in he closes the bag and utters his peculiar hoot.

WORK IN THE LODGE.

643.—So far we have described the work outside the lodge; it now remains to describe the work within it. The basket is "turned down" at night with observances described elsewhere (par. 291). From the time it is turned down until the final ceremonials in the morning, the work consists of singing the songs of sequence of the rite in their proper order. The singing begins when the Atsá'*l*ei depart from the medicine-lodge in the evening and continues until the Song of the Atsá'*l*ei is heard outside. The moment the song outside ceases, that in the lodge is resumed, and again the song in the lodge ceases the instant the signers outside are again heard. Thus, song is continued throughout the night, without interruption, either in the lodge or on the dance-ground, but never in both places together. There are many intricate rules connected with these songs, some of which have been learned and are related in the chapter on song; but there are many more which have not been discovered.

644.—The first of the songs of sequence sung in the lodge is perhaps the most musical of the night. It is the first of the Atsá'*l*ei Bigï'n and alludes to one of the Atsá'*l*ei without naming him. The following is a free translation of the first stanza:

1. Above it thunders.
2. His thoughts are directed to you,
3. He rises toward you,
4. Now to your house
5. Approaches for you.
6. He arrives for you,
7. He comes to the door,
8. He enters for you.
9. Behind the fireplace
10. He eats his special dish.
11. "Your body is strong,
12. "Your body is holy now," he says. See par. 933.

The second stanza is the same except that the first line is: "Below it thunders."

645.—After the dancers have sung their last song outside, the singers inside the lodge sing the four Béna *Halál*i or Finishing Hymns. The following is a free translation of the last of these:

I

From the pond in the white valley (alkali flat),—
The young man doubts it—
He (the god) takes up his sacrifice,
With that he now heals.
With that your kindred thank you now.

II

From the pools in the green meadow,—
The young woman doubts it—
He takes up his sacrifice,
With that he now heals.
With that your kindred thank you now. See par. 937.

At the pronunciation of a meaningless vocable (niyeoóo) in the refrain, the chanter puts his right hand under the eastern edge of the inverted basket which serves as a drum. As the last verse of the song is uttered he turns the basket over toward the west, makes motions as if driving released flies from under the basket out through the smoke-hole and blows a breath after the invisible flies as they are supposed to depart. During the singing of this song, an assistant applies meal to the lower jaw of the patient.

646.—The next labor of the chanter is to unravel the drumstick, lay its component parts in order and give them to an assistant to sacrifice. The way in which these acts are performed has been already described (par. 295). While unraveling, the chanter sings the song appropriate to the act. When the stick is unwound the chanter gives final instructions to the patient and all are at liberty to depart.

INSTRUCTIONS TO PATIENT.

647.—According to these instructions, the patient must not sleep until sunset. Shortly before that time he returns to the medicine-lodge to sleep there, and this he must do for four consecutive nights, although he may go where he will in the daytime. Under the threatened penalty of a return of his disease, he is forbidden to eat the tripe, liver, heart, kidney, or head of any animal, or to eat anything that has floated on water. If an ear of corn or a melon has dropped into water and floated it must not be eaten. These taboos must be carefully observed until he attends a celebration of the ceremony of to‘nastsihégo hatál; then he partakes of the peculiar composite mess prepared on that occasion and thereafter the taboos are removed.

TO‘NASTSIHÉGO HATÁL.

648.—There is a variant of the ceremony of the night chant which is called to‘nastsihégo hatál. This name has not been satisfactorily translated; but it seems related to the name for sacred water, tó‘lanastsi. Some of the rites and observances of this variant are described in the preceding pages (pars. 419, 647); but more extensive information in relation to them appears in the story of the Stricken Twins, the myth accounting for their introduction among the Navahoes. The rites, as described in the myth, differ in some respects from those of the night chant. The pictures of the two ceremonies differ somewhat and so do the songs. In to‘nastsihégo hatál there is a picture on the last day. The most notable difference is the omission, in the one form, of the public dance of the last night, which is so characteristic of the other form. To‘nastsihégo hatál is known as the ceremony of Kĭninaékai or the White House, while that of the night chant proper is known as the ceremony of Tsĕ‘nitsihogán or the Red Rock House.

649.—The author never witnessed this form of the ceremony and learns that it is rarely performed. The patient and his relations are to some extent at liberty to decide which of the two forms of ceremony they will have ; but they usually choose the night chant because, owing to the public dance of the last night, there is more merriment at it, and it attracts a larger concourse than the other form.

PART III.

Myths.

MYTHS.

THE VISIONARY.

650.—He of whom this tale is told belonged to the gens of *Thá‘tsini*.[23]   His name was Bi*tá*ha*t*íni[24] (the Visionary) and he lived at Tse‘gíhi.[1]   This shows how he came to be a chanter.   Whenever he went out by himself, he heard the songs of spirits sung to him, or thought he heard them sung.   He was the third of four brothers, the youngest of whom was named Nakiĕstsái.   His brothers had no faith in him.   They said : "When you return from your solitary walks and tell us you have seen strange things and heard strange songs, you are mistaken, you only imagine you hear these songs and you see nothing unusual."   Whenever he returned from one of these lonely rambles he tried to teach his brothers the songs he had heard ; but they would not listen to him.

651.—On one occasion the Visionary remained at home while his brothers and a brother-in-law (married to their sister) started out to hunt.   They went first to a place called Apahílgo*s* and thence they went further on to a place called Bĭs*tá*[25] and from here they began to hunt.   About the time they had reached Bĭs*tá*, the Visionary set out to follow them ; but it took him until sundown to reach Apahílgo*s*, and he said to himself : "I shall pass the night here."   He camped on this side of the cañon ; on the other side there was a cave in the cliff.   While he was camping he observed a vast multitude of crows going into this cave—the crows in those days were like people.   On the same side of the cañon and below where he stood there was another cavern, into which also he observed crows flying.   After a while they all passed into the caves and quieted down.

652.—In the middle of the night while he was lying down he heard a noise. He arose to watch and he saw a spark of fire flying across the cañon from the cave on his side to that on the opposite side, and soon after he saw another spark flying back.   Then he heard a voice proceeding from the cave on his side of the cañon calling (in a loud, singing tone) : "Ts*ĭ'*ni ts*ĭ*né, ts*ĭ'*ni ts*ĭ*né, ts*ĭ'*ni ts*ĭ*né, ts*ĭ'*ni ts*ĭ*né (they say)."[26]   "What do they say has happened ?" came the question in a similiar tone four times from the opposite side of the cañon.   Then from the cave beneath him he heard four times called : "They killed many, they say." "Whom did they say were killed ?" was the question that now came four times from the opposite side.   From the near side came four times the reply : " He-who-picks-on-the-back, He-who-sits-between-the-horns, and twelve big deer."[27] From the opposite side he next heard : "That is what has happened, they say." Again from the near side came : "The four men have killed deer enough (i.e., all they shall kill)" ; and from the far side : "It is well, so be it."   At length from the near cave the crows called : "It is well.   Begin the dance now" ; and those on

[159]

the far side replied: "Let you begin first." The crows were of both sexes in each place, yet because they sang on opposite sides of the cañon is the reason that to-day the yébaka and the yébaad stand opposite one another when they sing in the rites of the night chant. Then he heard the people on the near side of the cañon howl and begin to dance. Instantly the howl was repeated and the dance begun on the far side, and on both sides they danced at the same time. All night after this he heard them shouting, dancing, and singing, and heard them calling across the cañon from one side to the other. The last song they sang was the Bluebird Song, and with this they ended the dance at dawn. After this he heard the Crow People say they would separate and hunt for food. Before sunrise he observed the crows flying from the cave in every direction, and by the time the sun had risen no one seemed to be left in the caves.

653.—When the crows had all departed he set out to seek his brothers at Bistá. When he arrived there he found his youngest brother in the camp—the others were still out hunting—and he lay down. Soon after his arrival the other brothers came in from the hunt, but they brought no game; they all sat around the fire, smoked, talked, roasted some meat they had on hand from a previous hunt, and ate it. One of them said to the prophet: "What is the matter with you? Why do you lie down? Why have you come over here? We left you at home to take care of the hogán." The Visionary answered: "I started yesterday to follow you, but night came on at Apahí'lgos. I camped and heard there strange things, which I will tell you about if you wish to hear them." His eldest brother said: "There is no use in listening to you, you will tell us only of things you think you have heard—your foolish stories. We don't believe in you." The Visionary then said: "It is well. If that is the way you think, I shall tell you nothing." "Go on with your own talk," said the eldest brother to the others, "there is no use in believing him." So they talked about other things and did not refer to the Visionary's conversation again until late in the day.

654.—In the meantime, the brother-in-law had said nothing; he had been lying down and thinking about the Visionary. He was beginning to believe the prophet might be a truthful man, and on this occasion he thought it would be but right to listen to him, at least. He rose, rolled a cigarette, smoked, and meditated on the words of the Visionary. After a time thus spent in thought, he spoke, saying: "Let us listen to the words of our brother. How can we tell whether they are wise or foolish until we have heard them?" He tapped the Visionary coaxingly, familiarly, on the front of the thigh and said: "It matters not whether our brothers attend to your words; tell of what you have seen and heard and I will listen to you." "No," answered the prophet, "I will not speak while the others sit by in scorn and care not to listen." The brother-in-law spoke again, tapping him as before: "Tell your tale to me. I do not scorn you. I will listen." Then the prophet arose and said: "I shall tell you only the truth about what I have seen and heard at Apahí'lgos and all that I shall tell you is true"; and he related to his brother-in-law all the incidents of the previous night and all that he had seen and heard.   When the Visionary had done speaking, the brother-in-law declared: "I now truly believe in you, for yesterday we killed a magpie and a crow and we killed twelve deer."   The prophet then reminded them that he had heard the crows say that the party would kill no more deer, and the brother-in-law said: "Our brother has told us the truth in some things; we may feel sure that he has told us the truth in all.   We will kill no more deer on this nunt.   Let us return home to-morrow."   The eldest brother said: "It makes no difference what our brother predicts; he has not made the deer; he does not control them; we shall go out hunting to-morrow and we will kill some more."   "It is well," said the brother-in-law.   "Go out and hunt if you will.   I shall not go hunting.   I shall not tire myself for nothing."   That was the end of the day. Night came and they all went to sleep.

655.—At daybreak, next morning, the eldest brother got up and declared: "I am going out to hunt, I advise you all to go hunting."   The two eldest brothers left the camp to hunt while the brother-in-law and the youngest brother staid at home with the prophet.   The youngest brother now asked the Visionary: "Did you truly hear all that you said you heard?   Do not deceive me.   If you speak not the truth why should I stay here idle, and if you speak the truth why should I weary myself on a useless hunt?   Speak to me again that I may know what to do."   The prophet answered: "I have told the truth; you shall see for yourselves when our brothers return in the evening and bring no deer with them." So these three remained in camp all day and at evening the two elder brothers returned; but they brought home no meat with them.   "Now," said the brother-in-law to the unsuccessful hunters, "you see what our brother said was true. You have gone out and tired yourselves for nothing, while I have remained at home and rested myself."   But the eldest brother said: "I care not for what our brother says.   For all his tales I shall go out hunting again to-morrow and I shall not fail to bring home game," and thus ended this day.

656.—Next morning they got up early as they had done on the previous morning, and the two eldest went out to hunt; but the other two remained in camp with the prophet saying: "Why should we weary ourselves in vain?   We shall kill nothing if we go."   Those who went to hunt, having wandered all day, returned at night weary and empty-handed.   Those who had remained behind said nothing to the returning hunters, they waited for the latter to speak; but the tired men kept their mouths closed and lay down to sleep without speaking; and that was the end of this day.

657.—When morning came the two eldest ventured out again.   They still thought that no one controlled the deer; that no one owned them and that they would surely kill some on this day.   The others remained in camp as they had done before.   In the evening the hunters returned again unsuccessful.   On the way home the eldest brother thought to himself.   He began to think that the Visionary must have told the truth and that what he had heard and witnessed would account for their failure to find game.   When he entered the camp he threw his arrows in anger on the ground and said sulkily, " Where has a devil gone with the deer ?[38] I have hunted now four days and found none. I shall hunt no more, I give it up." The prophet answered : " It is as I told you, you can kill no more deer on this hunt. You killed the crow and the magpie when you went hunting. It is they who own the deer and they have spoiled your hunt. This is why you can kill no deer." They packed the meat they had killed four days before and got everything ready to leave on the following morning.

658.—They started for home early next morning and, after traveling a short distance, stopped near a place called *Depéhahatin*, on the brow of the bluff, to rest and smoke. While sitting there they observed four Rocky Mountain sheep that walked along the side of the bluff among the rocks and then turned off into a bend where they were hidden from sight. The elder brother bade the prophet to head them off in the bend and shoot them there.

659.—He ran, as he was told, and hid himself behind a mountain mahogany bush, near where he knew the sheep must pass out, and lay in wait. Presently they approached. He drew his arrow to the head and prepared to shoot ; but as he did so, he was seized with a violent trembling and spasm, found himself unable to release the arrow and the sheep passed unharmed. When the sheep had gone by, the spasm and trembling disappeared and he felt as well as ever. Then he ran ahead to another turn in the cliff to head them off again. Here he got behind a bush of the mai*t*á or coyote corn (*Forestiera*). Again the sheep approached, again he drew his arrow to the head, again he was seized with trembling and spasm and again the sheep passed unharmed. He stretched his limbs and worked his joints, saying, " What is the matter with me that I cannot shoot ? " When he came to himself again he ran once more to head the sheep off. His brethren watched all his acts from the top of the hill and wondered greatly. " Why is it," they said, " that he does not shoot when the bighorns pass him ? " The third time he headed the sheep off he got behind a juniper tree, but all happened as before, and the sheep passed unharmed. The brothers from their watch on the hill saw all this ; they saw him stretching his limbs and working his joints. They saw him run around a fourth bend to head the sheep off but then they saw him no more. At the fourth bend he got behind a cherry bush and drew his arrow to the head ; but just as he was about to release it the sheep threw off their masks and behold ! they were not sheep but holy ones (*d*ĭgí'ni *d*ĭné'). They untied their skins and showed themselves as the Gá*n*askĭ*d*i. (Par. 46.)

660.—In these days when we make the kethawns of *H*astséayuhi, to sacrifice in the ceremony of klé*dz*e *h*atál, we put first those of mountain mahogany in the east, because he first stood behind a mountain mahogany bush to shoot the sheep, we next put mai*t*á in the south because he next hid behind such a shrub to shoot, we then put kethawns of juniper in the west, because on the third occasion he hid himself behind a juniper tree, and lastly we place kethawns of cherry in the north, because the last time he tried to shoot the sheep he hid behind a cherry tree. See par. 399.

661.—The four Gánaskïdi now approached the prophet, bearing with them a skin and a mask for him to wear. They bade him strip himself of his clothes. He laid his left moccasin, his left legging, his bow and the arrows he held in his left hand, on the ground to the left of where he stood ; he laid his right mocasin, his right legging and the arrow he was about to draw, on the ground to his right ; he laid his shirt between them, and, on the top of this, he laid his head-band. After he had stripped himself they gave him the sheepskin and told him to hold it in his hand ; one of them puffed a breath on him, whereat the skin slipped easily over him and covered him. Then he took, along with his four companions, four steps which brought them to the edge of the cañon and here they stepped off. The place where they stepped off is known to this day as *Depéhahatin* or Place Where Sheep Come Up.

662.—The watchers on top of the bluff waited a long time for the reappearance of the prophet. At length they said, one to another : " Perhaps he has killed a sheep, and finds it too heavy to carry up the bluff ; some one should go to his help." So one of them descended the bluff to seek his brother. He followed the trail and soon came to the place where the prophet had laid down his clothing and weapons. From there, forward, no human footprint could be seen ; no track but that of the sheep leading to the precipice and disappearing at its edge. The hunter examined the tracks carefully and found to his surprise that, while up to the place where the clothes lay, there were tracks of only four sheep, further on there were tracks of five sheep and that each of these sheep had taken four steps to reach the edge of the precipice. He descended the walls of the cañon, which was terraced, and on three more terraces he observed the tracks of five sheep, each sheep taking four steps ; but beyond the fourth terrace no footprints could be found. He climbed the bluff again to where the clothes lay ; but these he did not disturb. He returned to his comrades on top of the cliff and related to them all that he had observed.

663.—" Now," said the brother-in-law, " what do you think ? How do you account for the strange things that have happened ? You would not believe what our brother told you, but his words have all come true. Now one of our brothers is lost to us." " True," said the eldest brother, " I did not believe what my brother said ; but I believe it now. And what is your counsel ? What have you to say about it ? What shall we do ? " They held a council together and determined how they should act.

664.—First they went down to where the clothes lay, to see what they should do about them and they examined the ground around there. They concluded to leave the clothes alone. Then they went back to their home at Tse'-gíhi. There they put into one sacred basket, turquoise, white shell, haliotis shell, and cannel-coal, and into another basket, specular iron-ore, blue pollen, life pollen, and corn pollen, singing as they did this. They took these things back to where the clothes lay. The second brother laid the baskets on the edge of the cliff where the tracks ended, and repeated the prayer to *H*astséyal*t*i, beginning :

*Ha*aábeya*d*e
Tsĭ'snad*z*ĭni, etc.

and he prayed to all the other gods, to whom we now pray in the rite of klé*dz*e *h*atál. When they had done praying, the Wind whispered to them and said : " Do the things I bid you and on the fourth day after this, early in the morning, your brother will return to you." Then they all went home.

665.—On the fourth night after this, as directed by Nĭ'lt*s*i, Wind, they spent the whole night in song and prayer and vigil as we do now on the fourth night of the the rites of klé*dz*e *h*atál. They sang the songs of Béna*s*a, and other songs. They sprinkled meal in the four directions. Early in the morning they began to sing the Bluebird Song, which begins with the words, *H*ayilká négo na*s*á (I am walking in the morning) [20] and as they were singing this the prophet appeared at the door. This night of watching we now call *T*oil*h*á*s*a Biklé, His Sleepless Night. On the next day, called Bit*si'n*, His Day, we kill sheep and prepare for the visitors to come to the rites of the klé*dz*e *h*atál.

666.—The brothers within the lodge now spread a buckskin on the ĭntsé'tla or wónigi (the center of the lodge behind the fire) with its head to the north ; on this they drew, in pollen, the figure of the Pollen Boy. (Plate II, C'.) They drew from the door of the lodge to the heart of the Pollen Boy figure on the ĭntsé'tla, a trail of meal, and on this four figures of footprints in meal. They first (near the door) made a figure of the print of the right foot, next of the left foot and so on. The prophet walked along the trail, placing his feet on the pictured footprints, and sat down on the figure of the Pollen Boy. As he sat, the eldest brother prayed and sang for him, and, when this was done, he put pollen on the soles, knees, palms, back, chest, shoulders, mouth, and crown of the sitting man and sprinkled it over his body from foot to head. Each of the others then placed pollen in his own mouth and on his own head and prayed. At last they begged the prophet to tell them his adventures.

667.—He said : " For a long time you have not believed my words ; but now you know that some things I told you were true. When you were out hunting I foretold that which came to pass." Then he told the story of his pursuit of the bighorns as you have already heard it, and he told his tale further. When he and the four Gá*n*askĭ*d*i jumped from the edge of the cañon, where the hunters last saw their tracks, they alighted on a very narrow ledge which ran along the face of the cañon wall and they followed this ledge until they came to a place called *H*astsé*d*espĭn or Place Where the Yéi Sit ; here they met *H*astséyal*t*i and *H*as-tsé*h*ogan. These sent word ahead to other yéi that they had with them a mortal man whom they were bringing home, and soon they met a multitude of the Yéi-*d*ine‘, which gathered around the prophet and gazed at him. There were *H*astsé-yal*t*i, *H*astsé*h*ogan, Dzaha*d*old*z*á, Gá*n*askĭ*d*i, *H*át*d*ast*s*ĭsi, *H*astsébaka, *H*astsé-baad, Nayénezgạni, *T*o‘bad*z*ĭst*s*íni, *H*astséol*t*oi, *H*ástsél*t*si, and *T*ó‘nenĭli. These were the 12 chiefs of the gods who had sent the younger Gá*n*askĭ*d*i to capture the prophet ; but besides these there was a multitude of holy ones of lesser degree. Many divine animals and birds were in the throng; among these he saw Coyote, Ni'yélni,[30] Bluebirds, and Yellow Birds. When he arrived at the home of the yéi he observed that they were preparing sacred objects and conducting rites and he said: "I desire to learn your rites and I will give you twelve large buckskins if you teach me." They said they would do this, and it was thus he came to learn the ceremony.

668.—Now the yéi sent out messengers to bring in the sacrifices which the brothers had laid on the brink of the cañon. Out of the ĭnklĭ'z — the precious stones and shells—they made five great bowls or baskets: a basket of turquoise, a basket of white shell, a basket of haliotis shell, a basket of cannel-coal and a basket of rock crystal. They had the power to take a small fragment and make it grow to any size and shape they wished. Then they put a sacred buckskin over each basket; they prayed and sang over them and jumped over each in four different directions. The prophet sat by and watched carefully all these rites and remembered them. One old yéi taught him the songs and he learned them more readily than any man has learned them since. The yéi made in his presence the masks and sang over them the songs of *Hozóndze*.

669.—On the following morning they displayed to the prophet a picture (yiká*l*). It was the picture of the whirling sticks which we paint now in the rites of klédze *hatál* (plate VI). The yéi did not draw it on sand as we do now; they had it on a sheet of some substance called naská. We do not know now what this substance was; it may have been cotton. They unfolded this sheet whenever they wanted to look at the picture. The yéi who unfolded it to show the prophet said: "We will not give you this picture; men are not as good as we; they might quarrel over the picture and tear it, and that would bring misfortune; the black cloud would not come again, the rain would not fall, the corn would not grow; but you may paint it on the ground with colors of the earth." When the picture was folded and put away they took the fragments of stones and shells left in the baskets and made of each fragment a great bead as long as the hand, creating in all a great pile which they divided among themselves. The yéi remained at home. At night they put on the ground, bottoms up, the two sacrificial baskets, which the prophet's brothers had given them, and beat them as drums while they sang. The songs sung that night were those of the Atsá'*l*ei. He learned all these songs that night, for he listened well till they ended their singing and went to sleep.

670.—On the second morning they displayed a sheet on which was painted the picture we call naak*h*aí yiká*l*, the picture of the dance of the yéi, such as we draw upon the sand (plate VII). They explained the picture to him and spoke to him as they had spoken of the picture of yesterday. He studied it all well, that he might remember it when he returned to his people. At night they turned down the baskets and sang the Songs of *Sĭ*'néo*l*e.

671.—On the third day they unfolded another sheet of naská, displaying the picture called Dsaha*d*oldzábe yiká*l*, or picture with the Fringe Mouths (plate

VIII).   At night they turned the baskets down and sang the songs of Aga'hoá-Gisĭ'n.   He listened to these with care and learned them well.

672.—On the fourth day no picture was displayed, but the Songs of Dsaha-doldzá or the Fringe Mouths were sung.   These are to cure headache, sore eyes, and contraction of the tendons of the lower extremities.   Such diseases were common among the Navahoes until these rites were introduced.   Two Yébĭtsai who came from the east sang the songs while they drummed on the inverted baskets.   Dsahadoldzá wore no mask then, although the actors who represent him now wear masks.   His body was naturally half red and half black; but the yéi told the prophet that when mortals came to perform these ceremonies they should wear masks and paint their bodies to look like this god.   By sunset many holy ones had gathered together from different parts to perform the dance of the last night, and when darkness came they were ready to dance the naakhai as we dance it to this day.

673.—But shortly before they began to dance, a yéi, called Hastséayuhi, who had not been with the crowd before, entered the lodge unseen by the others and asked the prophet to step out.   As soon as they were outside he took the prophet under his arm and carried him away.   He carried his captive, one after another, to the tops of the four great mountains that bound the land, and from the top of Depéntsa he carried him up into the sky.   As the prophet was going up into the sky he sang the song of Degoneĭstéhe (I am ascending), which he had learned among the holy ones on earth, and when he reached the sky he sang the song Agá'hoaie (Up above).

674.—Just as they were about to begin the dance the yéi missed the prophet, and there was a great commotion among them.   They looked for him in every direction; they called to one another and shouted; but nowhere could they find him.   When they had searched and inquired all around the camp, some went back on the trail by which they had brought him hither, but they could find no trace of him.   They all returned to the dancing-ground and held a council. Some one said in the council: "It is Hastséayuhi who has stolen our grandchild. No one else would be so mischievous.   He is the thief."   This soon became the opinion of all, and Hastséyalti was asked to go in search of the prophet.

675.—He went first to the east, to the summit of Tsĭsnadzĭ'ni, and of the gods there he inquired if they had seen his grandchild.   They told him that Hastséayuhi had come there with the captive and gone on west with him to Tsótsĭl.   Hastséyalti followed the captor and the captive from Tsótsĭl to Dokos-líd, and from there to Depĕ'ntsa.   At Depĕ'ntsa were the Bear People and many other holy ones.   It was one of these, a great insect named Don'tso, who told Hastséyalti where his grandchild had been taken.   Hastséyalti threw a couple of sunbeams up against the sky, making of them a trail, something like the ladders we see in Zuñi, and on these he ascended to Yaga'hogan, where Hastséayuhi dwelt.   The holy ones used to travel thus on sunbeams long ago. He went to the top of his ladder, and there meeting the eagle and other birds of the sky, he asked them where his grandchild was. "We do not know," they answered, "we have not seen your grandchild." *H*astséyal*t*i put his hand over his mouth and smiled and wondered where his grandchild was. In the meantime the prophet lay hidden in the corner of a shelf below where the ladder leaned against the sky. *H*astséyal*t*i had gone beyond this place. Soon he heard the voice of the prophet singing a song with the word *T*ágit*s*elgo*t*, meaning, You have gone too far. He returned to the place where he heard the voice and met *H*ast*s*éayuhi. "Where is my grandchild?" demanded the Talking God. "I know not," replied the thief, although at the same time he had the captive hidden behind him. *H*astséyal*t*i pushed *H*ast*s*éayuhi aside, beheld his grandson, seized the latter by the arm, and took him along.

676.—He threw a ladder of sunbeams down on Tsótsi*l*, and descended to the summit of the mountain. As the prophet was going down he sang the song Yagonis*l*é*l*e (I am descending). They went down the mountain side till they came to a place called Tsĭ'n*d*aspĭn, where they found all the yéi from Tse'gíhi, waiting their coming. As the yéi had held no dance at the place where they originally intended to have it, they now spoke of holding it at Tsĭ'n*d*aspĭn; but they counseled and talked and argued and at last concluded to hold the dance at Tsú*s*kai (Chusca Knoll). They all set out for Tsú*s*kai, and on their way they came to Hosta Butte and to a door on the side of the butte. Here he bade the others wait outside while he entered and spoke to those who dwelt within. He found there a number of the *S*ás*d*ĭne', or Bear People, and he said to them: "My grandchildren, we are on our way to Tsú*s*kai, to dance there." When he came out he said to his companions: "Those who dwell at Tsú*s*kai, within the mountain, are not the same as we, they are Mountain People." The next place the travelers came to was *T*ó'*h*askĭ*d*i, near Ní*h*otlĭzi, Brittle Earth, and after that they arrived at *T*ó'*h*at*s*i. The prophet thought to himself: "I know not this trail nor whither I am going." He looked before and behind and saw a multitude of the yéi preceding him and following him, and he sang this song:

> I walk on the top of the mountain
> Beside *H*ast*s*éayuhi.
> They go before,
> They come behind,
> I walk in the middle.

> I walk at the foot of the mountain
> Beside *H*ast*s*enetli'hi.
> They come behind,
> They go before,
> I walk in the middle. See par. 939.

677.—He was alarmed and began to weep. *H*ast*s*é*h*ogan and *H*astséyal*t*i observed his tears and said to him: "Do not weep. You will return yet to your home and to your people." They crossed a valley and got on top of another

ridge and here they stopped to eat something.   For the prophet they made gruel
in a yellow bowl and *H*ast*s*éayuhi administered it to him in four draughts, moving
the bowl from a different point of the compass at each draught, as we now do
when we administer the medicine in the rites.   While this was being done
*H*ast*s*éyal*t*i sang :

> I walk on high
> (But) in *H*ast*s*éayuhi's house
> They walk above me.   See par. 941.

678.—When the song was finished they all partook of food, and when they
were done eating they said : " Now we are all off to T*s*ú*s*kai for the dance."

679.—In those days T*s*u′*s*kai was a *h*og*á*n or hut.   All the yéi, whose names
have already been told and all the holy animals now assembled there to witness
the dance, and they made a great multitude.   The Eagle and the Owl were there,
and this is the reason why the feathers of these birds are used in the dance now.
All were dressed in their best.   The yéi were all dressed alike—so much alike
that you could no longer tell one from another.   They dressed thus because they
were going to ask the prophet a question.   They were going to ask him which
one among them followed him to the sky and rescued him.   They sat down around
the edge of the chamber, inside the mountain, and *H*ast*s*éyal*t*i and *H*ast*s*é*h*ogan
placed the prophet in the middle and bade him point out the one who had followed
and rescued him.   They told him that if he guessed correctly they would send
him home to his people ; but that if he did not guess correctly he should never
see his people again.   *H*ast*s*éyal*t*i and *H*ast*s*é*h*ogan then took their seats.   Now
as he sat, Wind whispered into the ear of the prophet :   " He who sits farthest
to the east is the one who followed you."   The prophet then pointed to this one,
who was *H*ast*s*éyal*t*i, and sang this song :

I.

1. Up on high he traveled for me,
2. *H*ast*s*éayuhi traveled for me.
3. Your holy body is now with me.

II.

1. Down below he traveled for me.
2. *H*ast*s*éyal*t*i he traveled for me.
3. Your holy body is now with me.   See par. 942.

680.—Although he had guessed aright, one half of the assembly still wished
to keep him while the other half wanted to let him go.   At length those who were
in favor of letting him go prevailed.   They said :   " If we send him to his home
he will teach his people our songs, the black cloud will be always with them, more
rain will fall, the grass and the trees will grow better.   He has guessed correctly.
He has won the right to go."

681.—Now came the fourth night from the time the prophet had descended
from the sky.   When darkness fell, the yéi turned the basket down again to beat

time to their singing. They bade the prophet, too, to turn down a basket and recite all the songs he heard. "If you remember them all you may go home in the morning," they said. He put the basket down and began to sing, and the yéi outside began to dance as we do now in the dance of the naak*h*aí. They had an unusually fine dance and a fresh lot of dancers came for each set of songs. In all 18 sets of songs were sung. He repeated them all without making any mistake, so when the birds began to sing in the morning they bade him go to his home; but before he left they told him: "The songs you have learned here you must teach to some of your brothers. We are sorry you are going to leave us; but when you have taught the songs to your people you shall return to us." As he departed the yéi sang a Bluebird Song—*Dó'li, dóli nigá'ni.*

682.—When he had passed through all the crowd of yéi and gone on he heard a voice behind him saying "T*s*u'!" (chooh). He stopped and looked all around to discover who had said this; but he could see no one. He started to walk on again, when again he heard the voice and turned to see who spoke; he looked more carefully than before, but all in vain. All these things happened a third time and he started once more to pursue his journey. When for the fourth time he heard the voice, he glanced quickly behind him and upwards and he beheld an owl sitting on a limb of a piñon tree. "Come nearer, my grandchild," said the owl. When the prophet drew near the owl continued: "There is one thing the yéi have not told you, and that is, how to prepare the stuff which they sprinkle on the hot coals to make a smell, the yá*d*i*d'*ini*l*. I have followed you to tell you this. The yéi fear the things they use in the mixture; that is why they have not told you about them." Then he told the prophet how the yá*d*i*d'*ini*l* was made. The owl told him not to go directly home, but to return to the place where he had left his clothes and gone off with the Gá*n*ask*ĭd*i. He did as he was bidden and found his clothes lying as he left them. He put them on and set out for his home at Tse'gíhi. How he was received and what was done with him there have been already told.

683.—He told his relations that the yéi had charged him to teach his people the songs he had learned; that they were good for disease of the eyes, and that on that very night, when darkness came, he would begin to sing them. At the appointed time his family were all ready and many of their neighbors had gathered, too, to hear the songs. He continued to sing all night, but when morning came not one of his audience could remember a single song. He sang all night for a second, and a third night, but no one could learn the songs. On the fourth night the prophet said: "It is because you give me nothing that you cannot learn. Pay me a fee and then you may remember what I sing." Hearing this the eldest brother gave the prophet twelve sacred unwounded buckskins (*t*okakéhi), and these were the skins which he afterwards gave to the yéi, as he had promised, for teaching him to sing the songs.

684.—All the time that the singing was going on the youngest brother, Nakiĕst*s*áhi, had lain behind his grandmother, seeming to be asleep. Now the others bade him get up and try to learn, and told him that if he tried, perhaps he could learn first. But his grandmother said: "No, he is stupid. His elder brothers have better minds than he. If they cannot learn the songs, how can he learn them?" For all that she caught him by the ear, made him rise, and bade him help in the singing. He got up sleepily, scratching his head and rubbing his eyes, which he seemed scarcely able to open; but he managed to sit down beside his brothers. They said, "Sit up in this way"—showing how to sit. He sat up at last, in a proper way, beside the prophet, and the latter said, "Perhaps you can learn the songs." But all this time the youngest brother had been deceiving his people; he had been quietly learning the songs while pretending sleep. They told him of the promised fee in deerskins. When the prophet had done singing, Nakiĕstsáhi began and sang the songs through, from beginning to end, without making a mistake. He pretended he had learned them all in one night. He had watched, too, all that was done during the previous nights, had listened to the descriptions of the rites, and had heard how the kethawns and sweat-houses were made. After this the prophet repeated all the songs and lore carefully over, for four nights more, and at the end of that time the youngest brother knew the songs and rites as well as the prophet knew them. These people all belonged to the gens of *Thá'tsini*, and it is from this gens that the songs have spread over the whole Navaho nation.

685.—Four days after this a man came from a distance, saying he had heard of the adventures of the prophet and of the songs and rites he had brought home with him. He said he had a blind son on whom he begged the prophet to test the efficacy of his songs. But the prophet answered that he had taught his youngest brother all the songs and rites, and that Nakiĕstsáhi was the one he must ask. The visitor gave a present of twelve buckskins to Nakiĕstsáhi, and the latter went off to sing over the blind boy. He sweated the boy four times in ceremonial form; he sprinkled for him on hot coals the fragrant yád id ĭni*l* and performed many other rites, but he had no dance. The blind boy recovered his sight and the youngest brother came home.

686.—Soon after he got home another man came who said his son had a headache and was deaf in one ear, and he offered a fee of twelve buckskins to Nakiĕstsáhi. The latter was ugly and stupid looking; he had never combed his hair until he learned the rites; but after that, he took more care of his personal appearance. He went to the lodge of the deaf boy; he made the kó*n*nike (par. 255), or sweat-bath, without the sweat-lodge, four times; he performed all the rites and sang the songs he had used with his former patient; he cured the boy and returned to his home.

687.—No sooner had he gotten back than a woman came to him who said that her daughter's mouth was crooked. She said she had heard of the wonderful power of the prophet's songs and begged that they might be tried on her child. Nakiĕstsáhi dug a hole in the ground "so big" (about the size of a bucket). Into this he put four hot stones, covering them with leaves of many kinds. He made the girl lie down and put her face over this. When he had sweated her face sufficiently, he applied to it a piece of skin cut from the centre of the forehead and nose of a bighorn. In addition to this, he performed rites and sang songs, and thus he cured the girl with the crooked mouth.

688.—Soon after he got home, another woman came who said her daughter was crippled—that her hamstrings were contracted and hardened. This time the shaman did not want to go. He pleaded that his voice was weak and that he was weary with his vigils. All those who heard him urged him to go; the woman offered him 32 buckskins and a large bowl of haliotis shell in which to mix his medicines, and at last he consented to accompany her. This time, in addition to songs and rites, he prepared the wol*thád* (par. 301), and for four days applied them four times to her limbs. In the end she walked in beauty, she recovered happily.

689.—The prophet then bade the shaman, Nakiĕst*s*áhi, to have more rites and a dance over the first patient that he treated, the boy that was blind and that now could see, and to apply to him again the medicine that had already cured him. The friends of the boy who had been deaf desired also that he should be present at the ceremonies. All consented to this, and a great yébo*g*an, or medicine-lodge, was built. When the house was finished the people took the young shaman over there, and he wanted to know how much they would give him for his services; for he required now a much greater fee than he had ever had before. All the rites which are now performed in the klé*dze hatál* were performed then.

690.—When the songs were being finished on the last morning it was noticed that many of the *d*ï*g*ín *d*ïné‘, or holy people, were gathered around. When the songs were done, these departed and after they had gone the people sought for the prophet, but sought in vain. They never saw him again. They thought he had gone back to the home of the holy ones, where he had learned the songs, but they never knew. Before he left he spoke to his youngest brother, saying: "I shall meet you once more; but when the meeting will be I know not."—Thus ends the legend.

691.—(There is a sequel to it, which the writer has not heard. It refers to the promised meeting of the prophet and his brother, which took place at Tsé‘ïntyel.) [32]

THE WHIRLING LOGS, A SEQUEL TO "THE VISIONARY".

692.—Bï*t*á*h*a*t*ïni, the Visionary,[24] had heard many tales about *T*ó‘nihili*n*, where the waters whirl, and of the *S*ï*l*néo*l*e, or cross of logs that moves around there on the waters, but he had never been to the place and was anxious to see it. When he returned to Tse‘gíhi from his first adventure among the holy ones, he determined to journey to the *S*ï*l*néo*l*e.[33] The particular spot where he lived at this time was called Tse‘ya*h*ó*d*ïlyï*l*, Dark Place under the Rock. For four

nights he considered various plans.   He had heard of the way in which Na*t*ĭ'něs-
*th*ani [34] had floated down the San Juan in a hollow log and he concluded to try
the same plan.   Like Na*t*ĭ'něs*th*ani, he had a grandmother and relations; but
unlike him, he had no trouble with his people.   He, too, had a pet turkey.   (See
" Navaho Legends," p. 160.)

693.—He went to the banks of the San Juan River and selected a dead
standing cottonwood tree.   He placed pieces of dry wood around the butt, and
by rubbing sticks together he started a fire to burn the tree down.   We do not
know how much he burned that day; but he had not burned the tree through,
when he extinguished the fire and went home.   When he got home, his grandmother asked him where he had been all day, and he told her he had been a great
way off, but told her nothing more; he wished to keep his purpose secret.   She
said: " Your pet turkey has been crying for you all day.   He is lonely when you
are gone."

694.—The first day he went to prepare his log, he used cottonwood branches
to make his fire; the second day he gathered on his way, branches of piñon which
he carried on his back to make his fire.   He remained at work until late on the
second day, and then he put out his fire and went home.   Again his grandmother
asked him where he had been during the day, and he replied: " I have been
walking around the land."   His grandmother said: " Your turkey has been
mourning all day again and would not eat.   Next time you go out to walk you
should take your pet with you."

695.—On the third day when he went out again to his work, he gathered
dead branches of cedar on the way and with these he made a fire at the tree.
Fearing that his grandmother had become suspicious of him and would watch
him, he came home by a circuitous route and approached the hut in a direction
different to that in which he had left it.   As he drew near he saw his grandmother
standing on a hill gazing in the direction in which he had departed in the morning.
He came up noiselessly behind her and startled her, asking: " What are you
doing here?   For what do you look in the distance?"   She said: " Your turkey
was in great trouble to-day.   He picked up nothing.   I offered him food, but he
would not eat.   He has not eaten for three days.   I feared he would run away.
He ran far to the east, but came back.   Feed him now, yourself."   The turkey
knew the thoughts that were in his master's mind; this is why he was troubled.

696.—On the fourth day, in order to deceive his grandmother, he started in
a false direction; but, as soon as he was out of her sight, he turned and went
toward the San Juan.   On his way he collected branches of spruce to make his
fire.   During these four days he had burned his tree down and burned off the
upper branching part so as to make a neat log.   When all this was finished he
put out his fire and went home by a circuitous way.   As he neared his home he
noticed his grandmother gazing in the direction in which he returned yesterday.
When they met she said: " Your turkey ran to the south to-day and was gone a
long time.   He was never away so long before.   I fear he wants to leave us.

He cries now all the time while you are gone, my grandson, and eats nothing. Give him something now to eat," and then she asked : " Where do you go every day ? Do you visit the holy ones ?" " No, I see them not," he answered. Yet she did not believe him ; she thought he went to see the *dïgíni*.

697.—On the fifth day the Indian went off again in a false direction — this time toward the east — but he soon turned in the direction of the north and went to his log. His thought now was, how long the log should be. He lay down beside it, but could not decide what to do. He arose, procured a slender pole and measured, with it, his own height ; to the measure he added two spans and decided to make the log of this length. He laid on dry cottonwood branches at the point he had selected and kindled a fire. Late in the day he extinguished the flames and went home in a roundabout way. From a distance he saw his grandmother standing on a hill and looking toward the east. He approached her from the west, and got close to her before she was aware of his presence. " Where have you been again to-day ?" she asked. " I have just been strolling around in the neighborhood of the hut," he answered. Again she told him how his turkey had cried in his absence and refused to eat. " He ran far to the west to-day and was gone a long time. I feared he would never return," she said. The Indian offered food to his turkey, but the latter ate very little and seemed sad. " Why do you grieve, my pet ? I am going nowhere. Why do you not eat ? You will be sorry if you starve yourself." The turkey went off and lay down silent and sad, no longer cheerful as he used to be.

698.—After eating his breakfast, on the sixth day, the man went south from the hut, before he turned and walked north to the river. On his way he collected piñon branches for his fire. When he got home in the evening, his grandmother told him that his turkey still cried, failed to seek food and refused it when offered and that he had run a long way to the west during the day.

699.—On the seventh day, when the Indian left home in the morning he started west ; but soon again turned toward the north and went to his log. On his way he gathered dead cedar branches for his fire. As before, when he came near home, he found his grandmother looking for him and for this he scolded her, asking her why she always watched him when he went away and when he came back.

700.—On the eighth day, when he left, he went directly north and on his way he gathered branches of spruce for his fire. This day he burned the log through, secured the piece of the desired length, put out his fire and went home. He saw his grandmother looking toward the north for his return. She told him that his turkey was still sorrowful and would not eat.

701.—On the ninth day he began his journey by going toward the east ; but soon he turned toward the north, went to his log and began to burn a hole in it lengthwise — to make it hollow by fire. He made his fire this day of cottonwood branches and put it out in the evening. Returning to his hut, he approached it from the south and saw his grandmother looking toward the east. She told him that his turkey had been happier during the day than it had been for many days ; that it had staid near the hut and picked up some food.

702.—On the tenth day, the Navaho departed in the direction of the south ; but eventually went to the north where his log was. He used piñon limbs to make his fire, and burned the hole still larger. Coming home, he approached from the west. When he met his grandmother she told him that his pet seemed still happier and more contented than he was yesterday and had eaten more.

703.—When he left the hut on the eleventh day he departed toward the west and he returned in the evening by way of the north. He used cedar wood for his fire and burned the hole still larger. In order that it might not burn too much to one side, he rolled his log from time to time ; this he did every day. When he returned in the evening he was seen coming from the east. His grandmother told him that his bird seemed very happy during the day and had picked up a good deal of food. The grandson said : " I am glad my pet feels happy."

704.—He went directly to the north on the twelfth day. With a fire of spruce he burned the hole completely through and made it large enough to hold his body. He scraped away the charcoal from the inside with a sharp-pointed stick. In coming home he approached the hut from the east and, as before, met his grandmother outside watching for his return. She told him that his pet was still happier and better. When he returned to the lodge the turkey gobbled loudly four times to welcome him.

705.—During the twelfth day the old woman visited her other grandchildren and told them that something troubled Bïtáhatïni, that he no longer staid at home as he used to, and that she feared he was preparing for another mysterious journey. His brothers advised her to speak cautiously to him and endeavor to find out what was going on. At night she said to him : " Where have you been, every day, for the past twelve days ? Have you been among the dïgíni as you were before ? You had dreams, you had visions, and they proved true. Do you have visions now again, and do you hear mysterious voices ?" He answered : " I see the holy ones no more. I hear no mysterious voices. I am but lonely here and I wander forth to cheer my mind." He slept little that night : he was thinking how he should plug the ends of the hole in the log.

706.—Next morning, while his grandmother still slept, he arose stealthily, took some chenopodium bread and meal of grass-seeds and made of these a bundle which he hid in his clothing. Then he went to his log, sat down beside it, and again considered how he should plug it. After awhile he arose, collected bark of cottonwood, bark of cedar, and bark of cliff-rose ;[35] these he pounded into a pulpy mass, tied into the form of a plug with yucca fibre and forced into the tip end of the log. He prepared another plug of the same material for the butt ; but to this he attached a long string of yucca so that he could pull it in after him when he got into the log. He provided himself with a long stick to enable him to push the plugs out whenever he wished. He put the log close to the bank of the river, entered it and drew in the plug at the butt. He rolled around inside the log till he caused it to tumble into the river. He had not floated far when the plugs began to leak, and soon the log, filling with water, sank to the bottom of the stream. He tried to push out the plugs with his stick, but failed, and became alarmed. He said: "It is all my own fault. Why did I do such a foolish thing? I have taken many risks before, but none so great as this. I used to be happy up on the dry land and in the sunlight. Now I shall drown. Oh! why did I do this?" And he wept.

707.—Heedful of the words of their grandmother on the previous night, two brothers of the Visionary went out on this (thirteenth) day to find his trail. They started at the hut; the elder went east; the younger went west; when they got some distance from the lodge they circled round to the south and when they met, they said to one another that they had discovered no tracks. They went back to the hut; the elder went west, the younger, east; they circled around until they met in the north and one said to another that he had found the fresh track of their brother leading to the north. They followed the trail till they came to the place where the log had been burned. Here they found the stump and the severed end of the log, the debris of the material used in making the plugs, and various traces of his work. They found where he had entered the log and rolled it into the river. They went back to their grandmother and said: "He has rolled himself into the river in a hollow log." The same day they returned to the San Juan, crossed it and walked a long way down its banks seeking for a trace of their brother, but in vain. They said: "Only the Thunder People, only those who dwell above in the clouds know where our brother has sunk beneath the river."

708.—Now the Thunder People began to make signals. Again and again flashes of lightning descended into the river and a rainbow appeared with its end sticking in one place out of the water. The holy ones in Tse‘gíhi beheld these signs and thought they must have some meaning for them, so they sent to *Tó‘neníli* (par. 117) to find out what they signified. Bearing his two magic water jars, he went to the river where the lightning was flashing and where the rainbow rose. He struck the water to the right with his black jar and to the left with his blue jar, uttering with each motion his peculiar call. As he did this the water opened before him; he descended to the bottom of the stream and found there the log nearly covered with sand. He heard a voice calling from within the log. "Who is there?" cried Water Sprinkler. "It is I, *Bĭtáhaƚíni*," said the voice. *Tó‘neníli*, in surprise, placed his hand over his mouth. He went back at once to his home in Tse‘gíhi and told what he had seen and heard. The people to whom he spoke sent word to their neighbors and these spread the news, so that at sunset a great crowd was gathered, and a council was held which lasted all night. As some doubted if it were indeed Bĭtáhaƚíni who was in the log, it was decided that a messenger should be sent to the hut of the Indian to see whether he was at home.

709.—In the morning *H*astséyalti was sent to inquire. He did not speak to the grandmother or to the brothers. He made signs to them which they understood, and they answered that it must surely be the Visionary who was in the log. They told him what had happened as far as they knew. By signs he bade the Navahoes to come to the San Juan with him. They came but they were helpless; they could not even reach the log and they begged him to do what he could. He asked them if they had the sacred jewels and other articles of sacrifice. They replied that they had. He directed them to put these in a haliotis shell and sink them in the river, up stream from the point where their relation lay,[36] as an offering to the holy ones, and he bade them, when they had done this, to go directly to their homes and not to look backward or spy upon the actions of the yéi. When *H* astséyal*t*i got home and told all these things, several of the yéi repaired to the place in the river where the log was submerged. When *T*ó‘nen*i*li had opened the waters, in the way in which he opened them before, four of the yéi went down and with their staves prized the log up out of the sand; but they found this no easy task. They tried to land the log on the south side of the river; but the current was so strong they could not do this and they landed it, instead, on the north side. They tried to pull out the plugs; failing in this, they called for Nayénĕzg̣ani, who, with his great stone knife, cut off from the butt the piece containing the plug and pulled the man out by the feet. It was found when he came out that only his head was dry. The log had filled with water up to his chin. With their staves the yéi poked the plug out from the tip end.

710.—After the Navaho came out of the log, the yéi asked him for what purpose he had entered it. He answered: "My purpose was to go to *T*ó‘nihili*n* where the logs whirl around and see the *S*í*l*néo*l*e. When I was with you before I often heard you speak of both, and I determined to go there; but I came near dying instead. I thank you for rescuing me." One of the gods said: "That is a trifling cause for which to risk your life. You have been to the great places of the holy ones and have seen much. The things you now wish to see are insignificant compared to those you have already seen." He answered: "You have taught me much; you have shown me much; I have seen all the sacred places except this and I shall never rest till I behold it. I am determined to go; for not until I have gone there shall I know all." "There is little to be seen there," said the gods, "and who are they that told you the *S*í*l*néo*l*e lay down the river from here?" The Navaho answered: "I have often heard your people talk of it, and know it must be down the river. I have seen the picture drawn and I want to see the place. I want to get the medicine you procure there. No one told me to go there. It was my own plan; but I came near finding the land of the dead instead of *S*í*l*néo*l*e." "You cannot go there," said the yéi. "But I must go," said the Navaho, "I must get the medicine and behold with my own eyes the strange place of which I have as yet only seen the pictures."[37] Four times the yéi said these words and four times the Navaho gave the same reply. At last the gods said: "Then you shall go. We must think over your words and determine how we can help you. Go now to your people; but at the end of four nights come back to us, and bring your pet turkey. On the third day you must wash yourself with amole and dry yourself with pollen and you must call in your neighbors to a feast in the daytime. On the fourth night you must again gather your friends and give them food, and all night they must sit up and sing the Songs of *Hozóni*. In the morning that follows the night of song, the yéi will come for you." After they told him this they took him to Tse'gíhi and from there sent him home.

711.—When he reached his home his grandmother said to him in anger: "You have been telling me lies. Every day when you came home you told me you were only wandering around the country because you felt lonely, and instead of that you were burning out a log in which to float down the river." He replied: "I told you as I did, because I knew if I spoke the truth you would not let me do as I wished. I had much trouble in consequence of following my own will; I am sorry that I lied to you; but now I shall speak the truth. I wish to tell my story." Then he related to her all his adventures; told her all the yéi had promised and all they had ordered him to do. "Heretofore," he said, " I wished to go in secret. Now that the gods help me, I shall let you all know when I am going. Do not mourn for me this time. I shall take my pet turkey with me, for so the gods have ordered, and I shall come home again in safety. The new mysteries I shall learn, will be of benefit to my youngest brother;[38] they will complete his knowledge and he will transmit them to others who will make use of them when he is dead. He will not be a great chanter until he obtains this knowledge. That is why I go to seek it. He thinks he knows all about the klédze *hatál*, but he knows not the half. Clean the lodge well and carry the dirt far away. Our relations and neighbors must sing all night. We must sing the Happy Songs of the Talking God, the Mountain Songs, the Songs of the House God and the Songs of the Grasshopper." He said then to his youngest brother, "Wash my turkey, even as you wash me, and dry him with corn-pollen. From the time I depart with the yéi until my return you must sing every morning the *Hozóni* Songs. When your songs are finished you must say a prayer for my safe return and scatter corn-pollen toward the east."

712.—The friends, as they were bidden, gathered and sang all night on the fourth night. Early in the morning Bĭtáhatĭni heard far and faint the first call of *Hastséyalti*; but no one else in the lodge heard it. Others heard the second and the third calls; but when *Hastséyalti* got near the door and uttered his fourth call, all heard it. The god lifted the curtain in the doorway and beckoned the Visionary to come forth. The latter, taking his pet turkey under his arm, and bidding his brother sing the *Hozóni* Songs till the day was bright, left the lodge. *Hastséyalti* laid down a short rainbow; the Navaho got on the middle, *Hastséyalti* got in front and *Hastséhogan* behind. "You my people," said the prophet, "must not look at us or see how we travel. Remain in the lodge. Continue with your song." He then began to sing himself; the rainbow began to move, and soon the three travelers were in Tse'gíhi.

713.—Here the Indian found a great crowd of holy people assembled and he found they had prepared for him a hollow spruce log such as they had formerly made for Na*t*í'nĕs*th*ani, but not so long. It had windows of crystal. When he was ready to go in, they opened the log at the butt end, but did not show him the rest of the log. After he got in, four gods, Nayénĕzgạni, *T*o'bad*z*ĭsts*í*ni, *H*ast*s*éol*t*oi and *T*ó'nenĭli, performed a ceremony over the log like that performed now over the the patient on the last day of the klé*dz*e *h*a*t*ál (par. 593 *et seq.*) As soon as *T*ó'nenĭli sprinkled water, a dense dark mist gathered around the log and around all the people who had assembled to carry it, so that no one, from afar, could see what they were doing. They lifted the log on rainbows and bore it to the river, while the dark mist followed and hid them. They bade the Indian not to speak while in the log, unless he spoke to himself or sang sacred songs, and they would let him know when they wanted him to get out.

714—After they launched the log it often floated close to the bank and had to be shoved out into the stream. Six gods—two Gá*n*askĭ*d*i, two *H*ast*s*é*h*o*g*an and two Dsaha*d*old*z*á — worked with their staves to keep the log in the channel. At dark they came near to a high, steep ridge of rocks [39] and here they pushed the log ashore so that it might not float away during the night.

715.—Next day when they reached the ridge of rocks, they found themselves stopped. Tiéholtsodi had dammed the water and they had to pull the log ashore again. The gods spoke to the Navaho through the log. " We must make a sacrifice to Tiéholtsodi. If you have the sacred jewels hand them out to us but do not speak." They took out one of the crystal windows of the log and the Navaho handed the jewels out through the hole. They placed the jewels in a white shell bowl and sank them in the stream which at once flowed on and carried the log with it. The liberated waters flowed so angrily that the gods found it difficult to keep the log in the channel. Night came on when they reached a place called Tlo'tsáhi Bĭ*lth*á*h*otyel,[40] where they pulled the log up on the north shore for the night.

716.—On the following day they floated the log down to *T*aha*d*o*t*lĭz, Blue Shore, where they found an eddy beyond which they could not make the log float. They sent *T*ó'nenĭli down the stream to see what was the matter. When he came back he said he had found a dam, but could not find the people who had built it. The Fringe Mouth of the Water and the Fringe Mouth of the Land were then sent to explore. When they returned they related that they had found those who built the dam, that they were the Flat Tails (Beavers) and the Web Toes (Otters), that with them were Fish and Water Coyotes. *H*ast*s*éyal*t*i and *T*ó'nenĭli were sent to talk to the Flat Tails and their companions. " Why did you build this dam ? " said the messenger. " Our grandson wishes to go down the river. We desire that you open the dam." The messengers and the Flat Tails quarrelled. " He shall not pass this place," said the Flat Tails. " He must pass. Open the dam," said the messengers. These demands and refusals were repeated four times. At length the Flat Tails said : " We must have sacrifices.

We must have the sacred jewels. It was to get these that we dammed the stream. You gave jewels to Tiéholtsodi to let your grandson pass; now you must give them to us. For him you put the jewels in a white vessel, for us you must put them in a blue one." Thus said all of the four peoples that were in the water. The yéi consented to this. They got from the Indian the sacred jewels and put them in the river. The dam was opened. The log floated on. As the waters fell the prophet inside the log sang the Na*h*osts*á*he Bigï'n, or Song of the Subsiding Waters. Then he thought of his turkey, and looking out through one of the crystal windows he beheld his pet on the bank of the river running along. He felt pity for the bird and thought to himself, " I fear my turkey will wear his feet off running." Then he sang a song about his pet.

717.—The log floated on well after it passed Blue Shore until it came to the the mouth of a stream which entered the San Juan from the south, called Tse‘*la*-ka*í*d*e*za‘ or Standing White Rock (Creek) ; here they found another obstruction. The water, instead of flowing on, accumulated and flowed back. The stream was choked by great bowlders of granite, between which lay mud and gravel. *T*ó‘ne-nïli went down to the dam, but could find no one. Next, two Dsaha*d*oldz*á* went there, but neither could they find any one. When they had returned, a grebe, floating on the water, spoke to *H*ast*s*e'yal*t*i, telling him that they who built the dam were the Turtle People, the Rough Frog People, the Green Frog People, and the Little Fish People, and that these people were hidden among the gravel. Again *T*ó‘nenïli went to the dam. He searched among the gravel, found these people, went back to his comrades and got *H*ast*s*é*h*o*g*an to go with him to speak to the builders of the dam. " Our grandson Bï*t*á*h*a*t*ïni wishes to go down and see the *S*ï*l*néo*l*e. Open this dam for us," demanded *H*ast*s*é*h*ogan. " We shall not open it. He must not pass here," said the Turtle People. When *H*ast*s*é*h*o-*g*an and the Turtle People had each thus spoken four times the latter said : " He may pass if he makes us sacrifices. It is to get these that we dammed the river. You gave jewels to Tiéholtsodi and the Flat Tails to let him pass. They are not the only ones who want presents. You must give something to us also. We desire cigarettes, corn-pollen, blue pollen, specular iron-ore and powdered shells. If you place these in a bowl of haliotis shell and sink them in the river above the dam, we will let your grandson pass." The sacrifices were put thus in the river ; the dam was broken open ; the water flowed on, bearing the log with it. The people of the water, who had built the dam, stood on the bank, watching the log as it passed. Among these was T*s*áltso, the Great Frog, who was particularly ugly, whose great eyes seemed about to pop out of his head, whose body was covered with warts. He smoked a pipe. He drew the smoke in through his mouth, but passed it out through his warts. As the log went by, the Indian peeped out through one of the crystal windows and, seeing T*s*áltso, four thoughts passed through his mind. His first thought was : " How ugly is T*s*áltso ! How big his eyes !" He spoke not ; but Great Frog, sitting on the bank, knew what was passing through the man's mind and he answered the unspoken thought thus : " Yes, my grandchild, this is just the way I look."   The second thought of the Indian was : " What a rough skin and what a swollen throat T*s*áltso has ! " and the latter answered the unheard thought : " Yes, my grandchild, this is just the way I look."   The third thought of the man was : " How strange he appears, with smoke coming out of the warts all over his body ! " and T*s*áltso said, in answer to the thought : " Yes, my grandchild, this is just the way I look."   The fourth thought was : " How thin and fleshless his legs are ! " and T*s*áltso responded to the thought : " Yes, my grandchild, this is just the way I look."   The yéi did not go far that day after they passed the dam. It soon grew dark and they drew the log up on the south side of the river.

718.—Next morning they had the usual trouble about keeping the log in the center of the stream.   It went on to the falls in the San Juan where the log of Na*ti*'něs*th*ani had stuck and here this log came down on its end and stuck too. The yéi tried to prize it up with their staves but they failed.   *H*astséyal*t*i went up to the Thunder People and begged their aid.   These threw down two ropes of lightning, passed them under the log and lifted it out of the mud.   As they were lifting the log, the Navaho sang four songs which are still sung and are called Klé*dz*e I*d*ní' Bigï'n.   The log went on again after this adventure ; but it had not gone far when darkness came and the yéi landed it on the north bank of the river for the night.

719.—They launched the log early on the following morning.   It moved along well until it came to a place where the river spreads out wide ; here it drifted toward the southern shore and stranded.   The yéi shoved it out into the stream again with their staves ; but they did not keep it floating long.   It soon moved toward the north shore where it again stranded ; but as darkness now came, the yéi let it stay where it stopped.   During the night it sank deep in the mud.

720.—When morning came again, the yéi tried, with their staves, to lift the log out of the mud but they did not succeed.   " Let us call upon the Rain to help us," they said.   *T*ó'nenili threw water from his jars four times against the sky and Ása*t*íni sang his rain songs.[41]   Soon copious showers descended ; the river rose ; the yéi worked with their staves, and got the log floating again.   After this it continued to rain and it rained too hard.   The thunder shook the earth without ceasing ; the lightning was continuous ; it was an awful storm.   They feared the log might be overwhelmed and the Navaho drowned.   " Can you stop this storm that you have raised ? " they said to *T*ó'nenïli.   He replied that he could.   He shook his bag of fox-skin toward the four quarters of the heavens as he now often does in the dance of the naak*h*aí, and each time he shook the bag he uttered his howl.   The clouds separated and let the blue sky appear ; they passed off in four different directions and the rain ceased.   When the yéi shoved the log out into the current it floated better than ever before because the river was high on account of the great rain.

721.—The log had not floated far when it came to a place where two ridges extended out into the water from opposite sides, making the stream very narrow. A cedar tree stood at the extremity of the southern ridge, a piñon tree at the extremity of the northern. A breath-feather was tied to the top of each tree. The log, floating crosswise to the stream, became lodged against the trees. The holy ones tried their best to release the log, but they could not; so they stopped and began to talk of different plans. It was *Hastséayuhi* and *Hastsédïltsosi* who had planted these trees for mischief. They accompanied the holy ones on this journey and pretended to be their friends; they even allowed the messengers to be sent down into the water as usual, yet they said nothing. *Hastséyalti* then proceeded to ask each bystander, in turn, if he knew how to move the log. Each in turn answered "No" until he came to *Hastséayuhi* who said that he and *Hastsédïltsosi* could do it, but that they must first receive gifts. To *Hastséayuhi* was given turquoise and white corn-meal; to *Hastsédïltsosi*, white shell and yellow corn-meal. The former went to the cedar on the south side, the latter to the piñon on the north. Each laid his sacrifices on the ground beside the tree at which he stood, twisted his tree four times, plucked it easily from the ground and planted it back in the place from which he had originally dug it. The piñon represented a man, the cedar, a woman; and therefore it is that now in the rite of the night chant, when we pull the mask off the patient by means of a tree we use a piñon in treating a man and a cedar in treating a woman. See par. 449.

722.—After passing the ridges of rock they came to a lake closely surrounded by high cliffs. The river flowed into the lake on one side and out at the other by two streams. The log floated to the middle of the lake and then circled around, sunwise, in constantly widening circles until it touched the shore near the rocky wall, on the south side, where the Fringe Mouths of the Water lived, and here it stopped with its butt to the south. *Tó'nenïli* pushed aside the waters in his usual way. *Hastséhogan* and *Gánaskïdi* pulled out the stopper and helped the Indian to get out of the log. At the same time the door of the house of the Fringe Mouths was thrown open. He entered and found many holy ones inside who awaited his coming. The chief of the Fringe Mouths said to him, "We have heard that *Bïtáhatïni* was coming to us; we have heard why he comes, and he comes not in vain. We shall give him what he seeks and then he will be a perfect chanter of the klédze *hatál*." The Prophet spoke not. The Fringe Mouths led him four times around the lodge, and placed him sitting in the south. It is for this reason now that the patient, when awaiting, sits in the south during the ceremonies of klédze *hatál*. Then they closed the door and bade him look down at the ground until they told him to lift his eyes. While he was looking down, they took from a shelf a sheet of cloud and spread it on the ground. When they bade him look up, he beheld the sheet of cloud covered with a picture in many colors and he saw four footprints and a trail drawn in white corn-meal extending from where he sat to the picture where was a bowl of water. He was told to arise and examine the picture more carefully, that it was called *Thaltládze Dsahadoldzábe yikál* or picture with the Water Fringe Mouths.[12]   After he had looked at it for a long time, the holy ones asked: " Have you observed the picture well? Have you got it fixed in your mind so that you will never forget it?" When he had replied "Yes," he walked as the yéi directed, on the tracks of meal to the center of the picture. He sprinkled pollen on the faces of the gods in the way we do it now (par. 509); he sprinkled it up the stem of each corn-plant and down its three roots, as he uttered the words " Hozógo naſádo." He placed corn-meal on the feet, chest and mouth of each divine figure, on the bases of the ears and the base of the tassel of each cornstalk. After this he picked up from each deposit a portion of the sacred meal and handed it to Hastsé-yalʈi. He stepped into the water in the middle of the picture, bowed his head and uttered this prayer:

> In beauty, I shall walk.
> In beauty, you shall be my picture.
> In beauty, you shall be my song.
> In beauty, you shall be my medicine,
> In beauty, my holy medicine.

When he had finished his prayer the yéi began to beat the drum and shake the rattle. A Fringe Mouth and a goddess entered masked and the prophet fell upon the ground in a fit. The yéi dragged his shaking body to the north of the central fire, and laid it, head to the north, face to the east. They rolled up the pictured cloud and laid it away on the shelf. At the same time the two divinities whose entrance had caused the convulsion, departed. When they had gone, the chief of the Fringe Mouths began to treat the patient by singing and making marks on the ground with the point of his rattle from the body of the patient outwards towards the cardinal points. He first made a straight mark in each direction and then a zigzag mark. The first song of the chief did no good; at the end of the second song, the patient straightened his fingers; at the end of the third song, his body became straight; and at the end of the fourth he sat up, but still he trembled. All that were in the lodge felt sorry for him, and four who were present prayed for him—one in the east, one in the south, one in the west and one in the north. They pressed to the sacred parts of his body the horn of a bighorn in the same manner that we do it now. They took two hot coals from the fire, and sprinkled on them, corn-meal. When he had inhaled the smoke of the burning meal they threw water on the coals and put them to one side. They took two more glowing coals from the fire and sprinkled yádid'iniʈ (par. 197) upon them. When he had sufficiently inhaled the fumes of this they threw water on the coals. The four coals were carried out of the lodge and deposited toward the north in a shady place where the sun could not shine on them. Bïʈáhaʈini went back to his seat in the south of the lodge and the yéi thus addressed him: " When the People upon the Earth treat a sick person in the ·rites of klédʐe haʈáʈ let them do to him as we have done to you. Truly they cannot draw a picture on a cloud as we do; but they may imitate it, as best they can, on sand. If the four songs we have given you do not cure him, let them make the prayer which we shall teach you, and if that does not cure, let them sing the Yikaígĭn or Daylight Songs." At last they told him he must go to the opposite side of the lake where he would hear the Songs under the Water and learn other mysteries.

723.—The Prophet left the lodge and again entered his log, which whirled around the lake four times and landed on the north shore with its butt to the north. Here he found a doorway whose bottom was on a level with the surface of the water, and he passed through it to a house where many holy ones sat. He was placed sitting in the south. The lodge belonged to *H*astséyal*t*i and *H*astsé*h*og̃an, but holy ones of all kinds were assembled there. When the Indian was seated, *H*astsé*h*og̃an asked him why he came. He replied that he came to see their pictures, to hear their songs and prayers, to learn how they made their medicines. *H*astsé*h*og̃an replied : " It is well, we can grant you what you seek. Now bow your head, gaze downwards and look not up until you are bidden." When he was told to raise his head and look, he beheld on the floor, drawn on a cloud, in many colors, the picture of those above one another.[43] He was told to rise and study the picture well. When he had gazed on it sufficiently he performed rites over it as the yéi directed. He put pollen on the masks of the gods ; he put meal on the feet, chests and mouths ; he took up the meal again and gave it to *H*astséyal*t*i ; he said a prayer such as he had said over the former picture ; but he did not fall into a fit and the ceremonies for the fit were not employed. There was no fumigation. They explained to him how to make the cold infusion and other medicines used in the rites. They told him of all the ceremonies that go with this picture, which are called *t*o'yunánd*z*e *h*atál or, chant beyond the water. After this they showed him another picture which was called picture of many dancers. Long years ago the Navaho chanters knew this picture and drew it, but it is now forgotten.[44] The Prophet thanked *H*astsé*h*og̃an for all that had been told him. He left the lodge and again entered his log. After he was in, the yéi plugged the butt end, through which he had entered, and shoved the log once more into the middle of the lake. The log circled around the lake four times and then floated away.

724.—The lake had two outlets ; one to the northwest, flowed to other rivers and to the ocean in the west ; one to the southwest, flowed into the whirling lake of *T*ó'nihili*n* which had no outlet and no bottom. It was on the latter stream that the log with the Indian inside floated and soon came to the whirling water which was surrounded by high steep cliffs. Here were the whirling logs he had so often heard of. When his log entered the lake it ran first toward the center, then it moved around four times, making each time a wider circle until it approached the shore and landed close to the inlet and south of it. The yéi pulled the plug from the butt of the log and helped the Indian to come out on the land. When he was out, they put the plug back again and told him to look around. He beheld the cross of sticks circling on the lake. It did not move on its own center, but turned around the center of the water.   The log which lay from east to west was at the bottom ; that which lay from north to south was on top.   On each of the logs, four holy ones were seated—two at each end, and all were singing a song the burden of which was " He comes for my sake."   Many stalks of corn were fixed to the logs ; but in the picture, as the Navahoes draw it now, we put only four.[45]   As Bĭ*táhatï*ni gazed, he wondered why the holy ones were doing as they did.   When this thought passed through his mind, they began to sing another song, one of the *Sï*né*ole* Bigï'n.   After this, they sang a third song, the burden of which was, " From the east he looks at me," and a fourth song, " The Rain brings pollen on the tassel."   The cross of logs went around the lake four times, getting closer to the shore each time, while the holy ones sang ; till at last it reached the western shore where they landed and went into their houses.   In the meantime the rain was falling so hard that when the cross of logs reached the western end of the lake, the Indian could scarcely see it.   The yéi who had come with him and guided his log, now led him around the southern shore of the lake to the western side.   Bĭ*táhatï*ni began to fear ; but his companions encouraged him, saying : " Fear not.   Your body is holy.   You are holy as you travel."   As soon as they said this, they commenced to sing a song beginning : "Nitsés *dï*gíni, Your body is holy."   He thought to himself, " I wonder what sort of a place I am going to," and as he thought this he sang the fifth *Sï*né*ole* Song.   As he walked he heard voices coming from the place he was approaching, saying : " Bĭ*táhatï*ni comes."   Hearing this, he sang the seventh Song of *Sï*né*ole*.   By the time he had finished the song he was near the door and he heard a voice in the lodge crying : " Bĭ*táhatï*ni is near."   His companions bade him sing a song of entrance which should last until he got into the lodge.   The holy ones inside the lodge cried : " One of the Earth People is coming.   He brings soft goods ; he brings jewels ; he brings fruits ; he brings good thunder ; he brings the he-rain and the she-rain.   He approaches in a beautiful way.   Before him it is beautiful as he approaches.   Behind him it is beautiful as he approaches.   Above him it is beautiful as he approaches.   Below him it is beautiful as he approaches.   All around him it is beautiful as he approaches."   As he passed through the door the holy ones in the lodge began a Song of Welcome.

725.—When he entered the lodge he found the *dï*gíni prepared to receive him.   The picture of the *Sï*né*ole* (plate VI.) was already spread upon the ground.   He was bidden to sit in the southwestern part of the lodge and study the picture.   After a while one of the yéi said to him : " The People upon the Earth have never been here before.   We have heard beforehand that you were traveling hither.   What do they call the place whence you come ? "   He answered : " I started on my journey from a place called Tse'ya*hód*ï*lyï*l ; from there I went to Tse'gíhi and thence I came here with your grandfather."   " And whither are you bound ? " they asked.   " I started to come here.   I sought to come no further than the *Sï*né*ole*," he replied.   When they asked him his name, he said : " Those who come with me call me Bĭ*táhatï*ni."   The *dï*gíni continued :

" We have heard of you at Tse‘gíhi ; we have heard of you at Tsúskai and other places which you visited, when you went out before in search of mysteries, and we know you have learned the mysteries of these places."   The Navaho said : " I am glad I have come among you ; that I bring good, beautiful meal ; that I bring good, beautiful pollen and other good, beautiful things.   This is the only holy place I have not hitherto visited.   I came here, my grandfather, to see your picture and to learn of your medicine.   Now I have beheld your picture.   The other holy ones know not how to draw it."   Someone now said : " Let us sing a song while he puts pollen on the picture" ; so they sang while he applied pollen and when the song was done he placed meal on the picture.   Some of those holy ones who had sat upon the logs while they were whirling around the lake now came forward, brewed the cold infusion which we use to-day in our rites, to make the patient feel light within, and sprinkled some of the infusion over the pictured logs.   When the sprinkling was done, the yéi bade the Navaho pick up from off the picture the meal he had deposited and put it in his medicine bag, for the meal had now become sacred and had the power to heal.

726.—When all the rites connected with the picture were done, the yéi told him that there was yet another medicine he must learn to make.   As this medicine must be prepared outside the lodge, all went out to see it made.   The work was done by a virgin boy and girl, children of the divine ones who had sat on the east limb of the cross of logs while it floated on the lake.   To the boy was given a turquoise bowl containing white meal ; to the girl a white shell bowl containing yellow meal.   While their father sat on the shore, the children went around, collecting crystals of frost from the plants that grew around the margin of the lake.   That which the boy collected and that which the girl collected, mixed with the meal, were placed in separate buckskin bags.   From these materials was made the azé *d*a‘tsos or frost medicine (par. 213) such as we administer to this day in the rites of klédze *ha̱tál* when the patient has fever.   The yéi then sang another song, the tenth *S*ĭ*l*néo*l*e Bigĭ'n, still sung in these days by the Navaho chanters when they administer the frost medicine.

727.—When the song was ended all returned to the lodge.   Here another picture [46] was shown to the Navaho, much like the one he had seen before, and rites similar to those of the first picture were performed.   After the rites were completed and the picture put away, the *d*ígíni said to the prophet :   " Now you have learned many mysteries.   With these you may treat your people when they are ill.   In this work you may help one another.   You will work for the sick ; they and their people will work for you.   While you sing in the lodge the others will bury your kethawns and perform many services for you."   As they prepared to leave the lodge they sang the eleventh Song of the *S*ĭ*l*néo*l*e, a song about plants. As they emerged from the lodge, hearing the voice of a grasshopper, they sang the twelfth *S*ĭ*l*néo*l*e Bigĭ'n, which is a Song of Anĭ*l*tá ni, the Grasshopper.

728.—They proceeded to the cross of logs on the shore of the lake.   As they approached the cross, flashes of lightning shot out of it.   They passed from the shore to the cross on a short rainbow.   The yébaka or male divinity to whom belonged the eastern arm got on the cross first — no one else was allowed to get on before him — the Navaho followed and the yébaad or wife of the eastern god got on after him.   The other divine ones boarded the logs in the order in which they had come off them.   Thus on the east limb of the cross there were three individuals ; but on each of the other limbs there were only two.   Before he got on the logs, the Navaho was bidden to close his eyes and to open them again as soon as he found himself aboard.   As soon as all were on the cross, it floated to the center of the lake, circled around the water four times as it did when he first saw it and landed at the place from which it had started.   Here all got to the shore on a short rainbow.   Each time, in going around, when the cross passed the landing-place the yéi asked the Navaho if he wanted to get off ; but each time he said " No " until the journey was finished.   On leaving the log, the yéi moved in an order (of precedence) the same as that observed on leaving the shore.   When all were on land, the yéi directed the Indian to walk around the shore of the lake toward the place where he had left his hollow log.

729.—As he walked, coming to a ravine in which were rose bushes, he saw a turkey picking hips.   He approached the bird ; but, to his surprise, it did not run away.   It allowed him to walk right up to it and then he discovered that it was his own pet turkey.   The pet ran around him, holding out its wings in joy.   The Visionary seized the bird, embraced it and said :   " I greet you, my pet.   I thought you had remained behind.   How did you get here ? "   As it was now growing dark, the Indian sought a place to sleep.   He selected a big cedar tree, scratched a place for himself to lie in the débris under the tree, put the turkey on an overhanging limb to perch, and lay down to sleep.   But for a while he could not sleep ; he grew chilly, and he said :   " My pet, I am cold."   Soon after, he fell asleep, and while he slept the turkey came down from the tree and covered him with its right wing.   The Navaho slept soundly the rest of the night.

730.—When he woke in the morning he found the wing of the turkey covering him and he was so warm that his skin was moist with perspiration.   When he woke he found that he was in a dark, narrow ravine where the sun did not shine ; but he soon found a sunny spot on a neighboring ridge and he sat down. He spoke thus to his turkey :   " My pet, I thank you for covering me last night. I slept well.   Now I shall give you something to eat."   He made a mush of meal of the seeds of tlo'tsózi (*Sporobolus cryptandrus*) for the turkey and, for himself, a mush of white corn-meal, in a yellow bowl which he always carried.   They both ate.   After eating, the turkey felt happy ; it ran around, picking up insects and other small objects to eat.   Together they walked along the ridge to the east until they came to a place where four streams flowed from the hill in different directions.   Then as a heavy rain began to descend, accompanied by great thunder and lightning, they sought shelter under a ledge of rock.   The lightning struck so close, all around, that the Visionary, thinking he was in danger, sang the fourth of the I*d*ní' Bigĭ'n or Thunder Songs, and blew his breath in four different directions.   The clouds with the thunder passed away in four directions — east, south, west, north—and the sun shone again.   They descended the hill to a place where the four streams joined into one; they came to a beautiful meadow where the water overflowed the land; they took four circuits around the meadow and as they walked the prophet thought to himself: " What a beautiful place this is for a farm.   I wish I had brought some grains of corn with me, or that I had asked the yéi for some, at the last place where I visited them.   At length he went to the center of the meadow where he met two *Hast*séyal*t*i and two *Hast*sé*hog*an ; one of each came from the lodge at the *Si*l*néo*l*e* and one of each were of those who had traveled with him.   They asked him where he had slept the previous night.   He pointed out the place ; he told them how he longed for seeds to plant a farm, and how sorry he was that he had not brought some with him.   Said the holy ones :   " It is a fine place for a farm, our grandson ; a fine place for a young man and a young woman to farm together.   The crops cannot fail here."   When they had spoken he sang another song, the first of the *T*aiké Gisi'n or Farm Songs, the burden of which is " I wish I had the seed."   One of the divine ones now said : " You have the seed.   Your turkey has it.   Go ask him ; but do not let him know it was I who told you." The Navaho approached his pet and thus spoke :   " My pet, this is a good place to plant.   Have you any seed ?"   The turkey held up its head, ran four times around its master, stood facing the east, shook its wings and dropped from them four grains of white corn.   It ran to the south and (facing south) dropped four grains of blue corn ; to the west, and dropped four grains of yellow corn ; to the north and dropped four grains of variegated corn.   Each time that it shook its wings and dropped corn, it gobbled.   The Navaho picked up the corn and went the to the east ; but the turkey did not follow him.   Again it went toward the east and shook from its wings four squash seeds ; to the south and shook out four beans ; to the west and shook out four watermelon seeds ; to the north and shook out four muskmelon seeds ; lastly it came to the center between all these points and shook out four tobacco seeds.   *B*i*tá*ḥa*t*ini came back to where the turkey was, picked up all the seeds, and returning to his place in the east, sang the second and third of the Farm Songs.   Now he and his turkey together wandered four times in increasing circles till they reached the edge of the meadow. From here, the man went to a neighboring gully and procured a piece of tsĭn-tlĭ'zi (*Fendleria rupicola*) to use as a planting stick.   They both returned, making four circuits to the place where they had been standing.   Approaching the east, the man dug a hole and, planting the white corn, sang the fourth Farm Song. Still continuing the same song, he planted the blue corn in the south, the yellow corn in the west and the variegated corn in the north.   He returned to the center and began the fifth Farm Song.   While singing this, he planted squash seeds in the southeast, beans in the southwest, watermelon seeds in the northwest and muskmelon seeds in the northeast.   Singing the sixth Farm Song, he planted to-bacco seeds in the edge of the field, beyond the others in four different places —

east, south, west, north. When the planting was done he erected four scarecrows made of branchlets secured to the ends of high sticks. These were not only to frighten away birds, but to show that the land was claimed. Again he circled four times around the field and went to the south to camp under a piñon tree. As on the previous night, the Navaho made his bed under a tree and put the turkey to perch on a limb above him ; but when he fell asleep the turkey came down from the tree and covered its master with its left wing.

731.—He slept well until daylight and woke warm and perspiring. They made a breakfast like that of the day before. When they had eaten, Bĭtáhatĭni said to the turkey : "Come, my pet, to the farm and see if all is well there." Taking four turns, as usual, they entered the farm, and found that the corn had sprouted, that its top had already appeared above the ground. The Indian sang the seventh Farm Song. They staid in the farm all day, pulling weeds, and at sunset went back to camp at the piñon tree where they had rested the previous night. The turkey, before it went to roost, plucked a feather from its right side close to the tail and gave this to its master for a blanket. The Indian laid the feather over him. It grew quickly in size until it covered him from head to foot, and it kept him warm all night; but as morning approached the feather became small again, and when he woke, it was but the size of an ordinary turkey feather.

732.—The Indian arose at sunrise and again prepared mush for himself and his bird, as on the two previous mornings. Before going to the farm he walked around it, to see if he he could find any tracks, to see if anyone visited the land. When, at length, he entered the farm, he found the corn had grown as high as his knee, and the weeds half as high. He went among the hills where wood grew and made a wooden hoe ; with this he returned to the farm and worked at cutting down the weeds until after sunset, when he returned to the piñon tree to sleep. As on the night before, the turkey gave him a feather for a blanket ; but this time the feather was plucked from the left side near the tail.

733.—It was late next morning when they arose from sleep. The turkey was the first to wake up. Mush was made as before, of corn-meal for the man and of meal of grass seeds for the bird. When they went to the farm they found that the ears on the corn were forming, and that the other plants were in bloom. The man spent the day hoeing weeds, while the turkey ran through the field and around it. When darkness came, they left the field in the usual way, and went off to camp at the piñon tree.

734.—On the following morning, after they had eaten the usual breakfast, they took four turns around the meadow outside the place where the plants were growing, then entered the farm from the east, and found that everything seemed ripe or nearly so. The Indian said : " My pet, we will stay by this farm ; we will not leave it." Going sunwise around the farm, he broke off an ear of white corn in the east, an ear of blue corn in the south, an ear of yellow corn in the west, and an ear of variegated corn in the north. Going round a second time, he

culled one squash in the east, one bean-pod in the south, one watermelon in the
west, and one muskmelon in the north.   He tied the corn in one bundle.   He
took all he had picked to the edge of the farm, where he kindled a flame by rubbing two sticks together, built a big fire of sagebrush, and put some corn in the
husk on the fire to roast.   He sat in thought, planning how he might cook the
other vegetables.   Just as he asked himself : " How shall I prepare the squash ? "
Tó'nenĭli and *Ásaĭni* appeared before him.   " Do you live here and till this
farm ? " said *Tó'nenĭli*, the Water Sprinkler.   " You have raised a fine crop of
corn.   We wish to see how much corn you have."   He led the gods into the
farm, walking sunwise and halting at the four cardinal points, showing them all
that grew there.   The divine ones asked him where he got his seeds and the
man replied that the pet turkey had dropped them from its wings.   When they
went back to the fire, after examining the farm, they found the corn was not quite
cooked, some parts of the husks were still green ; yet the Indian pulled one of the
ears out of the ashes.   He was about to eat it, when Water Sprinkler checked
him and said : " Do not eat that.   Cook it well first.   If you eat your green corn
before it is well cooked the frost will blight your field or the floods will wash it
out."   *Ásaĭni* asked the Navaho what he intended to do with the squash.   " I
was thinking," was the answer, " of cooking it in one or two ways, either baking
it in the ashes or toasting it before the fire."   " Never cook it in either way,"
said the holy one, " until it is perfectly ripe.   It is never ripe until the frost
comes, and the frost has not come yet.   If you bake it now, early frosts will blight
your crops or floods will wash them away."   As he said this he put his hand
under his blanket, drew out a great long earthen pot and continued : " Put your
squash into this, and put your bean in with it."   When the Indian had obeyed,
Tó'nenĭli poured into the pot his mixture of sacred waters (par. 209) which he
always carried with him, and, placing the pot on the fire, said : " Thus must you
cook your squash."   " What do you intend to do with the watermelon ? " asked
Water Sprinkler.   " I had thought of roasting it before the fire as I thought of
doing with the squash," replied the Visionary.   " Do not do so," said the god ;
" you must eat it raw.   If you throw it on the ground it will burst open.   Eat
then the soft red flesh within, but not the hard rind without.   If you cook the
watermelon now, the Indians will forever have to cook their watermelons."   The
divine one then asked the Navaho what he thought of doing with the muskmelon.
That, too, the Navaho said he thought might be roasted before the fire.   " Do
not cook it in any way," said *Tó'nenĭli*.   " Cut it open with a flint knife and eat
only the soft part inside.   If you cook it now, the Indians will forever have to
cook their muskmelons."   At last the yéi asked : " What do you think of doing
with the tobacco ? "   The Indian answered : " I know how to use that, for I have
seen the holy ones put it into reeds and smoke it."   " We came," said *Tó'nenĭli*,
" to teach you how to cook the food and tell you all about it that you should
know ; but we have yet other things to tell you.   On a dark, stormy night, when
the lightning flashes often, come here to your field and stand beside a stalk of the

white corn in the east. When a bright flash of lightning comes, pluck a leaf while the light shines. Do likewise with the blue corn in the south, the yellow corn in the west, and the variegated corn in the north. Go around the field again and do this to the tassels of the corn. Go around once more and cull by the lightning glare leaves from the other plants in your field. Go, at last, around the outside of your field and pull, while the lightning shines, leaves from the sunflowers, grass, and other wild plants you may find. Put all that you gather into a bag and take it to your camp with you." That very night the sky was covered with black clouds, the lightning flashed vividly, and Bĭtáhatíni, going to his field, did as Water Sprinkler had bidden him. See par. 203 *et seq*.

735.—On the following day he went out early to his field, culled various products in the manner of the previous day and cooked them as he had been told. Ásatíni had left the long pot with him, to use in cooking squash ; but had told him if ever he moved away from the farm he must return the pot. Just as he was beginning to prepare the food, *H*astséyal*t*i, the Talking God, and *H*astsého-*g*an, the House God, appeared before him. Each brought with him a young son and a young daughter. Bluebirds and many other beautiful birds of different kinds were now sporting and singing among the corn. By this time Bĭtáhatíni had built himself a small hut of sticks covered with weeds and earth. *H*astsé-yal*t*i said : "We have come to see your corn. You are now a great chanter and know many mysteries ; but there is one more medicine which you must learn how to use and we know that you collected the material last night." The two yéi, the four children, and the Navaho went into the hut and sat down. In a little while the children ran out. As they were gone a long while the parents missed them and said : "Where are our children ?" They looked out, saw the children in the field and called them. All the little ones at once returned to the hut except one of the boys, the son of *H*astséyal*t*i. "Where is your brother ?" asked the Talking God of the boy who had returned. "He has fallen asleep among the corn," was the answer. *H*astséyal*t*i, taking the boy with him, went into the field. There he found that his son had plucked some corn-silk, leaned against a corn-stalk and fallen into a swoon or trance. The child breathed, but was unconscious. The god returned to the hut and said to Bĭtáhatíni : "My son is ill in the corn-field, can you help him ? You People upon the Earth know much. We also know much ; but I know not how to deal with such an attack as he now has. Have you ever seen an Indian die thus in the field ? If you cure my son, I will teach you how to make the cigarette sacred to me." The Visionary only promised to try what he could do. Together the holy one and the man walked to the farm, circled around it four times, entered it from the east and went to where the boy was lying. The prophet laid the boy on his back with head to the east ; he pulled up four stalks of corn and laid them, radiating from the body, so that the tip of one pointed east, that of another pointed south, that of a third pointed west, and that of a fourth pointed north ; he made a cold infusion of the leaves collected during the storm of the previous night, and he sang Farm Songs. The boy sat up; consciousness was returning.   The prophet pressed the cornstalks to different parts of the boy's body as we now press sacred things to the body of a suffering man in the rites of the night chant (par. 135); he gave the cold infusion to the boy in four draughts; and the boy arose, in all things happily restored.   In these days, if a man becomes ill while hoeing or ditching in his field, or if he falls asleep in the field and awakes feeling ill, we treat him as the prophet then treated the son of *Hastséyalti*.   In return for his cure, the divine one showed the Navaho how his kethawns were made.   Each was a span long.   One was half black and half white; the other, half blue and half yellow.   As the corn had by this time become very ripe and hard,[17] the Talking God asked the Indian when he intended to gather his corn.   The man said he intended to gather it on the morrow.   "It is well.   We shall come and help you," said *Hastséyalti*.

736.—In the morning, when he went to his field, he found it again thronged with beautiful little birds that sang and disported themselves.   He plucked four ears of corn, one of each color.   From these he shelled some grains and gave them to his turkey; he roasted the rest for himself.   A great number of holy ones came to his field when he had done eating.   They plucked first a single ear of white corn in the east; then, with many hands, plucked the rest of the white corn and made a pile of it in the east.   They plucked all the blue corn and made a pile of it in the south; all the yellow corn and made a pile of it in the west; all the variegated corn and made a pile of it in the north.   But there were four stalks of corn, each bearing three ears, from which they plucked nothing; they reserved these for a future ceremony.   They passed around the field again sunwise, making a pile of squashes in the southeast, a pile of beans in the southwest, a pile of watermelons in the northwest and a pile of muskmelons in the northeast.   Lastly they culled the tobacco and placed it in four piles beside the piles of corn.   While the harvesting was going on the yéi saved some of the produce for themselves.   When the crop was all gathered the Indian sang the tenth Farm Song.   He measured the heaps of produce by his turkey.   Bidding the turkey to stand close to each heap, with its tail toward the heap, and to hold its head high, he found that each heap was level with the top of the turkey's head.   The visitors looked at the turkey in wonder while the prophet sang the eleventh Farm Song.   The chiefs among the holy ones gathered around *Bïtáhatïni* and thus they spoke to him: "Your turkey has done wonderful things before us.   It must be holy.   You have said that it bears upon it the white, the blue, the yellow, and the varigated corn; that it has the squash, the bean, the watermelon, the muskmelon, and the tobacco.   Tell us where it carries the white corn?"   "That," said the prophet, "is in the end of its tail where the feathers are white."   "Where is the blue corn?" they asked.   "That is around its neck," he answered.   "Where is the yellow corn?" they inquired.   "At the end of the small feathers above its tail," was the reply.   "And where is the mixed corn?"   "That is on its wings."   Thus, in answer to their questions, he told them that squashes were on the turkey's right side, under the wings, that the bean was in its snout (erectile process), that the watermelon and the muskmelon were on the left side under the wings and the tobacco in the feathers under the tail. "What is this?" said they, pointing to the beard. "That is the thing with which my pet combs itself," said the man. "Thus is my pet turkey dressed. Tell me now how your pet turkey is dressed," he said, speaking to *Hastséhogan*. The holy one answered: "I have no pet turkey. Things that belong to the water are mine. You have a wonderful pet. It has done wonderful things in our presence. Surely it is holy." The Visionary sang the twelfth Farm Song and when he had done singing he said to the holy ones: "Return tomorrow and help me to husk my corn." They all went home. He remained in his field until sundown and then went to his hut.

737.—As soon as the Visionary got through his breakfast on the morrow, the holy ones began to arrive. They came shouting all the way from their homes to the cornfield. *Hastséyalti* and *Hastséhogan* called them together at the eastern pile. They husked this pile first and husked the others separately, in turn, afterwards, moving sunwise. They took off most of the husk, but not all; they left a few of the leaves so that two ears might be tied together and hung over a string. They worked until sunset and finished the husking. Before they departed, the Indian cried in a loud voice asking them to come back the next day and carry the harvest home. They took toll for their labor and went away. The Indian and his turkey returned to the hut.

738.—When the holy ones approached, next morning, *Hastséyalti*, *Hastséhogan* and *Tó'nenĭli* came in advance and called the others together to work. They began with the eastern heap of corn and went around the field as they had done when culling the products. They carried them to a place southeast of the field and near the hut to the east. They piled them again in separate piles in the order in which they had lain in the field. They proceeded to erect a drying frame in the middle of the piles, thus: they set up forked supports, forming a four-cornered structure whose sides faced the east, the south, the west, and the north; on these they laid four stringers, and across the stringers many poles. They hung the tobacco on the poles. They tied the ears of corn in pairs and hung them on the poles over the tobacco—the white corn in the east, the blue in the south, the yellow in the west, the mixed in the north. When this was done the Visionary invited his visitors to come again the next day and they all went to their homes.

739.—When they arrived the next day, *Bĭtáhatĭni* asked the yéi to build him a good large house, not a dwelling of clouds, mists, rainbows and lightning such as the yéi dwelt in; but a solid house of wood, weeds, and earth, such as the Navahoes build, when many work together. Such a house they built for him that day. All of the yéi did not go to their homes that night. Some remained to have a ceremony with the corn.

740.—The stalks of corn, with ears attached, which had been saved for the rites and, when needed, pulled out by the roots, were laid in a row with their tips to the east, in the order, from north to south, of white, blue, yellow and mixed corn.   All the medicines the prophet had gathered on his journey were laid around the collection of plants.   The prophet sat down to the west of the whole group.   The divine one who enacted the part of chanter then began to sing.   He sang the first songs in the evening, and in the morning he sang the last songs, which were Yikaígïn or Daylight Songs.   Between these times other gods led in singing any songs of sequence they might know, and this was continued all night. Such was the ceremony of the vigil of the corn which is practiced among the Navahoes to this day.⁴⁸   When the singing was done, a prayer was said over the corn.   *Hastséhogan* said the corn should have its breakfast, for these stalks of corn were like men, they were living and must have food.   The Visionary proposed to given them a feast consisting of corn baked in the ground.   " Give them not such food," said the House God, " that is food proper for man, but not for corn.   My little daughter here has food for the corn.   It is dried meat of four animals—deer, antelope, elk and bighorn."   At the bidding of her father, the girl ground these meats into fine powder between two stones, put them into a bowl of white shell and mixed them, with water, into a material like mush.   " Who shall feed this to the corn?" asked the Navaho.   " My son, Water Boy, and the daughter of *Hastséyalłi*, Corn Girl, are to give the food," said *Hastséhogan*.   The children put water into a bowl of turquoise, for the corn must be given water to drink as well as food to eat.   It was to be sprinkled on the corn just as it is to-day sprinkled on pictures of the corn in our ceremonies.   To the boy the black or male plumed wands were given ; to the girl, the blue or female plumed wands. Twice, acting alternately, they sprinkled the different plants, beginning with the tobacco in the east.   Then, alternately, they placed the meat pulp on the tobacco and the corn and made motions as if placing it on the other plants.   While feeding the plants, the thirteenth Farm Song was sung.   Lastly, the Visionary, from bags of cloud, took a handful of tobacco for himself and gave a handful to each one of the visitors, who each departed as soon as he had received the gift. Before the Talking God left the lodge, he said to the prophet : " In the days to come, when you treat the sick among your people do in all things as we have taught you, and when you make a ceremony over your corn, do also as we have shown you.   Never give corn to eat of its own substance.   If you give it, corn will thereafter ever eat corn until all in the land is destroyed.   Then men will starve and have to eat one another, and thus destroy their own race.   Give unto corn, flesh to eat.   For like reasons corn must be fed to the masks in the ceremonies.   Should meat be fed to them, men would, thereafter, eat men."   Once, many years ago, when this ceremony of the corn was going on, and while the young virgin was grinding the meat to feed the corn, a wicked woman named Estsán Tsói, Ugly Woman, went out from the lodge and fed corn to the corn that was hanging on the poles of the drying-frame.   That year the people starved and men ate the flesh of other men.

741.—Before the visitors left, they said nothing to the Visionary about his ever leaving the farm, about returning to the home of his people or to his friends at Tse'gíhi.   Perhaps they expected him to stay and raise another crop.   Perhaps they wished to return, gamble with him and win his corn.   Even those who were his companions on the journey from Tse'gíhi to *Sĭlnéole* left without speaking of his departure.   But he had thought of going away, although he often said to himself : " I have here a great store of corn and other food which I am loth to leave." After he had remained four days and four nights at his hut, seeing no one but his turkey, he began to grow lonely.   In the meantime his friends at Tse'gíhi wondered where he was and what had become of him, until the sun sent down a sunbeam as a messenger to tell them that he was living near *Tó'nihilin* and had a farm there.   When they heard this, they dispatched *Hastséltsi*, the Red Yéi, to find their grandchild.

742.—On the morning after the fourth night of solitude, when the sun was about half-way between the horizon and the zenith, Bĭ*táhatĭni* and his turkey were sitting at the door of the lodge and looking east, when they heard afar the voice of Red Yéi sounding somewhat like the voice of a wolf, " Woo-oo-oo."   The call was repeated at short intervals four times, seeming louder and nearer each time. After the fourth call, *Hastséltsi* stood before them and greeted them thus : " *Haláhotsa* !   What are you doing here ?   I thought you had gone home long ago."   The prophet answered : " When I left the Whirling Waters I had it in my mind to start for home at once ; but I saw here a good place to make a farm, my pet had the seeds, and, with the help of the holy ones, I have raised and harvested a large store of food which I like not to leave, though I long to go home." The yéi said he wished to see the store of food, and the Navaho showed it to him.   " If it is your wish to stay with your corn, I shall return to Tse'gíhi and tell your grandfather, *Hastséyalti*.   Perhaps he will come to give you aid."

743.—When *Hastséltsi* got back to Tse'gíhi he told his adventures to *Hastséyalti*, told him about the farm, and about the great store of corn which the prophet was loth to leave.   " Where did he get the seed for his farm ? " said the Talking God, although he well knew all about the seed when he asked the question.   " He got it from his pet," said Red Yéi.   " Truly," said *Hastséyalti*, " he is the one who had it."   *Hastséltsi* continued : " Although he has a great store of food which he likes not to abandon, he is lonely on his farm and would be glad to have his grandfathers come to see him."   By grandfathers he meant particularly *Hastséyalti* and *Tó'nenĭli*.   Addressing these two, *Hastséhogan* said : " Go you, to-morrow, at daylight, to your grandson's farm ; take with you such things as you need to help him, and bring him back to Tse'ya*hódĭlyĭl*."   They procured different kinds of clouds and rainbows wherewith to make bundles of the corn and a short rainbow on which to travel.

744.—Next morning early they got on the short rainbow.   The House God blew on the bow in the direction of *Tó'nihilin* ; the two divine ones started on their journey, and in time arrived at the house of the Visionary.   The latter heard the approaching calls and went out to meet the gods.   The holy ones spoke not; but spread the white cloud on the ground, and made motion to the Indian to put his white corn and pumpkins on it.   He obeyed.   Thus, in turn, at their bidding, he put the blue corn and the beans on the blue cloud, the yellow corn and the watermelons on the yellow cloud, the mixed corn and the muskmelons on the black cloud.   When he had done this, they, by signs, bade him turn his back for a moment.   When he looked around again he saw that all had been made into four small bundles, each of which might easily be grasped by two hands. *Hastséyalti* took a bundle in each hand — the yellow and the black.   *Bitáhatini* took the white and blue bundles and carried his turkey under his arm.   *Tó‘nenïli* carried nothing; he kept his arms free so that he might wave them, and by this motion keep the rainbow moving.   *Hastséyalti* got on in front, the Indian in the middle, *Tó‘nenïli* behind, and thus they started back to Tse‘yahódïlyïl.

745.—A cloud moved with the rainbow all the way as they traveled.   When they got close to the prophet's old home, the cloud enveloped the rainbow so closely that the travelers could not be seen when at last they descended to the ground.   They landed on a level rock; opened the bundles in their proper order; threw out the white corn to the east, the blue corn to the south, the yellow corn to the west, the mixed corn to the north, and the other products at points between the piles of corn.   They laid these things on the rock, but not the cloudy wrappings, which they kept to take away with them.   Addressing the Indian, the holy ones said: "You have brought home with you good white corn, good blue corn" (and so on, mentioning all the products of the field).   "You have brought back good pollen, good clouds, good black mist, good lightning, good rainbows, good he-rain and good she-rain.   You have brought the medicines of the holy ones, their pictures, rites and Songs of the Farm.   Such are the good things you have brought back with you.   You know now all the mysteries of the *dïgíni*. There is nothing more for you to seek among them.   It is well for you that Sun Bearer sent a messenger to tell us, where you tarried, or you would have worked and planted next year for the holy ones of *Sïlnéole*.   They would have gambled with you and won everything.   You would have been a slave to them.   Hold in your memory the pictures, rites, and songs they gave you and teach them to others. In the years to come they will benefit your people and your people will thank you."   The house lay to the west of where they stood.   The yéi bade him turn his back toward them.   As he did so he heard a sound like "click."   When, in an instant, he looked around again, the yéi had vanished.   Bidding his turkey to remain where it was for a little while and then to follow him, he started for his home.

746.—When he entered the hut where his relatives dwelt, he found there his grandmother, his youngest brother and his niece.   They rejoiced to see him. "Greeting, my grandson!   Greeting, my elder brother!   Greeting, my uncle!" they said.   After they had welcomed him they asked; "Where is your turkey?" "I left him behind me, down the river," he answered.   They said: "That is what we feared you would do.   We begged you not to take him with you.   He brought us the he-rain and the she-rain, the cloud and the mist. What shall we do without him?" Just as this was said a loud gobble was heard outside the door and a moment later the turkey ran into the lodge. It ran around the fire and came up to each person in turn as if glad to meet again. They all laughed. The old woman said: " My grandson has been joking with us." The youngest son stepped outside, cried aloud that his brother had returned, and all within sound of his voice came running to the hut. There was great excitement, and many words of greeting and shaking of the hand. When all had become quieted, they sat down and the wanderer proceeded to tell of his adventures. He related to his people all that had happened to him while he was gone, and then he said: " I went to see pictures, to obtain medicines, to learn mysteries, to hear songs. I bring back with me all that I have seen and heard. It will benefit you, my younger brother, and it will benefit our people." " We thank you for bringing us all this knowledge," said the brethren. " In the days to come, those that follow us will do as you teach us." He bade them divide the vegetables among them and reserve some for seed. It is from these seeds that our seeds come to-day. Our people had no corn or pumpkins before the days of Bïtáhatíni. The meal he carried with him on his journey was supplied by the holy ones of Tse'gíhi. " Build now a lodge," he said, " in order that I may teach my youngest brother all that I have learned." By this time many people had gathered—so many that when each one brought a single stick for the lodge, they found they had enough, and the lodge was finished that day. The prophet and his youngest brother entered it, and a crowd gathered around. He told them all the things they must get for the kethawns and other properties of the rite, and he assigned to each a different task.

747.—On the next day, in the part of the lodge opposite the door, two metates or grinding stones were placed, one to the north and one to the south, in such a manner that two persons could grind corn on them while facing one another; and troughs edged with flat stones were made to hold meal. A screen of interwoven willows was erected to hide the grinders from observation. It was painted white and decorated with pictures of corn, clouds, rainbows, and lightning. It had, in the center, four square holes, through which bluebirds and other little birds of beautiful plumage appeared. On top of the screen, and suspended above it on strings, were more little birds. These were stuffed bird-skins, in the rites performed by the Indians—they could do no better; but in the houses of the yéi, where the Visionary first saw such rites, there were real birds. Those above the screen perched on strings of rainbow; while those at the holes in the screen passed back and forth singing. When all was ready in the lodge, Bïtáhatíni went outside. The rain was falling and the moisture was so thick and close to the ground that he could not see far. Yet the prophet beheld Hastséyalti with his young son, and Hastsézïni with his young daughter, approaching. They wore their masks, for only when wearing them do the gods make themselves visible to men. Hastséyalti, the Talking God said: " My son and the daughter

of *H*astsé*z*ĭni will prepare the medicines for you, for they are virginal."
*H*astsé*z*ĭni, the Black God, said : " I have medicines which I wish prepared for
me, after the other medicines are made. Here is a corn-plant that was stolen by
a crow ; here is white medicine ; here are cakes which we call nanĕská*d*i, with
holes in them and toasted on coals ; here is meal from sacred pictures, and here
is my talisman. Take these." All went into the lodge. Two sacred buckskins,
one north and one south, their heads near together, were stretched on the floor
between the grinding-stones and the screens ; and the medicines were laid on the
skins. The boy went to one of the metates ; knelt on his right knee ; took the
tsasd*z*ĭ'ni or small upper stone in his right hand ; lowered and raised it three times
before laying on the tsasd*z*é or nether stone. The girl, facing him, performed
similar acts at the other metate. The boy took medicine from the buckskin
beside him ; lowered and raised it three times ; when he lowered it for the fourth
time he laid it on the nether stone. The girl followed his example. Each
grasped one of the upper stones with both hands, ready to go to work at the
beginning of song. The youngest brother of the prophet, Nakĭĕst*s*áhi, was now
seated at the basket-drum, behind the screen with the children. All other occupants of the lodge were before the screen. The singers sang the first Metate
Song. The moment they began to sing, the children began to grind and the
youngest brother to beat the drum. So they continued until four songs, that
sounded well (harmonized) with the noise of the stones, were sung. The prophet
gave to each of the grinders a brush made of grass and a single owl feather,—the
kind of brush with which we now sweep off stones,—and he sang the fifth Metate
Song. While he was singing this, each grinder took up a handful of the powder
and swept it slowly off his palm into the trough until all was swept away. While
the sixth song was being sung the powder was all swept up and laid on the buckskins. The seventh Metate Song was sung. The prophet bade the girl grind her
father's medicines, and grind them quickly. The boy did not help in this work.
When she had finished, she put the powder on a fawn-skin belonging to her father
and gave it all back to him. The medicine was distributed, most of those in the
lodge got some ; but those who did not, received, instead, incense powder, yá*d*id'ĭni*l*.

748.—" Do not leave," said the prophet, " until we have taken up the screen
and carried away the sand on which the picture was painted." When this was
done he asked them to wait until he sang two more songs ; they waited and he
sang. All were going away happy. They pronounced many benedictions on one
another—the visitors on their host ; the host on the visitors. They sang two
Farewell Songs, Bĭ*th*áos*t*esĭn. Lastly the prophet said for all a prayer called
*H*o*z*ódze Só*d*isĭn, and the visitors departed.

*S*O, A VARIANT OF "THE VISIONARY."

749.—A family of eight persons lived at a place called Klé*h*a*l*t*s*i, Red Clay
Valley, near the San Juan Mountains. There were the father, the mother, five
sons and one daughter.

750.—One of the sons, next to the youngest, whose name was *So*, believed greatly in dreams and visions. From time to time he would wander away from home by himself, and when he returned he would relate various wonderful visions he had seen, and often when he woke in the morning he would tell of wonderful dreams, but his brothers only laughed at him.

751.—One day the four other brothers went hunting. They went to a spring near which they had erected a blind or breastwork of branches, from which they were accustomed to shoot deer that came to the spring to drink. They were but a short time behind the blind when they killed two young deer—a male and a female. They took the carcasses to one side to dress them. They cut the meat into thin sheets and spread it out on the branches of trees to dry. After they finished this work they went back to the blind to watch for more game. While sitting there, they looked at the tree where their meat was hanging, and they saw a crow and a magpie eating of the meat. They left the blind, crept up carefully behind the birds, killed them with their arrows and threw them away at a little distance from the tree. They had built a shelter and prepared a camp not far from the spring, and when they had killed the birds they went to this camp and hunted no more during the day.

752.—Next morning while they were sitting by the fire they beheld their brother, *So*, whom they had left at home, approaching. When he came he said to his brothers: "What have you killed?" They knew he pretended to second sight, so they winked at one another, laughed and made fun, and one said: "We have killed nothing." He asked his question four times, but they gave him only the same answer. Then he said to them: "I heard something as I came by the cañon of Agáʒalai. While I was walking along on the further edge of the cañon, I stopped to take off one of my moccasins, for some gravel had gotten into it. Then I heard a voice crying from the east across the cañon, 'Someone was killed yesterday, they say.' Immediately I heard a voice in the west crying, 'Who was killed, they say?' The voice in the east answered, 'He-who-sits-between-the-horns-dead and He-who-picks-on-the-backbone-dead.' [49] At last the voice in the west said, 'It is well. They ought to be killed. Wherever they see red meat they go thither.' I looked to the east to see who was speaking and I beheld an eagle; I looked to the west and I beheld a crow." When he had done speaking, his brethren told him that they had killed a crow, a magpie and two deer, and they said: "We believe now you have always spoken the truth, for only the spirits could have told you this."

753.—They determined to return home. They tied the dried venison up in four bundles and each of four hunters took a bundle to carry, but there was no bundle for *So*. They started, but he loitered behind and did not set forth until his brothers were gone. He set out by another trail for the same destination; but when he came to the edge of a cañon, he saw four fresh tracks of bighorn. He followed the tracks and soon came to a place where the sheep had gone down a very steep shelving rock. He took off his deerskin robe which had hair on it, folded it, sat on it and slid down the cañon wall.   He followed the tracks along the floor of the cañon for awhile and soon came to a place where the trail led up the opposite wall.

754.—When he climbed the opposite wall of the cañon he saw, near its edge, four bighorn or Rocky Mountain sheep walking quietly along.   He left their trail, ran by a circuitous route to head them off, hid behind a juniper tree near the path by which they were advancing, and when they came close to him he drew his arrow; but when he released it, it refused to leave the string; it remained and the sheep passed on uninjured.   Again he ran to head them off. This time he hid behind a piñon tree and when the sheep approached he again bent his bow; but again the arrow would not leave the string.   A third time he ran ahead of the sheep and hid behind a mountain mahogany bush; but for the third time the arrow failed to leave the bow and the sheep passed on.   A fourth time he ran ahead and hid behind a cliff rose, but all happened again as on the previous occasion.   A fifth time he ran ahead and hid behind another juniper to wait for the sheep; but, as they drew near, he felt himself becoming stiff and powerless; he was under a spell.   As he gazed he saw the skins of the mountain sheep drop from the approaching forms, revealing the figures of four Gánaskïdi, or humpbacked gods, such as we see them now in the rites of the night chant.   The Gánaskïdi seized the Navaho, disrobed him, laid down his clothes and proceeded to dress him in the skin of a mountain sheep.   "It is too tight, I cannot wear it," he said.   They bade him turn around in the direction in which the sun goes; he did so; the Gánaskïdi breathed on him as he turned, and when he had completed the circuit he found that the skin fitted him easily.   Then they took him in the direction of the cañon of Tse'gíhi beyond the San Juan River.

755.—As they were traveling on a beaten trail, the prophet walking in advance of his companions, he suddenly disappeared from their sight.   They looked for him in all directions but could not find him.   Then one of them sought the aid of Hastséyalti and the latter came bringing with him his talking kethawn [50] and his six magic strings.   The strings were of different colors, and each was wound loosely in a separate ball.   He took first the white string and, holding one end of it, threw it to the east; it flew with the speed of lightning to the far east; but returned to his hand as rapidly as it went and he knew from this that what he sought was not in the east.   In like manner he threw his blue string to the south, his yellow string to the west and his black string to the north; but each, in turn, came back instantly to his hand.   Then he took his spotted string and threw it downwards; the end of it stuck and did not return.   "Does anyone live down there?" he asked the Gánaskïdi.   "Yes, down there is the dwelling of the Nï'ltsiye, Wind Gods," they said.   They examined the ground and soon found a hole through which they all descended to the dwelling of the Wind Gods and there they found So.   They spoke to him and begged him to come with them; but he did not listen to them, he had lost his reason, the Wind Gods had cast a spell upon him and taken his mind away from him. *Hastséyalti*, holding in his hand his talking kethawn, walked once, sunwise, around *So* and by this motion restored to him his mind. He listened now to the voices of his friends, and they all came forth and proceeded on their journey to Tse'gíhi.

756.— The four elder brothers, when they left the camp where they had killed the deer, went home. At the end of four days, as *So* did not return they began to wonder where he was and to feel concerned. They had a long talk about him and at length concluded to go back to the place where they had last seen him and trail him from there. They tracked him to where he slid down the rock, to where he went along the floor of the cañon, to where he clambered up the opposite wall and to the place where he left the trail of the sheep and ran to head them off ; they saw, too, where he had waited behind the juniper for the game to pass. They traced him to all his halting places till they found at last where he had encountered these strange people and there they found his clothes lying on the ground. Heretofore they had followed the tracks of four sheep and one man, but further on they saw the tracks of five sheep and no human footprint. Of these they saw tracks to show that only four steps had been taken, and beyond these no trail of any kind could be seen. They could only suppose that *So* had been changed by the spirits into a sheep and they said : " Alas ! our brother has often told us about his visions of the spirits and now we see that they have changed him into a bighorn and taken him away from us. How can we tell whither he has gone ? We should not have left him behind us. He is lost. Now we have naught to do but to return to our people and take his clothes with us." And they prayed to the spirits who took their brother, that they might, some day, restore him again to his home.

757.—When *So* and the Gánaskïdi arrived at the edge of the cañon at Tse'gíhi they stopped. He looked down into the cañon and saw at the bottom two *Hastséyalti* surrounded by a number of other yéi, a vast crowd of them. While he stood there a thunderbolt fell close beside him, but did no injury to him or his companions. There was a spring of water where they stood and beside that spring they waited until one of the *Hastséyalti*, seeing them from below, came up to meet them and led them down the wall of the cañon. As they advanced, the yéi picked up the sticks and stones that obstructed the path, so that they descended with ease to the bottom until they stood among the throng of yéi. These were gathered for the performance of a great ceremony of nine days duration and this was the last day of the rites ; hence the great crowd.

758.—The yéi led him and his four companions into a great medicine-lodge which was not like the Navaho medicine-lodge of to-day. It was in a great cavern in a cliff and there were four compartments in it. They led them through three of these rooms into a fourth and when they had entered this a yéi stood at the door to keep intruders out. *So* now looked around him. He saw hanging horizontally along the eastern wall of the room a long pole, painted white, from which twelve white masks were suspended ; on the southern wall he saw a pole painted blue, from which twelve blue masks hung; on the western wall he saw a pole painted yellow, from which twelve yellow masks hung, and on the northern wall he saw a black pole, from which twelve black masks hung. He found a great number of people were already in the lodge; among them was Nayénězgạni. One of the four Gánaskĭdi addressed the assembly, saying: "See! we have brought with us an Indian." To this Nayénězgạni said: "You should not have brought him. The Indians are a bad people. We do not want them among us," and he pointed to a place away from the center of the lodge, where he bade them sit down. Then a noise like thunder was heard and Nayénězgạni bade one of the yéi to look out and see what caused the noise. When the yéi returned he said he saw a great multitude descending the wall of the cañon in the direction from which their five visitors had come and that they seemed to be more of the same people. Again the noise of thunder was heard and again Nayénězgạni sent out one of the yéi to look. When this messenger returned he said: "It is Klĭ'stso, the Great Serpent, who approaches." A moment after Klĭ'stso entered the lodge, and crawled around it four times. The first time he crawled on the toes of the surrounding visitors; the second time on their knees; the third time on their chests; the fourth time on their mouths; then he sat down on the floor and said: "Why have you not invited me to this ceremony? This is the way you always treat me. When you have a merry time you never let me know about it." Nayénězgạni was the boholní' or master of this ceremony and he said, when the snake was done talking: "We will give you a smoke. So make no more complaints," and he handed him the pipe to smoke.

759.—Again they heard a peal of thunder on the brow of the cañon and Nayénězgạni sent out Hastséyalti to see who was coming. When the messenger returned he related that twelve birds called tsĭdĭltói were coming. Soon they entered the lodge and Nayénězgạni offered them the pipe. When they were done smoking he told them to be gone. These twelve birds came from a mountain which is east of Bear Spring.

760.—About this time Coyote had come into the lodge unobserved and they had passed the pipe to him, not noticing who he was. He had run in behind the ring of people next to the wall. At length his presence was discovered and Nayénězgạni sent Hastsézĭni to drive the intruder out. Four times did Coyote thus sneak in and four times was he driven out. When he was being expelled for the last time, Nayénězgạni said to him: "I want you to stay out. You have no right here and no interest in our ceremonies. You must not return again."

761.—About this time Nayénězgạni observed that there were other uninvited intruders in the lodge and he drove everyone out so that the following only remained: Nayénězgạni, To‘badzĭstsíni, Léyaneyani, Tsówenatlehi (these four were brothers), Hastséyalti, Hastséhogan (these two were nephews), Dsahadoldzá, Gánaskĭdi, Klĭ'stso, Hastsézĭni, four Atsá‘lei, Naěstsán, Yádĭlyĭl, Tsó‘hanoai, Kléhanoai, the four Wind Gods (Nĭ'ltsi-dĭlyĭl, Nĭ'ltsi-dotlĭ'z, Nĭ'ltsi-litsó, Nĭ'ltsi-lakaí) and Tó‘nenĭli.[51]

762.—When all the intruders were gone Nayénĕzgạni went to a corner where there was a pile covered with a blanket of darkness. He removed the blanket and revealed a heap of twelve human skulls ornamented with turquoise earrings. He spread a blanket of white daylight on the floor; on this he laid the skulls (in a row), four large bundles of powdered medicine, and four small bundles of powdered medicine, making eight in all. He untied all these bundles; they contained the medicines of the ănḷíhi—the fatal medicines which the Navaho witches use when they slay their enemies. They are made from the flesh of dead men, taken from different parts of their bodies, dried and ground to a fine powder. When the dreadful bags were opened Nayénĕzgạni said: "Let all of you keep your places sitting in a row." He took a little of the medicine out of each bag, as much as he could grasp with the tips of the fingers of one hand, and gave to each person present. The big snake was the last to whom he gave the drugs. All the others tied up the medicine in little bags or in the corners of their robes or shirts. But the snake was perfectly naked and could find no place to put the medicine for safe keeping but in his mouth, so he put it there and that is why the mouth of the serpent deals a deadly poison now.

763.—Next, four sheets of sky were brought forth. A white sheet was spread on the floor in the east; a blue sheet in the south; a yellow sheet in the west and a dark sheet in the north. On each of these sheets was painted a picture, which the Navaho was told to study with care, and remember. When he had done, they rolled up again the sheets of sky and Nayénĕzgạni said: "Such pictures you must teach your people to draw. They cannot do this on sheets of sky as we do; but they can grind to powder stones of various colors and draw their pictures on sand."

764.—"Now," said Nayénĕzgạni, "let us go out and dance, for all is ready outside for us to begin." And they went forth to where there was built a great circle of branches, such as we make now in the rites of the mountain chant,[12] except that instead of one opening, as we have now, there were four openings in the circle. This was because, there in the land of the yéi, the dancers did not go in and out at the same gate, as ours do; but when a party entered from the east, having danced, it passed out at the west, and when a party entered from the south, it passed out at the north. Basket-drums had been laid out for the musicians to play on. The yéi took So along with them in order that he might learn the dance.

765.—Soon after they entered the circle two persons came in from the east, Hastséyalḷi and Hastsébaka; the former bore a bag of corn-meal and the latter a great stalk of corn having twelve ears. Hastséyalḷi strewed corn-meal to the four cardinal points — to the east, to the south, to the west, to the north, whooping at each act his usual call. As he scattered the meal, Hastsébaka followed his motions by waving the cornstalk to each of the four points. Then Hastséyalḷi, his hand extended to the west, held aloft a pinch of corn-meal and let it fall into a hole already dug in the ground. Where the meal fell Hastsébaka planted the stalk of corn and they filled the earth in around it. When this was done the four Atsa'ḷei entered.   They made such motions as our dancers make at this day with their rattles, sweeping them downward to the west and to the east, and whooping their call at each motion (par. 615).   They stood, as usual, with their faces to the west to begin to sing.   They opened their mouths and endeavored to sing, but no sound issued — they had lost their voices.   The leader made, with his rattle, the usual sign for them to stop, and they stood still.   Nayénĕzgạni then said : " This must be the spell of the Coyote.   It is he who has taken away the voices of the singers, in revenge for being turned out of the lodge."   He sent *H*ast*s*éyal*t*i to summon the Coyote who waited outside the corral ; but the messenger returned saying that Coyote refused to come.   Nayénĕzgạni sent *H*ast*s*éyal*t*i out a second, a third and a fourth time with peaceful words to the Coyote, begging him to enter the corral, but still the Coyote would not come.   When he refused for the fourth time Nayénĕzgạni became angry and said : " Go forth and drag him in whether he wishes to come or not.   When we wanted him not in the medicine-lodge, he entered unbidden, now when we desire his presence in the dark circle he will not come."   Now the youngest brother of Nayénĕzgạni, named Tsówenatlehi, seeing that his eldest brother was wroth said : " It will avail nothing to be angry with Coyote ; wrathy words and loud commands will not influence him ; offer him some gift for his services and then perhaps he may enter and help you."   Na-yénĕzgạni said : " It is well.   Let us do as you say.   We will make him god of the darkness, of the daylight, of the he-rain, of the she-rain, of the corn, of all vegeta-tion, of the thunder and of the rainbow," and he sent *H*ast*s*éyal*t*i out to repeat these promises to the Coyote.   " It is well," said Coyote, when *H*ast*s*éyal*t*i had spoken, " though I fear the people in the dark circle may laugh at me when I enter and pray to my god to have the voices of the singers restored."   He entered the circle, went up to the east of the great cornstalk, stood facing it on his hind legs, raised his fore legs as high as possible and let forth a long coyote yelp.   These acts he repeated at the south, at the west and at the north ; but at the north he followed the long yelp by several short ones.   When he was done he went to one side and sat down ; the singers tried again to sing and found their voices restored to them, strong and sweet.   When the four dancers, with *H*ast*s*éyal*t*i the Yébĭt*s*ai, making five in all, had finished they went out at the opening in the west of the circle.

766.—The next set of dancers came in at the south.   They were fourteen in number—*H*ast*s*éyal*t*i, *T*ó'nenĭli, and twelve ordinary dancers such as we have now in the dance of the naak*h*aí.   Different parties of such dancers kept coming and going alternately by the east and the south entrances.   *S*o sat and watched all this time.   When it came about the hour of midnight he was growing hungry. Many of the divine ones offered him food, and he was inclined to accept it, but there was a dark cloud at his left ear ; in it was the spirit of darkness which whispered to him : " Eat only when the Yébĭt*s*ai gives it to you," and at his right ear was the dark wind of the north, which whispered : " If you take the food you will never see your people again."   These spirits knew the thoughts of all the assembly, and even before one had spoken he revealed the thought to *So*, and prompted the answer. So he fasted and waited until after midnight, when he went to the Yébĭtsai and said : " Sĭtsaí, my grandfather, I am hungry. Will you give me something to eat ? " Yébĭtsai wore around his waist a white sash ; this he removed, laid on the ground and spread open, when there appeared among its folds a beautiful white water bottle that looked like white stone, a bag of corn-meal, and a very small cup made of white sea-shell. The Yébĭtsai mixed in the cup a little of the corn-meal with a little of the liquid from the bottle, making a cold paste or mush which he gave to *So* to eat, and *So* ate from it with two fingers as is the custom with the Navahoes. He ate and ate till he was filled full and could eat no more ; but much as he ate he never reduced the contents of the cup in the least. When he was done he handed the cup back to the Yébĭtsai who emptied it with one sweep of his two fingers and gave the morsel to the Navaho. The cup remained empty, and the Yébĭtsai folded up again in his sash the vessels and the bag of meal.

767.—Now Yébĭtsai went along with the dancers and paid no further attention to *So* for a while ; but when the dance was all done, and day began to dawn and the crowd began to disperse he came to where the Navaho had been sitting, to look for him ; but the Navaho was not there. The Yébĭtsai sought for him in all directions, four times through the crowd, and inquired of many if they had seen him ; but could find no trace or tidings of him. The Yébĭtsai brought forth his magic strings of different colors. He took his white string, and holding one end of it, threw the rest to the east ; it fled with the speed of lightning to the far east, but returned to his hand as rapidly as it went, and he knew from this that the missing Indian was not in the east. In like manner he threw his blue string to the south, his yellow string to the west, his black string to the north, and his spotted string to the nether world, but all returned instantly to his hand. Then he took his second blue string and threw it towards the zenith ; there the end stuck and did not return to him. From this he knew that *So* had been taken into the heavens, and he said : " Up there is my grandchild. I will follow him." *H*astséyal*t*i, the Yébĭtsai, was a holy one of great power. He took two sunbeams and laid them side by side so as to form a raft or platform ; on these he floated up to the heavens, and up through the hole in the sky, which is right above the summit of Tsótsĭ*l*. Arrived on top of the sky he found the track of *So* and of the god *H*astséayuhi who had stolen him. The tracks led to the south, and following them he soon came in sight of four rows of blue houses, toward which he now saw *H*astséayuhi hastening with the captive. He quickened his pace and soon overtook the fugitives. He seized *So*, took him away from the captor and back to the sky-hole over Tsótsĭ*l*. " Now *S*ĭtsówe, my grandchild, we are going down again," he said. They stood on the sunbeam raft and floated back to the summit of Tsótsĭ*l*.

768.—From the summit of Tsótsĭ*l* they traveled through the air on white sunbeams till they came near to the place where dwelt the kindred of *So*, and here they descended to the earth. *H*ast*s*éyal*t*i said then to the Navaho : " Now my grandchild, you can travel faster than ever you did before ; but I do not wish you to go home to-day. You must travel a little way and sleep on your road to-night ; early to-morrow you will reach the lodges of your people. You must tell them that my voice is ominous, and that if one hears it something strange will happen to him or his people the same day. When I travel among the Navahoes I shall wear the skins of *d*óli as signs that I am *H*ast*s*éyal*t*i." As *H*ast*s*éyal*t*i spoke to *S*o they stood side by side. When the former ceased to speak, the Navaho looked around to where he had stood, but the god had vanished. *S*o looked up ; he beheld in the east great white clouds ; in the south, great blue clouds ; in the west, great yellow clouds ; and in the north, great black clouds. He said : " I wonder whither my grandfather has returned ? Has he gone to the white clouds ? Has he gone to the blue clouds ? Has he gone to the yellow clouds ? Has he gone to the dark clouds ? " Then he began to weep and said : " Good-bye, Grandfather, I wonder whither you have gone."

769.—From the place where *H*ast*s*éyal*t*i left him, *S*o went but a little way when he came to a cañon into which he descended and constructed on the bottom a small circle or corral of brushwood with an opening to the east. As he sat there all alone after dark, he beheld approaching him from the east a figure dressed in white. It had white shirt, leggings and moccasins, a white head-dress trimmed with owl-feathers and great staring yellow eyes. It was Naĕst*s*á, the Owl. He now entered the enclosure, passed by way of the southeast to the south and there sat down. After sitting awhile in silence Owl said to the Indian : " Whence come you, and where is your home ? " and *S*o answered : " I am just wandering around in these parts. I have no home." Naĕst*s*á asked these questions four times, but got always the same answer. At length the Owl said : " Twelve days ago some of the yéi took a Navaho with them to Tse'gíhi, and I think you are the man. Is it not so ? " And *S*o answered that he was indeed the man. Then Owl asked : " What did you learn there ? " and *S*o told him of the dances he had witnessed, of the pictures he had seen, of the songs he had heard sung, and the prayers he had heard prayed. " How many songs have you learned to sing, how many prayers have you learned to repeat, and how many kethawns have you learned to prepare ? " *S*o related all that he had learned. " Was that all they taught you ? " said Owl, and *S*o answered : " Yes, that was all they taught me." " It is well," said Owl, " but there are other things to be done ; they have not taught you all ; this is because even the Yébĭt*s*ai, themselves, are afraid to reveal these things. There are six more kethawns, they are those of *t*ihi*d*iaí, ayá*s*bĭtsos, t*s*ĭdi*s*á*s*i, t*s*ĭdĭ*l*tsói, t*s*ĭdibé*z*i and ko*nd*i*d*itlít, and that is all. The Owl explained to the Navaho how all these things were made, and the two remained together until the day began to dawn, when Owl departed.

770.—From this camp the Navaho went directly to the lodge of his people, and these said to him when he returned : " Greeting, our child. Greeting, our brother," and they embraced him and wept over him. They said: "You have often told us of your converse with the spirits, but we only laughed at you. Now we know that you spoke the truth, for you have been taken away by them and have been with them many days." Then his mother said: "My child, stay here and leave us no more." His father said: "Yes, my son, your mother's words are good, listen to her and leave us no more." His elder brothers said: "Yes, younger brother, we have been sad while you were gone. Leave us no more." His sister said: "Older brother, you have been long gone, we have wondered where you were. Do not leave us again. Remain forever with your people." From that time they watched him closely and anxiously. He did not go out of their sight for twelve days and twelve nights.

771.—At the end of this time he said he felt lonely, that he would like to take a little walk. He went out, taking his bow and arrows, and saying he was going to hunt deer. About noon, as he wandered on, a Nĭ′ltsiye appeared to him and said: "You have many more things to learn, and the gods desire to teach them to you. You must learn where the different gods live in Tse‘gíhi, and you must come to these again. Then he took So off with him to Tse‘gíhi, to the same part that he had visited before. But on his first visit he did not observe what he observed now, that there were four pueblos or rows of pueblo dwellings; in the east was Kĭnɫakaí, or the White House; in the south was Kĭndoɫĭ′z, or the Blue House; in the west was Kĭnɫĭtsó, or the Yellow House; in the north was Kĭndĭɫyĭ′l, or the Dark House. The chief of the White House was Naklétso, or Big Wolf; the chief of the Blue House was Maídoɫlĭz, or the Kit-fox; the chief of the Yellow House was Naɫuĭ′tso, or the Puma; and the chief of the Dark House was Klĭ′stso, or the Big Serpent. Poles of corresponding colors hung on the walls of the houses inside. The rooms were small, but whenever the inmates wanted to have one larger they had only to puff a breath at each of the four walls and the room expanded to the desired size.

772.—They took So into the White House and into the room in which Hastséyalti lived. Hastséyalti said to him: "My grandchild, when you were here before did you observe all these pueblos that you see now?" and So answered: "No, my grandfather, and I did not see many things which I now behold." Hastséyalti continued: "Sĭtsówe, my grandchild, when you were here before we sent four akánĭnĭli, messengers, to summon the holy ones from all parts of the land. We sent one to Tsĭ′snadzĭni, one to Tsótsĭl, one to Dokoslíd, and one to Depĕ′ntsa[2]; to the chief of each one of these mountains we sent a messenger. Did you find out all this when you were here before?" So replied: "No, I was so busy watching the motions of the Yébĭtsai and of Tó‘nenĭli that I did not see what other things were done." The yéi said: "It was thus we sent out our messengers. But there are many more things for you to learn. We have much to explain to you. You must stay here with us; you must not return soon to your people. There is a trail going up on the east side of the cañon and there, at the brow of the cliff, is a place called Tsásidasakad, Standing Yucca; there is another trail going up to the south of here, and beside it, at the brow of the cliff, there is a place called Tsósaka*d*, Standing Spruce Tree.   To the west of us a trail ascends the cañon wall, and beside it is Tsĕ'ni*h*ogan, the Cave House where you entered the cañon.   To the north a trail ascends, and near it, at the edge of the cliff, is Tse‘es*t*ágisaka*d*, Standing Mountain Mahogany.   Now I will show you where all our neighbors dwell.   Let us first follow the trail to the east, by the way of Tsási*d*asaka*d*."

773.—Then these two, *H*astséyal*t*i and *S*o, by themselves, went upon the eastern trail, and they traveled on to the east until they came to the mountain of Tsïsnad*z*ï'ni, where they entered a house of four rooms made of sheets of white daylight.   Here the prophet was shown two kinds of kethawns, [52] by the god of the mountain, Tse‘gá*d*ini*t*ïni A*s*iké, Rock Crystal Boy, and the god said to him : " I am the god of the insane.   When you wish to restore to reason a person who has lost his mind, you will make such kethawns as I have shown you, and you will bury them in the ground with their points directed to this mountain, as a sacrifice to me for a cure."   From Tsïsnad*z*ï'ni, *S*o and his conductor went to Tsótsï*l*, where they entered a house of four rooms made of blue sky.   Here he was shown another pair of kethawns like those seen at Tsïsnad*z*ï'ni, except that they were painted blue. The god of the mountain said to him : " These also are for the cure of the insane, they must be buried in the ground with their tips directed toward Tsótsï*l*, as a sacrifice to me for a cure."   From Tsótsï*l* *H*astséyal*t*i and *S*o went to *D*okoslí*d*, where they entered a house made of the yellow evening light.   Here dwelt Na*t*á*l*kai A*s*iké, White Corn Boy, and Na*t*á*l*tsoi A*t*é*t*, Yellow Corn Girl.   They exhibited to *S*o two kethawns similar to those he had seen at Tsïsnad*z*ï'ni, except that they were painted differently ; the male kethawn was white, and the female yellow.   They said that these kethawns also had influence over the mind, were to cure insanity, and should be buried in the ground with their tips pointed toward *D*okoslí*d*, or the west, to gain the favor of these gods.   From this place *H*astséyal*t*i took the Navaho to *D*epĕ'ntsa, and into a house made of darkness, where they found *Th*ad*i*tí A*s*iké, Pollen Boy, and Anï*l*táni A*t*é*t*, Grasshopper Girl.   These showed the Navaho two kethawns which were like those he had seen before, except that they were painted black, and they said : " These also are to cure insanity.   Bury them in the ground with their tips to the north, towards these mountains, if you would invoke our aid.   Then the yéi and the Navaho went back to Tse‘gíhi, to the home of the Yébïtsai, and here *H*astséyal*t*i said : " There are still more yéi for you to know, and in time I will show you them all."

774.—They next took the trail which led out of the cañon to the south, by way of Tsósaka*d*.   This time the Indian had six companions on his journey ; there were *H*astséyal*t*i, who was always the spokesman and always walked in advance, *H*astsé*h*ogan, *H*astsébaka, *H*astsébaa*d*, *T*ó‘nenïli, and *H*astsé*z*ïni the fire god who always bore fire — a burning wand of shredded cedar bark.   When they had climbed out of the cañon, they went first to a place called Natséskï*t* where they entered a white house made of cedar wood, inhabited by Coyotes who made masks. *Hastséyalti* told the Coyotes that he had with him an Indian, a dweller on the earth, and the Coyotes answered, "Dzódaakola. It is well." *Hastséyalti* said to his party : "We must continue on our journey," and they went on to a place called *Degózitla* where they found a Fox living. The spokesman said to the Fox : "We have an Indian with us. Do you like this?" and the Fox replied : "It is well." They journeyed on and came next to a place called Tse'ya*h*ótsi*tal* and here they found the Owl, Na*ĕ*sts*á*, who had met him many nights before and spoken to him when he was camped alone. *Hastséyalti* said to the Owl : "We have an Indian with us," and the Owl answered : "I know the man. It is well." From this place they journeyed on till they came to Ki*n*áhi and here they found Tsĭdĭl*t*ói, Shooting Bird. *Hastséyalti* told him the same as he had told the others and received the same reply. From Ki*n*áhi they traveled on to Ki*n*hitsói where *Hastséayuhi* dwelt, and from there to the White House in the Chelly Cañon where they met some of the Gá*n*askĭdi. At each place *Hastséyalti* spoke as he had spoken at the other places and received the same reply. They came up from the Chelly Cañon, and came down through the Cañoncito Bonito (where the Agency is now), and went southward through the valley to Tse'*d*ezái, where they found *Hastséd*ĭl-tsosi, a yéi with a black face and a whistle, who dwelt among the rocks in a cave. Inside of his house there was a white rainbow. Again *Hastséyalti* said : "We have a Navaho with us," and the god replied : "It is well." They went on south from here to a place called Tsé'no*t*oz or Striped Rock, where they found the Nĭ'ltsi *D*ĭné' or Wind People. "We have an Indian with us," said *Hastséyalti*. "It is well," said one of the Wind People, and then to the Navaho, "Henceforth you will be one of the gods. You have breathed them in. They will be in the ends of your toes, in the ends of your fingers, and all through your body." They next came to a place called Kaítso, where stood the home of *T*ó'nenĭli, to which he now returned saying : "This is my home ; that of *Hastséyalti* is far away in Tse'gíhi ; but when anything happens that concerns us both we meet at some place between our homes and hold a council." They traveled on and came next to a place called Náta*h*asai where stood the home of *Hastséhog*an, but not he who accompanied the party. His house was made of blue sky ; on top of it grew four spruce trees ; a white spruce in the east, a blue one in the south, a yellow one in the west, and a black one in the north. On the top of the eastern tree there was a pigeon ; on the top of the southern tree, a bluebird, on the top of the western tree a bird called nikéni, and on the top of the northern tree a yellow-shouldered blackbird. As the visitors entered the house all the birds whistled. *Hastséyalti* said, as usual : "We bring with us an Indian," and *Hastséhog*an answered : "It is well ; but now it would be well for you to take him to the house of his people. His father, his mother, his brothers, and his little sister must long to see him again and no doubt his heart yearns to see them once more. Take him to his home." They left this place and came to *Haskánh*atso. Here they found Coyotes, called Mai-natlé*l*e or Changing Coyotes. They were yéi converted into Coyotes or having the forms of Coyotes. They wore masks as did the Coyotes seen before, but they differed from those in other ways.   They had blue faces and yellow feet.   From the house of the Coyotes they journeyed on past Naho*d*oóla, past Sa*n*sĭltsóz, above Acoma, past *L*é*z*bai*t*o‘, past Dsĭ*l*d*z*o*l*tsĭ′ndi, Envy Mountain, to the north of Tsótsi*l*, to a place called Béikĭ*th*otyeli, Broad Lake.   Usually there is a broad sheet of water there, but when they came there was no water, the bed of the lake was dry.   They started to cross this dry plain when a bighorn came running from behind, touched *S*o as he passed, and ran on ahead of the travelers. But the instant the bighorn touched him, *S*o became blind, and after that his companions had to lead him onward by the hand.   They went next to a place called Kaid*z*ĭtsí.   From there they went to Tse‘bĭnaasé*l*yi, thence to In*d*ĕstsíia‘ and thence to *T*o‘alt*s*íd*i*, where they tarried awhile in a rock shelter, mixed some corn-meal with water, and ate.   In that rock shelter we still see the pictures of the masks or faces of these yéi.   When they had finished their meal they went to *T*ĭstsósĭn*d*eskĭ*z* and from there they journeyed on to Ná*h*odeskĭ*z* where they rested for a short time.   While they were sitting, *H*ast*s*é*z*ĭni laid down the firebrand which he had hitherto carried, and when they rose to journey on he forgot it and left it behind him.   When they arrived at Yé*d*asĭtahi, Where Gods Sit High, *H*ast*s*é*z*ĭni remembered his firebrand and said to his companions: "Siké (My boys) I have forgotten my firebrand and left it behind.   What shall we do?" and they replied: "We may as well leave it there.   We can use it in the future." That fire burns there to this day.   It is now a burning coal-bank.   *H*ast*s*éyal*t*i said: "Perhaps, in the days to come great misfortunes may befall mankind, war and disease; then you may go back to your firebrand, light from it four other fires, each at a different point and burn the world up."   Pursuing their journey, they came next to Dsĭ*l*nahasklĭ′*z*i, and next to Tse‘at*s*áhi.   As they were passing this rock an antelope ran up from behind, as the bighorn had run up at Broad Lake, and touched *S*o.   The moment he touched the Indian, the latter was stricken with "the warps" [53] (nalt*s*í) and thenceforward his companions were obliged to carry him.   The next point on their journey was Tse‘kiétsi, where there were pictures on a rock, and passing this they came to a steep rocky mountain which lay directly across their path.   Some advised that they should cross the mountain by the shorter and more difficult trail, while others advised that they go around the mountain by the longer and easier trail; but they at last decided on the shorter trail, hoping by it to reach Tse‘gíhi the sooner.   Thence they went home to Tse‘gíhi.

775.—The companions of *S*o took him in and laid him down on a level piece of ground (plaza) in the middle of the four rows of pueblo buildings.   They went into the White House in the east, where Great Wolf was chief and asked for a medicine-man who could cure blindness and the warps; but Maítso answered that there was no one among his people skilled in curing these diseases.   They went into the Blue House where Fox was chief and made the same request; but the chief answered them as Great Wolf had done.   They went to the Yellow House in the west where Puma was chief, and there they met one of the twelve

Gánaskĭdi who bade them bring the invalid in to them. They took him in, as directed by the Gánaskĭdi. A long pit was dug to the east of the front door and in this a fire was made. They placed pieces of firewood so that their tip ends were directed to the east. When the wood was reduced to red coals, they covered these completely over with a layer of fresh piñon branchlets; over the piñon they laid a covering of fresh cedar branchlets; over these they laid a covering of the plant tsĕ'ʐi, and on top of this they laid a covering of ʈoikáʈ. They carried the Indian out and laid him upon this pile, his head to the house. They covered him with a sheet of darkness, a sheet of blue sky, a sheet of yellow evening sky, and a sheet of white daylight. They let him lie there awhile until he began to perspire profusely. They applied to the sacred parts of his body the eight plumed wands. After this was done he arose somewhat straighter than when he lay down, but still needing assistance, and walked with one man supporting him. His sight was partially restored. They took the plants and branches with which the fire had been covered and laid them among the branches of a tree which stood to the east. They took the coals out of the pit and cast them away. The Gánaskĭdi said to the Indian: "When you find one of your people afflicted as you have been you must do to him as we do to you." This was all done early in the morning and after the work was over, the whole party sat in the house all day and did nothing more.

776.—The next day, early in the morning, a similar ceremony was performed on the south side of the house, and on the third day it was performed on the west side. After the third sweating he was able to see fairly well and could walk a little without assistance. On the fourth day the work was repeated in the north, with the head of the patient toward the house as on the previous occasions, and when the work was done the patient was as well as ever. He could sit or lie anyway he chose.

777.—Then So said: "I would like to return to my people to-day," and the yéi said: "It is well." He returned to his home in Kléhaʈsi on a rainbow. He went back to his mother; he went back to his father; he went back to his brothers; he went back to his sister. They were wild with joy; they threw themselves upon him and all embraced him at once and all wept at once. He had been gone sixteen days. They asked him where he had been and what tidings he had to tell, and he answered: "If you wish to hear the news, build a hut on the east side of our dwelling." "No," said the youngest brother, "the houses of the yéi are in the east. If we build you a house as they build theirs you may become one of them, and they will take you away from us forever. Let us build you a house in the west." And So said: "It is well." So they built a hut to the west of their dwelling and completed it in one day, and that night nothing was done.

778.—The next day he bade one of his brothers to get for him a piece of the root of tsásitsoz (*Yucca angustifolia*). He said: "You must collect it in this way: scrape the soil away from the root with your hand. With a stone arrowhead cut out a piece about so long (indicating on his extended palm the distance from the wrist joint to the end of the middle finger). When you have cut out this, rub the divided ends of the plant with corn-pollen, place them together, pack earth around them, and they will grow together again. Bring the piece that you cut out to me." When the piece of root (*t*álagos or *t*álawuc) was brought, *So* directed his sister to prepare with it a bowl of suds. He directed that five branchlets of spruce be brought; these he laid on the floor of the lodge in a group,—one east, one south, one west, one north, and one in the center. On this, in the center, he placed the bowl of suds. He selected his youngest brother as the one to whom he should teach the rites. He made the latter disrobe and wash himself all over with the suds. When the bath was done he directed another brother to rub the candidate all over with white corn-meal to dry him. When this was done, *So* began to tell his family (directing his speech more particularly to his youngest brother) all his adventures, from the first day when he pursued the bighorns into the cañon until the day of his last return. When he had finished his story he began to teach his brother the sacred songs. He remained in the lodge twelve days and twelve nights teaching his brother the songs, describing the ceremonies, showing him how the kethawns were made, and imparting to him all that he had learned during his sojourn among the yéi. When he had done, he said: " Now, younger brother, that is all. You must do all these things exactly as I tell you. If you make any mistakes you will become blind and warped and crippled; your mouth will be twisted. As long as you live, I want you to do all these things exactly as I have shown you how to do them. Now, my younger brother, I am going to leave you again." As he said these words he vanished. His brother was looking at him as he spoke; but, all at once, he saw him not.

779.—When *So* left the medicine-lodge, he rode on the white thunder to the top of the mountain called Tsolíhi, and from there he went again to the home of *H*astséyal*t*i at Tse‘gíhi. *H*astséyal*t*i said to him : " My grandchild, I see you have returned." *So* answered : " Yes, my grandfather, I have returned. I like no longer to live among my own people. I feel lonely there. I love better the dwellings of the yéi." " It is well, my grandson," said the yéi. " If you love us better than your own people you may stay with us and we will plant gardens for you." Some of the yéi then went out and planted for him corn, squashes, melons, and beans. *H*astséyal*t*i said to him : " Tell me which one of these houses you would like to live in, and you may take one of the yébaad for a wife." *So* answered : " I will take a house for a dwelling, but I do not wish yet to wed any of the women. Sometimes I will go around among them and visit them." Besides the yéi who dwell in the four rows of houses there were many more living in cave-houses high up on the side of the cañon. Looking up at these he observed that many women were gazing out from the caves and from the windows of the houses, and he sang a song to them.

780.—In twelve days from the time the corn was planted, the silk began to form and the little squashes and melons had grown "so big" (sign : about the size of a hen's egg). *So* had told *Hastséyalti* that he had related all his adventures to his youngest brother and had taught him concerning all the ceremonies, sacrifices, pictures, songs, and prayers. *Hastséyalti* said : " Your brother has learned all but one thing and that is how a certain picture is to be drawn." The yéi drew the picture for *So* and said : " We will go to your brother's home and draw this picture and return the same day. There is no reason why you should sleep there to-night." *So* wept to think he would have to return again to his people, for he had learned to love the yéi.

781.—They all traveled—*So* and his six companions of old—on a rainbow, from Tse'gíhi toward *Depĕ'ntsa*. As they went along they often saw the heads of yéi, male and female, sticking out from under the roots of trees, from under stones and from springs and swamps. When they got near his former home, his companions said : " There is the house of your people. Go thither and teach your brother what we have shown you. We shall wait here till your return ; come back to us when the sky is red."

782.—When he met his brother he said : " There is yet one thing more for you to learn, it is a picture," and he drew the picture for his brother. When he had done he spoke again, saying : " I draw this picture only to let you know how the picture looks, but you must not try to draw it yourself. When you have your dances, and sing your songs, you may make all the other pictures I have shown you ; but not the one I show you now." So the Navahoes do not draw this picture now, and don't even know what it was.

783.—*So* then said : " Younger brother, I shall now leave you forever ; you will never see me again ; but when the summer comes you will watch for the storms, and when you see the he-rain you will say, ' There is my brother,' for I shall be in the storm you behold." As he spoke he disappeared and has never since been seen except in the thunder showers of the summer.

THE STRICKEN TWINS,

MYTH OF *TO'NASTSIH́ÉGO HATÁL*.

784.—This is a story about songs, which first became known to some of our people who lived at a place called *Īndĕstsíhonia'*, which is south of and near Tsé'ĭntyel,[54] or Broad Rock in the Chelly Cañon. They were learned from holy people of the cañon. Here in the woods, dwelt a family of five Indians : a grandmother, her daughter, her daughter's husband, and two children of these, a boy and a girl. They were poor ; they had no sheep and no corn ; they lived on woodrats, seeds, and wild fruit.

785.—The granddaughter, who was fourteen years old, but not yet a woman, went out one day to the east of the lodge to hunt for *haskán*, or yucca fruit.[17] While she was gathering the fruit, she heard a strange voice in the woods as if someone were speaking to her in her own language. When she came home she related the occurrence, but no one seemed to pay attention to her. The family thought they had no neighbors. The next day she went to the south of the lodge, and the third day she went to the west, to gather *haskán*. On each occasion she heard again the strange voice, and when she came home she told what had happened, but no one heeded her.

786.—On the fourth day she went to the north, in the direction of Tsé'intyel. While she was gathering *haskán* under a cedar tree, she suddenly became aware that someone was standing beside her, and looking up she beheld a man. It was the *Hastséyalti* or Talking God of Tsé'intyel, dressed in his mask and plumes and garments of fine buckskin, just as *Hastséyalti* is dressed in the Navaho ceremonies now. She was bashful and hung her head when she beheld the fine stranger. "Why do you hang your head? Whence do you come?" he asked her, although he knew all the time who she was and where she dwelt, and that she was alone in the woods. Then he asked her many questions, but she only hung her head and rubbed her feet together, as bashful virgins do when a man speaks to them.

787.—He asked her these questions four times and on the fourth time he added: "Why do you not answer? Are you deaf? Are you so ugly that you are loth to look up?" At this she laughed and said: "I fear to speak to you; you are such a fine man and a stranger besides." He sat down under the cedar tree near her, and said again: "Whence do you come?" She answered: "I have lived in this neighborhood a long time." Then in turn she asked him where he lived, and she said: "It is strange I have never seen your tracks in these woods, nor the tracks of anyone but those of my own people." "I have been speaking to you for four days," he answered. "Why have you not seen me before? My home is in Tsé'intyel. I have seen and known you for a long time. I know the time you started out to-day, and that is why I came over here to meet you. I have come to seek you in marriage; but I will not coax you or persuade you against your wishes. If you do not wish to marry me, it is well." She replied: "I have never been married before. We are not fitted for one another. You are too fine a man for me. You are dressed in beautiful clothes, while I am covered with poor rags. Then I fear my relations will scold me if I marry without their consent, and I fear to speak to them." "You need tell no one about it," he said, "and I will do the same; such is the custom among my people; we marry in secret and tell no one." "I am too poor to wed you," she said again. "I have never been married and I fear I cannot keep the secret." "But I want to marry you," he persisted. "It is for that reason I have sought you. No one need ever know what we have done"; and so he continued to persuade her until he had asked her and been refused four times. But at last she consented, and they made mutual vows of secrecy. * * * *

788.—When *Hastséyalti* left her on this first occasion, she sat long and pondered on what she had done. She was filled with remorse and wept. She feared to go home and face her parents lest they should learn her secret and kill her, but at length she loaded her basket of *ha*s*k*án on her back and went home.

789.—When she got home her lips were parched in consequence of her anxious thoughts; but she said nothing. They expected her to speak again of the voices she had heard; but she spoke not and they asked her no questions. During the three following days she met *H*ast*s*éyal*t*i again in the woods every day when she went out to gather fruit; but after the fourth meeting he came no more. She kept her secret well; but at length her people began to notice a change in her appearance. Four months after meeting *H*ast*s*éyal*t*i she felt strange motions within her. She wanted to tell her sensations; but all her relations kept silence and no one led her on to speak.

790.—At the end of the ninth month twin boys were born to her; and then her relations, who had in the meantime removed their habitation, began to question her. "When we lived at In*d*ĕst*s*í*h*onia‘," they said, "on three different days, when you returned from gathering *ha*s*k*án, you told us you heard voices in the woods; when you came home on the fourth day your lips were parched and you said nothing. Was this the time when you knew the father of your children?" She made no answer. They kept this questioning up constantly for four days and four nights, taking turns and keeping her from sleeping, thus hoping to force her to tell her secret. At length she said that someone must have known her in her sleep, and that she knew not who the father of her children was. Then her grandmother threatened to kill her if she did not confess; but her brother thus pleaded for her: "Ask her no more. Do not fret her to death with questions. She knows no more than she tells you. Our numbers are few, it is well they are increased; there are two more men in the family; let us be thankful. Perhaps the *d*ígíni (holy ones) have done this and perhaps they may send us more."

791.—After this they moved to various places in the neighborhood of their first home—to Tse‘tláha*h*ast*s*i, to Klétsoi*d*eza‘ and to Ki*l*tsóibi*h*otyel, and they lived in these places eight years while the boys grew to be fine-looking boys. They looked much alike now and were of just the same height. At the age of eight they began to wander a good deal from home. They often walked far away and their people watched them closely lest they might some day wander too far away and be lost. They watched them hard all summer and all winter. Most of the time they made them sit behind the fireplace so that they could not easily slip out unobserved; but whenever they got out they were found again far away.

792.—In the ninth year they had to watch them more closely than ever. One day, about the time of the year when they were born, the boys one morning asked permission to go out saying they would return soon; but they did not soon return and the elder people went out to bring them in. The latter sought to follow the footprints of the boys; they found four tracks of each leading eastward from the lodge and there were no more,—there the trail ended. They then hunted in different directions until sunset, when they gave up the search. They came home very tired and lay down early; but they could not sleep. The next day they took an early breakfast and spent all the day searching for the boys, but could not find them. They sought the boys again all day on the third day, but in vain, and when they got home in the evening they talked for a long time over the events of the day and they wondered how the tracks had ended so mysteriously and how the boys could have gone away and left no trail. On the fourth day they hunted once more until sunset without success and when they returned to the hut at night they said: "Let us search once more for the children and if we do not find them let us give up the search." They remembered that when the children were born, they had scolded the mother, threatening her life; that only the pleadings of the brother saved her, and that he then said he thought the twins might be the children of one of the *dǐgíni*. Now they talked of all this and the mother said she believed her children had gone to seek their father. On the fifth day the family sought again for the children without success; they returned weary to the lodge some time before sundown and began to talk of the lost children. While they were speaking the children suddenly entered the lodge, the elder bearing the younger on his back—the one was blind, the other was lame.

793.—"A*h*aláni, *s*a*s*tsǐ'ni—Welcome, our children," said the elders and they wept and rejoiced over the returned ones. They asked the children where they had been and what had happened to them, and the children told this story: They had not wandered far from the lodge on the day of their departure when they came to a rock-shelter where they sat down to rest. While they were seated the roof of the shelter closed over and entrapped them. In the cave thus formed they remained (as they now found) four days and four nights in utter darkness. On the fifth day the rocks were opened by the god *H*ast*s*é*d*ǐltsosi (pars. 824, 825,) and they were allowed to come out. Then they found that one was lame and the other was blind, and they thought of the way of traveling by which they came home, that the one who could walk should carry on his back the one who could see. They thought it was *H*ast*s*é*d*ǐltsosi who had imprisoned them in the rocks and cast the evil spell upon them.

794.—Now their people tried to cure the children by every means they could think of; they tried sage-brush and other herbs, but all without avail and at last they abandoned all attempts as hopeless. In the meantime the children became a sore trouble to the family which had always been poor and found it difficult to make a living for themselves. Here now were two grown children to be provided for besides, who could gather no food and had to be attended as if they were babies. They became at last weary of the children. They upbraided the mother bitterly for having given birth to such progeny; they implored her again to declare who was the father of her children and they said to the children "Begone. Go where you will, but leave us. Go far away and die somewhere." Then the children counseled together. "Our people are weary of us," they said. "What shall we do?" The cripple said to the blind one: "We must leave here.

You carry me out and I will guide you on your way. We shall pick berries while we can find them. When the berries fail we shall play, and when we are too weak to play we shall lie down and die." " Get on my back then," said the blind one, " and let us leave." So the cripple mounted on his brother's back.

795.—They left the lodge, traveled some distance to the east, and sat down on the edge of a cañon to rest. " Here," they said, " we shall spend the night, and in the morning we shall go elsewhere." When they rose next morning they thought they would have nothing to eat, but they soon discovered lying near them two cakes made of the seeds of tlo*t*áhi (*Chenopodium fremonti*) baked in the ashes. One said to the other : " It is our father that has brought us this food. Let us be thankful." When they had eaten they counseled as to which way they should travel that day, and they concluded to go to the south. The blind one bade his brother to get on his back again ; they went to the south the same distance that they had traveled the day before to the east, and they stopped for the night. When they woke next morning about sunrise, the cripple turned on his side and saw, within his reach, four fine ripe *h*askán fruit. He told his brother ; they both gave thanks to the giver, lighted a fire, and roasted the *h*askán. After they had eaten they held another council and decided to go to the west. They traveled in this direction till they came to the edge of a cañon, where they spent the night. When they rose on the fourth morning it was late ; the sun had risen high. The cripple found lying near him four ears of corn in the husks ; but the husks were partly opened and he saw that the first ear of corn was white, the second blue, the third yellow, and the fourth had grains of all colors. They gave thanks to the one who had given them the corn. They lighted a fire, roasted the corn, and divided equally between them, taking two ears each. It was *H*ast*s*éyal*t*i who had laid the food beside them every night while they slept, and the corn which he now gave them was from the home of the yéi at Tsé*'*intyel. All this time they did not go very far from their home and they did not keep going in one direction, for they still hoped that some of their relations might come looking for them. They held another council. " You must decide on the trail for to-day," said the elder. " No," said the younger, " you must decide for you are the older brother." They went that day to the north, the blind boy carrying the cripple as usual ; but they did not yet go very far from the hut for they still had hopes that their people might take pity on them and seek them. When night came they lay down to sleep and said : " To-morrow we shall decide which way we shall travel." All this time they had slept warm every night, they knew not why ; but it was because *H*ast*s*éyal*t*i had covered them with t*s*a*l*yé*l* be*l*klá*d*i, the blanket of darkness. In the morning, before they woke, he came and took it off.

796.—It was nearly noon on the fifth day when they woke. The cripple, as usual, was the first to wake. When he opened his eyes he saw near him a small bowl, " so big " (about two inches) with something yellow in it which he supposed to be a mush made of corn-pollen, and he tasted it. When each had eaten four morsels of the mush he declared to the other that his hunger was satisfied and that he cared to eat no more, although there was some food left in the little bowl. The blind one asked : "How much is left?" The cripple looked again and answered : "It is as full as ever." Then they began to talk about what they should do with the mush in the bowl ; but while they were talking *Hastséyalti* came, unperceived, and took the bowl away. The boys hunted a long time for the bowl and went a good distance from their camping-place to find it ; but they could not find it, so they gave up the search and sat down to consider what they should do next. "We have camped for four nights near the house of our kindred," said one to the other, "yet no one has come to seek us as they used to do. Truly they must have abandoned us." Then the boys wept and the younger said : "You are the elder, you must say what we shall do now." Then the elder said : "Let us go to the north, to Tsé'gi (Chelly Cañon). We have heard that the *d*ígíni dwell there. Perhaps they may take pity on us." The blind boy took the cripple on his shoulders and they traveled northward until they reached the cañon. They descended by a trail that led past some rocky pinnacles called Tsé'nesgé*l*, and past Tsé'íntyel and they camped in the valley below Tsé'íntyel that night. They slept warm for their father as before, unperceived by them, covered them with the blanket of darkness.

797.—In the morning, early, they were aroused by the distant call of *Hastséyalti*, "Wu'-hu'-hu'-hú!" The blind boy woke first. The call was repeated, as usual, four times, each time louder, and immediately after the fourth call *Hastséyalti*, their father, appeared to them, and addressed them, saying : "Whence come you, my grandchildren?" He addressed them as grandchildren although he well knew they were his own sons. The blind boy said to his brother : "Look well, and tell me what sort of a person this is who calls us his grandchildren." The cripple replied : "It is none of our people. This man wears beautiful plumes on his head and is dressed in fine clothes. He must be one of the *d*ígíni." "Look closer, younger brother," said the blind boy, "and tell me more about how he looks." "I am ashamed to look again," said the cripple, "he is so beautifuly dressed, he is such a grand man." "Whence come you," the holy one asked again and again. When he had asked for the fourth time one of the twins replied : "We come from Ín*d*ests*í*hzonia'. There dwell our mother, her brother, our grandfather and grandmother and great-grandmother. Our people drove us out and told us to begone. We wept and came away." "And why did they drive you out?" asked *Hastséyalti*. The twins then told him their story : how they had wandered to the rock shelter ; how the shelter had closed around them and held them fast ; how at length when the rocks were opened they found that one was blind and the other lame ; how the blind boy took the lame boy on his back, and how they found their way home. They told what means had been tried to cure them and how their grandparents at last got tired of them and drove them away. In few words they told the story of their lives ; but when he asked them how they came to be disabled they could only say they did not know. "I will think if something may be done to help you," said *H*ast*s*éyal*t*i. He had in his hand a little bowl that, to the boys, seemed to be the same bowl out of which they had eaten the day before ; it contained a fine white meal called yĭs*te∕*kaí.[11] He bade the cripple mix a little water with this and make a paste. The boys ate till their hunger was completely satisfied, yet when they were done the bowl was as full as in the beginning ; but *H*ast*s*éyal*t*i put it to his lips and emptied it with one lick of his tongue.

798.—He said then to the twins : "See yonder great rock (pointing to Tsé‘-ĭntyel), on its east side there is an arch of rainbow. Touch the rock under the rainbow arch and you may enter ; but tell no one who it was that showed you the way. The *d*ĭgíni (holy ones) dwell there." Then he disappeared. The boys went as they were bidden. They saw on the rock an arch of rainbow, but the bow was only of two colors, and they saw no door under it ; but when they touched the rock as they had been told to do, a door flew open and they passed through. They came into a chamber where they saw no one ; but in the opposite wall they beheld a door and over this there was an arch of rainbow of three colors. They touched this door as they had touched the first wall and it flew open, revealing a second chamber. They stood outside the door a little while and peered in, but they saw no one, and entered. Then they observed in the opposite wall, another door, and over this a rainbow arch of four colors (*i. e.*, a four-colored rainbow). They passed through the third chamber and struck the door. When it flew open it revealed another apartment. This, too, was empty, but in the opposite wall was a door and over this a rainbow arch of five colors.[14] The door was covered with beautiful rock crystals that gleamed like stars. On beholding it the lame boy cried out to his brother : "This door shines so brightly that I fear to touch it, and I am ashamed to enter such a beautiful house." They stopped before the door and counseled with one another for some time ; at last they said : "What will it avail us if we return ? And perhaps this is the last door. Let us go on." So the cripple touched this door and it flew open as the doors before had flown open. When they looked first into the fourth room they saw no one, but when they had gotten to the middle of the room the cripple became conscious that they were not alone ; looking around he found the place filled with the holy ones ; he was ashamed and hung his head. The blind one stopped, for he heard voices. The *d*ĭgíni knew the twins were coming and were waiting for them.

799.—The chief, *H*ast*s*é*h*o*g*an, was talking. "Which one among you," he said, "has revealed to the People on the Earth[55] the way to our house ? These are the first of them we have ever seen in our dwelling. It must be someone here who has betrayed the path. Which one is it ?" Nayénĕz*g*ani, who was there, said : "It is not I." *T*o‘bad*z*ĭst*s*íni, his brother, said : "It is not I." Then *H*ast*s*éol*t*oi, Dsaha*d*old*z*á, Gá*n*askĭ*d*i, *H*ast*s*ébaka, *H*ast*s*ébaad, *H*ast*s*é*lt*si, *H*ast*s*é*z*íni and even *H*ast*s*éyal*t*i, the guilty one, each in turn denied that he had revealed the way. "We have never visited or spoken with the People on the Earth," some said. Others said : "Ask *H*ast*s*éayuhi, he is a great rambler ; he goes everywhere ; perhaps it is he who has told." But *Hast*séayuhi spoke : "It is true, I go everywhere and travel far, yet I never met these people." Some accused *Hast*séd*i*ltsosi, saying he too was a great rambler, but he denied as *Hast*séayuhi had done. They accused *Hast*séel*tod*i, but he denied it and said he was a person fond of home who never traveled much. Some suggested that *T*ó'nen*i*li might be the guilty one, as he was a great buffoon and was always going about and playing pranks ; but he declared his innocence. "*Hast*séĕltlihi is another who travels much. Let him speak. Perhaps he had dealings with these people," said another ; but *Hast*séĕltlihi denied that he had ever spoken with the People on the Earth (Ni'na*h*oká*dd*íne').[55] These mentioned were all chiefs among the *d*ígini, and when they had done questioning the chiefs they questioned all of inferior degree who were present ; but all these too denied that they had told any of the People on the Earth how the house might be entered.

800.—When the holy ones had all been questioned, *Hast*séhog̣an began to question the boys. "Whence come you ? Are you holy people or are you People on the Earth ?" "We are of the People on the Earth," the boys answered. "We come from Ĭn*d*ĕsts*ih*onia', which is over in *that* direction (pointing). We were born and reared there, and there dwell our mother, our uncle, our grandfather, and grandmother." The yéi asked them how they came to be, —the one blind and the other crippled. The children told the whole story of their misfortune and wanderings ; how they were driven forth from their home, and how they came to wander into the Chelly Cañon. When they had finished their story, *Hast*séhog̣an asked them (four times) which one among those present had revealed to them the way to enter the home of the holy ones, but they replied that no one there had told them. Then he asked : "Why do you come to us ? What is it that you want ? Of what were you thinking and of what were you talking when you entered here ?" "We came to find some one who would take pity on us," said the blind one. "I came to have my eyes restored, and my brother came to have his limbs restored as they were before the evil spell was cast upon us." "I know not how to cure either the blind or the lame," said *Hast*séhog̣an, "but here is Nayénĕzg̣ani, who can cure you." At this Nayénĕzg̣ani said he had not the power, but that his brother *T*o'bad*z*ĭsts*í*ni had. *T*o'bad*z*ĭsts*í*ni said he did not know how to cure these maladies but that *Hast*séol*t*oi did. They all knew how to work the cure ; but they did not want to take the trouble. So in turn each of the following gods, Dsaha*d*oldzá, Gá*n*askĭ*d*i, *Hast*sébaka, *Hast*sébaad, *Hast*sél*t*si, *Hast*sézĭni, *Hast*séyal*t*i, *Hast*séayuhi, *Hast*séd*i*ltsosi, *Hast*séel*tod*i, *T*ó'nen*i*li, and *Hast*séĕltlihi were called upon, and each in turn denied his power to cure. *Hast*séhog̣an turned to them all and said : "Are there none among ye who can make the blind to see and the cripple to walk ?" With one voice they all said " No," though they all lied. Then he told the children of a place called Tsé'bĭniyi, near Tsé'ĭntyel, where holy ones also dwelt, among whom they might find some one who could cure them. The blind boy took the cripple on his back and departed.

801.—They went on toward Tsé‘bïniyi. As they were crossing an arroyo the cripple saw some cactus with ripe fruit; bidding his brother to stop, he dismounted and both set to eating the fruit. While they were eating the divine ones of Tsé‘ïntyel sent word to those of Tsé‘bïniyi that the strangers were coming to them. When the boys approached the rock they saw a rainbow arch of two colors; they touched the rock under this arch and at once a doorway opened for them. They stood a moment outside and the cripple peered in. " How does it look inside?" said the blind one. "The room is empty," said the cripple " It looks just like the first room we entered at Tsé‘ïntyel, and on the opposite wall I see a rainbow of three colors." They passed through this vacant apartment, touched the door under the rainbow, and the door opened as before to allow them to pass. Thus they went through three chambers, as they had done at Tsé‘ïntyel, until they came to a shining crystal door under a bow of five colors, such as they had seen at Tsé‘ïntyel. They touched this and entered the fourth apartment, which at first seemed empty as before; but when they reached the middle of the room they found it filled with the holy ones, who had heard of their coming and awaited them there. These seemed to the children to be just the same people they had met at Tsé‘ïntyel and their father was among the number. He was in hope that some of the other yéi might do something to cure his children. This was always on his mind and for this reason he went around from place to place wherever they went. *Hastséhogan* was speaking in an angry voice. He said: " These are people who should never have been allowed to enter here. They smell badly. They should be put out. What do you want from us? (this to the twins). If you wish to have your diseases cured why do you come to us? The People on the Earth understand how to treat disease. Whence do you come, and who told you there was a house here?" One of the boys replied that their home was at Ĭndestsĭʰonia‘, and he went on to tell the whole of their sad story, all over again. "We went to Tsé‘ïntyel to be cured but the divine ones there said they could not cure us and sent us here. It was they who told us of your house. Is there no one among you who can make the lame to walk and the blind to see?" "No," said *Hastséhogan*, "among all the holy ones here there are none who can help you; but there are other *dïgïni* dwelling near who can help you. Try those at Kĭninaékai" (White House, par. 390). Hearing this the twins departed.

802.—The sun was setting when they came out. While they were on the trail that led to Kĭninaékai darkness fell on them as they reached an old ruin, which was a ruin even in those ancient days, and here they lay down and slept. When they wakened in the morning the cripple saw two ears of roasted corn, one yellow and one white, lying beside them. He told his brother what he had found and the blind one said: " Let us thank the giver. You eat the yellow ear and I shall eat the white one." When they had eaten the corn he said: " Let us go on. We have nothing to hope from those we left behind; they even gave us nothing to eat. If those we are going to visit cannot cure us they may at least take pity on us and give us some food." The people of the White House had been notified by their neighbors of the approach of the strangers; they had held a council and had determined to admit the boys into the houses at the bottom of the cliff but not into those in the cave above. As the boys came around a jutting cliff and came in sight of the White House, a great crowd was gathered to receive them, at the bottom of the cliff, for those at the White House had heard of this strange pair and their odd way of traveling. The father of the boys was among the crowd. When they arrived where the crowd stood the cripple said to his brother: "We are surrounded by a multitude of *d'ígíni* who are so beautifully dressed that I fear to look at them. I fear to approach them;" but the blind one made answer: "It is of no use that we change our minds now. We cannot go home, we have no home to go to."

803.—The crowd opened for them and they entered one of the houses. "Why do you stand?" said one of the *d'ígíni*. "Why are you not seated? Sit down and rest until the chiefs come down from Kĭninaékai. They may have something to say to you." In a little while the chiefs came and one of them was accompanied by two sons and two daughters. "Who are these people?" said one of the chiefs, "To what race do they belong?" Those standing around replied: "We know nothing about them; we know not whence they come; we have never seen such people before." At length the father of the twins said: "I know something about them. They belong to a race called the Ni'na*h*oká*dd*ïne', or People on the Earth. Have you never heard of them?" The chief answered: "Yes they are something of that kind. I know what they are now." Then turning to the twins he said: "What do you seek? The People on the Earth know nothing of this place. They never come down here." "Grandfather," said the elder boy, "it is not for nothing that we come this way." Then he told briefly the story of their lives and their misfortunes and ended by saying: "We came hither hoping to find some one who could cure us." "Do you bring fine beads with you?" asked the chief. "Do you bring with you white shell? Do you bring turquoise? Do you bring haliotis shell? Do you bring cannel-coal? Do you bring rock crystal? Do you bring tobacco? Do you bring feathers of the bluebird? of the yellowbird? of the eagle? of the turkey?" And thus he asked them, one after another, if they brought the sacred things which the holy ones demanded for the treatment of disease (par. 235). To each question the children answered "No," and at last they said: "We bring none of these things. We are poor. See how we stand. We have not even moccasins or leggings to protect our limbs from the thorns of the cactus." *H*ast*s*é*h*og*a*n then said: "I know not how to cure your diseases; but ask these people around you; some of them may know." Then turning to the assembled crowd he asked: "Do any of you know how to cure the diseases of these children?" They all said "No," except the father of the twins, who was present and he said nothing. They all looked closely at the children but no one offered food. *H*ast*s*é*h*og*a*n said: "There is another place here which is the home of holy ones. It is the branch of the cañon that comes from the north and it is called *Lǐtsǐthaa'* Red Promontory.   There perhaps they may help you."   Hearing this, the blind boy took the cripple on his back and the two departed.

804.—The holy ones rose as their visitors left and then the voice of *Hastsé-yalti*, their father, was heard.   He said : " I am sorry none of you will help these children.   In every place they have been they have hoped that some one would offer to cure them ; but no one offers."   They all listened to his voice and were quiet.   When he had spoken some one asked : " Why do you plead for them ?" He answered : " Because they are things for us to pity.   One is blind and he carries the helpless one who sees.   They are poor, hungry and helpless.   It makes me sad to look at them.   Some one should take pity on them.   This is why I spoke for them.   The People on the Earth, I pity them all."   *Hastséhogan* then said : " Surely we would take pity on them and cure them, but they bring not the gifts which we must receive when we cure disease."   The twins did not hear these remarks.   They were far on their way returning when the last words were said about them.

805.—They passed by Tsé'bǐniyi on their way and one proposed that they stop there again but the other said : " Alas ! no.   They would not help us before and they surely will not help us if we try again."   As they passed, the people of Tsé'biniyi looked at them from their doors and windows and said : " There go those people returning who came to see us yesterday."   The people of Tsé'ǐntyel were also at their doors and windows on the lookout for the strangers ; they thought the twins were coming back to them ; but when the children got near Tsé'ǐntyel they turned to one side and passed by.   For as they approached Tsé'ǐntyel the cripple said : " Let us go back to Tsé'ǐntyel, we now draw near to it " ; but the blind one said : " It would be of no use.   They did not help us before and they would not help us now."   " I see the *dǐgíni* at their doors," said the one.   " They only laugh and mock us," said the other.   So the children went on up to *Lǐtsǐthaa'* to find out what kind of a place it was and if the people there would be kinder to them than the others were.   As they neared the place the cripple saw that some people stood outside waiting for them.   The *dǐgíni* here had heard that some of the People on the Earth were coming to visit them.   This house was in a cliff of red sandstone and it had rainbows to show where the doors were, like those in the other houses they had visited.   When they got near the house the multitude had disappeared and no one was to be seen.   They went up, touched the rock under the rainbow as they had done elsewhere and a door opened for them.

806.—When they entered the first room they saw it was red, like the red rock of the outer cliff ; but the room was empty and the boys talked between themselves and said they thought no one lived there ; but soon they beheld a rainbow arch on the opposite side and touching the wall under this a door opened and they entered the second chamber.   Crossing this they touched the wall under another rainbow and soon entered a third chamber.   On the opposite wall of the third room there was no rainbow but a *sá'bĭtlo̱l* or sunbeam instead and under this there was no crystal door as there had been in the other houses; but the wall was smooth and even, like the face of a cliff. They began to fear that no one lived here but soon they heard the sound of voices beyond the wall; they touched it; a door opened for them and they stepped into the fourth chamber. They found the room filled with holy ones called *Hastsé̱ltsi* or Red Yéi (par. 96). The Red Yéi were all standing as the boys entered and they looked down on them. These holy ones were more numerous and finer looking than any they had seen before and they had many young men and young women among them. "Who are these strangers who have come to see us?" "To what tribe do they belong?" "Who knows them?" Such were the questions which the Red Yéi asked of one another, and the answers were: "We know them not," "We have never seen such people before." During the time the yéi were talking, the blind boy stood in the middle of the floor bearing the cripple on his back. The father of the twins was present again and at length some one asked him if he knew who the strangers were. He only answered: "They belong to a race called the Ni'na*hoká̱ddĭ*ne' or People on the Earth." The chief then bade the boys to walk around the room from the east, as the sun moves, back to the east again. He bade them be seated in the center of the room and asked them why they had come to visit the house of the Red Yéi. "I am blind," said the elder boy, "my brother is crippled. We hope that some one may take pity on us and cure us. We have been sent here by the holy ones of Kĭninaékai. Our mother has tried all remedies she could think of, but has done us no good and has given us up to die. We want to find some one who will pity us and cure us; but besides we are now very hungry and would thank you for something to eat." "Have you a basket of turquoise?" asked the chief. "No" they answered, "we have not." "Have you a basket of white shell?" he asked, but again they said they had not. Thus he went on and named one at a time all of the sacred gifts (par. 235) and asked the twins if they had it; but to each question they said "No," and at last they said: "We are poor. We have nothing. We know not how to get these things ourselves and there is no one who will give them to us." "You must have these things to offer us, or we cannot help you. I cannot cure your eyes if you have not these things. I cannot cure your limbs if you have not these things," said the chief. "But perhaps the *Hastsé̱hogan* of Tsé'ĭntyel may help you and here now among us is *Hastséyalti* of Tsé'ĭntyel (indicating their father); perhaps he may cure you. Besides, it is not our province to cure. We are the bearers of the whip. We are the people of racing. It is our duty to punish those runners who lose in the race" (par. 96). Being again refused, the blind one took the cripple on his back and set forth on his journey. As they left they heard *Hastséyalti* saying to the chief of the Red Yéi: "You should take pity on these people; they may be relations of yours."

807.—They went toward Tsé'ĭntyel and soon after they were gone their father quitted the house at *Lĭtsĭt*haa', and laid on the trail, where the boys must pass, some branches of *hastséta* (*Lycium pallidum*) covered with ripe fruit. The boys ate of these berries till they were satisfied and continued on their way. They went up to Tse'íntyel and knocked on the wall under the rainbow of two colors as they had done before, but the door did not open. They knocked four times, harder each time, but still the door opened not. After the fourth knock a voice was heard crying from within : "Who stands there ?" and one of the boys replied : "It is we who have been here before, one bearing the other on his back." The voice from within cried out : "You cannot enter here. Go over to Tsé'bĭniyi ; perhaps there they will let you in." The twins said, one to another : "It will profit us nothing to remain here. Let us do as we are bidden. Let us go to Tsé'bĭniyi, perhaps there the door may open for us." When they got a little distance from Tse'íntyel, the cripple looked back and saw the people outside looking at them and laughing.

808.—They went to Tsé'bĭniyi and knocked as they had done at Tsé'íntyel, but the door opened not and no one spoke. Thus they knocked four times and waited each time for something to happen. After the fourth knock a voice within cried : "Who is it that wishes to enter ?" and one of the twins replied : "It is two who were here before, one bearing the other on his back." The voice within called again to them saying : "You cannot enter here again. Go on once more to Kĭninaékai, perhaps there the yéi may open the door for you." So the twins went on to Kĭninaékai, to the place near the house at the base of the cliff where they had met and talked with the *d'ígíni* on the previous occasion. Here they stood for some time hoping some one would come out to speak to them ; but nobody coming, they sat down and waited a while longer. At length they saw some one approaching. He was the *Hastséyalti* of Kĭninaékai. "Do you still loiter around here, grandchildren ?" he said. "I pity you, I am sorry for you ; but there is no use in your staying in this cañon. All the holy ones are laughing at you, and none of them will help you." "Very well, our grandfather, we loiter around here only because we still hope that some one may take pity on us. We have heard that the holy ones can cure our diseases, and it is for this reason that we remain." "It is no use, your remaining here. We can do nothing for you. Leave this cañon and go elsewhere." "It is well," said they. "We shall do as you bid us." When they had thus promised *Hastséyalti*, the cripple said to his brother : "Elder brother, you are the elder, say you which way we shall now go." But the elder brother would not decide, so they sat and counseled a long time about what they should do. In the end they decided to go back to their old home again, and they turned their faces toward Ĭnd'ĕstsíhonia'. When they had gone a little way, the cripple looked back toward Kĭninaékai and saw the people there, gathered outside of the houses, laughing at the twins and mocking them. They slowly climbed the walls of the cañon and went on to their old home.

809.—From a distance their people saw them coming and said : "Here are those troublesome children coming back to us again." When the children arrived at the door of the hut their people forbade them to enter; they told them in angry tones to begone; they did not even offer them anything to eat. The children said one to another, "There is no use in our trying to enter here. Let us go back to *Lĭtsĭtʰaa‘* again." "But what shall we do in the meantime for something to eat?" "Let us go where the *hastséta* (*Lycium* berries) grew, we may find some more berries there to eat." They went back over a place called *Lĭtsóideza‘* (Yellow Earth Sticks Up). The sun set at a place where they had encamped before and here they lay down and slept.

810.—At daylight next morning they were wakened by the voice of a yéi. It sounded as usual four times, each time louder and nearer, and after they heard the last call, their father approached them. "There is no use in your coming hither," he said. "The people here will never help you. Go to Tsé‘zĭni (Black Rock), the *dĭgíni* there may take pity on you and cure you." Then he gave them of *yĭsᵗelkaí* (a fine white meal[11]) mixed with pollen in a bundle about the size of the doubled fists, and a small yellow cup, of such size as might be surrounded by the thumb and index finger. "Do not use much of this meal," he said; "only so much as you may pinch up thus (with tips of four fingers and thumb). Put it into the bowl and mix it with water. Should you meet some one who asks you what you live on and where you get your food, never show them these things, never tell them that you have them, and should they find them on you, never say that *Hastséyalᵗi* of Tsé‘ĭntye gave them to you." Before he parted with them he said: "You will meet me again in other places." They had not gone far on their journey when they found themselves near Tsé‘ĭntyel again. The people of this place came out to look at them and laugh at them, but *Hastséyalᵗi* did not laugh. He said: "You should not laugh at these poor children. Perhaps they are your kindred."

811.—At Tsé‘zĭni there were two houses in a black rock, one to the east, another to the west. The children approached the one in the east, and saw a rainbow of two colors hanging over a black door. They touched the door; it flew open and they entered a room whose walls were made of smooth *pászĭni* or cannel-coal. The room was empty. Then, as in the other houses, they passed through two more doors and two more empty rooms, all lined with the black *pászĭni* until they came to the fourth door, over which hung a rainbow of five colors. When they arrived at this door they heard voices on the other side of it. When they entered the fourth apartment they had to descend a flight of four steps, so when they reached the floor they found themselves near the middle of the room and surrounded with an assemblage of *dĭgíni* of two kinds—the *Hastsézĭni* or Black Yéi and the *Tsóskagi*. Unlike the yéi at other places, these had no fore-warning of the approach of the twins and were not aware of their presence until the children stood in their midst. The yéi bade the children be seated and asked them: "How did you know that there were houses here?" The children remained silent. " Did the *d'igíni* of Tsé'ĭntyel tell you? Did those of Kĭninaé-kai tell you? Did those of *Lĭtsĭthaa'* tell you? We have heard of your visit to these places. We have heard of the strange pair who travel around, one bearing the other on his back. Tell us of your travels. Tell us what happened to you at these different places." The children spoke: "We have been to Tsé'ĭntyel; we have been to Tsé'bĭniyi; we have been to Kĭninaékai at the foot of the cliff, and we have been to *Lĭtsĭthaa'*. At all these places we met the holy ones but they refused to help us and sent us on to another place. A second time we re-turned to every place, for they told us a second time to go to them; but on our second journey we were not even allowed to enter the houses. Voices from within told us to go on. When at all places we had been told that on one could help us, we left the cañon and returned to our old home at Ĭnděstsĭhonia'; but there we were driven away with angry words, by our own people. Then we came here hoping that some of the holy ones at Tsé'zĭni might take pity on us." "At what place were you, when they told you to come here? Where were you when you were told that your legs and eyes could be cured here?" "At every place we were sent to another place. · At last we were told to come here." "Did you get anything to eat at the places you visited?" "No, we got nothing to eat." "Were you born, the one blind and the other a cripple?" "No, we were born sound. We are twins." "Who was your father?" "That is a question we have asked our mother and she has told us she does not know." Such were the ques-tions asked by the yéi and such the answers given by the twins. Then the yéi said: "We can cure the eyes of the blind and the limbs of the lame, and the holy ones you have visited should have the same power; but there are certain gifts we should receive before we can perform the cure. Have you white shell? Have you turquoise?" and thus he named all of the sacred things that the yéi require. To each question the children answered "No" and when he had named them all, they said: "We are poor, we have none of these things and we know not how to get them." "Alas, we cannot cure you unless you bring these offerings with you," said the yéi. "Go hence to Tse'*haltál* (Fallen Rock); perhaps there they may cure you for nothing. Here we cannot. There is no use in your waiting here." So the cripple mounted on the back of his blind brother and they went away. See par. 102 *et seq.*

812.—They went along the edge of this Black Rock and they came to Beikĭt-*halkaí* or White Lake; thence they went to Nágoselĭni or Place-where-tobacco-pipes-are-made,[56] and thence to *Sá*yitsósi or Slender Sand-hill which was a house in those days. As they approached the house they met *Hazél* kai, White Squir-rel, who said to them: "Do not seek to enter that house, you were not told to go there, you were bidden to go to Tsé'*haltal*. Keep on therefore until you find it." They went on in the direction of Tsó*ns*ĭla, but as they approached it they met one of the *Sásd*'ine or Bear People, who said: "Do not come hither, this is the way to Tsó*ns*ĭla.[57] Go on in that direction to Tsé'*haltal*, as you have been told." After they parted with the Bear Man they went to Pe*sl*ĭtsi'bigel, Queue of Red Knives, and next they went to Tsé*haltal*. This name means Fallen Rock, for it appears in this place as if a part of the mountain had dropped out. There was a little open park in the woods at the foot of this mountain, and as the twins were crossing the opening the dwellers of Tsé'*haltal* beheld them coming. At this place there was a *H*astséyal*t*i and a *H*astsé*h*og*an*, as there were at all the other dwellings of the holy people, and they were the chiefs. When the twins were observed, *H*astséyal*t*i told *H*astséel*t*od i to go and meet the travelers and see who they were. When *H*astséel*t*od i met them he said : "Are you Ni'na*h*okádd ïne ?" and they answered : "We are." "From what place do you come ?" he asked. "We come from a place called Tsé'z̆ïni. It was the holy ones there who told us to come to the place called Tsé'*haltal*." "Sit here, then," said the yéi, "until I go back and tell my people who you are that are coming to them." When *H*astséel*t*od i returned he related that the travelers were a strange pair who had been sent to them by the gods of Tsé'z̆ïni ; that one was blind and one was crippled and that the blind one bore the cripple on his back. "Why do they come, and what shall we do about their coming ?" said the chief. "They probably come here for a purpose since they were sent here," said the messenger. *H*astséel*t*od i was then sent back to walk in front of the twins and lead them in,—so he went over to them again and they followed him to the house. They did not have any doors to open this time, for *H*astséel*t*od i, going in advance, opened the doors for them.

813.—They passed, as in other places, through three empty rooms and in the fourth room they found the people assembled and waiting for them. The doors of the different rooms had rainbows over them ; but besides a bow of five colors the door of the fourth room had, on each side, dark kethawns (ke*t*án d'ï*l*yï'*l*). The chief asked them to sit down and asked them to tell their story, who they were, whence they came, and what they sought. The cripple briefly related their history from the beginning and ended saying : "We have visited all these places and in all we have been refused help. In the last place we visited they told us to come here ; they said they thought you could help us, and so we have come in the hope that you might do so." *H*astséyal*t*i said : "The people at Tsé'z̆ïni were mistaken about me at least, I cannot help you ; but here is *H*astsé*h*og*an*—perhaps he may have the power to cure you." But *H*astsé*h*og*an* denied his power to heal, and thus each of the other chiefs in turn, being asked, said they had not the power to heal the children. The *H*astséyal*t*i directed that they be taken out of the house and be led around it sunwise until they reached the north ; that there they be carefully directed how to get to *T*óïntsa and that they be told to go to that place. All was done as he had bidden and the twins departed for *T*óïntsa (Tunicha Mountains).

814.—As they were approaching this place the people saw them coming, while they were yet a good way off, and *T*ó'nenĭli, the Water Sprinkler, was sent to meet them, to see who they were and, if they were the People on the Earth, to bid them approach no nearer. When *T*ó'nenĭli met them he said : "Who are you ? If you are of the Ni'na*h*okádd'ïne' you cannot enter our house and must

come no nearer." The children answered : " We are truly of the Ni'na*h*okádd*ï*ne';
but we have already been in the houses of other divine ones. We have been in
Tsé'*h*alta*l* and the people there showed us the way to your house and told us to
come hither." " Sit here then and wait," said *T*ó'nen*ï*li, " till I return to my
people and tell *H*ast*s*éyal*t*i what you have said. Perhaps he will bid you to come
to him." When *T*ó'nen*ï*li went back he told *H*ast*s*éyal*t*i what he had heard from
the children and he described them and the queer way in which they were traveling. " It is well," said the chief, " bring the children hither. We have never
seen any of the People on the Earth and we would all like to know how they
appear." *T*ó'nen*ï*li went back to the children and led them to the house — he
going in advance. They did not need to open the doors on this occasion, either,
for *T*ó'nen*ï*li, going before them, did this.

815.—They passed as usual through three empty rooms and through four
doorways. Over each doorway was a rainbow such as they saw in the other
houses. The last doorway was not only arched by a rainbow of five colors but
it had on one side a black kethawn and on the other a blue kethawn. The fourth
room in this abode was the handsomest they had seen yet in any of the abodes ;
the walls were lined with gleaming crystals that emitted a beautiful light, and
they found the room thronged with people who stared rudely at them. *H*ast*s*é-
yal*t*i bade them be seated and turning to those who sat around, said : " Do not
look so curiously at the children. Wherefore do you stare at them so ? " Then
he said to the children : " I hear you are of the Ni'na*h*okádd*ï*ne'," and the children
answered : " We are." " And I learn that you come here from Tsé'*h*alta*l*." They
replied : " Yes, the *d*ïg*í*ni of Tsé'*h*alta*l* sent us here." " And where do you come
from beyond that place ? " he said. " We come from *Ï*n*d*ést*s*í*h*onia' ; we were born
there," they replied. " Were you born thus maimed ? " he continued. " Was
one of you born blind and the other born lame ? " " No," they said, " we were
born sound," and then they went on and rehearsed the sad story of their lives as
they had often told it before. They named all the houses of the *d*ïg*í*ni they had
visited and told how they had been repulsed there ; but they never told the things
that *H*ast*s*éyal*t*i of Tsé'*ï*ntyel had forbidden them to reveal. " When we left
Tsé'*h*alta*l* they told us to come here and that is why we are here now. We hope
you can cure us. We have heard you holy ones know everything. We were
happy in the old days when both of us could see and both of us could walk, and
we want to find some one who will restore us again as we were in those happy
days." When they had finished their story *H*ast*é*syal*t*i said : " The People on
the Earth have many things which we have not ; but which we would be glad to
have. They have cigarettes and enjoy the pleasure of smoking ; they have white
beads and turquoise and haliotis shells," and thus he went on, naming as others
before him had named, the sacred things that the y*é*i prized (par. 235). " When
we heard you were coming we hoped you might be bringing these things with
you." " We are poor, we have nothing," said the twins. " Had we had these
things before, we need not have come so far as this. We have heard before that

the yéi wanted these." "Why, then, have you come here, if you bring not the gifts with you. If you had these to offer we would cure you. There is still one holy place you have not visited. It is called Tse'gíhi; go there and try what the *d*ígíni will do for you. Perhaps they will take pity on you and cure you for nothing." Tó'nenïli then led the twins out (*H*asts*é*yal*t*i had told him to do this); he led them sunwise around the house until they reached the north. Thence he led them to the top of a high hill; here he pointed out to them the walls of a cañon far to the north, and he told them to mark the spot well, for there, said he, was Tse'gíhi.

816.—Tó'nenïli left them and they went on from the top of the mountain till they came near the cañon. "Are you sure this is the place?" said the blind one. "Yes, I know this is the place that was pointed out to me," said the cripple. Suddenly and to their great surprise, the sun went down, for they had not noticed how the day was passing, and it soon became too dark for them to travel. "It is night, elder brother," said the cripple, "we can go no further"; and they lay down to sleep south of the cañon. Next morning the blind one awoke first, and said: "Younger brother, is it day?" "Yes," answered the other awaking; "the sun has arisen." "Are you sure this is the place they pointed out to you?" "Yes, I am certain." "Is the cañon far away?" "It is not many steps more, elder brother." The cripple then mounted on his brother's back, and they went on to the edge of the bluff overlooking the cañon. Here they sat down, and the cripple scanned carefully the chasm before him. It was very deep; he could not see the bottom; the walls were deeply channeled where the water ran down, and no trail could be seen. As he sat there looking and thinking, he saw a rainbow slowly forming and stretching from the cliff on which they sat to a shelf of rock on the opposite cliff. His attention was next attracted by the distant sharp barking of a small dog. Carefully scanning the rocky shelf on the opposite side of the gorge, he observed such a dog tied there. It was a watch-dog of the holy people. *H*asts*é*yal*t*i in his house also heard the dog barking, and he said: "Our dog never barks unless he sees something strange. Go forth, *H*asts*é*el*t*o*d*i,[58] and find out why he barks." *H*asts*é*el*t*odi went to where the dog was tied, but saw nothing. He mounted the rocks a little higher, looked in the direction to which the dog's nose pointed and saw, at last, the boys seated on the opposite brow of the cañon. He had never seen such people as these before and, wondering who they could be, he went down to his home to tell what he had seen. "Why did you not go to them and find out who they were?" said *H*asts*é*yal*t*i. "Go now and see them, and when you come back tell us." Before the boys were aware that any one was coming, *H*asts*é*el*t*od i stood before them. "Whence come you and what people are you?" said the yéi. "We come from *T*ó*ï*ntsa, and we are the Ni'na*h*oká*dd*ïne' or People on the Earth." "We have never seen the People on the Earth before. They know not this place. Whither are you going?" "We are journeying to a place called Tse'gíhi. At *T*ó*ï*ntsa we saw *H*astseyal*t*i and *H*asts*é*hogan. They showed us the way hither and bade us come here."

When the boys had made these answers, *H*ast*s*éel*t*o*d*i returned to his house (which was on the same side of the cañon the twins were on—the dog was tied on the opposite side, that he might the better watch the approach to the houses) and told what he had heard. "Are they fine-looking men? Are they well dressed?" asked *H*ast*s*éyal*t*i. "No," replied the other; "one is lame and one is blind; they are lean and dirty, and clad in rags." Then there was a council among the yéi. "Shall we let them in?" it was asked. "Yes, let us allow them to enter," said many. "We wish to see what the People on the Earth look like." *H*ast*s*éel*t*o*d*i was therefore sent back again to the boys, and told to walk in front of them and lead them in. He went back and bade the boys follow him; but he told the cripple not to look backward as he advanced, to keep his eyes carefully bent on the ground.

817.—They descended twelve steps down the side of the cañon to the first apartment, or house, twelve steps more to the second, twelve steps more to the third, and twelve steps more to the fourth. The cripple saw not if there were doors to the apartment; he saw neither how they entered nor how they left them. He was still bidden to keep his eyes on the ground as they entered the fourth room —they knew not if there were doors, or how they entered—but when they got to the middle of the room some one told them to sit down and look around them. "I shall sit down, but it is no use for me to try to look around," said the blind one, "for I can see nothing. You look around, younger brother, and tell me what you see." The cripple described the apartment to his brother. It was a large square room with a high ceiling, at the top of the wall next to the ceiling there was a horizontal painted streak (frieze)[59] of yellow corn-pollen, and below this there was a streak of blue as broad as the streak of yellow. Crystals were set in the walls, to give light, and rainbows over doors. "Whence do you come, and why do you wander here?" queried *H*ast*s*éyal*t*i, when the twins were seated. "We have been to *T*óintsa. We went there to be cured — the one to have his eyes restored, the other to have his limbs restored. They would not cure us there, but told us to come to Tse‘gíhi, and perhaps we could be cured here. Therefore we come to you. We have had a long and a painful journey." "Where were you before you went to *T*óintsa?" asked the yéi, and in reply the boys related the story of all their adventures. "We have been driven forth from one place to another. Some places we have visited a second time, and were not even allowed to enter. At length we went to *T*óintsa, and from *T*óintsa we were sent to Tse‘gíhi, the place where we now are and where we are telling the story of our wanderings." "Now," said *H*ast*s*éyal*t*i, "you have been to many holy places, and have seen many holy ones. Where have you been told that your eyes and your legs would be restored as they once were?" "We have been to many holy places, but everywhere they told us that they could not help us." "If the others could not help you, neither can we," said the yéi. But he asked: "Have you white shell? Have you turquoise?" and thus he asked them, as others had done before, if they had brought with them the sacrificial things.   To each question the boys replied "No," and at last they said: "We know of no way of getting them.   How can we catch birds when one of us is blind and the other crippled?"   *Hastséyalṭi* then asked in turn each of the yéi present if he could cure the children, and each in turn said he could not.   *Has-tséelṭodi* was then bidden to take the children out and show them the way to *Depĕ'ntsa*, the San Juan Mountains.   As he took them forth he made them precede him, and he again bade them not to look around.   This caution was given lest the children, seeing the rainbows over the doors, might be tempted to touch them.[60]   The yéi took the children out to the place where he first met them, here he made them walk around sunwise, stopped them in the north, showed them where the San Juan Mountains lay, and told them to go there. The cripple said: "The mountains seem very far away."   "But they are not," said the yéi.   "Go there, and you will find the road is short."

818.—They left him and went straight towards the mountains.   He watched them till he saw them entering a ravine on the mountain side and then he returned to his house.   They were toiling slowly up a hill when suddenly the sun set, and they camped for the night where the darkness overtook them.   In the morning they were wakened by the cry of *Hastséyalṭi*: "Wu'hu'hu'hú."   They had heard this before and knew it well.   As before, it sounded faint and far at first, it was repeated three times, each time louder and nearer, and soon after the fourth call they saw *Hastséyalṭi* approaching them.   He clapped his hands together; he put one hand over his mouth as if he were surprised,[61] and he asked the boys who they were and whence they came.   They answered: "We are People on the Earth and we have traveled a long and weary journey."   Without waiting for further questions they went on to relate the whole story to the yéi. "We have been to all the holy places," they said, "and have been sent from one place to another in hope that some one might take pity on us and cure us.   At the last place we went to they sent us to these mountains."   "I am sorry for you," said *Hastséyalṭi*, "I shall return to my home and speak to *Hastséhogan*.   I am not the head chief there; I can do nothing without consulting *Hastséhogan*." When he got back to his house, he said to the chief: "Two of the People on the Earth come this way.   They desire to enter our house.   What say you?" "How do they look?" said *Hastséhogan*.   "Do they look grand and well dressed (bígĭs)?"   "No, they look repulsive and dirty (ĭntsóye)," replied the other.   "I understand that the People on the Earth have plenty of white shell and turquoise and haliotis and pászĭne and all the other things that we require.   Do these two people come provided with them?"   "That I cannot answer," said *Hastséyalṭi*.   "Return then to them and ask them," said the other.   *Hastséyalṭi* named to them the sacrifices that the yéi demanded and asked the children if they had brought them. "Alas! we have none of these things," they replied, "we are poor and helpless, our people have driven us forth to die.   We have hoped to find pity in the holy places and to be cured without reward."   The yéi bade them remain where they were and promised to go back and speak once more for them, and tell that they had none of the sacred things, but hoped to be cured without paying. So he went back and told this to *Hastséhogan*. The chief said : " We will not let them enter unless they bring the gifts. Besides, they are not the kind of people we wish to come to us ; they are filthy and ragged. Go back to them and tell them how they can get to *Tó'nihilin*, where the water runs into the ground. Bid them to go there, and tell them they cannot enter here." *Hastséyalti* returned to the children and told them all this. " At Tó'nihilin," he said, " are many of the holy ones. It is there that *To'badzĭstsíni, Hastséoltoi*, the *Hastsébaka*, the *Hastsé-baad* and the other relations of *Nayénĕzgani* dwell. There perhaps they may cure the blindness and the lameness." " It is well," said the cripple, " we will go there and see if they will take pity on us ; " so he got on his brother's back and they started. *Hastséyalti* climbed up on the summit of *Depĕ'ntsa* and watched the boys till they got down into the valley of *Tó'nihilin* and out of his sight ; then he went to his home and his people asked him : " Whither have the children gone ? " He replied : " They have gone down into the valley at *Tó'nihilin*." See pars. 692, 724.

819.—*Tó'nihilin* is a lake surrounded by mountains. The boys descended to the shores of the lake on the northeast, and they walked sunwise around the lake until they stood on its western shore. Then they looked back in the direction in which they had come and they beheld three gods approaching them. These were *Nayénĕzgani, To'badzĭstsíni*, and *Hastséoltoi*. The gods approached them from the east, one after another, they passed to the south and approached them from that side and thus they did in the west and in the north, in somewhat the same manner as these three gods to-day, in the ceremonies of the night chant, approach the ailing man (par. 595). The cripple said to his brother : " Three of the *dĭgíni* approach us." " How do they appear to you ? " said the blind boy. " One is black, one is red, one has a blue face and carries a quiver of puma skin." When the *dĭgíni* had encircled the children and come around again to the east, Nayé-nĕzgani asked : " Whence come you, my grandchildren ? " and they replied : " We come hither from *Depéntsa*, our Grandfather." " What people are you ? " said the god. " We are the People on the Earth," replied the twins. " We came first to Tse'gíhi from a place called Ĭndĕstsíhonia'." " We have heard of you at Tsé'ĭntyel," said the holy one, " the *Hastséyalti* at that place has told us about you." " We have been to all the holy places," said the children and they named all the places they had visited. " They have been talking about curing us. They have sent us from one place to another. At the last place to which we went they would not let us enter, but sent us on here, and that is the reason we are here now." " We have heard of you," said Nayénĕzgani again. " We have heard that one of you could not see and that the other could not walk. We have some thoughts of helping you, but you must go first to a place called Apahĭ'lgos, and there you will hear from us again." This was the first time that no one had mentioned to them any of the sacred articles, or asked them for these gifts. *Hastséoltoi* led the children to the top of a neighboring hill, pointed out to them the bluffs that bordered the cañon at Apahï'lgo*s* and described to them carefully the way to get there.

820.—"Look close to all these things and mark well the spot to which we are bound, my younger brother," said the blind one. "I have observed all the landmarks," said the lame one ; "we shall surely get there," and on they trudged till they got to Apahï'lgo*s*. The lame boy said : "We have now arrived at the place that was pointed out to us. We stand on the brow of a very deep cañon." "What does it look like ? Do you see any trail by which we may descend ? Do you see the houses of the holy ones ?" "I see neither house nor trail," was the answer. As he said this and glanced up the cañon he became suddenly conscious that a rainbow spanned the cañon below him. He turned to look at this ; the bow vanished as suddenly as it had appeared ; yet during the moment the bow had lasted a yéi had crossed the cañon and climbed its walls. The moment the bow disappeared this yéi, called *Hátd*ast*s*ï*s*i (par. 53), stood before the boys. "Are you the People on the Earth ?" he said, "Such people have never been seen here before. They do not come this way." "Yes," said the boys, "we are the People on the Earth. We are poor, we are unfortunate. Behold us ! We have been to *Tó*'nihili*n* to get cured and the people there have sent us here." "We have heard of you from the other holy places," said the yéi, "and that is the reason I have come up here to meet you. Do you seek my dwelling ? Then stand behind me." He made a rainbow, they stepped on it behind him and in a moment they found themselves far below, on the opposite side of the cañon, standing in front of a door over which hung two parts of a rainbow,—the yellow and the green parts.

821.—The door opened before the yéi and they passed into an empty chamber, on the opposite side of which was another door overhung by a rainbow of three colors. As in other places they passed through three empty chambers in all, and through doors over which hung rainbows,—there was a rainbow of five colors over the last door. When they entered the fourth room they found it thronged with people who awaited them there, and the boys stood until they were bidden to sit down. Now it was one of the *H*ast*s*ébaad who spoke to them. She asked them what people they were and whence they had come, and when they had answered her, she said : "We have heard of you before. We have heard of you at Tsé'ïntyel. We have heard of you at Tse'bíni. We have heard of you at Kïninaékai," and thus she named all the holy places which they had visited. "All the people in this room have heard of you. Now, tell us why you have come to us." "We have come," said the children, "to be cured of our ailments. Every place we have visited we have hoped for the same thing. The reason we have been to so many places is, that at no place have they sought to help us, but have sent us on to another. We had a grandfather and a grandmother once, but they got tired of us and sent us out to die." "We have heard that the People on the Earth know many things ; we thought they knew how to cure the lame and the blind," said the yéi. The children answered : "Our grand-parents have tried every medicine they could think of to cure us, but all failed, and they told us to go away." Then the yéi named the sacred things (par. 236) and asked the children if they had them. The children said: "We have none of these things. That is the reason we have visited so many places. We hoped to be cured without bringing these gifts." The *H*ast*s*ébaad paused a moment and then said: "We will think of what you have told us; we will counsel about it. At all the holy places you have visited they are now counseling about you. You will hear from us again some time. You will know what our councils decide to do. But while we are talking about you, you must go to Ts*ĕ*'ni*h*o*g*an (a place of cliff-houses) where the Dsaha*d*oldzá, Fringe Mouths, dwell." *H*át*d*asts*ĭ*si was told to take the children away to the top of a neighboring mountain and show them the way to Ts*ĕ*'ni*h*o*g*an. He motioned to them to proceed and he followed them. When he got outside he formed another rainbow; they stood on this and in a moment found themselves on the top of the mountain. Here the yéi pointed to a distant range of high cliffs and to a dark spot or hole on the face of the cliff and said: "Go straight over to that place. There are *d*ígíni dwelling there who may cure you or give you advice what to do."

822.—The children descended from the mountain into a cañon, and followed up the cañon till they came to the spot which *H*át*d*asts*ĭ*si had pointed out to them. It was a great cave about half way up the face of the cliff. They saw no way of getting there so they sat down to think about it. While they sat in thought a sound like that of a rattle proceeded from the cave. Soon after, a number of people appeared at the mouth of the cavern and then descended on a rainbow to the foot of the cliff. One side of the body of each was colored blue, the other side red; their faces were of a natural tint. They had streaks of lightning on their bodies. The boys sat facing the east. Three of the yéi, a *H*ast*s*éyal*t*i, a Dsaha*d*oldzá (par. 39) and a Yébaad, approached the boys from the east, then retreating and moving sunwise they approached them in the south, the west, and the north. When they got around to the east again they asked the boys who they were and whence they came. When the boys had answered, the yéi said: "There are few people who are admitted to the house of the Dsaha-*d*oldzá. You cannot enter here." "We come not of our own wish," pleaded the boys, "we come because the yéi of Apahĭ'lgo*s* sent us here. Therefore we had hoped you might let us enter. We have been to other holy places asked to be cured of our ailments, but everywhere we have been asked if we had certain things to offer (naming them). We have told them we had them not, and we tell you now that we have not these things and are not able to get them." "I am sorry," said *H*ast*s*éyalti, that you have not these things. Had you had them you might long ago have been cured of your ailments. But now you must go to *D*epéhaha*t*in (Where Sheep Come Up, par. 661). They who live there know how to cure blindness and lameness. Go to them and hear what they will say to you. In every place where the holy ones dwell they are talking about you." *H*ast*s*éyal*t*i himself went this time with the boys to show them their way. He pointed out to them a high cliff of white stone and said to them : "Go neither to one side nor to the other ; let your path be straight for that cliff."

823.—They went on till they came to the brow of the cañon on whose opposite wall the white cliff arose. The cripple found that the walls of the cañon were terraced and that steep cliffs separated one bench from another. He saw no trail by which they could descend ; but he soon perceived a rainbow that slanted down from the brow to the bottom of the cañon. "Surely," he thought, "the people here knew we were coming and are prepared for us." The cripple soon heard the rainbow rattle and saw it shake, and he heard a distant musical voice (it was the voice of Gánaskĭai, par. 46) crying "Iyahánga." "I hear a voice far down in the cañon," said the cripple. "I hear nothing," said the brother ; "what does the voice say?" "It says 'Iyahánga,'" replied the cripple. Four times this voice was heard, nearer and clearer each time ; but it was not until the fourth call that the blind boy heard it. After the fourth call the cripple said: "Here comes some one. He has horns on his head and a hump on his back. He bends over like an old man, and walks slowly, leaning on a staff." The yéi approached the boys from the east ; he walked around them sunwise as other yéi had done, approaching them and retreating again in the south, the west, the north, and when he got back to the east he turned to them and asked them whence they came. "We come from Tsĕ′nihogan," they replied, "and are on our way to Depéhahatin. We were told at Tsĕ′nihogan that we would find here a people called Gánaskĭdi. Tell us, are you one of these people?" "Yes, I am one of the Gánaskĭdi. If you wish to enter my house get behind me on this rainbow," said the yéi. They did as they were told and soon found themselves far down in the cañon, standing on a narrow ledge on the same side of the cañon as that of the place from which they started. The rocky wall before which they stood was steep and smooth. No door was visible, but the figure of a Rocky Mountain ram was depicted on the wall and under it was a white spot. The cripple said to his brother : "Here we stand on a small narrow ledge with a precipice above us and a precipice below us, and no hole in the rock. I see not where we can go." "Hold your tongue," said Gánaskĭdi ; he struck the white spot with his staff and a doorway opened before them, disclosing a vacant apartment, into which the boys entered after the yéi.

824.—The walls of this room were smooth and no opening could be seen in them ; but on the wall opposite to the one through which they entered there was another picture of a mountain sheep (ewe) and under this a blue spot was painted. The yéi struck this spot with a staff and again a door opened. They passed through another chamber in which they found no one. It was like the first in appearance except that under the figure of the sheep (a ram) there was a yellow spot. When the yéi struck this, a passage opened into another empty chamber. On the opposite wall of the third chamber there was a picture of rain and under this a black spot. When Gánaskĭdi struck the black spot a doorway opened into the fourth chamber and when they entered it they found it filled with people.

The walls of this room were beautifully decorated, and the cripple told his brother that this was the most beautiful room they had yet entered. On the east wall white clouds were painted and above them a white fog; on the south wall blue clouds and above them a blue fog; on the west wall, yellow clouds and above them a yellow fog; on the north wall, black clouds and above them a black fog. On the walls, too, there were objects like the heads of Rocky Mountain sheep without bodies, but they looked as if they were alive; on the east there was a white ram's head; on the south a blue ewe's head; on the west a yellow ram's head, and on the north a black ewe's head. On the horns of the white head in the east there was crooked lightning; on the horns of the blue head in the south was straight lightning; on those of the yellow head in the west was crooked lightning and on those of the black head in the north was straight lightning. On each wall there was a large crystal stone which emitted light and made the room bright, and with each stone there was a special charm or remedy to cure disease: in the stone of the east there was a remedy for blindness; in that of the south a remedy for lameness; in that of the west a remedy for deafness, and in that of the north a remedy for the crooked face (lateral facial paralysis). They felt as they stood in the room, as if rain were falling on them. They felt a sense of mist and moisture.[62] After a long time of silence one of the yéi said to the cripple: "Have you seen everything?" and the boy answered: "Yes I have seen all." The yéi then said: "There are certain articles (naming them) which we demand of you. All the men here, young and old, know how to cure the blind; but they must have these articles or they cannot do it. If you come, bringing these, we can cure you; if you bring them not we cannot cure you." The cripple said: "We bring them not, we are poor and helpless. We know not how to get them." "Then," said the yéi, "we will counsel about you. At all the other holy places they are talking about you now. Go from here to Hastsé-daspĭn, where dwell the Hastsédiltsosi or Squeaking Yéi, who squeak like mice. You think you have been to all the holy places but you have not; there is one more place for you to visit. Go there before you give up trying and see what these people will say to you." The chief who spoke told the Gánaskĭdi who brought them in to take the boys out again. He opened the walls and closed them again with a touch of his staff. When they passed out under the sky they got on a rainbow, in the order in which they got on before; and before they knew what had happened to them, the boys found themselves back on the brow of the cañon, at the spot whence they came. Here Gánaskĭdi pointed out to the cripple some rocky pinnacles which rose on a distant plain and bade him go there and be careful not to pass beyond the pinnacles.

825.—The boys went as they were told and sat down at the base of one of the pinnacles. No one had told them what they should do when they got here, but now Little Wind (Nĭ'ltsiazi) whispered to them: "Hold your heads down and look not up, or you will be whipped." They did thus and immediately heard the squeaking, mouse-like voice of the yéi. He came so fast you could hear the wind rushing by him and he bore in his hand a scourge made of four leaves of yucca. He ran around the boys four times, sunwise, stopped and ran around them again, four times in the opposite direction. For this reason it is that one of the kethawns made for these gods, in the rites of this day, has a spiral line passing around it four times sunwise while the other kethawn has a spiral line passing four times around it in the opposite direction. He stopped in the east and turning to the boys asked them who they were. They replied that they were the People on the Earth. Said the yéi: "You are the first of your kind that ever came here. We have never seen people like you before. Who sent you hither and what do you come for?" "We come from *Depéhahatin*, and we come to be cured. It was the Gánaskĭdi who sent us here and showed us the way. We do not come here of our own notion." "Did the Gánaskĭdi tell you you must not look at me?" said the Squeaking Yéi. "He did not tell us so," they said. "Then why do you look down? Why do you not look up at me?" "We heard the great noise of your coming. We feared you and dared not look up." "Where did you come from first? What tribe of the People on the Earth are you?" "We come from Inděstsĭhonia'." Thus he questioned them and thus they answered him. Then he said: "The holy ones themselves fear us. Even they must be whipped before they can enter our house. For this reason very few of them ever visit us. You had better go to some other place. We are cruel people who dwell here. We whip every who comes near us. Go yonder to Tsótsĭl (Mt. San Mateo) on whose summit the *Hast*séayuhi dwell. I know not what they will say to you there; but I bid you go."

826.—The cripple mounted on his brother's back and they set out for Tsótsĭl. They got in time to the foot of the mountain and then they slowly climbed to the top. There is a hollow place at the top of the mountain like a bowl (or a crater). They sat on the edge of this hole. As they sat they heard a loud noise as of a great wind approaching and soon a violent tempest began to blow. The wind grew stronger and stronger and the sand and dust grew thicker and thicker in the blast until the cripple could not see an arm's length before him. At the height of the storm *Hast*séayuhi and *Hast*séeltlihi appeared before the boys, coming out of the storm. One holy one said to the other: "I wonder what these two strange boys are sitting here for. One is blind and the other is crippled, yet they have climbed to the mountain top." The two gods, like the *Hast*sédĭltsosi, bore scourges and they were just as fond of whipping. The boys said they were Ni'na*h*okáddĭne that they had just come from *Hast*sédaspin and that the people there had sent them. "They told us that *Hast*séayuhi and *Hast*séeltlihi live here. Perhaps you are they of whom we were told." "Why came ye here," said the gods, "and what do you desire?" "We have been to many holy places," said the boys (naming them in the order in which they had visited them), and at each place we hoped to have our eyes and our limbs restored to us as they were before; but at each place they sent us to another place and at the last place, *Hast*sédaspin they sent us here, and that is why we are now at the top of Tsótsĭl." The yéi

said : " He who spoke to you at *H*ast*s*é*d*aspĭn, was mistaken.   We do not make
cures for the People on the Earth.   You might have been cured elsewhere, but
not upon Tsótsĭ*l*.   We who live on this mountain whip those who enter our
dwelling and those who enter once belong to us forever.   They never can leave
us or return again to their people.   There is no use in your staying here.   Go
down to the foot of the mountain (pointing to the southwest) and there you will
find a place called Ts*ĕ*′n*d*aspĭn.   Holy ones dwell there ; but we know not what
they may say to you."   Then they pointed out to the boys the way to Ts*ĕ*′n*d*aspĭn
and the boys departed.

827.—As the yéi of Tsótsĭ*l* and the yéi of *H*ast*s*é*d*aspĭn whipped their visitors
and the former also held their visitors captive, they were seldom seen by the other
yéi and rarely had intercourse with them, so they did not know when the boys
were coming to them, and the yéi of Tsótsĭl sent no message to those at Ts*ĕ*′n-
*d*aspĭn that the twins had gone there ; yet the latter had heard from friendly yéi
of the wandering boys, were on the lookout for them, and from afar saw the boys
descending the mountain.   The *H*ast*s*éyal*t*i of this place told *H*asté*l*pahi to go
out and meet the boys on their way.   When he met them he asked them whence
they came and whither they were going.   They replied that they had been to see
the *H*ast*s*éayuhi on Tsótsĭ*l*, that the latter had sent them to Ts*ĕ*′n*d*aspĭn and to
this place they were going.   The yéi said : " I come from Ts*ĕ*′n*d*aspĭn ; my people
have already heard of you and of your visits to the other holy places.   Follow
me."   The house at Ts*ĕ*′n*d*aspĭn was covered with black cloud, the door was of
black cloud, the black cloud extended to where they stood and held on it a rainbow.   They stood on the rainbow and soon found themselves at the door of the
house.

828.—*H*ast*s*é*l*pahi had in his hands two fox skins ; he held them together in
front of him and then pulled them apart ; as he did so the curtains of clouds rolled
back from the doorway and the three entered a vacant room which they crossed,
the yéi leading.   In this way they passed through four doorways and three vacant
rooms.   The second doorway had curtains of blue cloud ; the third had curtains
of black fog and the fourth, curtains of blue fog.   The fourth room was full of
people who were standing and talking to one another.   The twins were told to sit
down.   *H*ast*s*éyalti questioned them, they answered him, and this was what they
said : " Whence do you come ? "   " We come from the summit of Tsótsĭ*l* where
we met *H*ast*s*éayuhi."   " Have you been elsewhere ?   Is that your home ? "   " It
is not our home.   We made but a short stay there.   We were reared this side of
Tsé′ĭntyel at a place called Ĭn*d*est*s*í*h*onia‘."   " Did the People on the Earth rear
you ?   Was your mother one of them ? "   " They reared us and our mother was
one of them."   " Were you born maimed as you are ? "   " We were born sound
and well."   " Who was your father ? "   " We have asked our mother that question and she has told us she did not know."   " How came you, the one to be
blind, the other crippled ? "   he continued.   Here the boys told the story of how
their misfortune befell them, how their relations had tried to cure them without

avail and had driven them forth to die; they told all their wanderings among the holy places and named them, and they told how the holy ones had refused to cure them unless they gave certain articles which the twins did not possess and knew not how to get. "We have heard of you at these places," said the yéi. "We have heard of you as the pair who traveled, one bearing the other on his back. At what places were you offered food?" "We have never been offered food," said the boys. "You have been to many holy places," said the yéi, "but there is one more place for you to visit. Perhaps we will see you again. Perhaps you will yet find out who your father is. The other holy place is Tsúskai.⁶³ There dwell *H*astséyal*t*i, *H*astsé*h*ogan and many other holy ones." When he had said this, he told *H*astsé*l*pahi to take the boys to Akï*d*anas*t*áni (Hosta Butte) but not to go to the top of the Butte, as the Bear People were there and they might delude the boys to enter; but to go around it and from the opposite side to show the boys where Tsús*k*ai was. *H*astsé*l*pahi guided the boys as he was bidden, showed them where the hill of Tsús*k*ai rose in the distance and told the boys to go straight there.

829.—When they crossed the cañon of Bahastlá the people of Tsús*k*ai saw them and said: "Here they come, the blind boy carrying the cripple." When they reached *T*ó'*h*at*s*i they were again seen and the people at Tsús*k*ai said: "They come now from *T*ó'*h*at*s*i." When they got to the foot of the mountain at Tsús*k*ai, *T*ó'nenïli the Water Sprinkler was dispatched to go down and meet them. When the cripple saw the yéi coming, he said: "The old man we met at Tsé'*h*al*t*a*l* approaches us." The yéi walked around the boys saying, "Yuw yuw yuw yuw," something like the yelping of an Indian dog. He put his hand over his mouth and asked, in astonishment: "Are you not cured yet?" He carried a wicker bottle garnished with spruce twigs and filled with water; pouring a little of the water into the hollow of his hand, he sprinkled it on the path they were to travel in the direction of Tsús*k*ai, Instantly the clouds gathered, rain began to fall, and a rainbow formed; *T*ó'nenïli took the lead; the boys got behind him on the rainbow and in a moment they found themselves up at Tsús*k*ai, standing outside of a door (or curtains) made of black cloud.

830.—*T*ó'nenïli held up together before his face his water jar and a fox-skin; he pulled these apart and as he did so the curtains of cloud rolled away and they all passed between these into an empty chamber. As in other houses the boys had visited before, there were three empty chambers and four doors. The curtain doors of the second chamber were of blue cloud, those of the third chamber were of black fog and those of the fourth chamber of blue fog. When the boys entered the fourth room they found there *d*igíni of all kinds. They entered at the east and were led all around the room before they were told to sit down. The holy ones of Tsús*k*ai knew who they were and all about their history, for the holy people at the other places had told these things; yet they asked the boys all the questions that had been asked at the other holy places, for they wished to hear how the boys would tell the tale themselves, and the boys answered as they had always answered before. When the boys had finished their story the yéi asked: "Have you the dark kethawn (ke*t*án *d*ï*l*yï*l*) and have you the blue kethawn (ke*t*án *dot*lï'z) that belong to us?" "We have them not," said the twins. "Have you white shell? Have you turquoise?" (and so on, naming the sacred articles). "Neither have we any of these," said the twins. "One of us is blind; the other is lame; we are poor; we have no way of getting them." "You have traveled far," said the yéi, "and have visited many places, but all was of no use, and there is now no other holy place for you to go to. It was because you did not have the sacred offerings that you have failed. Had you had the offerings you would have been cured. There are many *d*ïgíni in this house but they know not how to cure you. The people of Tsé'ïntyel are now talking about you and are trying to find a way to cure you. All the chiefs of all the holy places you have visited are assembled in council and you will meet them there. When you leave here, go straight to Tsé'ïntyel and go not back to your mother's home." Tó'nenïli now led the boys out and to the top of Tsúskai and he pointed out to them Tsé'ïntyel and showed them the way to get there. He said: "On your way avoid carefully the place called *T*ó'*d*ïl*t*o, and go to the south of it. Avoid also the place called Ni'*h*altsï's (Hole in the Ground) and go to the south of it; the Bear People live there. Avoid also the place called Dsï*ld*asaáni and go to the north of it. The Bear People and the Deer People both live there."

831.—The children went as they were directed, and when they had passed Dsï*ld*asaáni they took the direct route from there to Tsé'ïntyel. When they reached Kiltsóibïla*h*otyél the holy ones at Tsé'ïntyel saw them approaching. The chiefs of the holy places had already gathered and were in council. They were talking about their *H*ats*s*éyal*t*i (who was not present at the council), of why he had pleaded the cause of the children and why he had said: "Perhaps they are relations of yours." The boys came down the path of T*s*áapani.[64] When the yéi saw the way they were about to descend, they placed certain weapons on the trail to see if the boys would pick them up. Dsaha*d*old*z*á laid his bow first; it was the bow of darkness, made of black wood with sinew on the back. He laid with it two arrows of great potency made of a wood called tse'ïskï'*z*i and feathered with quills from an eagle's tail. *Th*atlát*s*i Dsaha*d*old*z*á (Fringe Mouth of the Water) next laid on the trail his bow made without sinew, of the wood called tsé'*t*kani and two arrows which were made of tsïntlï'zi (*Fendleria rupicola*) and plumed with feathers of the atsé-*l*ïtsói or yellow-tail (*Buteo borealis*). *H*ast*s*éol*t*oi laid her weapons next upon the trail. Hers was a good bow made of wood called atlï'nbigest*s*i. Her arrows were made of reed and plumed with small eagle feathers. The quiver and bow-case were laid with these and this is why the quiver is now always carried by *H*ast*s*éol*t*oi in the ceremonies. Lastly *H*ast*s*é-yal*t*i (father of the twins) laid down a poor bow of cedar with the leaves left on the end, and arrows of rose which were tipped with a harder wood and plumed with owl-feathers. These four gods laid their weapons down in different places along the trail and went home, while *T*ó'nenïli hid himself on the bluff where he could observe the trail and see which set of weapons the boys would take.

832.—As they came along the path the cripple cried out : " Oh, elder brother ! Here in our path lies a beautiful black bow with sinew on the back and two beautiful arrows that point to the east. Let us take them."   " Alas !" said the elder brother, " they are too fine for such poor people as we. We must not take them, they are not intended for us."   When they came to the next pile the cripple cried : " Here on our trail lies another bow with arrows that point to the south."   " And how do these appear ? " said the elder. " They are beautiful and well wrought, but not so fine as the first," said the other.   " The arrows have points of stone and are plumed with the feathers of the yellow-tail."   " Ah, these are also too good for us ; we must not lift them," said the blind boy. When they came to the third lot of weapons the cripple again called to his brother saying : " Once more a bow lies on our path and with it are two arrows whose heads point to the west."   " What do these look like ? " said the elder. " They are beautifully formed," said the younger, " and a beautiful bow-case and quiver of puma-skin lie beside them."   " Even these are too fine for us," said the blind boy.   " We must not take them. They are not for us."   When they came to the fourth lot of weapons the cripple called again to his brother : " Another bow lies on our path with arrows that point to the north " ; and the blind boy asked : " How do these appear ? " The younger brother answered : " They are rudely formed ; the bow is of green cedar from which the leaves have not even been cut off ; the arrows are tipped with wood, not stone, and they are trimmed with owl-feathers ; they are poor."   " Then they are suited for poor people. Let us take them," said the elder, crouching down and picking the weapons up from the ground. When *Tó'ínenli* beheld this from his place of watching, he hastened back to Tsé'íntyel and told the chiefs, in council, what he had seen.   Then *Hastséhogan* turned to *Hastséyalti* saying : " Why have you not told us that these were your children ? Why have you denied them and let them wander all over the land hungry and disappointed ? Had you told us who they were, they might have been cured long ago." [65] *Hastsáylti* replied : " At one place I told you that perhaps they were kindred of yours. Could I have more plainly said they were my children ? Why did you not understand me ? " Still the chief upraided him. " Why did you let them starve ? Had we known they were of our own people we would at least have given them food and not have let them go forth from our doors hungry."   *Hastséhogan* then said to *Gánaskïdi* : " You own all the (wild) sheep. Take one over to *Tsáapani* and leave it there for the boys to kill." (For the yéi supposed the boys had been fasting all the time and they knew not of the miraculous food their father had given them). So, at a place on the trail where there was a black spot on the rock, a sheep was placed standing for the boys when they should come along.

833.—Soon, as they advanced, they espied the sheep not far away. The cripple said : " There is a Rocky Mountain sheep near our trail. Shall we not kill it ? "   " Alas !" said the blind boy, " our arrows are not sharp enough and our bow is too weak."   " Still, let us try," said the other ; " it sees us not. Perhaps we may creep closer to it." "Tell me, then, which way to walk and where to stop," said the elder. They advanced slowly closer and closer to the sheep; the cripple whispered to his brother to stop; he drew his bow and let fly. The arrow struck the sheep on the temple and bounded back, yet the sheep fell and moved not. The boys went up on top of the rock where the sheep lay, and found it dead. Gánaskĭdi was watching them from a hiding-place in the rocks, and when he saw the boys had killed the sheep he went back to Tsé'ĭntyel to relate what he had seen. Nayénĕzgạni was sent out with his big knife to skin the sheep, for the yéi knew the boys had no knife, and he was told to cut for the boys and give them to keep a piece from the end of each horn,—about a finger's length,—the gristle from each ear, the water from each eye, a strip of skin from the nose and forehead including the nostrils, and the two tendones Achillis. Nayénĕzgạni traced with his knife down the median line of the sheep's body, uttering his peculiar low groans as he did so; he cut the skin along the lines he had traced; he removed the skin and he cut out the parts he had been told to take. When he had done all this the boys said they had no fire to cook the food, therefore when he went back to Tsé'ĭntyel he told the yéi that the boys had no way of making fire, and Hastsézĭni was sent to make fire for them. He carried with him a burning brand of shredded cedar bark, such as the god carries to this day in the rites of to'nastsihégo hatál (pars. 104–107); he went to where the boys were, built a fire for them, and said: "When you have eaten your fill come over to Tsé'ĭn-tyel; but before you start gather all the meat you have left, fold it back in the skin, and leave the bundle back on the rock where you shot the sheep (there it was to come back to life again). "Thanks, our uncle," said the boys; "we have long hungered for meat." When they had finished their meal, they did as they were bidden and went on toward Tsé'ĭntyel. When they got to the floor of the cañon, they heard a voice saying: "Come hither." It was the voice of a bat; but at the same time Nĭ'ltsĭazi, Little Wind, whispered to them: "Listen not to the voice, but go on to Tsé'ĭntyel." But the voice persisted in saying: "Come hither," and Little Wind kept on saying: "Heed not the voice, but go to Tsé'ĭn-tyel." The boys kept on, and as they neared Tsé'ĭntyel the yéi sent the father to meet his children. When he came to them, he said: "My children (ye who were born for me), I am your father. If I have failed to say so before now it was not my fault. Your mother bade me be silent."[66] The cripple said to his brother: "My elder brother, here is the yéi who met us before several times; he who first told us to go to Tsé'ĭntyel, he who gave us the white meal and the little bowl to mix it in, and now he calls us his children." "Yes," said the yéi, "I am your father. It was I who gave you the meal and the bowl, and you did not go hungry on your way, but had plenty to eat. I am glad you have come back here. We have counseled about you. You will yet be cured. The blind will be made to see and the cripple to walk. Follow me!" And they went after him to Tsé'ĭntyel.

834.—There were many people standing outside when they entered. The first, and second, and third rooms, which were empty when the boys visited the place before, were now thronged, as was also the fourth room.   The yéi shook hands with the children[67] and bade them welcome, saying: "You had a hard time with us before and were cruelly treated, but we knew not you were our kindred."   And those who stood near called them by various terms of relationship.   One said, "My sons," another said, "My grandsons," another, "My younger brothers," others, "My cousins," "My nephews."   The apartments and doors were so crowded that the boys had scarcely room to pass through.   In the middle of the floor in the fourth room were spread naskán or embroidered blankets, such as the Oraibes make.   After the boys had been made to walk around the room sunwise they were made to sit on these blankets with their faces to the east, and then *Hastséhogan* spoke to them: "I could not help you before because I did not know you were my children.   This is why you have gone without profit to all the holy places (naming them in the order visited).   Had your father not denied you it would have been different."   Then he told them why the different sets of bows and arrows had been laid on their path, and how they found out by the weapons they took who their father was.[65]   The yéi ordered some of the food called yïstĕlkaí to be mixed for the children, and he said to the people: "Gaze not upon them while they eat; if you do they will be bashful and will not eat all they want."   The food was given to them in a small yellow bowl, which seemed scarcely to hold a mouthful, but they both ate from this bowl until they were satisfied, and then the bowl was as full as in the beginning.   They handed the bowl back to their father, saying: "We can eat no more."   He emptied the bowl with one sweep of his finger, and it remained empty.   "Where shall we cure these boys?" said one; "shall we do it here or at Kïninaékai?"   "Let us take them to Kïninaékai and do it there," said another; and this is what they decided to do.   Their father, *Hastséyalti*, was bidden to go in advance, leading the children, and the whole crowd started for Kïninaékai.   They wanted to see them cured just for the same reason that the Navahoes now go in crowds to witness a great healing ceremony.   They all went first to the north side of the cañon, to the foot of the cliff, and they stopped there a while to talk about the ceremony of cure.   Some proposed to have the ceremony performed just where they stood; but the father of the children said: "Let us not be in haste.   Let us go on with care.   Let us try to make a sure cure.   It is my fault that the boys have traveled so far and suffered so much.   Now, let us do the best we can for them."

835.—After talking a while they all agreed to make a sweat-house such as is made to-day in the rites of klédze *hatál*.   The sweat-house was built; it was adorned on top with pictures of the rainbow and the lightning; the light of a rock crystal was made to shine into it; twigs of spruce were placed on the floor for the boys to sit on, and four hot stones were put in to make the room hot.   Before the blind boy went into the sweat-house they put into his eyes a mixture made of the water from the eye of a sheep and a plant or medicine called nakétïn.   Before the cripple went in the tendones Achillis of the sheep were pressed to his limbs, and the juice of a plant called azénaol*thá*d*e* (chewed, par. 304) was spit upon them and rubbed in. After the boys entered, the opening of the sweat-house was covered with curtains or blankets of blue cloud, of black mist and of blue mist, and the yéi charged the boys strictly on no account to talk in the sweat-house. "If you get too warm and want to come out, touch the curtain with the hand." The lodge soon grew very hot and the boys began to perspire freely; after a little while the blind one became conscious of a faint light streaming in under the curtains and the cripple felt he could move his legs a little. Their joy was so great that they forgot what the yéi had told them. "Oh! younger brother," cried one, "I see." "Oh! elder brother," cried the other, "I move my limbs." In an instant the rainbow, the lightning, the curtains of cloud and mist, and the sweathouse itself vanished and left the boys sitting on the open ground with nothing but the four stones beside them and the spruce-twigs under them, the one as blind, the other as lame as ever. The yéi were angry. *H*ast*s*éyal*t*i their father and *H*ast*s*é*h*og*an said to them: "You are fools. You were bidden not to speak. It is your own fault if you are not cured. You must have no ears that you did not hear. Perhaps that is why the *d*ïgíni have driven you away from their houses— because you would not listen to what was said to you." Though the people around still called them their children, they upbraided them; they said, "It would have cost you nothing to be cured; but you have broken the charm by your own folly. Now you will have to pay and all the holy ones here demand the sacred articles they have always demanded, and these must be both good and beautiful. (Here the articles are all mentioned again, par. 236.) These holy ones have been calling you their children; that is the reason we would have cured you without pay." Ah! had these boys kept quiet in the sweat-house that day our people could now all have their diseases cured without paying for the cure; but because they spoke and had to pay, the Navahoes have, ever since, been obliged to make gifts in order to be cured. "Go anywhere now. Go where you will, only begone," said the yéi.

836.—So the poor blind boy told his brother to mount again on his back. They walked in sadness down the cañon and mourned for what they had done. They now knew not what way to go nor what trail to take; they had no purpose; they wept as they walked along and as they wept they began to sing. At first they sang only meaningless syllables; but after a while they found words to sing. They cried to music and turned their thoughts to song. The holy ones still stood grouped behind them, and, hearing the song, said one to another: "Why do they sing?" "I wonder what they are singing about?" and they sent the father of the children to bring them back. When *H*ast*s*éyal*t*i overtook them he said, "Come back, the yéi wish to see you again and speak to you." The blind boy replied, "I shall not go back. They have told us, in anger, to begone. They are only making fools of us." But the cripple urged: "Let us return once more and find out what they wish to say." When they returned some one asked them: "What were you singing as you went along?" They answered: "We were not singing.

We were crying." " And why did you cry ?" " We cried because you bade us go away and we knew no longer where to go." The yéi still persisted : " What kind of a song did you sing ? We surely heard the words of a song," and the boys said : " We were not singing, we were crying." When the yéi asked this question for the fourth time the cripple spoke : " We began to cry, and then we sang ; we turned our cry into a song. We never knew the song before. My blind brother made it up as we went along, and this is what we sang :

> From the white plain where stands the water,
> > From there we come,
> Bereft of eyes, one bears another.
> > From there we come.
> Bereft of limbs, one bears another.
> > From there we come.
> Where healing herbs grow by the waters,
> > From there we come.
> With these your eyes you shall recover.
> > From there we come.
> With these your limbs you shall recover.
> > From there we come.

> From meadows green where ponds are scattered,
> > From there we come.
> Bereft of limbs, one bears another.
> > From there we come.
> Bereft of eyes, one bears another.
> > From there we come.
> By ponds where healing herbs are growing,
> > From there we come.
> With these your limbs you shall recover.
> > From there we come.
> With these your eyes you shall recover.
> > From there we come.   See pars. 944, 945.

837.—When the yéi had heard the boys' song they counseled once more and at last they said : " We must never turn our children out again, blind, crippled and helpless as they are," and they said to *H*ast*s*éyal*t*i of Tsé'*z*ïni, " Send them to Áyakini (the Moki towns) and to *Th*ála*h*og·an[68] and tie up for them the things they are to use there." He tied up, each in a separate bundle, the four following things : (1) a living kangaroo rat (naas*t*é) ; (2) t*s*o*s*, a worm ; (3) níyol, the wind—a talisman to produce wind ; (4) four migratory grasshoppers (nahas-t*s*ági). These he wrapped in a black cloud and put in a pouch that hung on one side. Thus they instructed the boys : " Go to the Mokis and let the rat loose in their fields ; he will scratch up the seeds and they will see that their crops will be destroyed if they do not get rid of him ; then they will give you valuable presents to kill the rat or take him away. When you have taken the rat away the corn will grow well ; but when it is a hand's breadth above the ground turn your worm loose in the fields ; he will begin to eat the tender shoots ; then they will give you presents to get rid of the worm.   When the corn puts forth its tassel take out the wind, and let it loose ; it will blow the corn down, and when they see their crops again in danger they will give you more presents to still the wind.   When the ears begin to fill, turn out the grasshoppers to devour the crops ; then they will give you things of value to call away the grasshoppers.   But be careful not to call these in too soon—not till you get all the things you have demanded.   First get four unwounded buckskins, and in these you will place the other articles according as you get them, baskets, feathers and all."   They gave the boys a short rainbow, about a finger's length, to keep, and they gave an arched rainbow, about eight paces long, for them to travel on.   They bade the boys go down the Chelly till they came to the mouth of the cañon, and then to *Háhastyel.*   They laid the rainbow down, bade the boys stand on it, the cripple to shut his eyes for a little while and then open them.

838.—The boys stood on the bow ; their father gave a puff of wind and the bow started.   The bow stopped for a while ; the cripple opened his eyes and found that they were a little way from Kĭninaékai.   After this he kept his eyes open to the end of the journey.   The bow went by jumps or frequent stops along the road they desired to go.   In a little while they came to *Háhastyel.*   They had been bidden, when they started, to go to the western end of the first Moki mesa, to the last town (Walpi), and they kept on with the rainbow to near the foot of the cliff there.   The Mokis saw them coming and said : "Two ugly creatures approach us.   We know not what they are."   When the boys got to the foot of the mesa, where the trail begins to ascend, the people on top could see them no longer.   Then the twins folded up their rainbow, put it in their pouch and climbed the hill to Walpi.

839.—When they arrived at the top of the mesa the Mokis gathered around them, threw small stones and pieces of filth at them and mocked them.   One stuck his finger in the blind boy's eye and asked him why he couldn't see.   The boys tried to enter a house, but the Mokis would not let them.   The people brought out broken fragments of food in baskets ; but when the boys tried to help themselves, the baskets were snatched away.   Thus did the Mokis continue to tease the children.   They staid around the villages four nights, during which the Mokis gave then no shelter and nothing to eat ; but they had the magic bowl their father had given them to eat from and they had the blanket of darkness to cover them at night and keep them warm.   During this time the people of the villages were planting their corn.   Every day they went down to their fields in the valley and the boys went with them, although the Mokis continued to tease them —to offer them food and take it away again.

840.—At the end of the fourth day, when the Mokis had planted their crops, the boys remained in the fields for awhile after the planters had gone home, and turned their rat loose.   Then they went up and slept on top of the mesa.   When the Mokis went down in the morning to visit the fields they saw where the rat had begun his mischief and they came back howling : " Our crops will be ruined, the rats have gotten among them." The rats multiplied in one night and became very numerous. The Mokis tried to catch the rats, to destroy them. They tried to dig them out, to drown them out, to trap them; but they kept on increasing and eating up the seeds. Every day they replanted the hills where the rats had been at work; but when they visited the fields on the following day they found their seeds again destroyed. This went on for four days. The old men and the old women returned weeping from the fields and saying: "Alas! we shall have no food to eat in the winter that is coming." Then the chiefs of the Mokis held a council, and some one spoke saying: "We hear that the People on the Earth know many things. There are two of them here among us now. Let us call them into our council; perhaps they may help us." The young men laughed at this and said: "They are blind and crippled; they are poor and ugly; they can know nothing." But the old men said: "It is no harm to ask them. Let us try. All our own ways have failed." So the chiefs went to the twins and asked them if they knew of any medicine that would drive the rats away. The blind boy answered, "I am blind and can do nothing. Perhaps my brother knows something that will help you." One of the chiefs said: "The corn belongs to us all. If you help us, every one will give you something, and you shall have all the tsé'asté (paper bread, par. 223) you want to eat." "It is well," replied the cripple; "we shall try to help you." Then the chief called aloud to the people and bade them bring tsé'asté, to bring an unwounded buckskin (par. 257) and any valuables they did not need, and place these beside the boys as gifts; to bring hanikaí (meat and corn boiled together) and plenty more of their best food. When they had eaten their fill, the boys said: "We will go down into the fields; but when we go the Mokis must retire to their houses; no one may look down to see what we are doing. If any one glances at us over the edge of the mesa it will spoil all our work, it will undo what we have done."

841.—The boys went down into the fields, caught four of the rats, wrapped them up in a dark cloud, put them in their pouch and came up again on the mesa where the Mokis were. They told the chiefs to tell the people that no one must go down into the fields for four days and four nights, and that no one must even look down during that time. The chiefs then told the boys to go round among the people and eat anywhere they chose; that they would be welcome at any house. The Mokis now became very kind to the twins. At the end of the fourth night, the Mokis went to their fields; they found that their corn had grown a hand's breadth in height; that all their other crops were doing well; and they saw no more tracks or traces of the rats; the animals seemed to have all disappeared. When the Mokis returned from the fields they thanked the boys, saying: "Our corn, our beans, our squashes, our melons, are all growing well."

842.—For a while after this, the Mokis were very thankful and very kind; but they soon forgot the good services which the boys had rendered them, thought they would need nothing more from them, and began to annoy them again; they would poke incandescent sticks in their faces; they would throw dirt on them ; one would push over another so that he would fall on the boys ; they would poke fingers in the boys' eyes, and at last they refused to give them food. The boys got weary of this, left the Mokis and set out for *Thálahog*an. While the boys were crossing the valley the people of Moki gathered on the brow of the mesa, laughed at the boys and made vulgar jokes about them.

843.—When the twins arrived in *Thálahog*an the people there received them as the people of Moki had done, with ridicule and contempt. Food and objects of value were offered to them and then snatched away and all the tricks that were played on them at Moki were played on them again at *Thálahog*an. The people at this place were now busy hoeing their corn which was about a span high. The boys followed the people to the field and at sunset or thereabouts, when the till-ers went home, and the fields were all deserted, the boys turned their worm loose among the corn. When they went back to the pueblo that night the people would give them no place to sleep in the houses, so they slept outside on a pile of ashes.

844.—When the people went out next morning they found their young corn infested with worms that were gnawing the roots. All the people in the village who were able to walk—men, women and children—went to gather the worms in bowls and baskets and they worked all day until after sunset—then they went home. The corn that was gnawed all withered at the tops. This destruction and this labor of the people kept on for four days, at the end of which time, scarcely a hill of sound corn could be seen. There was weeping and wailing in the pueblo. The people cried : " We shall starve this winter, for the worms have eaten all our crops." A council was held and some one arose in the council and said : " We have heard that these boys who are among us, the blind one carrying the cripple, banished the rats from the fields of the Mokis ; perhaps they can do something to chase away the worms that now destroy our crops." The young men, like the young men at the Moki towns, laughed at these words, saying : " They are blind and crippled, they are poor and ugly, they know nothing " ; but the elders said : " It is no harm to ask them. Let us try what they can do." Then one of the principal chiefs among the men and one of the principal chiefs among the women went together to seek the boys, and meeting the latter begged them to help in driving away the worms. The blind boy said : " I know nothing and can do nothing, for I am blind ; but ask my brother who can see, perhaps he can help you." " What will you ask us in return for chasing these worms ? " said the chiefs. " We are all crying for our corn. Destroy the worms and you shall have all you want to eat, you shall be welcome at every hearth." The cripple de-manded first two unwounded buckskins, which when he got he spread out as he did also the skin he got from the Mokis. One skin was to receive food and the other the various jewels, baskets, feathers and other valuables which he next de-manded and received. The people brought them, too, a great mess of meat stewed with corn and alkán, or sweet bread (par. 221).

845.—The boys then told the chiefs as they had told those of Moki, that the people must remain in their houses, and not look toward the field while the boys were at work and that after their return the people must not visit their fields, or go in the direction in which they lay or look toward them. After these orders had been announced from the housetops, the boys went among the corn, caught four of the worms, wrapped them in dark cloud, put them in their pouch and returned to the village. At the end of the fourth night after this the people of *Thálahogan* visited their fields. They found that their corn had sprouted about a hand's breadth in height and that the beans, squashes and melons had also grown well above the ground. Indeed it was not necessary to visit the fields to see that all was well again, for those who stood on the hill-tops near the village could observe that the field looked green once more. The people returning from the fields boasted about their crops. Some said: "My corn is *so* high" (making signs); others said: "Mine is higher than that"; and thus they talked, but all said that not one more worm could they see. While the corn was still in danger of being lost the people were very kind to the boys; but as soon as they thought it was out of danger, again they began to persecute the twins in various ways as the people of Moki had done, and at last, after four days of this torment, they even refused them food.

846.—After the end of the fourth night, the boys went down into the fields with the people; when the latter returned in the evening to the village, the boys remained behind and planted the wind in the ground. After this the wind blew so hard for four days that it broke the young corn and blew it prostrate. Again all the people of the town, who were able to work, went into the fields. They raised shelters of weeds to the windward of the hills of corn and set up stones to keep the windbreaks in position, but these did not preserve the corn from the great force of the storm. The old men said to the younger men: "We bade you to be kind to these boys and not to persecute them; but you would not heed us and now again our crops are being destroyed." Two of the chiefs among the women and one of the chiefs among the men now went to the boys, and calling them affectionately "our grandchildren," begged them to assist in stilling the storm. Four times they begged the children and four times the latter refused to help them, saying: "Your people laugh at us and torment us. We are poor and ugly. What do we know about the wind and how to stop its blowing?" While they begged the boys the women petted and caressed them. "You People on the Earth[55] know much; you can still the wind for us as you chased away the worms," they said. At length the boys yielded and said: "We will try to help you; but you must give us all that we ask for. When we helped you before you paid us in old rags, in cast-off articles of clothing, in scraps of food. We will take such things no longer, we must have things new, fine, valuable, and we must have the best and freshest of your food. On the first occasion we had two unwounded buckskins from you, now we want three more," and then the boys demanded all the sacred articles which the yéi had told them to get among the people of the pueblos. The three chiefs returned to the council and told there what the boys had said and what they demanded: "We live on corn," they said. "If the corn is destroyed we die.   These boys promise to save us if we give them these deer-skins and jewels and feathers.   If we have no corn we shall have no mush, or sweet bread or paper bread, or stews of corn and meat or any of the savory dishes that are made out of corn.   Therefore, we should give the boys what they ask for, in order that they may stop the wind."   The people then went forth and began to lay down their treasures before the boys.   They first spread the three deerskins and on one of these they piled paper bread and other articles of food, and on the other skins they piled clothing, baskets, precious stones, feathers, pollen, and all the other treasures that the boys had asked for.   Yet they did not put the best that they had on these buckskins, just as we do not give away the best we have, if we can help it.

847.—The boys now having told the chiefs to instruct the people, as they had instructed them before, went into the fields, dug up the wind they had planted, wrapped it in black fog, tied the bundle with a rainbow, put all in their pouch and went back to *Thálahogan*.   At the end of the fourth night, after this, when the restrictions placed by the boys had ended, the people visited their fields once more.   The storm had ceased, the corn was all straight again and nearly in tassel, the squashes, beans and melons were all in blossom.   "You should be thankful to these boys," said the chiefs to the people.   "You should laugh at them no more.   You should cease to annoy and revile them."

848.—During the days of their trouble the people of the village were very good to the boys, they invited them to eat in every house ; but after the winds had ceased and the crops had begun to flourish again, they no longer invited the boys to help themselves from the bowls.   They began to revile and curse the boys ; "*Itáhotsïndi* !"[69]   Go to the Devil's place.   In*d*áznaal !   May you die !   We shall take away from you the fine things we have given you.   We shall kill you" ; such were the words they said.   It was the young men of the town who counseled to rob and kill them ; but the chiefs said : "No.   Let them depart in peace ; but they must depart."   Boys of their own age shot at them with blunt arrows so as to hurt but not to wound them.   The twins hung around the village and stood all this abuse for four days, and then they made up their minds to go back across the valley to the villages of the Mokis.

849.—When they arrived at Áyakini the Mokis were hoeing their corn which was now in tassel and the boys went with the laborers to the fields.   There the youths of Moki teased the maidens—pointing to the twins they said : "There are husbands for you."   The boys said to one another : "We have only one more kind of medicine—that is our grasshoppers ; let us see what they can do."   After sunset, when the laborers went home, the boys went to the center of the fields. They picked out a stalk immediately to the east of the center and in its tassel put a grasshopper.   To the south of the center in a tassel of corn they put another grasshopper ; to the west of the center they put a third grasshopper, and to the north a fourth.   This done, they returned to the mesa and slept on the edge next to the cornfields that night.

850.—During the night the grasshoppers increased and did great destruction; they ate off the leaves and the silk of much of the corn, and they ate the covering from the stalks. When some of the Mokis descended to the fields in the morning, as it is always their custom to do during the growing season, and found the fields swarming with grasshoppers and saw what damage had been done, they howled like wolves. This is a common signal among these people; they use it to call the people together from a distance in time of danger and even when they kill a deer. After the call was sounded many more people came down from the mesa; when these were shown the grasshoppers and the injury which had been done they were sent off, young and old, to gather cedar bark, to make fires in order to smoke the pests out. But this plan did not work well; the grasshoppers would rise from the place where the smoke was and settle down immediately in some other part of the field where there was no smoke instead of leaving, as the Mokis had hoped they would do. They tried the smoke all day without success.

851.—Early next morning the boys heard a herald crying on the housetops. He gave orders that all people, even to the smallest children, that were able to walk, should go to the fields that day. The children, he directed, should catch grasshoppers, put them in baskets, carry them beyond the fields and kill them, while the men were to remain in the fields tending the fires and chasing the grasshoppers with branches. Thus the people toiled all day, yet, by the second night the grasshoppers had spread not only over the fields of Áyakini, but over those of *Thálahogan* as well. At *Thálahogan* the people were evidently doing the same as those of Moki, for the smoke of their fires could be seen across the intervening valley. The twins had an easy time up on the mesa all day; they did not go down into the fields; but sat in the sun and enjoyed the sight of the Mokis fighting the grasshoppers. Perhaps they whistled through their teeth.

852.—Next morning they again heard the crier on the house-tops bidding the people to go out and do as they had done the day before. On the previous day they had gathered bark and branches for their fires; but to-day they gathered grass and greasewood and all sorts of inflammable herbs. But for all their work the grasshoppers did not leave or diminish, and at night there was little left of the corn but the stalks. Meanwhile the smoking was going on over at *Thálahogan*, as actively as ever, and the twins sat on the brow of the cliff and watched and rested. Some of the people came home very late that night, for they had worked as long as there was light to see, and they ate their suppers and went to bed very tired. Many said: "There is no use in going back to the fields to-morrow. The pests have eaten all the leaves and have begun on the stalks. They will devour these tomorrow, and there are more of them now than ever." The chiefs did not sleep at all that night, so great was their anxiety; but they determined not to give up, and bade the crier call to the people again next morning.

853.—On the fourth morning some had given up all hope, refused to go to the fields and staid at home; others were reluctant, but went at the entreaty of the chiefs. When the people went to the fields, the stalks of corn had disappeared, nothing was left but short stumps, and the grasshoppers were busy even on these. The watermelon vines, squash vines, and beans were similarly devoured. By noon the corn was all gone to the roots. All the laborers went home, disheartened, before the sun was half way down the west and told the old women what had happened. These began to wail: "Alas for our little children; they must starve and die, for we have no corn wherewith to feed them."

854.—There were sad councils that night which lasted all night at the Moki towns and at *Thálahogan*. The young men, as well as the old, joined in the councils. Thus they spoke in the council: "Only the roots of our corn and beans are left, starvation and death are before us. All the methods that we have used in past years to drive away the grasshoppers we have tried this time, but without avail. We have made more smoke, we have killed more grasshoppers, we have worked harder than ever we did before; but the grasshoppers increase in numbers. They have conquered us. What shall we do?" At length some one said: "Where have the twins gone, the blind one bearing the cripple?" and the answers came: "We saw them on the brow of the cliff this morning as we went to the fields"; "We saw them on the side of the mesa this morning. Perhaps they are now asleep among the rocks." A crier was sent to the housetops to call out and find what had become of the boys. The first chief cautioned the people: "Never frighten these boys again. Torment them no more. Curse them no more. You have done wrong." The chiefs had now begun to suspect that the boys had brought the grasshopper plague on them in revenge for bad treatment. The second chief said: "Ever since these boys came among us we have had misfortune. If I find them in the morning I shall kill them and throw their bodies down over the cliffs." Several of the young men who heard this announcement were rejoiced and shouted: "That is what should be done with the boys! Let us fling them down over the cliffs!" Then a gray-haired old woman spoke: "We would be fools to kill them. If they have destroyed the crops, perhaps they can save them as they did before. Let us first beg them to help us as they did when the rats troubled us, and if they refuse or are unable to help us, then it is time to talk of killing them." The first chief said: "The words of the woman are wise.[70] I think as she does. Let us first ask the boys if they can help us. They did it before; they may do it again." The chief of *Thálahogan* was at this council with some other head men of that place. He said: "It might not be lucky to kill them. If they have the power to bring on these plagues and the power to stop them, perhaps if we killed them we would never raise crops any more." At last, all agreed to the proposals of the first chiefs. No one slept that night.

855.—Early in the morning the crier on the housetops inquired for the boys. They had slept during the night under a ledge of rock on the side of the mesa next to the fields, and were discovered at last on the side of the mesa near where they had slept. Early, too, the people of the Moki rose and ate their breakfast, and then sent six of the head men and six of the head women to the boys to talk with them. The old woman who interceded for them on the previous night was the first to speak. After she had embraced them and called them by tender names—"my children, my grandchildren," etc.,—(and this made the boys feel proud) she said: "You came to our help when the rats were eating our corn; you helped us again when the worms were destroying it; you saved us once more when the wind was blowing our corn down; you can help us now when the grasshoppers are devouring it. Drive away the grasshoppers from our fields and we shall be your friends forever. No more shall our young men and boys annoy you; no more shall they curse and revile you; no more shall you go hungry; no more shall you sleep on the cold rocks without a blanket. You shall live as our own people live. Whenever you enter a house food shall be set before you," and she made them many other good promises. The boys replied: "Thrice before have you made us just such promises as these, and thrice we have saved your crops from being lost; but as soon as your danger was over you forgot all your fine promises; you mocked us, you laughed at us, you tormented us, you drove us out of your houses, you did not give us a scrap of food to eat nor a blanket to cover us when we slept at night, out of doors, on the cold bare rocks of the mesa." Then the first chief repeated all the promises of the woman, and assured them that the Mokis would not again forget their word. He continued: "We are People on the Earth like yourselves.[55] We are not d'ígíni. Help us this once more and you shall be forever after treated as one of ourselves. This is the chief among the women; I am the chief among the men. We pledge you our word: hereafter you shall be to us as our own children." The other ten members of the delegation came forward and repeated all the promises that the first two had made, not only for all the people but each for himself personally, and all embraced the children and called them by the names of relationship. The boys responded: "We have heard all this before. We know now how much you mean of what you say. Were we to kill the grasshoppers and save your crops again, just as soon as you felt safe you would look kindly at us no more. You would shoot blunt arrows at us, throw dirt on us, poke your fingers in the eyes of the blind one, and refuse us food and shelter. Besides, there is no use in your coming to us, we know nothing about grasshoppers." But the chiefs repeated all their promises over and over again, and ceased not to implore their aid. Four times the boys asked: "Are your words true?" and four times the chiefs responded: "Our words are true. We speak for the whole people. The rest must keep the pledges that we make. What we promise, all the people promise," "If we help you this time," said the boys, "we want no more scraps or leavings of food, we want no second-hand clothes, we want no more inferior things, we must have the best of everything. First, we must have four more large and fine unwounded buckskins, and we must have an abundance of other skins, doeskins, fawnskins, antelope skins, and furs. We must have turquoise ear-drops as long as the finger, besides turquoise of lesser size. We must have beads of all kinds. We must have fine necklaces containing shells of all kinds, the best of coral and cannel-coal. We must have woven fabrics of all kinds—the best from everybody's house. We must have the five jewel baskets," and then the boys demanded all the rest of the sacrificial things that the yéi required, saying : "All these things must be of the best. Now, give us these and we will try to save what is left of your corn." "Stay, then, where you are," said the chiefs, "while we return to our people, tell them what you demand, and ask people whom we know have these things to give them up." A chief went back to the village and harangued the people. He repeated all that the boys demanded. He asked first for the sacred buckskins, then for the common skins, and after these for the other articles. Many were reluctant, and refused to give ; but the chief said : "Fear not to give them. When the boys have chased away the grasshoppers and saved the crops, we will kill them and get all our wealth back again." When they were told they should get their hard wealth—their beads—back again, they were satisfied and began to lay them down. They put them in pots, carried them out and emptied them on the buckskins. The boys tied up the other treasure also, including the fine food. Then they made the chiefs stand guard over the treasures (there had been some thefts on the previous occasions).

856.—They repeated all the previous instructions, telling the people to hide and not look toward the fields during their absence, and then the boys went down into the fields, where they had placed the first four grasshoppers. They approached the eastern grasshopper from the east. Going sunwise they approached the southern one from the south, the western one from the west, and the northern one from the north. They folded them all in a black cloud, tied the bundle with a long band of rainbow (much pantomime on the part of the story-teller), and put the bundle in their pouch. After they had done this they said a prayer ; they prayed that the Mokis might have all the corn, all the black clouds, all the abundant rains, and all the harmless lightning they desired. A moment later the boys were on top of the cliff at the villages ; they had come up on a trail of rainbow. "Go back to your houses now," said the boys to the chiefs who were guarding the property. "You shall have plenty to eat this year ; you shall have abundant black clouds ; you shall have abundant rains ; you shall have beneficent lightning. We have prayed for all these things for you. But you must keep your word to us and feed us well. We shall abide with you here for a while and eat with you, and the people must not visit their fields nor look toward them for four days and four nights." During these four nights the people could not sleep for they were anxious about their wealth, lest the boys should escape with it ; yet they were anxious about their corn, too, and feared to injure the boys lest the spell which the latter had cast on the grasshoppers might not work.

857.—On the morning after the fourth night, the people went down to their fields and found their corn as good as ever. The ears were forming. The melon vines had grown long and little buttons of melons had appeared on them ; so with the squash vines. The beans were in blossom. Rain was falling on the farms of Moki and on the farms of *Thálahog*an. As soon as the rain began to fall on themselves the people of Moki came home, and when they returned the boys had their goods all wrapped up so tightly with a band of lightning that they formed a very small package. The Mokis had visited the fields before breakfast ; when they returned the chiefs bade them eat in haste, as they intended, immediately after eating, to kill the boys and get back all their property. While the people were eating, the boys were on the edge of the cliff walking from place to place ; but they were closely watched all the time, for the chiefs had placed guards outside to observe them till the others finished their meal.

858.—Suddenly the boys disappeared from the edge of the mesa and the watchers ran back announcing this to the chiefs. " Run and see whither they have gone," was the order. In a moment the messengers returned, crying : " They are already at the foot of the mesa." The people rushed forth from their houses with clubs in their hands, and ran down the side of the mesa after the boys. When the pursuers got to the edge of the first ravine, on the trail the boys had taken, the fugitives had reached the top of a low rise just beyond it. When the crowd reached the top of this rise, expecting to find the boys just on the other side of it and to overtake them in a moment, they found to their astonishment that the boys were a long way off. When out of sight of their pursuers the boys cast their rainbow before them and went rapidly forward. While in sight, they moved slowly, for the blind boy could only walk with the cripple on his back. The Mokis ran fast, meantime, and when the boys had ascended the next rise their pursuers were but about thirty paces behind them ; but when the latter mounted the ridge the fugitives were at least four hundred paces ahead. By this time the Mokis began to throw the sweat from their faces and many of them got tired and abandoned the chase ; yet whenever the boys were seen they were slowly walking. The Mokis continued to pursue them up the neighboring valley and in the direction of the Chelly Cañon. When they came to a place called *Lĭt*naikaí, White Horizontal Smoke, most of them became exhausted and gave up the pursuit ; but a few kept on till they arrived at Tsĕ'tsĕlsaka*d*, Lone Oak, and here the last one threw himself on the ground exhausted. " Farewell, my beautiful beads ! Farewell, my precious necklace ! Farewell, my rare turquoise basket ! You are gone forever ; I shall never see you again." Such were the cries the baffled pursuers uttered. But the boys did not hurry, they seemed to the waiting group they left behind to go more slowly than ever. The group at White Smoke remained there, hoping soon to see their comrades return, bringing their valuables with them ; but when their friends came back empty-handed, the people who had stayed at White Smoke, too, began to weep and cry farewells to their lost property as those at Lone Oak had done. From the latter place the boys went toward Kǐninaékai on their rainbow by jumps.   At Tse‘hestsídahaska‘, where there is a lake, they stopped to drink and eat some of their paper bread and other delicacies which they had obtained from the Mokis.   They went next to a place called To‘diníhi, where there is a wall of stone.   When they passed through a gap here, the holy ones of Kǐninaékai saw them coming and Hastséhogan sent Hastséeltodi to meet them in Tsǐnlí Valley.

859.—When Hastséeltodi met them he asked them what they had done. They answered: "We have done all that we were told tŏ do and we have returned laden with the best of jewels and with all the sacred things we were bidden to get." "I shall return to my kindred before you, and tell them this," said the yéi. "If you bring all the things we have demanded of you, perhaps you may be cured." When Hastséeltodi returned and told his story to his kindred, Hastséhogan said: "We rejoice to hear they have an abundance, and that everything they have is of the best. We must divide with our neighbors. Go out to all the other holy places and tell the people to come in." When the boys arrived at Kǐninaékai they did not enter any of the houses ; they stopped at the bottom of the cliff where they found a crowd gathered to meet them.

860.—The yéi spread a blanket on the ground for the boys to sit on ; Hastséyalti came down from his house, went where the boys sat, and asked them what they had done. The boys related all their adventures and told at greatest length all the trouble they had had in getting home. "What, O father, were your thoughts about us while we were gone? We have suffered much and escaped many dangers in getting these things for you ; but we have gotten all that you commanded us to get" ; and they mentioned by name all the treasures they carried "'Tis well," said the old man ; "now you shall have your eyes cured and your limbs cured, and you shall walk as well and see as well as you did before the evil spell was cast upon you." The dǐgíni of Lǐtsíthaa‘, being the best runners, a courier was sent to them with news of the boys' successful return, and they were asked to spread the news to all the other holy places. Soon the holy ones from many places assembled at Kǐninaékai—the young gods hoped to get a share of the jewels and the elders hoped to get a smoke. They had sent word to the Hastsézǐni or Black Gods to hasten their coming, as they are the keepers of the fire and as they travel slowly. They stop to make a fire often on their journeys, and lie down to rest at the fire before they move on again (par. 111). On this occasion they did not arrive until sundown on the fourth day after they were sent for, and the dǐgíni had to wait their coming. When the Black Gods arrived, all the gods were present, and then they held a council to determine if the promised healing ceremony should be held at Kǐninaékai, at Tsé‘ǐntyel, or where it should be held. They talked all night about this. Some one said : "Kǐninaékai is an unlucky place for the boys. We began the rite here before and it was broken. If we begin here again something unfortunate may happen. Let us go elsewhere."

861.—It was decided to go to Tsé‘ǐntyel, and in the morning they all set out for that place, the boys walking in the middle of the crowd.   They all walked to the low hills that skirt the foot of Tsé'íntyel, near the place where the two creeks join,[54] and here they chose a place where the ceremony was to be performed. *Hastséhogan* of Tsé'íntyel then asked if anyone had brought with him the necessary medicine, but all answered that they had left their medicines at home. He told them their assistance would not go unpaid, that all who helped would receive presents for their help.   "Go home and get your medicines," he said.   "Return here at the end of four nights and in the meantime spread the news of the coming rite again, so that those who have not heard before may hear now, but send no message to the *H*ast*s*étso, Great Yéi, and Klĭ'*s*tso, Great Serpent.   They are evil ones who must not know what we intend to do."   He said to the boys : "Go back to your home at Ĭn*d*ĕstsí*h*onia' and see once more how your kindred there will greet you.   But tell them not what has happened since last you left them. Tell them not that you have found your father or that the holy ones have promised to cure you."

862.—The boys left Tse'íntyel as they were bidden, and got back to Ĭn*d*ĕstsí*h*onia', where their mother dwelt. As they approached the house their uncle saw them a little way off and cried out : "Here come these ugly boys again.   I supposed they had starved to death long ago ; but still they live, and again they return to us.   Let us drive them away."   Their grandmother came out and advanced to meet them.   "Begone!" she said.   "We chased you away before. Why do you return to us ?   We wish never to see you again.   Go far away and starve."   One of the boys, hearing this, said to the other : "I am sorry we came back.   We have heard cruel words we did not expect to hear."   But the other replied : "I feel neither sorry nor ashamed.   We came not here of our own wish.   It was the holy ones who sent us, and we did right to listen to them. Our mother and her people do not want us to be of the People on the Earth. Let us go back to the holy ones and remain with them forever."   Yet for all these brave words their minds were sad and they sat down and wept.   When they had dried their tears, one said to the other : "We must never go back to our mother's lodge again.   Let us return at once to Tsé'íntyel where they have promised to cure for one his eyes, and for the other his legs.   Some day we may be able to do a service for the holy ones.   Some day they may ask us."   So the one mounted upon the back of the other, and they set out on their return journey.

863.—When they got back to Tsé'íntyel their father asked them : "What did your people say to you at your home?"   He named each one of their relations and asked what each one said.   "Our grandmother met us at a distance from the house," they answered, "and forbade us to approach nearer.   She told us we were dirty and ugly, that they were tired of us, and she bade us begone. She alone spoke to us.   The others came not near us."   "Look no more at your mother or at your mother's people," said the yéi.   "When we have cured you, we will find a place for you.   We have sent word to all the holy places you have visited.   A great crowd will be here to-night."

864.—The boys remained all day down near the bank of the stream. About sundown the crowd began to gather. At the foot of the rock of Tsé'intyel the council was held as to how the ceremony should be conducted and how the medicines should be prepared. The medicine-lodge for this occasion was built of stone; its ruins may still be seen near Tsé'intyel; but the Navahoes now build the medicine-lodge of wood and earth. After the council was ended at night they made and sacrificed circle kethawns (par. 300 *et seq.*). Thus ended the work of the first day.

865.—(The rest of the myth is taken up mostly with a description of the rites, given with a certain incompleteness which indicates that it is intended for the ears of those who have already witnessed the rites and understand the allusions of the speaker, without a full description of all the work. As the rites are described in another place more fully than the narrator of this myth gave them, it is considered unnecessary to repeat this part of his tale; but some incidents will be here mentioned, which are strictly mythical or belong to that form of the ceremony known as *to'nastsihégo hatál* (pars. 648–649). The whole of the myth of The Stricken Twins accounts for the origin of this form, or its introduction among the Navahoes.)

866.—On the morning of the second day cigarettes were made for the Owls, for Aga'hoá' Tsïlké, for *H*astséyal*t*i and for *H*astséd*i*ltsosi. When these had been sacrificed the sweat-house was constructed. Its frame was made of two rainbows: one, a female, extending from north to south and the other, a male, extending from east to west (plate II, A). They covered this frame with a black cloud and curtained the doorway with an unwounded buckskin and a black fog. Mortals cannot build such a sweat-house as this, so to-day we do the best we can by making one of the sticks and clay and painting a picture of the rainbow on the outside. The medicines used were tsóltsïn (par. 215), klédze azé (par. 203), *d*á'tsos (par. 213), and naké*t*in (par. 345) and besides they used the parts of the mountain sheep which the boys had killed. The naké*t*in was mixed with the water from the sheep's eye and put in the eyes of the blind boy, with instructions to him not to let it drop out. They were told with many warnings not to talk in the sweat-house and reminded of their former folly in the sweat-house near Kïn-inaékai. *H*astséyal*t*i and *H*astsébaad were designated to treat the boys, and those divine ones, when the songs of the sweat-house were done, approached from the east and threw aside the curtains. *H*astséyal*t*i with a downward sweep of the hand beckoned the boys to come forth and motioned to them to sit on embroidered Moki blankets which had been spread for them. *H*astséyal*t*i made massage on the blind boy, holding two black plumed wands with the tip of the sheep's horn in the right hand and two black plumed wands with the strip of skin from the sheep's nose in the left hand. *H*astsébaad operated on the cripple holding two blue wands and a tendo Achillis of the sheep in each hand. When the whole party returned from the sweat-house to the lodge, the boys were placed first on a Moki blanket. The cripple now felt as if he could stretch out his limbs, but as he had been told to say nothing about his feelings or his treatment till all was done, he kept silent. After the pollen was administered two unwounded buckskins were spread with their noses to the east; a picture of the Pollen Boy was drawn on each skin and one of the boys was placed sitting on each. There they prayed to Dsahadoldzá of Tsĕ'nihogan on the east; to Gánaskĭdi of Depé-hahatin on the south, to Hastséhogan of Kĭninaékai on the west, and to Hastsél-tsi of Lĭtsíthaa' on the north, that the eyes of the blind and the limbs of the lame might be restored as they were before. The boys were then both clothed with the evergreen dresses and the masks of antelope skin, as is done to-day (par. 357 *et seq.*) masks were made from the skins of two young twin antelopes which Tó'nenĭli captured at Dsĭldasáni, Porcupine Mountain. Nayénĕzgani and To'badzĭstsíni, cut off the evergreens with stone knives and after the fragments of the dresses were carried out all lay down to sleep.

867.—On the morning of the third day, after six kethawns had been made and buried in the usual form, two ditches were dug and that form of the sweat known as kónnike was used on the boys. No pictures were drawn; but the same medicines were used as on the previous day and the same treatment employed by the same gods. While they were sweating, unwounded buckskins and black clouds were put over the boys, and underneath them, in the order named, from below upward, were the following seven substances: juniper leaves, piñon leaves, spruce leaves, *Gutierrezia*, a plant called tsé'aze, *Boutleloua* grass and winter-fat (par. 255). Hastséyalti sang the Ásatĭni Bigĭ'n or Songs of the Long Pot. When the yéi tried to cure the boys before near Kĭninaékai they intended to do it in one day, but now they had no such intention. At night the boys were each clothed in six hoops made of the materials the same as those on which they lay while taking the sweat, as is done to-day. When these hoops had been removed and torn to pieces the work of the day was done. See par. 419.

868.—On the fourth day, before sunrise, some went out and tied a white downy eagle-feather to the top of the piñon sapling that was selected to remove the masks in the ceremonies at night. Then cigarettes were made for Hastsé-yalti, Dsahadoldzá, Gánaskĭdi, Hastséltsi, Hátdastsĭsi, Hastsézĭni, Tó'nenĭli, Hastsédĭltsosi and four of the Tse'thadepé or Rocky Mountain sheep. After these were planted they made a sweat-bath the same as on the first day; except that they built it to the west of the medicine-lodge. After the sweat was done, the cripple was able to walk by himself to the medicine-lodge but not strongly and the blind boy could distinguish light more plainly than he had done before. Their father collected the yucca which was to wash them in the afternoon. Hastséeltodi and Tó'nenĭli collected the earth from the center of a field — each bringing earth for a different boy — which was to be used in making the circles of mud. Tó'nenĭli collected the water and Hastséeltodi collected the spruce twigs. With all these, two mud platters were made as they are made to-day (par. 437). A turquoise basket was placed in one of the circles for one of the boys and a white shell basket in the other circle for the other boy. *Hastséyalti* and *Hastséhogan* of Tsé'bĭniyi made the lather, each in a separate bowl. As they began to work it up *Hastsézĭni* began to sing the *Tsalyél Bigĭ'n* or Darkness Song as it is sung at the lather-making to-day (par. 439). When the boys had been washed in the suds and rinsed off in clean water they got on the Moki blanket and were dried with corn-meal while the Estsánatlehi *Bigĭ'n* was sung. It was *Hastsézĭni* who applied the pollen to the vital parts, *Hastséĭyalti* it was who cut the piñon tree that had been adorned with an eagle-feather in the early morning, and it was *Tó'nenĭli* who dug the hole between the boys in which the tree was planted. *Tó'nenĭli* put a mask on the blind boy, while *Hastséeltodi* put one on the cripple. *Hastséyalti* sprinkled the meal and *Hastsébaad* planted the tree. The tree was bent and tied to both masks, first to the blind boy's and then to the cripple's and when it flew back it drew both masks with it. The tree was taken out and deposited by the gods who had planted it. In the meantime, at Tsé'ĭntyel they were preparing the supper of many dishes which is eaten on the fourth night. The virgin boy and girl who mixed the cold gruel for the communal feast that came later and sprinkled the masks were children of *Hastséhogan*. 12 unwounded buckskins were spread for the masks and the treasures which the boys had brought from Moki. These filled the turquoise basket and four other sacred baskets to overflowing. A haliotis basket, a black basket and a crystal basket were filled with all the different kinds of pollen that came from Moki. These baskets were laid behind the masks and Moqui blankets were spread over them. About midnight the song of Hyĭdĕzná was sung and the masks were shaken as we do it in these days (par. 469, 470). It was *Hastséyalti* who made the smoke and blew it on the masks. Singing was kept up all night until daylight; then another bowl of lather was made for *Hastséyalti* to wash his head before he set out on his journey to take kethawns to *Tóĭntsa*.

869.—On the morning of the fifth day, when *Hastséyalti* returned from burying the kethawns, the yéi uncovered the baskets that contained the jewels, feathers and pollen and found that all these things had increased marvelously during the night. Now all the wealth which the boys had brought from Moki was divided among the assembled yéi. The division, for justice sake, was made by four—*Hastséhogan* of Tsé'ĭntyel who sat in the east, *Hastséyalti* of Tsé'ĭntyel who sat in the south, *Hastséhogan* of Kĭninaékai, sitting in the west, and *Hastséyalti* of Kĭninaékai, sitting in the north. From the hands of these *Hastséhogan* of Tsúskai gave out the spoils to the males who stood around and *Hastsébaad* of Tsúskai gave them out to the females. Owls, foxes and other animals were there and each got a share. But *Hastsézĭni*, the chanter, got more than all the others. He got a share of the jewels equal to that of any other and in addition he received five sacred baskets, six unwounded buckskins and the embroidered blankets. He got, too, most of the feathers and the different kinds of pollen.[72]

870.—*Hastsétso* and Klĭ'stso,[73] the evil ones, lived in a house near that of *Hastsézĭni*, and the insect *Dóntso* stood guard for them. His usual place was at the smoke-hole of their house, where there were two big black rocks; now he was in the medicine-lodge watching the division of the treasures; but he was so small that no one observed him.

871.—As soon as the division was completed *Dóntso* ran home and got up to his place on top of the lodge. As he did so some dirt fell on the floor below where *H*ast*s*étso was sitting and the latter was angry. It was because he and *K*li´stso were so inclined to wrath that they were not invited in when the treasures were divided. But the insect told *H*ast*s*étso what he had witnessed in the medicine-lodge and named all the precious things he had seen divided. *H*ast*s*étso rose from his bed and asked where this took place. The insect replied that he had seen it in a medicine-lodge at the foot of Tsé'intyel. The Great Snake, hearing this, rose in anger and said: "Why was I not invited? Let us go over there. Come with me." But *H*ast*s*étso said: "No, I would do better to go alone. I have a better mind than you. I can speak better. I shall go alone to these holy ones and tell them what I think of their conduct." On the north side of the door there was a black fog, on the south side a black cloud. The cloud was folded with lightning inside. As soon as *H*ast*s*étso pulled back the cloud to pass out lightning flashed, thunder pealed and rain fell. As he ran down on the black rocks toward Tsé'intyel it rained on his path and the lightning struck in all directions around him, smashing trees and rocks. When the people in the medicine-lodge beheld the violent storm they said: "*H*ast*s*étso is coming;" they were alarmed and all fled to Tsé'intyel except four—the two boys, their father and *H*ast*s*éz*ĭ*ni, the chanter. The boys and their father were alarmed though they fled not; but *H*ast*s*éz*ĭ*ni was not afraid. He said: "I fear not *H*ast*s*étso." As the latter approached the lodge the lightning struck violently all around it. *H*ast*s*éz*ĭ*ni had possession of fire. That is why he did not fear the one that was coming.

872.—*H*ast*s*étso ran into the lodge where the four were and roared in an angry voice: "I hear you have had a great dividing of treasures among you. They were given out freely to all; but I got none. Why did you not invite me to come and get my share?" "All that you have heard is true," said *H*ast*s*éyal*t*i, "and if you are angry I will give you a smoke; that is all you wish for; you do not care for the turquoises and other precious things; they are of no use to you." Hearing this *H*ast*s*étso spoke to the storm cloud: "My cloud, I have been promised a smoke. Cease to rain and cease to lighten." The cloud withdrew itself a little way off toward the side from which it had come; but it still staid threateningly near, though the rain ceased to fall and the thunder was heard no more. *H*ast*s*éyalti then made for his visitor a cigarette which he painted black, filled with mountain tobacco,[7] sealed at the end with moistened pollen and lit with the sun. When the visitor had smoked he received a goodly store of finished beads and a bag of tobacco. *H*ast*s*étso was a chanter too; but he knew only seven songs. *H*ast*s*éz*ĭ*ni gave him twenty songs and *H*ast*s*éyal*t*i gave him ten; so that he had now thirty-seven songs to sing when he treated the sick. *H*ast*s*étso said he was thankful for what he had received; that the songs would help him in his healing rites; that he would enjoy smoking the tobacco; that the jewels would look well upon him, and that he did not care to possess the other things that came from Moki. They told him he must divide with *K*li'*s*tso. He said: "It is well. I have nothing more to do here. Go on, my children, treat the twins well. Farewell my grandchildren," and departed. He went over to where the black cloud hung. As soon as he was hidden under its folds the thunder began again to roar and the lightning to flash, and these continued until he got within the door of his house.

873.—When *H*ast*s*étso had gone home, *H*ast*s*éyal*t*i sought the runaways, bade them return to the medicine-lodge and told them what had happened while they were gone. When all had returned to the lodge there was another council and this was what they said: "Our boys can now see and walk as well as ever; but they are not altogether restored as they once were; their backs are bent, their limbs are crooked; their hardships have deformed them. We must not let them stay as they are; we must make handsome men of them." They spread two embroidered Moki blankets on the floor and made the boys stand on them. They asked to whom should fall the task of straightening them out. After much talk it was decided that the two daughters of *H*ast*s*é*h*og̱an of Tsé'ĭntyel should perform it. The maidens being called they came and stood facing the boys, not close at first, but a little distance off,—the elder facing the one who had been blind, the younger, the one who had been crippled. The plumed wands (par. 279) were handed to the girls;—the blue wands to the younger who stood in the south and the black to the elder who stood in the north,—and the girls advanced and pressed the wands to the trunks and limbs of the boys. Behind the girls as they wrought stood two sons of *H*ast*s*é*h*og̱an of Tsé'ĭntyel, brothers of the girls, erect and comely youths, which it was intended that the twins should be made to resemble. When the girls had finished the massage with the plumed wands the twin boys were changed in form and feature, they became tall and straight and fair to behold and looked like the sons of *H*ast*s*é*h*og̱an.[74] Then the girls said, pointing to the twins: "Behold our ugly brothers! See how ugly we have made them!" And this is why, to this day, a Navaho maiden speaks of her younger brother as her ugly brother, no matter how fair he may be to look on. After their forms had been straightened their father brought them some clothes. For one he brought white mocassins, white leggings, buckskin pantaloons, an embroidered shirt, a head-dress decorated with eagle-plumes, a necklace of white beads and ear-drops of turquoise. For the other he brought embroidered mocassins and leggings, fringed buckskin pantaloons, an embroidered buckskin shirt, a head-dress trimmed with the feathers of the yellow-tail, and jewels the same as those brought for his brother; an embroidered blanket was given to each. When the twins were arrayed in all these fine garments they looked so much like the handsome sons of *H*ast*s*é*h*og̱an that it was difficult to tell one pair from another. The boys then left the medicine-lodge and went to another house.

874.—When it was dark the yéi said: "Let us turn down the basket and sing" (par. 291). "Come on the trail of song," called the crier from the door of the lodge. The boys returned, the basket was turned down and the singing began. The boys were seated in the middle of the lodge; but when they saw the other yéi crowding in through the door to hear the songs, they were seized with tsĭdĭlʇáʻ (hypnotic convulsions). The yéi said: "We must not go on with the singing while the boys are in this condition, we must cure them first," so they stopped the song and bade the father and Tóʻnenĭli to undress the twins. They were laid on their sides with their faces to the east, a buckskin was spread over them. Hastsézĭni arose and sang a song, and he then proceeded to treat the boys as the shaman to this day treats those who fall into the trance in the medicine-lodge. When the twins recovered from their trance they took their seats in the lodge and the yéi began again to beat the basket and sing. When the singing was done, the basket was turned up. The evil influences that had gathered under it were blown out through the smoke-hole of the lodge, the fragrant yádidĭniʇ was burned for the boys to smell and the work of the night was done.

875.—On the morning of the sixth day, Hastséelʇodi and Tóʻnenĭli went out early to get the pieces of sandstone of different colors and the charcoal which were to be powdered and used in making a picture. After they returned others went to work and ground these substances to powder between hard stones. Then the yéi spread out over the floor of the lodge a black fog on which to paint the picture. "Truly," they said, "The People on the Earth can never draw their pictures on a fog; but they can spread sand on the floor and that will do as well." Several now went to work; the picture of Sĭʇnéole (plate VI) was drawn and the plumed wands were set around it. The twins were summoned and the picture was sprinkled and all the ceremonies performed on it as they are done to this day. When these were over, the sheet of fog, with the picture on it, was folded up, carried out of the lodge and thrown away under a tree.

876.—The yéi who were not at work in the lodge spent the day mostly in sports and those who worked joined them when the rites were done. They played the game of seven chips, nánzoz and many other games. They ran foot-races. On all these sports they made bets and the betting was high. At dark the call to song was heard at the door of the lodge, the basket was turned down and the Sĭʇnéole Bigĭʻn or Songs of the Whirling Sticks, 14 in number, were sung. As the last song was finished the basket was turned up; then the twins were fumigated and the work of the day was done. The boys did not sleep in the medicine-lodge that night though others did.

877.—On the morning of the seventh day a black cloud was spread on the floor of the lodge and on this was drawn Hastséhogan beyikáʇ, or the picture of the House God.[75] It was Hastséhogan who was to treat the twins to-day, and while the painting of the picture was going on he prepared himself. He did not remove his clothes; he only whitened his hands and he left the lodge concealing his mask under his blanket. There was no bowl of water in the center of the picture and there were therefore no acts connected with the bowl, otherwise the

observances were much the same as those of the day before. A stalk of corn
was painted in the center of this picture as it is done to-day and the boys were
placed sitting, one on each side of this pictured stalk on a level with the lowest
ear. In these days only one person is usually treated at a time and he is seated
directly on the cornstalk. When he had completed the massage of the boys he
shouted once into each ear of each boy thus giving four shouts. In these days,
when only one person sits on the picture the god shouts twice into each ear and
thus gives four shouts. When *Hastséhog*an departed, the boys were fumigated
as before,—two coals being placed before each to receive the incense; the cloud
picture was taken out and thrown on the ground, under a tree, north of the
picture of the previous day.

878.—Those who worked not in the lodge, spent the day again in sports and
in gambling. After dark the basket was turned down and forty-three songs were
sung. Forty of these were *Hastséhog*an Bigĭ′n, or Songs of the House God, but
besides these, three songs were sung at the turning up of the basket drum.
Again the boys were fumigated and left the lodge. Had the yéi planned to
have a dance of the naak*h*aí on the last night, the dancers would now have gone
out and practiced on the ground in front of the lodge; but as there was to be no
such dance, all lay down and went to sleep.

879.—On the morning of the eighth day a black fog was spread on the floor
of the lodge and Dsaha*d*oldz*á*be yik*á*l or the picture with the Fringe Mouths, was
drawn even as it is done in the medicine-lodges of the Navahoes to this day (plate
VIII). The ceremonies connected with the picture were like those of the day
before. The ceremonies on the twins outside of the lodge were performed by
*H*astséyal*t*i, Dsaha*d*oldz*á* and a Yébaad (par. 577). When the fumigation was
done and the coals extinguished the black fog on which the picture was drawn
was thrown away a short distance to the north of the picture of the previous day.
The afternoon was again spent in games. At night the Dsaha*d*oldz*á* Bigĭ′n, or
Songs of the Fringe Mouths, were sung. These are 12 in number and in addition
to these there is one song for turning up the basket, making 13 in all sung during
the night. At the close of the songs the boys were again fumigated and left the
lodge to sleep elsewhere.

880.—On the ninth morning all rose earlier than usual. A black cloud was
laid out for the picture of this day—the *H*astséz*ĭ*nibe yik*á*l or picture with the
Black God. Hastséel*t*odi brought in the bark of a lightning-stricken tree, with
two leaves of yucca; of these was formed the *h*a*n*o*l*yél or bundle of fuel which
*H*astséz*ĭ*ni was to carry that day on his journey. Four cakes of blue corn-meal
(nan*ě*sk*ád*i) made into one bundle were also provided for him and with these two
bundles he set out. When he returned to the lodge, nearly at sunset, the twins
were standing side by side, facing the east — the one who had been blind being
north of his brother. The twins were bidden to lie down as the god approached
and he walked over them as is done in the ceremonies to-day. The boys then
entered the lodge, followed by *H*astséz*ĭ*ni who performed ceremonies on them

and on the picture. Then he left the lodge to take off his mask. When he returned all the spectators departed to their homes. The sun had now set. (Pars. 102–116).

881.—At dark the call to song was again heard and the twins entered the medicine-lodge. On this occasion they sat in the northwest part of the lodge after passing around the fire sunwise from the door in the east. All night the singing was kept up and the boys sat in the lodge not being allowed to sleep during the whole time.

882.—Early in the morning a buffalo-robe was spread to the east of the lodge door with its head pointing east. The boys were placed standing on this, while the masked gods performed a ceremony of succor. These gods were *H*astséyal*t*i from T*s*ú*s*kai, Dsaha*d*oldzá from Ts*ĕ*'ni*h*og-an and Gá*n*aski*d*i from *D*epé*h*a*h*a*t*in. All the other gods who performed rites of succor on the boys went to the west when they had done; but these gods departed to the east. When they were gone, the boys and the chanter returned to the lodge and smeared their chins with corn-meal. The four final songs were sung, and as the last was finished the basket was turned up. It was now daylight and the boys returned to the lodge where they had slept. The last thing done was to dispose of the yucca drum-stick. The fibres of which it was made were unwound to the accompaniment of song, straightened out, laid together butt to butt, taken toward the east, put lightly in the forks of a tree and sprinkled with meal and pollen, while the prayer was said (par. 295). This ended the healing ceremony.

883.—After the ceremony was over another council was held among the yéi to decide what should be done with the boys. Some proposed that they should stay with their father; but others said: "It is not well that they should remain among us for they belong to the People on the Earth." At last it was decided to put the boy who had been blind at Tse'*d*esdzái (sandstone pinnacles near Fort Defiance) where he should control the thunder storm and where the people might pray to him when they wanted rain; and to place the other at Tse'ni*h*okĭ'*z* (near Navaho Springs) where he should become *D*iní'yasĭ*t*ai, the guardian or god of animals. The boys dwell at these places still.

884.—But before they went to their new homes they tarried for a while among the People on the Earth and taught them the rites which they had learned from the holy ones of the Chelly Cañon.

PART IV.

Texts and Translations.

Texts and Translations.

SONGS.

GENERAL REMARKS.

885.—The task of recording these Navaho songs is not easy, and when they have been satisfactorily reduced to writing the labor of translating them is beset with many difficulties. It is often no easy matter to determine the meaning of an English song from hearing it sung. The difficulties are increased in a strange language. The Navaho poets greatly distort their words to make them fit their tunes. They employ all figures of euphony defined by our writers besides some to which our terms do not well apply. A word is often distorted in Navaho song so as to become homophonous with a totally different word in prose and thus the student may be led far astray. The shamans themselves often differ in explaining such terms. Many archaic words appear in the songs for which the Navahoes have only traditional meanings or none. Many meaningless vocables are introduced for the sake of meter and rhyme and such vocables are as essential, and must be repeated as faithfully, as the most significant words.

886.—Among written tongues, known to thousands of the most learned scholars, in translating from a dead to a living language, or even in translating from one living language to another, particularly in poetry, the work is often unsatisfactory and subject to much criticism. The best poets in the English tongue may not make their meaning clear to the most intelligent English readers. Our scholars differ as to the interpretation of many passages in Shakespeare. Recognizing these facts, it must not be supposed that the translations from an unwritten savage language, which follow, are offered as perfect. But they are the result of long and careful study, aided by the most learned Navaho singers and by the best English-speaking and Spanish-speaking interpreters whose services could be procured. Many times the combined knowledge of all these have failed, and the author's own understanding of the etymology of the Navaho language, obtained during a period of twenty years' study, had to supply the deficiencies.

887.—He simply offers the work as the best he can do. But here stand the texts. Perhaps when the present pagan cultus of the Navahoes is dead, when " I want to be angel " has supplanted " Hyĭdĕzná " in the worship of this people, some student of the language more skillful than the author may arise to interpret more correctly the spirit of these songs.

[269]

888.—Another difficulty with Navaho songs is that, without explaining, they often allude to matters, which the hearers are supposed to understand. They are not like our ballads—they tell no tales. He who would comprehend them, must know the myths and the ritual customs on which they are based.

889.—Although there are some separate songs for special occasions, the majority of the songs of this ceremony, as well as of other ceremonies practiced by the Navahoes, are what the author has, in previous works, called songs of sequence. Such songs are divided into sets, which must follow one another in an established order, and the songs within each set must be sung in a certain order. To change the order would be considered inimical to the success of the ceremony. Some of these songs are sung during the progress of the ceremony, and a certain set may be appropriate to a particular rite; but a majority are reserved for the last night, when they are sung inside the medicine-lodge (pars. 643–645). Then, it is customary to finish some sets, which have been sung in part during the previous days, as well as to sing certain sets that belong to the last night only. Not all the songs of sequence are sung even on the last night, if time be wanting; but those omitted by the shaman are repeated in his next ceremony, to the exclusion, perhaps, of others. The rules governing songs of sequence are very intricate and we cannot explain them all.

890.—The following is a list of the songs of sequence sung on the last night, in the order of their occurrence, with the Navaho name of each set, a free translation of the same and the number of songs in each set:

1. Atsá'lei Bigǐ'n,	Songs of the First Dancers,	12.
2. Tsé'ni Gisǐ'n,	Songs in the Rock, or Cave Songs,	16.
3. Sĭlnéole Bigǐ'n,	Songs of the Whirling Logs,	12.
4. Á'saṭini Bigǐ'n,	Songs of the Long Pot,	12.
5. Tsalyél Bigǐ'n,	Songs of the Darkness,	10.
6. Dsahadoldzá Bigǐ'n,	Songs of the Fringe Mouths,	12.
7. Gánaskǐdi Bigǐ'n,	Songs of the Humpbacks,	12.
8. Depé Bigǐ'n,	Songs of the Bighorns,	8.
9. Nanṭí Gisǐ'n,	Suspension Bridge Songs,	12.
10. Taiké Gisǐ'n,	Farm Songs,	12.
11. Tse' Bigǐ'n,	Songs of the Rock,	8.
12. Idní' Bigǐ'n,	Songs of the Thunder,	16.
13. Aga'hoá Gisǐ'n,	Songs on High, Summit Songs,	26.
14. Hastséhogan Bigǐ'n,	Songs of the House God,	40.
15. Hastsézĭni Bigǐ'n,	Songs of the Black God,	10.
16. Nayénezgani Bigǐ'n,	Songs of Slayer of the Alien Gods,	10
17. Yikaígǐn,	Daylight Songs,	20
18. Béna Hatáli,	Finishing Hymns,	4.

Total songs of sequence of last night,   252.

891.—The following is a list of some of the songs of sequence sung on the preceding days, but not repeated on the last night:

In*d*iá‘ Bigĭ'n,	Songs of the Plumed Wands,	32.
Tsĕ'nit*s*i*h*ogan Bigĭ'n,	Songs of the Red Rock House,	10.
*H*od itlá*t* Gisĭ'n,	Songs in the Trembling Place,	7.
Anĭl*t*áni Bigĭ'n,	Songs of the Grasshoppers,	5.
Dsĭ*l* Bigĭ'n,	Songs of the Mountains,	6.
*H*astséyal*t*i *H*ogán Bigĭ'n,	Songs of the House of the Talking God,	12.
Total,		72.
Total of both lists,		324.

892.—In addition to these, there are sets of songs sung before the last night, in which the number of component songs is not known, and there are single songs for special occasions. These together bring the total number up to about 400. Texts and translations of only 30 are given in the present work, although the author has recorded many more. In some sets, a number of the songs are so much alike — differing only in music, in arrangement of words, or in meaningless syllables—that it was believed it would not be instructive to publish more than one or two samples. Some of the songs have been published in previous works.

893.—It must require much study on the part of the unlettered shaman, with unlettered teachers, to commit to memory all these songs, with their meaningless vocables and their various tunes, and to remember the proper order in which they must be sung. But in the latter part of his labors his recollection is assisted by myth. Connected with these rhymes, are tales which give clues to their order. Some of the myths recorded in the present work serve this purpose. There is a version of the Origin Legend[3] into which songs of sequence of another ceremony are introduced. But some of the sets have their own special myths to explain their meaning and indicate their order. A vast amount of mythic lore pertains to this ceremony, which has not been recorded.

894.—Usually a Navaho sacred song has a prelude to each stanza and two kinds of reiterated endings, one for the verse and one for the stanza. For convenience in this work, the former is called the burden and the latter the refrain. Preludes, burdens and refrains are often meaningless, or of doubtful meaning.

895.—Many of these songs have been sung by Indians into the phonograph, and the cylinders are now preserved in the American Museum of Natural History in New York. The number of each cylinder, where the song has been thus preserved, is given after the text, in the following pages. The late Prof. John Comford Fillmore, has noted the music from several of the phonographic records. Some of his melodies have appeared in " Navaho Legends."

896.—In his book entitled " Navaho Legends,"[3] and in his papers, " The Mountain Chant: A Navajo Ceremony,"[12] " Navajo Gambling Songs "[20] and " Songs of Sequence of the Navajos,"[54] the author has discussed the subject of Navaho poetry at greater length. To these works, the student who desires further information is referred.

AGA'*HOA'* GISĬ'N.   SONG ON HIGH OR SUMMIT SONG.   No. 1.

897.—Aienáya*n*.

I.

Yanehóho halanáe'ee (four times).
Yanehóho ha*n*aia*n* (twice) ea*nanan*.
(Meaningless prelude).

1. Aga'*h*oa'á*d*e,   *d*asĭzíni   eee,
   From a high place,   he stands above, high,

2. *H*ast*s*eniayúhi,   *d*asĭzíni   eee,
   *H*ast*s*éayuhi,   he stands above,

3. " Nitsési   *d*igĭ'ngo,"   *d*asĭzíni   eee.
   Your body   is holy,   he stands above.

Yanehóho hanea*n*aina (twice) yanehéhe ya*n*aia*n*.
(Meaningless refrain).

II.

(Repeat prelude).
1. Niyaki*nh*osá*d*e,   *d*asĭzíni   eee,
   From a house below,   he stands above, or high,

2. *H*ast*s*eneistlí*n*e,   *d*asĭzíni   eee,
   *H*ast*s*éyal*t*i,   he stands above,

3. " Nitsési   *d*igĭ'ngo,"   *d*asĭzíni   eee.
   Your body   is holy,   he stands above.

(Repeat refrain).

FREE TRANSLATION.

I.

898.—From a place above, where he stands on high,
      *H*ast*s*éayuhi, where he stands on high,
      (Says) " Your body is holy," where he stands on high.

II.

From a house below, where he stands on high,
*H*ast*s*éyal*t*i, where he stands on high,
(Says) " Your body is holy," where he stands on high.

899.—One idea the hymnist seeks to express is, that the gods, in response to prayer and sacrifice, descend from their lofty homes to cure the patient, and when they do so, assure the patient that his body is holy, i. e., that he is cured. *H*ast*s*éayuhi is mentioned elsewhere in this work. The name of *H*ast*s*eĭstli*n*, apparently a form of *H*ast*s*éyal*t*i, has not been heard by the writer, except in the songs. Another idea conveyed is that the first named, and superior, god dwells on top of a high cliff, while the inferior god lives in a cliff-house below the summit, yet high. Kĭn, or ki*n*, means a stone house or pueblo dwelling. This is the first song sung on the first night. Cylinder No. 7.

KE*T*ÁN BIGĬ′N. SONG OF THE KETHAWNS. No. 1.

FIRST SONG SUNG IN PAINTING CIGARETTES.

I.

900.—Biázi   yéyeyéye*n*   ka̧*t*   *ha*d*a*nis*t*é (repeat).
Its little one   (no meaning)   now   it is prepared.
ea*nanan*an   éhehéhéa*n*   a*nanan*aiee.
(All meaningless).

⎱ Prelude and
⎰ refrain.

1. *H*ast*s*ene*h*og*á*ni,   ka̧*t*   *ha*d*a*nis*t*é.
*H*ast*s*é*h*og*a*n,   now   it is prepared.

2. Náholnĭs   biázi,   ka̧*t*   *ha*d*a*nis*t*é,
Tell   its little one,   now   it is prepared,
i.e., little messenger,

3. Bikéd*z*e   ka̧*t*   nĭltsábaka,   ka̧*t*   *ha*d*a*nis*t*é,
Toward its trail   now   rain male   now   it is prepared,

4. Ka̧*t*   ná'yila*d*o*l*élgo,   ka̧*t*   *ha*d*a*nis*t*é.
Now   where it will hang,   now   it is prepared.

II.

(Repeat prelude).

5. *H*ast*s*eneyal*t*íhi,   ka̧*t*   *ha*d*a*nis*t*é.
*H*ast*s*éyal*t*i,   now   it is prepared.

6. Ké*t*ani   biázi,   ka̧*t*   *ha*d*a*nis*t*é,
Kethawn   its little one,   now   it is prepared,

7. Bikéd*z*e   ka̧*t*   nĭltsábaad,   ka̧*t*   *ha*d*a*nis*t*é,
Toward its trail   now   rain female,   now   it is prepared,

8. Ka̧*t*   ná'yila*d*o*l*élgo,   ka̧*t*   *ha*d*a*nis*t*é.
Now   where it will hang,   now   it is prepared.

901.—A free translation of this song is given in paragraph 320. Ná'yila refers to the resemblance of an approaching shower to a hanging curtain. For the meaning of he-rain and she-rain see par. 16. As *H*ast*s*é*h*ogan is mentioned first and is associated with the he-rain, while *H*ast*s*éyal*t*i is mentioned second and associated with the she-rain, it shows that the former is here considered the superior. See par. 32. Cylinder 68.

KE*T*ÁN BIGĬ′N. SONG OF THE KETHAWNS. No. 5.

A TOBACCO SONG.

I.

902.—Ahéye   hooé   hóoooé   ho (twice).
Ahéyeyehó   ahéyeyehoé   a*nanan* (etc.),
(Meaningless prelude).

1. Ka̧*t*   ná*t*o   *l*ĭtsói   yée   nĭs*l*í*n*.
Now   tobacco   yellow   with   I am.

2. Ka̧*t*   bĭ*t*áni   tyéli   yée   nĭs*l*í*n*.
Now   its leaf   broad   with   I am.

3.	Bĭ'la*t*a	*d*o*t*lĭ'*z*i	yée	nĭ*s*lí*n*.			
	Its blossom	blue	with	I am.			
4.	*T*áaya	*s*ĭké	holón^{i}go	na*s*á,	nagái	yée	nĭ*s*lí*n*.
	Under the leaf (?)	my feet my trail	it has	I walk,	that	with	I am.

Ahéyeyehoé ahéyeyehó ahéyeyehoé a*n*a*n*a*n*a*n* aié.
(Meaningless refrain).

II.

2.	Ka̧*t*	bĭ*t*áni	tsózi	yée	nĭ*s*lí*n*.
	Now	its leaf	narrow	with	I am.
3.	Bĭ'la*t*a	dsĭ*l*kaíi	yée	nĭ*s*lí*n*.	
	Its blossom	mountain white	with	I am.	

(The rest as in stanza I.)

903.—For free translation see par. 322. There are four stanzas in the whole song, each of which refers to a different kind of tobacco. Concerning these four kinds, see note 7. The first stanza probably refers to *Nicotiana palmeri;* the second refers to *Nicotiana attenuata*, the dsĭ*l*ná̧to, or mountain tobacco of the Navahoes. The third and fourth stanzas have not been recorded. The first word in the fourth line, *T*áaya, is said to have no meaning, but in poetic form it might mean under the leaf. If such were the case, the free translation would have to be modified. Ye, here pronounced yée, is translated, with, but it might be more exactly rendered, by means of. Cylinder 70.

KE*T*ÁN BIGĬ'N. SONG OF THE KETHAWNS. No. 7.

904.—Aienáa*n*.

I.

*H*a*t*akeyugaíeee a*l*nanalgéli*s*ie (repeat).
(Doubtful) he crosses on it to me.
Hea*n*a*n*a*n*
(Meaningless).
} Prelude.

1.	T*s*égi	naye*h*olaíe	keyúnani	a*l*nánalgelie.
	Chelly Cañon	across	from the other side	he crosses on it.
2.	Klóozos	*d*o*t*lĭ'*z*i	nánĭ*t*i'	a*l*nánalgelie.
	A slender string	blue	stretching horizontally	he crosses on it.
3.	Ke*t*áni	*d*o*t*lĭ'zi	nánĭ*t*i'	a*l*nánalgelie.
	Kethawn	blue	stretching horizontally	he crosses on it.

Eheyeyea*n*.
(Meaningless).

II.

(Repeat prelude).

1.	T*s*égi	naye*h*olaíe	keyúnani	a*l*nánalgelie.
	Chelly Cañon	across	from the other side	he crosses on it.
2.	Klóozos	*l*akaíe	nánĭ*t*i'	a*l*nánalgelie.
	A slender string	white	stretching horizontally	he crosses on it.
3.	Ke*t*áni	*d*ĭ*l*yĭ'*l*i	nánĭ*t*i'	a*l*nánalgelie.
	Kethawn	dark	stretching horizontally	he crosses on it.

905.—For free translation see par. 330. The following story of the shamans explains the meaning of this song. In old days there was something like a spider's web (a sort of suspension-bridge) hanging across the Chelly Cañon at the Monuments or Captains (one of the monument rocks is now called Nasd*z*é, the Spider) and the holy ones of the cañon used to cross on this bridge. There was a blue string or bridge, on which *H*ast*s*éayuhi crossed, and a white string on which *H*ast*s*éyal*t*i crossed. Poetic licenses are taken with many words in this song, thus: naye*h*olaíe=na*h*olaí, klóozos=klózos, nán*ĭt*i'=nantí', a*l*nánalgelie= a*l*nánalgel. Cylinder 71.

KE*T*ÁN BIGĬ'N. SONG OF THE KETHAWNS. No. 10.

I.

906.—N*ĭ*zógo   niye yéyeyéye   nayílniyáhi·
In a beautiful way   (meaningless)   again with he arrives.
     Hea*nana*n   éyeyé yeyéa*n*.
     (Meaningless).

} Prelude.

1. *H*ast*s*ene*h*og·áni   yéyeyéye   nayílniya'.
   *H*ast*s*é*h*og·an   (meaningless)   again with he arrives.

2. Naholn*ĭ's* biá*z*i   yéyeyéye   nayílniya'.
   A message   his little one   (meaningless)   again with he arrives.

3. Bikéd*z*e   n*ĭ*ltsabakái   k*ạt*   nayílniya'*d*olé*l*.
   Toward its trail   rain male   now   again with he will arrive.

II.

(Repeat prelude).

1. *H*ast*s*eneyaltíhi   yéyeyéye   nayílniya'.
   *H*ast*s*éyal*t*i   (meaningless)   again with he arrives.

2. Ke*t*áni   biá*z*i   yéyeyéye   nayílniya'.
   Kethawn   his little one   (meaningless)   again with he arrives.

3. Bikéd*z*e   n*ĭ*ltsabaá*d*i   k*ạt*   nayílniya'*d*olé*l*.
   Toward its trail   rain female   now   again with he will arrive.

907.—For free translation see par. 333. In this, as in the first Kethawn Song, a superior position is assigned to *H*ast*s*é*h*og·an. *H*ast*s*ene*h*og·áni and *H*ast*s*eneyal*t*íhi are poetic forms. Naholn*ĭ's* biá*z*i is more correctly translated, little tell; but that means a little message, for the kethawn, with its symbolic paintings and accompaniments is not only a gift to the god, it is a message to him. Cylinder 74.

*H*AST*S*ÉYAL*T*I BIGĬ'N. SONG OF *H*AST*S*ÉYAL*T*I. No. I.

I.

908.—*T*i,   *t*i   béna*s*oie;   *t*i,   *t*i   béna*s*oie (twice).
This,   this   with I walk;   this,   this   with I walk.
     Bena*s*áio   ai*s*é   kolané.
     With I walk   (?)   (?)

} Prelude.

1. Ka*t*   *H*astseyal*t*íhi   bénasoie.
   Now   *H*ast*s*éyal*t*i   with I walk.

2. Biké   elá   bénasoie.
   His feet   these are   with I walk.

3. Bĭtsá*t*   elá   bénasoie.
   His limbs   these are   with I walk.

4. Bĭtsís   elá   bénasoie.
   His body   this is   with I walk.

5. Bĭní   elá   bénasoie.
   His mind   this is   with I walk.

6. Bĭné   elá   bénasoie.
   His voice   this is   with I walk.

7. Atsé   alkaí   naki*d*á*t*a   béitsos   bénasoie.
   Eagle   white   twelve   his plumes   with I walk.

8. *S*ĭtsĭ′dze   *h*o*z*ógo   bénasoie.
   Me before toward   happily, in a beautiful way   with I walk.

9. *S*ĭké*d*e   *h*o*z*ógo   bénasoie.
   Me behind from   in beauty, happily   with I walk.

10. *S*ikĭ′gi   *h*o*z*ógo   bénasoie.
    Me above   in beauty, happily   with I walk.

11. *S*iyági   *h*o*z*ógo   bénasoie.
    Me below   in beauty   with I walk.

12. *S*ĭna*d*áltso   *h*o*z*ógo   bénasoie.
    Me around all   in beauty   with I walk.

13. Sa*n*anagaí   biké   *h*o*z*ógo   bénasoie.
    In old age   trail   in beauty   with I walk.
    wandering

14. Nĭslĭ*n*go   bénasoie.
    It is I, I am   with I walk.

II.

Same as stanza I, except that in the 1st line *H*ast*s*é*h*o*g*an is substituted for *H*ast*s*éyalti, the 8th and 9th lines are transposed, and so are the 10th and 11th.

909.—For free translation see par. 336.   Béna*s*oie is a poetic form of béna*s*a. Elá is a form of alá'.   Cylinder 86.

THA‘DZÉ BIGĬ′N. SONG OF THE SWEAT-HOUSE. No. 1.
CALLED ALSO TSÉ‘NI GISĬ′N OR SONG IN THE ROCK.

910.—Ainá.

I.

Ya*n*anáne   eeée   (seven times repeated)   a*n*an*á*n   aié.
(Meaningless prelude).

1. Tsĕ′nit*s*í*h*o*g*án   la*t*é,
   Rock Red House   there,

2. *S*ĭ′la*t*áni   yáyegó ;
   I am there   (no meaning);

3. Éni*sh*áe   yáyegó
   Half way in   (no meaning)

4. Tsáno*h*áni   yáyegó.
   I have arrived   (no meaning).

5. Ts*ĭ*'na*t*áni   hy*ĭ*d*ĕ*zná   a*n*ána*n*án   aié.
   The corn-plant   shakes, stirs   (no meaning).

II.

(Same as stanza I, except as follows) :

1. *Thá'do*t*lĭ'zh*ogán   la*t*é.
   Water Blue House   there.

5. Nanisée   hy*ĭ*dezná   a*n*ána*n*án   aié.
   Plants, vegetation   shakes, stirs   (no meaning).

911.—A free translation is given in par. 338. There is little doubt that some special mythical explanation for this song exists, but none has been obtained. For Ts*ĕ*'nits*ĭh*og*á*n see par. 568. The Blue Water House is said to be a pond or lake below the Red Rock House ; but the name may be introduced here for the sake of antithesis. Ts*ĭ*'na*t*áni=ts*ĭ*l natán. Nánise signifies all kinds of plants, vegetation. One informant said that the third line meant i*d*ní'*h*áya, or the thunder comes up. Cylinder 84.

THA'DZÉ BIGĬ'N. LAST SWEAT–HOUSE SONG.
ONE OF THE SET OF TSÉ'NI GISĬ'N OR SONGS IN THE ROCK.

912.—Aiena.

I.

> *D*oliwóoóe, *d*oliwá*n*aná*n*e (twice).
> *D*oliwá*n*aná*n*é (three times) a*n*ané.
> (Prelude. *D*óli = bluebird).

1. Ts*ĕ*'nits*ĭh*ogán   la*t*é   *h*anisá*n*   a*n*ané,
   Red Rock House   there   it grows   (meaningless),

2. Ts*ĭ*na*t*átso   *h*anisád*z*ĭn   *h*anisá*n*   a*n*a*n*é,
   Corn-plant, great   it grows out   it grows,

3. Ehyél*t*i   b*ĭt*á*d*ia'yego   *h*anisá*n*   a*n*a*n*é,
   On both sides   its ears join   it grows,

4. B*ĭ*ts*ĭ*gai   its*ĭ*go   *h*anisá*n*   a*n*a*n*é,
   Its silk   is red   it grows,

5. *L*á*n*a*n*   ts*in*   ni*t*íyigo   *h*anisá*n*   a*n*a*n*é,
   In one   day   it ripens   it grows,

6. Keá*n*a*n*d*ĭ*ld*z*ĭ'*s*go   *h*anisá*n*   a*n*a*n*é   a*n*a*n*a*n*.
   Increasing rapidly   it grows.

> *D*oliwá*n*aná*n*e (twice) a*n*a*n*a*n* aié.
> (Refrain. *D*óli = bluebird).

II.

(Repeat prelude).

1. *Thá'do*t*lĭ'zh*ogán   la*t*é   *h*anisá*n*   a*n*a*n*é,
   Water Blue House   there   it grows   (meaningless),

2. Ebeskánitso   *h*anisádz*i*n   *h*anisá*n*   a*n*ané,
   Squash-vine, great   it grows out   it grows,

3. Ehyélti   niánigo   *h*anisá*n*   a*n*ané,
   On both sides   close together   it grows,

4. B*i*la*t*á   *l*itsóigo   *h*anisá*n*   a*n*ané,
   Its flower   yellow   it grows,

5. *Lánan*   kle   ni*t*íyigo   *h*anisá*n*   a*n*ané,
   In one   night   it ripens   it grows,

6. Keána*nd*íld*zi*sgo   *h*anisá*n*   a*n*ané   a*n*ana*n*.
   Increasing rapidly   it grows.

(Repeat refrain).

913.—For free translation see par. 342.   *D*óli is the bluebird, *Sialia arctica* or *S. mexicana*.   *D*oliwá*n* is a poetic expression referring to the voice of the bluebird.   Ts*i*na*t*átso = ts*i*l-natá*n*-tso.   Other words are modified for poetic reasons.   Cylinder 87.

DS*I*L BIG*I*'N. SONG OF THE MOUNTAINS.

I.

914.—Bélanas*á*aá   bélanasóoó   (repeat).
   (Prelude.   Bélanas*á*aá = b*i*l nás*a*, with him I walk).

1. *H*od*i*gíni   la*t*éye   ye   bélanas*á*aá,
2. *H*od*i*gíni   la*t*éye   ye   bélanas*á*aá,
   A holy place   therein   a god   with him I walk,

3. Ts*i*snadz*i*'nie   ye   bélanas*á*aá,
   Ts*i*snadz*i*'ni   a god   with him I walk,

4. Ds*i*lnan*t*ä*i*   nan*t*ánie   ye   bélanas*á*aá,
   Mountain chiefs   a chief of   a god   with him I walk,

5. Sá*n*a nagaíie   ye   bélanas*á*aá,
   In old age wandering   a god   with him I walk,

6. Biké *h*ozóni   b*i*néye   *t*iyée   ye   bélanas*á*aá.
   The trail of beauty   his mind (?)   with this (?)   a god   with him I walk.

II.

3. Tsots*i*'*l*iee   ye   bélanas*á*aá.
   Tsóts*i*l, San   a god   with him I walk.
   Mateo Mt.

(The rest as in stanza I).

III.

3. *D*ókooslí*d*ie   ye   bélanas*á*aá.
   San Francisco Mt.   a god   with him I walk.

(The rest as in stanza I).

IV.

3. *D*epĕ'ntsaïe   ye   bélanas*á*aá.
   San Juan Mt.   a god   with him I walk.

(The rest as in stanza I).

(Repeat prelude and add) : Kolagá ainá.

915.—For free translation of this song see par. 352. For reference to sacred mountains see note 2. The expressions Sána nagaí and Biké hozóni are found in various songs and prayers, usually at or near the end. Occasionally they come in one line as in the Hastséyalti Bigĭ'n, par. 908, but more commonly they are separated in two contiguous lines as in this song. Poetic licenses are often taken with the words. Sána nagaí means literally, he wanders or travels in old age; or we might say, old age wanders. Biké hozóni signifies, his trail of terrestrial beauty, his happy trail, feet or footprints. But, liberally translated, the two expressions joined mean a happy old age and they are used as a prayer or benediction for such good fortune, as when we say : " Long life and happiness to you," or, " May I live a long and happy life." In different connections, it has been found advisable to translate these words with different English equivalents. Cylinders 94, 95.

NAYÉNĔZGĄNI BIGĬ'N. SONG OF NAYÉNĔZGĄNI.
SUNG AT THE APPROACH OF THE WAR GODS.
I.

916.—Hoyéyeyé yinál, hoyéyeyé yinál,
    Hoyé yinál, hoyé yinal, hoyé yináaál,
    Niyó hoyéyeyé yinál, hoyéyeyé yinál,
    Hoyé yinál, hoyé yinál, niyó.
      (Prelude. Hoyé = a place of the yéi or gods. Yinál = he strides forward. The rest is meaningless).

1. Kạt   Nayénĕzgạni   yinál.
    Now   Nayénĕzgạni   strides forward,
                               advances.

2. Agá'dahozá'   yithá'   yinál,
    The high summits   among   he strides,
    Hoyéyeyé   yinál.
    In a place of gods   he strides.

(Refrain much like prelude).

II.

(Repeat prelude).

1. Kạt   To'bádzĭstsíni   yinál,
    Now   To'badzĭstsíni   he strides,

2. Nikédahozá'   yithá'   yinál.
    The low points   among   he strides.

(Repeat refrain).

917.—For free translation see par. 368. Yinál conveys the idea that the god strides from summit to summit—that he advances thus striding. Cylinders 38 and 98.

NAYÉNĔZGĄNI BIGĬ'N. SONG OF NAYÉNĔZGĄNI. No. 9.

918.—Yoliwán anan (etc.).
    (Meaningless prelude).

1. Nayénĕzgạni,
    Nayénĕzgạni, Slayer of the Alien Gods,

2. Ka*t*   s*ĭ*n*ĭ*s*n*lígo.
   Now   that I am.

3. T*s*ohanoaíe
   The Sun Bearer

4. S*ĭl*   *h*ána*tah*asgo,
   With me   arises,

5. S*ĭl*   ní*tah*asgo,
   With me   journeys,

6. S*ĭl*   ína*tah*asgo,
   With me   goes down,

7. S*ĭl*   nína*tah*asgo ;
   With me   remains ;

8. T*o*soé*d*a   ahéna   ahéna.
   He sees me not   (meaningless).

II.

1. T*o*'bad*z*ĭst*s*íni.
   T*o*'bad*z*ĭst*s*íni.   Child of the Water.

3. Klehanoaíe
   The Moon Bearer

(The rest as in I.)

FREE TRANSLATION.

I.

919.—The Slayer of the Alien Gods,
       That now am I.
       The Bearer of the Sun
       Arises with me,
       Journeys with me,
       Goes down with me,
       Abides with me ;
       But sees me not.

II.

The Child of the Water,
That now am I.
The Bearer of the Moon
Arises with me,
Journeys with me,
Goes down with me,
Abides with me ;
But sees me not.   Cylinders 39 and 93.

NAYÉNĔZGA̧NI BIGĬ′N.   A SONG OF NAYÉNĔZGA̧NI.

I.

920.—Na *to*'liná   *to*'liná   *to*'linaá'   *to*'liná   *to*'linaá'.
       He *to*'liná   *to*'liná   *to*'linaá'   a*n*a*n*he'hé'.
            (Meaningless prelude).

1. Ka*t*   Nayénĕzgạni   *sĭnĭslĭngo.*
   Now   Nayénĕzgạni   that am I.

2. *Sĭtasáseke,*
   Wherever I wander,

3. *Sĭtsĕ'dze*
   Before me

4. Tsĭn   ni*ta*deskaígo.
   Wood   scattered around white.

5. Ayolé*l*ego   ye*n*ye*n*ye*n* ;
   He makes it   (meaningless) ;

6. *S*ĭlagaá*st*ĭni   a*n*a*n*he'hé'.
   I cause it   (meaningless).

II.

(Repeat prelude).

1. Ka*t*   *T*o'bad*z*ĭstsíni   *sĭnĭslĭngo.*
   Now   *T*o'bad*z*ĭst*s*íni   that am I.

2. *Sĭtasáseke,*
   Wherever I wander,

3. *Sĭkésde*
   Behind me

4. *T*o'   nĭta*d*eskaígo.
   Water   scattered around white.

(5 and 6 as in stanza I).

FREE TRANSLATION.

I.

921.—I am the Slayer of the Alien Gods.
    Where'er I roam,
    Before me
    Forests white are strewn around.
    The lightning scatters ;
    But 'tis I who cause it.

II.

    I am the Child of the Water.
    Where'er I roam,
    Behind me
    Waters white are strewn around,
    The tempest scatters ;
    But 'tis I who cause it.

922.—The fourth line of the first stanza refers to trees recently stricken by lightning and showing the white wood where they are rent. The word for lightning does not appear ; but the shamans explain that lightning is meant, so the word lightning is inserted in the fifth line of the free translation. The fourth line of the second stanza refers, say the shamans, to water beaten to foam by high winds.   Although no equivalent for wind appears in the text, the word tempest is added in the fifth line of free translation to make clearer the meaning of the song.   Many meaningless syllables are omitted from the text.   Words are much changed for poetic reasons, thus: *Sïlástïn*, I did it or caused it, is changed to *Sïlagástïni*.   For Slayer of the Alien Gods and Child of the Water see pars. 73–88.   Cylinders 39 and 93.

THAOKĬ'S BE*H*AKINÁLDZO.   TO SWEEP *THAOKĬ'S* OFF   ITH.

923.—Ainá.

I.

Éye i'ye' (four times).
Nahéye nahéye a*n*a*n*a*n*a*n*ai ee*n*.
(Meaningless prelude).

1. *Hó*zani ;   si'wane   nayayaíe   a*n*ha*n*e.
The corn comes up ;   the rain descends   (meaningless).

2. Na*s*owé,   na*s*owé   a*n*ha*n*e.
I sweep it off,   I sweep it off   (meaningless).

II.

(Repeat prelude).

1. *S*íwani ;   *h*ózani   nayayaíe   a*n*ha*n*e.
The rain descends ;   the corn comes up   (meaningless).

2. Na*s*owé,   na*s*owé   a*n*ha*n*e.
I sweep it off,   I sweep it off   (meaningless).

924.—For free translation see par. 370.   The words *h*a'*h*ozáne, *s*ihiwáne, appear together in many songs of this ceremony and are sometimes the only significant expressions of a song.   Traditional meanings are assigned to them ; their etymology is not evident.   The former, although apparently related to *h*ozóni, noting terrestrial beauty, is said to mean, the corn comes up, or the corn grows, and the latter to signify, the rain descends.   They are varied much for prosodic reasons.   The abbreviated forms given in this song are rare ; those given above in this paragraph are the most usual.   The redundant *h*a'hwizánaha and *s*ihiwánaha are sometimes heard.   For other forms see lines 14 and 17 of the Atsá'*l*ei Bigï'n, par. 931.   It is a common feature of the songs, as in this song, to have the words transposed in different stanzas.   Cylinders 38, 98.

A*K*A*N* BENÁTSA BIGĬ'N.   SONG OF THE MEAL RUBBING.

A SPECIAL SONG OF ESTSÁNATLEHI.

925.—1 Bĭtsi'si   nanógan.
His body   it is rubbed away.

2. Estsanatléhi*s*i   na*n*ógan.
By Estsánatléhi   it is rubbed away.

3. Na*t*án   a*l*kaíye   na*n*ógan.
Corn   white with   it is rubbed away.

4. Bikenagá*d*be   nanógan.
   Its roots made of   it is rubbed away.

5. Bĭ*t*ala*t*aíbe   nanógan.
   Its leaf-tips made of   it is rubbed away.

6. Ka*t* bĭ*d*a*t*ó'be   nanógan.
   Now   its dew made of   it is rubbed away.

7. Bĭtsela*t*aíbe   nanógan.
   Its tassel made of   it is rubbed away.

8. Bĭ*thad*ĭ*t*ĭnbe   nanógan.
   Its pollen made of   it is rubbed away.

9. Ka*t*   bĭ*d*etsébe   nanógan.
   Now   its grain made of   it is rubbed away.

10. Sá*n*a-nagaíbe   nanógan.
    In old age wandering   it is rubbed away.
    made of

11. Biké-*ho*z*ó*be   nanógan.
    Its trail of beauty   it is rubbed away.
    made of

926.—For free translation see par. 442. Prelude and many meaningless syllables are omitted. A*l*kaíye (third line)=*l*akaíye. Metathesis is frequent in Navaho songs. Three other stanzas are the same as this except that corn of other colors is mentioned. Cylinder 105.

HYĬ*D*ĚZNÁ. WAKING SONG.

SUNG IN SHAKING THE MASKS DURING THE VIGIL OF THE GODS.

I.

927.—Hyĭ*d*ĕzná   (four times).
      He stirs   (prelude).

1. Bĭ'*th*a   *h*ayolká*l*i   hyĭ*d*ĕzná (twice).
   Among   the lands of dawn   he stirs.

2. *H*ayól   bĭ*thad*ĭ*t*íni   hyĭ*d*ĕzná.
   Dawn   its pollen   he stirs.

3. Ka*t*   sa*n*á   nagaíe   hyĭ*d*ĕzná.
   Now   in old age   wandering   he stirs.

4. Ka*t*   biké   *ho*z*ó*ni   hyĭ*d*ĕzná.
   Now   his trail   beautiful   he stirs.

Hyĭ*d*ĕznáï,   hyĭ*d*ĕznáï,   hyĭ*d*ĕzná.
He stirs,   he stirs,   he stirs.

The remaining stanzas — there are eighteen in all — are like the first, except in the 1st and 2d lines as follows : (The burden, hyĭ*d*ĕzná, twice repeated, ends every line.)

II.

1. Bĭ'*th*a   na*h*otsói.
   Among   place of horizontal yellow, evening land.

2. Na*h*otsó   bĭ*thad*ĭ*t*íni.
   Evening land,   its pollen.
   the west,

III.

1. Ka*t*   *H*astseyal*t*íhi.
   Now   *H*ast*s*éyal*t*i, Talking God.
2. Ka*t*   bĭltsó   *l*akaíe.
   Now   his skin   white.
           mantle

IV.

1. Ka*t*   *H*ast*s*e*h*ogáni.
   Now   *H*ast*s*é*h*ogan, House God.
2. Ka*t*   *t*lapanakaíe.
   Now   loin-cloth white.

V.

1. Ka*t*   Dsaha*d*oldzáï.
   Now   Dsaha*d*oldzá, Fringe Mouth.
2. Ka*t*   ĕtĭ'n   *d*ĭ*l*yĭ'*l*i.
   Now   bow   dark.

VI.

1. Ká*t*i   Ga*n*askĭ'*d*i.
   Now   Gá*n*askĭ*d*i, Humpback.
2. Ka*t*   ná*t*ozĭs   *l*akaíe.
   Now   tobacco-bag   white.

VII.

1. Ká*t*i   *H*at*d*astsĭ'*s*i.
   Now   *H*at*d*ast*s*ĭ'*s*i.
2. Ka*t*   yĭské   *l*akaíe.
   Now   leggings   white.

VIII.

1. Ka*t*   *H*ast*s*ebakáï.
   Now   *H*ast*s*ébaka, Male Divinity.
2. Ka*t*   yú*d*i   al*th*asaíe.
   Now   soft goods   of all kinds.

IX.

1. Ka*t*   *H*ast*s*ebaádi,
   Now   *H*ast*s*ébaad, Female Divinity.
2. Ka*t*   ĭ'nklĭz   al*th*asaíe.
   Now   jewels, brittle things   of all kinds.

X.

1. Ka*t*   Nayenĕzgáni.
   Now   Nayénĕzgani, Slayer of Alien Gods.
2. Ka*t*   bĭ*th*a*d*ĕldzáï.
   Now   his stone necklace.

XI.

1. Ka*t*   *To*'badзĭstsĭni.
   Now   *To*'badзĭstsĭni, Child of the Water.
2. Ká*t*i   bĭtsatló*l*i.
   Now   his ear-pendants.

XII.

1. Ka*t*   *H*astseol*t*ói.
   Now   *H*astseol*t*ói, Shooting Goddess.
2. Ka*t*   na*s*tuitsói.
   Now   puma.

XIII.

1. Ka*t*   *H*astseĭ*l*tsíhi.
   Now   *H*ast*s*é*l*tsi, Red God.
2. Ká*t*i   yo*l*ĭtsíhi.
   Now   red beads, coral.

XIV.

1. Ka*t*   *H*ast*s*eiзĭ'ni.
   Now   *H*ast*s*éзĭni, Black God.
2. Ká*t*i   yo*l*akaíe.
   Now   white shell beads.

XV.

1. Ka*t*i   *To*'nenĭ'li.
   Now   *T*ó'nenĭli, Water Sprinkler.
2. Ka*t*   *to*'*l*anastsíhi.
   Now   mixed waters.

XVI.

1. Ka*t*   T*s*ohanoaíe.
   Now   T*s*óhanoai, Day Bearer.
2. Ká*t*i   *h*ad*at*éi.
   Now   pendant of haliotis.

XVII.

1. Ka*t*   Klehanoaíe.
   Now   Kléhanoai, Night Bearer.
2. Ká*t*i   *th*adĭséli.
   Now   pendant of shell.

XVIII.

1. Ka*t*   Estsanatléhi.
   Now   Estsánatlehi, Woman Who Changes.
2. Ká*t*i   naniséhi.
   Now   vegetation, plants of all kinds.

928.—For free translation see par. 470. Hyĭd̆ĕzná, translated, he moves, or he stirs, is usually said of vital movements only. It is said when a man or animal, previously at rest, shows signs of life. Although the masks, in the rites, are shaken by the shaman, they are supposed, in a poetic or religious sense, to move of their own accord. The word is related to the name for life-pollen, i'yi*d*ezná (par. 187). For explanation of the dawn pollen and the evening pollen (stanzas I. and II.) see par. 190. For the expressions Sá*n*a nagaí and Biké *h*ozóni see par. 915. Cylinders 1, 2, 3, also 65, 66, 67, and 187, 188, 189. The song is so long, it took three cylinders to record it.

ATSÁ‘*L*EI YE*DAD*IGLÉ*S*.

SUNG WHEN THE FIRST DANCERS PAINT THEMSELVES WITH GLE*S*.

929.—E'a*n*aníye   yelo   *d*ïgíni   *h*ai*d*iglé*s*   kóla nína.
(No meaning)   with   a holy one   paints himself,   (no meaning).
                                              applies gle*s*,

1. Ka*t*   Nï'ltsa   Á*s*ike   yélo   *d*ïgíni   *h*ai*d*iglé*s*   kóla nína.
Now   Rain   Boy   with   a holy one   paints himself   (no meaning).

2. Ka*t*   bïtsis*l*akáa   ka*t*   kos*d*ïlyï'*l*i   yélo, etc. (as above).
Now   the surface of his body   now   cloud dark   with.

3. Ka*t*   bïtsis*l*akáa   nïtsabïzóle   yélo, etc.
Now   the surface of his body   mizzling rain   with.

4. Ka*t*   bïtsis*l*akáa   ka*t*   *t*o'bïzóle   yélo, etc.
Now   the surface of his body   now   water bubbles   with.

5. Ka*t*   bike*l*a*t*áa   ka*t*   *t*abïtáe   yélo, etc.
Now   his toes   now   to the ends   with.

6. Ka*t*   bï*l*a*t*áa   *t*o'ása   *d*ïlyï'*l*i   yélo, etc.
Now   his finger tips   water pot   dark   with.

7. Ka*t*   bïtsis*l*akáa   atsá   a*t*sósi   yélo, etc.
Now   the surface of his body   eagle   feathers   with.

(Repeat prelude).

930.—For free translation see par. 603.

ATSÁ‘*L*EI SONG.

SUNG OUTDOORS DURING THE DANCE.

931.—1. Óhohohó éhehehé héya yéya.
2. Óhohohó éhehehé héya héya.
3. Hówani hówowówowów owé.
4. Hówani hówowówowów owé.
5. Hówani hóa hówani ho.
6. Hówani hóa héya heáhi oowé.
7. Héya heáhi óohó.
8. Óhohohó héya heáhi ehéyeyíyayéa.
9. Oahóa hóa howóa.
10. Éyehéyehéye óhoahó.
11. Éyehéyehéye óhoahó.
12. Éyehéyehéye.
13. *H*ábi níye *h*ábi níye.

14. *Ha'hozánaha   s*ihiwánaha.
   The corn comes up   the rain descends.

15. Ts̆ına*t*áa   bĭ'*l*niya.
   The corn plant   with it arrives.

16. Aíaheóo   aíaheó.

17. *S*ihiwánaha   *h*ohezánaha.
   The rain descends   the corn comes up.

18. *To*'biá*z*i   bĭ'*l*niya.
   The child-rain   with it arrives.

19. Aiaheóo   aiaheó.

20. Óhohohó   éhehehé   héya   héya.

II.

15. Nanisée   bĭ'*l*niya.
   Vegetation   with it arrives.

18. *Thad*ĭtíni   bĭ'*l*niya.
   Pollen   with it arrives.

(The rest as in stanza I).

(All vocables without interlinear translations have no meaning).

932.—For free translation and remarks see par 617. For *To*'biá*z*i see note 22. For information concerning the words in lines 14 and 17 see par. 924. Cylinders 8, 9, and 127, 128.

ATSÁ'*L*EI BIGĬ'N. SONG OF THE FIRST DANCERS.

FIRST SONG SUNG INSIDE THE LODGE ON THE LAST NIGHT.

I.

933.—Ówowówowówowé (repeat).
   (Meaningless prelude).

1. Yú*t*a   *h*ódoní*l*   yegó.
   Above   it thunders   (no meaning).

2. Nódze   nádĭzkéz   yegó.
In your direction   for you he thinks.

3. Nódze   ná*d*itsá'   yegó.
In your direction   for you he rises.

4. Ka*t*   nikĭ'niyá   yegó.
   Now   to your house.

5. Ná'*h*o*d*éya   ya   yegó.
For you he approaches.

6. Ka*t*   no*h*ániyá   yegó.
   Now   he arrives for you.

7. Ka*t*   no*t*ániyá   yegó.
   Now   he is at the door.

8. Níhyilí*n*ya   ya   yegó.
   He enters to you

9. Yúna   *d*éya   ya   yegó.
Yúni, place   he approaches.
behind the fire

10. Bígel   gíyiyá   yegó.
His special   he eats.
article, dish
11. Nítsis   *hátayá*   yegó.
Your body   is big, strong.
12. Nítsis   dígĭn   kạ*t*   *sisí*   yegó.
Your body   holy   now   I say.
Ówowówowówowé   (repeat).
Ánanánanánané.
(Meaningless refrain).

II.

1. Yúya   *hód*oníl   yegó.
Below   it thunders.
(The rest as in stanza I).

934.—For free translation see par. 644.   Cylinders 42 and 125.

ATSÁ*L*EI BIGĬ'N. SONG OF THE FIRST DANCERS. No. 6.

I.

935.—1. Tsĭ*d*a   *ha*ʻaá*sd*e   nó*dz*e   *d*éya.
Truly   from the east   to us   he approaches.
2. *S*ogán   *d*ĭlyĭ'*l*iye   nó*dz*e   *d*éya.
Trumpet   black, with   to us   he approaches.
3. *Dot*lí'zi   biá*z*i   yíka   *d*éya.
Turquoise   little   for it   he approaches.
4. Dsáa*d*e   níya   haié.
Hither   he has arrived   (?)
5. Dsáa*d*e   holó   haié.
Hither   is some   (?)

II.

1. Tsĭ*d*a   iaʻaá*sd*e   nó*dz*e   *d*éya.
Truly   from the west   to us   he approaches.
2. *S*ogán   *dot*lí'*z*iye   nó*dz*e   déya.
Trumpet   blue with   to us   he approaches.
3. *D*ĭlkósi   biá*z*i   yíka   *d*éya.
Smooth shell   little   for it   he approaches.
4. Dsáa*d*e   níya   haié.
Hither   he has arrived   (?).
5. Dsáa*d*e   holó   haié.
Hither   is some   (?).

936.—This song is said to refer to some of the four gods represented by the First Dancers (par. 607), who come, one from the east and one from the west for the gifts of turquoise and shell offered to them. *S*ogán is said to be the name of a wooden trumpet or flute formerly used in the ceremonies; but it is much like the Navaho word for "my house." One shaman declared that this song is sung also in the rites of yói *hatál* or the bead chant. The last line seems to mean, Here are your sacrifices. Take them. If one is looking for tobacco and you offer him yours, you say, dsá*de* holó=here is some. Prelude, refrain and meaningless vocables are omitted.

BÉNA *HATÁLÍ.* FINISHING HYMN. LAST.

937.—Aíená.

I.

Niyeóoo niyeóoo niyea*nan*áni.
(Meaningless prelude).

1. *H*alkai*d*éya *t*ó'saka a*nan*ánti—
From the white valley water lies (meaningless)—

2. Tsǐkéyo *t*ookláa*d*a—
Young man believes not—

3. Bigél ana'gléa*s*go
His sacrifice prepared

4. Kạ*t* nayé*d*oa*s*go,
Now he picks up (a short thing),

5. Aígebe kạ*t* ǐn*d*áz*d*otli*n*.
With that now he heals.

6. Aígebe kạ*t* nikéyo a*s*éhe kạ*t* nani*d*óne.
With that now your people thanks now give you.

Niyea*nan*ánaie.

Niyeóoo niyeóoo niyeóoo niyea*nan*áni (repeat).
(Meaningless refrain).

II.

(Repeat prelude).

1. *H*altso*d*éya *t*ó'sǐla' a*nan*ánti—
From the green valley waters lie in pools (meaningless)—

2. Tsǐkéyo *t*ookláa*d*a—
Young woman does not believe—

3. Bigé*l* ana'gléa*s*go
His sacrifice prepared

4. Kạ*t* naye*d*olé*l*go,
Now he will pick it up,

5. Aígebe kạ*t* ǐn*d*áz*d*otli*n*.
With that now he heals.

6. Aígebe kạ*t* nikéyo a*s*éhe kạ*t* nani*d*óne.
With that now your people thanks now give you.

(Repeat refrain).

938.—For free translation see par. 645. Antithesis is a favorite figure of the Navaho poets, and this song contains an antithesis which we often find in their compositions (See par. 945)—a contrast of landscapes, of the beginning and end of a stream in the Navaho land. The story of many a stream in New Mexico and Arizona is this: It rises in a green valley in the mountains where it forms a series of little ponds, connected by a small rivulet, and flows down to the lower plains, where it spreads into a single sheet of water and sinks. Its surplus may never reach the sea, or reach it only in a very rainy season. This lake may be of good size during the summer rains; but as the dry season approaches it shrinks, leaving on the surface of the ground a white saline efflorescence called alkali in the West. This "alkali flat" is the *h*alkai of the Navahoes. The green mountain valley is the *h*altsó mentioned in the song. The adjective *l*í'tso contained in this word means yellow; but it also designates a light yellowish green. The composite flora gives a yellowish tint to the mountain meadows. The male is associated with the sterile, unattractive alkali-flat, in the first stanza, while the female is named with pleasant mountain meadow in the second stanza (see Symbolism of Sex, pars. 16 and 17). Some meaningless syllables have been omitted from the above text. Some words are modified for prosodic reasons. Cylinders 49 and 117. For other Finishing Hymns hear cylinders 47, 48, and 119.

A SONG OF THE VISIONARY.

SUNG WHILE TRAVELING.

I.

939.—1. Aga'*d*a*h*ozái' *th*aisá.
    On a place above among I walk.

2. *H*ast*s*éayuhi bĭnĭ'*s*ki hwiĭs*l*í*n*.
   *H*ast*s*éayuhi   beside him there am I.

3. *S*ĭts*i*'d*z*e *h*óyona',
   Before me one walks,

4. *S*ĭké*s*d*e* *h*óyona',
   Behind me one walks,

5. Alní'i hwiĭs*l*í*n*.
 In the middle there am I.

II.

1. Nike*d*a*h*ozái' *th*aisá.
  On a place below among I walk.

2. *H*ast*s*enet*l*íhi bĭnĭ'*s*ki hwiĭs*l*í*n*.
   *H*ast*s*éyal*t*i   beside him there am I.

3. *S*ĭké*s*d*e* *h*óyona',
  Behind me one walks,

4. *S*ĭts*i*'d*z*e *h*óyona',
  Before me one walks,

5. Alní'i hwiĭs*l*í*n*.
 In the middle there am I.

940.—For free translation see par. 676. Here is another of the many instances of antithesis to be found in these songs. Meaningless syllables are omitted from this text.

A SONG OF *HASTSÉYALTI*.

SUNG BEFORE EATING.

I.

941.—Aienaá*n*   oooóe   oóe   oóe.
  Aienaá*n*   oooóe   eeeeáhi   a*nanan*   aié.
(Meaningless prelude).

1. Aga‘*dah*ozái‘   *th*aisá   klégo   oo   woa*nanan* ;
On a place above   among I walk   at night (?)   (meaningless) ;

2. *H*ast*s*éayuhi   ka*t*   so*g*áni   yayeyóoo
*H*ast*s*éayuhi   now   my house   (meaningless)

3. *S*iyági   na‘hwína‘   niininé‘.
Above me   he moves along   (meaningless).
  A*nanan*   eee.
   (Meaningless).

942.—It would seem that there should be another stanza antithetic to this ; but it has not been recorded.   For free translation see par. 677.

SONG OF THE VISIONARY.

HIS SONG OF RECOGNITION.

I.

943.—1. Agá‘*h*oyoa‘   nagáne   s*ĭ*nisá‘,
     A place above   he traveled   for me I think,

2. *H*ast*s*éayuhi   nagáne   s*ĭ*nisá‘.
*H*ast*s*éayuhi   he traveled   for me I think.

3. Nitsís   *d*ĭgíni   ka*t*   s*ĭ*lní‘
Your body   holy   now   is with me.

II.

1. Niyáke*h*ozá‘   nagáne   s*ĭ*nisá‘,
A place below   he traveled   for me I think,

2. *H*ast*s*éneatli*n*   nagáne   s*ĭ*nisá‘.
*H*ast*s*éyal*t*i   he traveled   for me I think.

3. Nitsís   *d*ĭgíni   ka*t*   s*ĭ*lní‘.
Your body   holy   now   is with me.

944.—Free translation, par. 679.   Meaningless syllables omitted.

SONG OF THE STRICKEN TWINS.

945.—Aienán*an*.
I.

Éeeé   niyá (three times)   a*nanee*a*n*.
(Prelude. Níya = we arrive).

1. *H*alkai*d*éye   *t*o‘sakáa   *l*á*d*e   niyá.
From the white valley   water standing alone   from there   we arrive.

2. Bĭnäï   ĕ'tĭn   nahyí'ke,   láde   niyá.
His eyes   none   one bearing another, from there   we arrive.

3. Bĭtsáti   ĕ'tĭn   nahyí'ke,   láde   niyá.
His limbs   none   one bearing another, from there   we arrive.

4. Azé   haniésiye   to'   haniésiye,   láde   niyá.
Medicine   where appears   water   where appears,   from there   we arrive.

5. Estíyebeye   niná   nahostlínye,   láde   niyá.
With this   your eyes   recover, restored again, from there   we arrive.

6. Estíyebeye   nitsát   nahostlinye,   láde   niyá.
With this   your limbs   recover,   from there   we arrive.

Yeananeean.
(Meaningless refrain).

II.

(Repeat prelude).

1. Haltsodéye   to'sĭlá'a   láde   niyá.
From the green valley   water in a chain of pools   from there   we arrive.

2. Bĭtsáti   ĕ'tĭn   nahyí'ke,   láde   niyá.
His limbs   none   one bearing another,   from there   we arrive.

3. Bĭnäï   ê'tĭn   nahyí'ke,   láde   niyá.
His eyes   none   one bearing another,   from there   we arrive.

4. To'   haniésiye   azé   haniésiye,   láde   niyá.
Water   where appears   medicine   where appears,   from there   we arrive.

5. Estíyebeye   nitsát   nahostlínye,   láde   niyá.
With this   your limbs   recover,   from there   we arrive.

6. Estíyebeye   niná   nahostlínye,   láde   niyá.
With this   your eyes   recover,   from there   we arrive.

(Repeat refrain).

946.—For free translation see par. 836. The singers are supposed to express the idea that they have traveled all over the land from high green mountain tops to low desert plains searching for remedies and have been vainly promising one another that such remedies would be found. For a discussion of the words in the first lines of both stanzas see par. 938. In this song, as in many others, whole lines and words within lines of one stanza, appear in another, but in a different order. As usual, many words here are changed from their ordinary forms for prosodic reasons. Thus the last word, nahostlínye appears ordinarily as nahastlé, or with the first syllable joined to a preceding word, as in the ordinary prayer ending, hozóna hastlé (see par. 963). Na signifies, again.

ÁSATĬNI BIGĬ'N. SONG OF THE LONG POT. No. 1.

I.

947.—Ahé   hoé   hoé   hooé   (repeated).
(Meaningless prelude).

1. Ha'hwizáne,   sihiwáne,   óstĭnie   eee !
The corn comes up,   the rain descends,   O long pot !

2. Sihiwáne,   ha'hwizáne,   óstĭnie   eee !
The rain descends,   the corn comes up,   O long pot !

3. Mosél   mosél.
The water trickles   the water trickles.
(on the leaves).

II.

(The same as stanza I., except that lines 1 and 2 change places).

948.—The name ásaᵗíni or ésaᵗíni, changed here by commutation, syncope and paragoge to ósᵗínie, is applied to a long earthen pot, no longer used. A whole squash could be cooked in it. There was a god also who bore this name (par. 734). For remarks on lines 1 and 2 see par. 924. The meaning of mosél is traditional. The meaning of the song is obscure and may depend on some myth not obtained. Cylinder 13.

ÁSAᵗÍNI BIGĬ'N. SONG OF THE LONG POT. No. 2.

I.

949.—Ói   ohowówi (etc.)   wí'yan   wí'yan.
   (Meaningless prelude).

1. Tsílnaᵗaatsói,
   The great corn-plants,
2. Bĭᵗhakóisa-leói.
   Among I walk.
3. *Sï'ᵗan*   bĭ'ᵈĭsni'-golá';
   My corn   I speak to;
4. *Sï'dze*   *dá'ᵈĭlnĭ'se*   ói.
   Toward me   it holds its hands out.
   Wí'yan   wí'yan.
   (Meaningless refrain).

II

1. Epeskanitsói.
   The great squash vines.
(The rest as in stanza I.).

FREE TRANSLATION.

I.

950.—1. My great corn-plants,
   2. Among them I walk.
   3. I speak to them;
   4. They hold out their hands (leaves) to me.

II.

1. My great squash-vines,
   2. Among them I walk.
   3. I speak to them;
   4. They hold out their hands to me.

951.—That is to say: I and my crops greet one another. Untranslated syllables have no meaning. Many meaningless vocables omitted. Cylinder 13.

YIKAÍGĬN. DAYLIGHT SONG. No. 12.

I.

952.—Bǐ′za holóone. bǐ′za holó (repeat) bǐ′za holó, bǐ′za holó.
(Prelude.   Bǐ′za holó = he has a voice).

1. Tsí*h*ayilkánigo *d*óla aní‘.
Just at dawn   *Sialia*   calls.

2. Áya*s* *d*o*t*lǐ′zie bǐ′za holó,
Bird   blue   his voice   has,

3. Bǐ′za holónigo bǐ′za *h*o*z*ó,
His voice   he has   his voice   beautiful, melodious,

4. Bǐ′za *h*o*z*ónigo, hwí‘he ǐnlí‘.
His voice   beautiful,   glad   it flows.

5. *D*óla aní‘ *d*óla aní‘ i a*n* ee, (etc.).
Sialia   calls   *Sialia*   calls   (meaningless).

II.

(Repeat prelude).

1. Tsína*h*otsói *d*óla aní‘.
Just at evening twilight   *Sialia*   calls.

2. Áya*s* t*s*olgá*l*ie bǐ′za holó.
The bird   t*s*olgá*l*i   his voice   has.

(The rest as in stanza I.).

FREE TRANSLATION.

I.

953.—He has a voice, he has a voice.
1. Just at daylight *Sialia* calls.
2. The bluebird has a voice,
3. He has a voice, his voice melodious,
4. His voice melodious, that flows in gladness.
5. *Sialia* calls, *Sialia* calls.

II.

He has a voice, he has a voice.
1. Just at twilight *Sialia* calls.
2. The bird t*s*olgá*l*i has a voice.
3. He has a voice, his voice melodious,
4. His voice melodious, that flows in gladness.
5. *Sialia* calls, *Sialia* calls.

954.—The Navaho poets appreciate the value of rhyme ; but they usually secure it by the addition of meaningless syllables.   In this song we have rhyme without distortion of words or meaningless additions to the final words of the verses.   *D*óli, changed here to *d*óla, is the ordinary Navaho name for the bluebird, *Sialia arctica* or *Sialia mexicana;* it is here translated *Sialia* because in the second line of stanza I, the bird is called Áya*s do*tlĭ'*zi*, which means, literally bluebird. T*s*olgá*l*i is a bird, not identified, that sings in the evening. Another song of this set—Yikaíg*ĭ*n, Daylight or Dawn Songs—similar in meaning to this song, but differing from it in music, is given in "Navaho Legends," [3] page 28. Cylinders 41 and 106.

T*SALYÉL* BIGĬ'N. SONG OF THE DARKNESS. No. 2.

955.—Aiená.

I.

Aió aió aió aiá (etc.) ya haiá*n* haiá*n*.

(Meaningless prelude).

1. *H*á'hwi*z*áni éeé,   *s*íhiwáni   éeé.

   The corn comes up,   the rain descends.

2. Ésamóos   éeé,   ésamóos   éeé.

   It foams,   it foams.

II.

(Same as stanza I., but reversing the order of words in the first line).

956.—This is sung during the rites of the amole bath (par. 439). Ésamos refers to the foam on the infusion of yucca root. For an explanation of the words in the first line see par. 924. Cylinder 110.

T*SALYÉL* BIGĬ'N. SONG OF THE DARKNESS. No. 3.

957.—Aiená.

I.

Hóonen nóhonen nohá (repeat) nohá*nanán*.
Neye neye a*nanan* (repeat) aia*nana*naié.

(Meaningless prelude).

1. *S*ĭ'ka   *d*óli   *d*éya,   *s*ĭ'ka   *d*óli   *d*éya.

   For my sake   bluebird   approaches, for my sake   bluebird   approaches.

2. *H*ang*ad*iína,   *H*á'hwi*z*áne   eee ;

   The rain sprinkles,   the corn comes up.

3. *H*ang*ad*iína,   *S*ihiwáne   eee.

   The rain sprinkles,   the rain descends.

   Eeee a*nana*naié.

II.

(Same as I., but reversing order of lines 2 and 3).

958.—*H*ang*ad*ína, changed by epenthesis in the song, is said to be an archaic word. It means that the rain comes in occasional heavy drops as it sometimes does at the beginning of a shower. See par. 924. Cylinder 110.

SĬLNÉOLE BIGĬ'N. SONG OF THE WHIRLING LOGS, LAST.

I.

959.—1. Ánĭłáni   *d*éyaya.
    Grasshopper   arrives.

2. *Há‘aásde*   *d*éyaya.
    From the east   arrives.

3. *T*áetsóhi   *d*éyaya.
    The great corn   arrives.

4. *T*ó‘biázi   *d*éyaya.
    The child-rain   arrives.

5. *H*óhozógo   *d*éyaya.
    In a way of beauty   arrives.

II.

1. Ánĭłáni   *d*éyaya.
    Grasshopper   arrives.

2. *Í*a‘ásde   *d*éyaya.
    From the west   arrives.

3. Nánisée   *d*éyaya.
    Vegetation   arrives.

4. *T*hád*it*íni   *d*éyaya.
    Pollen   arrives.

5. *H*óhozógo   *d*éyaya.
    In a way of beauty   arrives.

960.—A free translation of this song is unnecessary. For the meaning of *t*ó‘biazi see note 22. Many meaningless syllables are omitted. Hear cylinders 11, 12, for four Songs of the Whirling Logs.

PRAYERS.

GENERAL REMARKS.

961.—The prayers of this ceremony are numerous and many of them have been collected and translated by the author; but the texts of only four are given. These illustrate the general character of the prayers, in which there is often much sameness. The most interesting prayer of the ceremony is that of the Atsá‘*l*ei repeated at the beginning of the outdoor rites of the last night. As the text and translation of this (or one of its four parts, rather) is given in " Navaho Legends " [3] it is not presented in this work; but the free translation appears in par. 613.

962.—The most of the prayers are of a kind which we designate as dialogue prayers. Such supplications are given out by the shaman, one sentence at a time; after each sentence he pauses to allow the patient to repeat it. Thus said, these invocations sound much like Christian litanies; but they differ from litanies in these respects: the devotee repeats the exact words of the priest instead of giving a response and the congregation does not join.

963.—These dialogue prayers all have at or near the end the words *H*ozóna *h*astlé (*Hozó* na*h*astlé, or *Hozóna h*astlí*n*, as sometimes pronounced) meaning, It is done in beauty, It is finished happily, which is analogous to the Christian amen. If a prayer is divided into parts or sections, like those of the first prayer which follows, *Hozóna h*astlé is repeated twice only at the end of each section, until we come to the last ; at the end of the completed prayer, it is repeated four times.

964.—Navaho prayers, then, have some features in common with Christian orisons, yet they show, in their spirit, no indication of the influence of Christian teaching. They are purely pagan compositions and are evidently of ancient origin. Only in one of the following prayers (par. 981), is there any evidence of modern growth ; this is, where the shaman, praying for his own benefit, asks for sheep, horses and beeves.

965.—The usual scheme of a dialogue prayer is this : The name of the god addressed is mentioned, flattering attributes are sometimes added, and, if there are other individual gods of the same name (as in the case of *H*ast*s*éyal*t*i) his residence may be specified. He is told that sacrifices have been prepared for him, and he is asked to remove the spell of disease. At once (whether a cure is effected or not), he is assured that it is removed, and exulting expressions of recovery follow. Then the god may be asked to bestow various blessings on the supplicant and on his kindred.

966.—In addition to the dialogue prayers, the shaman repeats, on different occasions, monologue prayers for his own benefit and that of his people ; but not for the cure of the patient. One such prayer is here given (par. 981). No god is named in it, and there is no mention of a sacrifice. The most elaborate monologue Indian prayer the author ever heard, has been published under the title "The Prayer of a Navajo Shaman."[9] This interesting composition is not in the form of a supplication,—although it is intended for one,—but is in the form of a narrative.

967.—Besides saying the audible monologue prayers the shaman often prays in silence ; so does the patient, and so do others who participate in the rites or are merely present in the lodge. Some of the occasions on which such mental prayers are especially appropriate, have been mentioned. Monologue prayers may be formulated or extempore.

968.—In addition to the lengthy prayers, there are a number of formulated, short, devotional expressions—benedictions or ejaculations they may be called— which are used when kethawns are deposited and on various other occasions. Texts and translations are given of the more common of these benedictions. See pars. 985–989.

PRAYER FOR KETHAWNS OF THE SECOND DAY.
FIRST PART. PRAYER TO THE OWL GOD.

969.—1. Naests*á*.
   Owl.

2. Nigél   *i*slá‘.
Your sacrifice   I have made.

3. Na*d*é   hilá'.
For you a smoke   is prepared.

4. *S*ïké   *saádï*tli*l*.
My feet   for me restore (future).

5. *S*ïts*át*   *saádï*tli*l*.
My lower   for me restore.
extremities

6. *S*ïts*í*s   *saádï*tli*l*.
My body   for me restore.

7. *S*ï'ni   *saádï*tli*l*.
My mind   for me restore.

8. *S*ïné   *saádï*tli*l*.
My voice   for me restore.

9. *Tädï*ts*in*   naa*d*ïlíl   *saádi*le*l*.
This very day   your spell   for me take out.

10. *Tädï*ts*in*   naalíl   *saan*ï'nla'.
This very day   your spell   for me is removed.

11. *S*ïts*ádze*   *t*ahï'n*dï*nla'.
Away from me   you have taken it.

12. Nïzágo   *sï*'tsa'   nénla'.
Far off   from me   it is taken.

13. Nïzágo   nastlí*n*.
Far off   you have done it.

14. Á*dï*ts*in*   na*ded*está*l*.
To-day   I shall recover.

15. Á*dï*ts*in*   *s*áha*dad*ol*t*ó'.
To-day   For me it is taken off.

16. Á*dï*ts*in*   *sït*áha   *dï*noké*l*.
To-day   my interior   shall become cool.

17. *S*ï*t*áha   nĕzkázgo   t*sïd*esá*l*.
My interior   feeling cold   I shall go forth.

18. *S*ï*t*áha   nĕzkázgo   na*s*á*d*o.
My interior   feeling cold   may I walk.

19. *T*osa*t*yéhigo   na*s*á*d*o.
No longer sore   may I walk (or, I walk).[76]

20. *T*oso*ho*do*d*elnígo   na*s*á*d*o.
Impervious to pain   may I walk.

21. *S*ï*t*áhago   sólago   na*s*á*d*o.
My interior   light   may I walk.

22. *S*ána'   nï*s*lí*n*go   na*s*á*d*o.
My feelings   lively   may I walk.

23. *H*ozógo   na*s*á*d*o.
Happily,   may I walk.
in terrestrial beauty

24. *H*ozógo   kós*dïl*yï*l*   senahotlé*d*o.
Happily   clouds dark   I desire (may I have) abundant.

25. *H*ozógo   senahal*t*ï'n*d*o   senahotlé*d*o.
Happily   abundant showers   I desire.

26. *H*ozógo   nanisé   senahotlé*d*o.
Happily   vegetation   I desire.

27. *Hozógo*   *thad*itín   senahotlé*do*.
    Happily   pollen   I desire.

28. *Hozógo*   *dató'*   senahotlé*do*.
    Happily   dew   I desire.

29. *Hozógo*   na*s*ádo.
    Happily   may I walk.

30. *Hozógo*   dá*s*e   elkǐ'd*z*e   a'   hwení*d*o.
    Happily   (not translated).

31. *Sĭtsĭ'd*z*e*   *hoz*ó*do*.
    Me before   May it be happy, or beautiful.
                             } Transposed in second

32. *Sĭké*de*   *hoz*ó*do*.
    Me behind   may it be beautiful.
                             } and fourth parts.

33. *Siyági*   *hoz*ó*do*.
    Me below   may it be beautiful.

34. *Sĭkĭ'gi*   *hoz*ó*do*.
    Me above   may it be beautiful.

35. *Sĭná*   *d*áltso   *hoz*ógo   na*s*ádo.
    Me around   all   beautifully   may I walk.

36. *Hoz*óna   *h*astlé.
    In beauty   it is finished.
    (happily) again

37. *Hoz*óna   *h*astlé.
    In beauty again   it is finished.

SECOND PART. PRAYER TO *H*AST*S*ÉAYUHI.

970.—0. Aga'*h*oági.
      High above.

1. *H*ast*s*éayuhi.
    *H*ast*s*éayuhi.

24. *Hoz*ógo   á'*d*ĭlyĭl   senahotlé*do*.
    Happily   mists dark   may I have abundant.

(31 and 32 transposed. The rest as in the first part).

THIRD PART. PRAYER TO *H*AST*S*ÉYAL*T*I.

971.—0. Niyakégi.
      Beneath.

1. *H*ast*s*éyal*t*i.
    *H*ast*s*éyal*t*i.

(The rest as in the first part).

FOURTH PART. PRAYER TO THE TALKING (ECHOING) ROCK.

972.—1. Tse'ĕtlíhi.
    Tsé'yal*t*i', Talking Rock.

(The rest as in the second part, except that at the end " *Hoz*óna *h*astlé " is repeated four times).

973.—For free translation see pars. 325–328.

PRAYER FOR KETHAWNS OF THE THIRD DAY.

FIRST PART. TO THE TALKING GOD OF THE WHITE HOUSE, FOR THE FIRST LONG KETHAWN.

974.—1. Kininaékaigi.
House of Horizontal White
(White House) in.

2. *Hayolkál*   naid'ilnáha.
The morning light   he rises with.

3. *Hayolkál*   yilnadiáha.
The morning light   he moves with.

4. *Hastséyalti.*
Talking God.

5. Nigél   ĭslá'.
Your sacrifice   I have made.

6. Na*dé*   hilá'.
For you a smoke   is prepared.

7. *Haké*   haád'ĭtlil.
His feet, or   for him restore
the feet,   (as they were).

8. *Hatsát*   haád'ĭtlil.
His lower   for him restore
extremities   (future).

9. *Hatsís*   haád'ĭtlil.
His body   for him restore.

10. *Háni*   haád'ĭtlil.
His mind   for him restore.

11. Hwiné   haád'ĭtlil.
His voice   for him restore.

12. Ád'ĭstsin   náalil   haád'ilel.
To-day   your spell   for him take out.

13. *Tád'ĭtsin*   náalil   haanénla'.
This very day   your spell   for him is removed.

14. *Hatsádze*   tahĭ'nd'ĭnla'.
Away from him   you have taken it.

15. Nĭzágo   hatsa'nénla'.
Far away   from him it is taken.

16. Nĭzágo   nastlín.
Far away   you have done it.

17. *Hozógo*   nadedotál.
Happily   he shall recover.

18. *Hozógo*   hahadadoltó'.
Happily   for him it is taken off.

19. *Hozógo*   hatáha   d'ĭnokél.
Happily   his interior   shall become cool.

20. *Hatáha*   honĕzkázgo   ĭndzagádo.
His interior   feeling cold   may he move around.

21. *Hozóna*   hastlín   (hastlé).
In beauty again   it is finished.

22. *Hozóna*   hastlín.
In beauty again   it is finished.

23. *Hozógo* na*s*ádo *s*ïtsówe.
   In beauty   may you walk   my grandchild.

24. *Hozóle*l kóo*t*e.
   It will be beautiful   thus.

SECOND PART. TO THE HOUSE GOD OF THE WHITE HOUSE, FOR THE SECOND LONG KETHAWN.

975.—2. Na*h*otsói nai*d*ïlnáha.
      The evening light   he rises with.

3. Na*h*otsói yi*l*na*d*i*t*áha.
   The evening light   he moves with.

4. *H*ast*s*é*h*ogan.
     House God.

(The rest as in the first part).

THIRD PART. TO A MALE DIVINITY, FOR THE FIRST SHORT KETHAWN.

976—1. Bï*l*na*z*do*t*lï′z.
       With blue face.

2. *H*ast*s*ébaka.
   Male divinity.

(From the 5th to the last lines, inclusive, the same as the first part).

FOURTH PART. TO A FEMALE DIVINITY, FOR THE SECOND SHORT KETHAWN.

977.—1. Bï*l*nidsotsói.
      With yellow under chin.

2. *H*ast*s*ébaad.
   Female divinity.

(From the 5th line to the last, inclusive, the same as the first part).

FIFTH PART. TO A MALE DIVINITY, FOR THE THIRD SHORT KETHAWN.

978.—(All the same as the third part).

SIXTH PART. TO A FEMALE DIVINITY, FOR THE SECOND SHORT KETHAWN.

979.—(Same as the fourth part, except that the words *Hozóna h*astlí*n* are repeated four times instead of twice).

980.—For free translation see pars. 383–387.

MONOLOGUE PRAYER OF THE SHAMAN DURING THE VIGIL OF THE GODS (par. 472).

981.—1. *Hozó* ke*h*atí*n*do.
     In beauty,   may (I) dwell.
     happiness,

2. *Hozógo* na*s*ádo.
   In beauty   may I walk.

3. *Hozógo* *s*aha*t*ói ke*h*atí*n*do.
   In beauty   my male kindred   may (they) dwell.

4. *Hozógo*   sezáni   ke*hat*í*ndo*.
   In beauty   my female kindred   may (they) dwell.

5. *Hozógo*   sĭsikél   na*hal*t*índo*.
   In beauty   my young men   may it rain on.

6. *Hozógo*   sĭséke   na*hal*t*índo*.
   In beauty   my young women   may it rain on.

7. *Hozógo*   sĭnantáhi   na*hal*t*índo*.
   In beauty   my chiefs   may it rain on.

8. *Hozógo*   ní'yi   na*hal*t*índo*.
   In beauty   us   may it rain on.

9. *Hozógo*   ní'yi   nan*t*á*do*.
   In beauty   (for) us   may corn grow.

10. *Thád*i*t*in   kehyetígi   na*hal*t*índo*.
    Pollen   in the trail of   may it rain on.

11. Ni'yitsĭ'*dze*   *hozógo*   na*hal*t*índo*.
    Before us   in beauty   may it rain on.

12. Ni'yiké*de*   *hozógo*   na*hal*t*índo*.
    Behind us   in beauty   may it rain on.

13. Ni'yiyá'   *hozógo*   na*hal*t*índo*.
    Below us   in beauty   may it rain on.

14. Ni'yit*s*íga   *hozógo*   na*hal*t*índo*.
    Above us   in beauty   may it rain on.

15. Ni'yiná*de*   *d*áltso   *hozógo*   na*hal*t*índo*.
    Around us   all   in beauty   may it rain on.

16. *Hozógo*   na*s*á*do*.
    In beauty   may I walk.

17. Yú*d*i   so*s*á*do*.
    Soft goods   may I acquire.

18. Ĭnklĭ'z   so*s*á*do*.
    Hard goods (jewels)   may I acquire.

19. *Lin*   so*s*á*do*.
    Horses   may I acquire.

20. *D*epé   so*s*á*do*.
    Sheep   may I acquire.

21. Béka*s*i   so*s*á*do*.
    Beeves   may I acquire.

22. Sá*n*a   nagaí.
    In old age   wandering.

23. Biké   *hozó*.
    Trail   beautiful.

24. Nĭ*s*l*í*ngo   na*s*á*do*.
    Lively   may I walk.

PRAYER TO THE WAR GODS AND THE GODDESS OF THE CHASE.
FIRST PART. TO NAYÉNĔZGANI.

982.—1. Nayénĕzgani.
    Slayer of the Alien Gods.

2. Nigél   ĭslá'.
   Your sacrifice   I have made.

3. Nadé   hilá'.
For you a smoke   is prepared.

4. Sïké   saádïtli*l*.
My feet   for me restore (future).

5. Sïtsá*t*   saádïtli*l*.
My lower   for me restore.
extremities

6. Sïtsís   saádïtli*l*.
My body   for me restore.

7. Sï'ni   saádïtli*l*.
My mind   for me restore.

8. Sïné   saádïtli*l*.
My voice   for me restore.

9. Á*d*ïsts*in*   naalí*l*   *s*áadile*l*.
To-day   your spell   for me take out.

10. Á*d*ïsts*in*   naalí*l*   saanï'nla'.
To-day   your spell   for me is removed.

11. Sïtsád*z*e   *t*ahï'n*d*ïnla'.
Away from me   you have taken it.

12. Nïzágo   sïtsanï'nla'.
Far off   from me it is taken.

13. Nïzágo   nastlí*n*   (or na*h*astlí*n*).
Far off   you have done it.

14. *H*ozógo   na*d*e*d*está*l*.
Happily, in a   I shall recover.
beautiful way,

15. *H*ozógo   sáha*d*a*d*oltó'.
Happily   from me it is taken off.

16. *H*ozógo   sï*t*áha   *d*ïnoké*l*.
Happily   my interior   shall become cool.

17. *H*ozógo   tsï*d*ĕsá*l*.
Happily   I shall go forth.

18. *H*ozógo   na*s*á*d*o.
Happily   may I walk.

19. *T*osat*y*éhigo   na*s*á*d*o.
No longer sore   may I walk.

20. *T*osoho*d*o*d*elnígo   na*s*á*d*o.
Impervious to pain   may I walk.

21. Sï*t*áhago   sólago   na*s*á*d*o.
My interior   light   may I walk.

22. Sána'   nï*s*lí*n*go   na*s*á*d*o.
My feelings   lively   may I walk.

23. *H*ozógo   na*s*á*d*o.
Happily   may I walk.

24. *H*ozóna   *h*astlé   (or *h*astlí*n*).
In beauty again   it is finished.

25. *H*ozóna   *h*astlé.
In beauty again   it is finished.

SECOND PART.

983.—(Same as the first, except that the first line consists of the name of *T*o'badzïstsíni, Child of the Water).

THIRD PART.

984.—(This has the name of *Hastséoltoi* for the first line.　After that it is the same as the first part to the 23d line, inclusive.　Then the prayer ends thus):

24. *Sïtsï'dze*　　　*hozógo*　　　nasádo.
　　Me before toward　happily, in beauty,　may I walk.

25. *Sïkéde*　　　*hozógo*　　　nasádo.
　　Me behind from　　happily　　may I walk.

26. *Siyági*　　　*hozógo*　　　nasádo.
　　Me below in　　happily　　may I walk.

27. *Sïkï'dze*　　　*hozógo*　　　nasádo.
　　Me above toward　happily　　may I walk.

28. *Sïná*　　*dáltso*　　*hozógo*　　　nasádo.
　　Me around　　all　　happily　　may I walk.

29. Sána　　nagaí,　　biké　　*hozó.*
　　In old age　travel　his trail　beautiful.

30. Nïs*lí*ngo　　*d*ïsnï'.
　　I am lively　　I say.

31. Sána　　nagaí,　　biké　　*hozó.*
　　In old age　travel　his trail　beautiful.

32. Nasïstlé.
　　Again I am done,
　　or finished, I am well again.

33, 34, 35, 36. *Hozóna*　　*hastlé*　　(repeated four times).
　　　　　　In beauty again　it is finished.

Cylinders 6, 77, and 78.

BENEDICTIONS.

I.

985.—*Hozódo.*
May it be terrestrially beautiful, happy.

II.

986.—*Hozógo*　　nasádo.
　　In a beautiful　may you (or I)
　　or happy manner　walk.

III.

987—*Hozólel*　　ko*t*é　　*s*ï*ts*ówe.
　　It will be beautiful　thus　my grandchild.

IV.

988.—*Hozolel*　　ko*t*é.
　　It will be beautiful　thus.

　　Hozógo　　　nasádo　　ko*t*é　　*s*ïts*ó*we.
　　In a beautiful manner　may you walk　thus　my grandchild.

989.—There are other forms embodying the same ideas as the above.　Certain favorite passages of the prayers, such as those given in par. 969, lines 31–35 (second person), may be used as parting benedictions among friends and relations. An old man, in making a benediction, such as III. and IV., may say *s*ïtsówe, my grandchild, to a young man; but a young man must say *s*ïtsaí, my grandfather, to an old man.

Notes.

Notes.

Remarks.—Some of the information contained in the following notes has already appeared in the notes of "Navaho Legends"[3] and in the text of that and other works by the author; but its repetition here could not be avoided without greatly impairing the value of the work. In a few cases, we have even repeated the exact words of the previous notes, fearing that we could not improve on them. On the other hand, most of the material is new.

1. North of the San Juan River, in Colorado and Utah, are a number of cañons abounding in ruined cliff-dwellings. Tse'gíhi is one of these cañons; but the author does not know which. It is often mentioned in the myths as the house of numerous yéi or gods who dwelt in the cliff-houses in ancient days. They are thought to still abide there unseen. The name, which means, Among the Rocks or, In the Cliffs, resembles closely, both in sound and sense, that of Chelly Cañon in Arizona. Chelly is but a Spanish spelling of Tsé'gi, Tséyi, or Tséyi, the Navaho name, which often takes different forms, g and y being interchangeable, also s and s. The Navaho for "in the Chelly Cañon" is Tséyigi. The two names are easily confounded.

2. There are many mountains in the Navaho land which are supposed to be the homes of divinities and therefore sacred. But there are seven of an especially sacred character and four of these seem to be regarded as of the highest sanctity. The seven sacred mountains are these: Tsïsnadzï'ni, which is believed to be Pelado Peak, north of the pueblo of Jemez, New Mexico; Tsótsïl, which is San Mateo Mountain, otherwise called Mount Taylor, New Mexico; Dokoslíd, which is San Francisco Mountain in Arizona; Depě'ntsa, which is the San Juan Mountains in Colorado; Dsïlnáotïl and Tsolíhi, which have not been identified, and Akïdanastáni, which is Hosta Butte in New Mexico. The first four named are those of the highest sanctity and the ones most frequently mentioned in the myths. They are considered as bounding the Navaho land, although Navaho camps may be found beyond, and the Navaho reservation is far within their limits. According to the myths they were once closer together and formed the boundaries of the habitable world. Tsïsnadzï'ni is the sacred mountain of the east. Although San Mateo and San Francisco mountains are almost in the same latitude, the former is regarded as the sacred mountain of the south. The latter is the sacred mountain of the west. San Juan is the sacred mountain of the north. Whenever, in this work, we speak of the "Navaho land" we mean the country bounded by a line which just includes these four mountains.

3. Navaho legends, collected and translated by Washington Matthews, etc. Boston and New York. Published for the American Folk-Lore Society by Houghton, Mifflin & Company, 1897. Pp. VIII, 299. The Origin Legend of the Navahoes is given in this work.

4. As stated in note 2, the Navaho sacred mountain of the south is Tsótsïl. The name might, for etymological, but not for phonetic reasons, be better written Tsó'dsïl. It is derived from tso, great, and dsïl, a mountain. It is called, by the Mexicans, San Mateo; but on September 18, 1849, it was named Mount Taylor, "in honor of the President of the United States," by Lieut. J. H. Simpson, U. S. Army. On the maps of the U. S. Geological Survey, the whole mountain mass, to which it belongs, is marked "San Mateo Mountains" and the name "Mount Taylor" is reserved for the highest peak, which is 11,389 feet above sea level and about twelve miles distant, in a direct line, east by north, from McCarty's Station on the Atlantic and Pacific Railroad.

5. Yéitso, whose name, derived from yéi and tso, signifies Great Yéi, genius or god, was the greatest and fiercest of the anáye,—the alien or inimical gods. He is mentioned in many myths; but is described most particularly in the Origin Legend.[3] He was an anthropophagous giant, who sought to devour the children of the Sun, but they eventually overcame him. His home was at

Tsótsï*l*, or San Mateo Mountain,[4] from the summit of which he descended every day to drink at a lake near the present village of San Rafael. Here he was slain by Nayénĕzgạni and scalped by *T*o'bad*z*ïst*s*íni.

6. The Navahoes, like most other North American tribes, have a tradition that they originally came to the surface of this world from a lower world — that their origin was subterranean. They now endeavor to locate the place of this mythological emergence. They say it is in a small lake surrounded by precipitous cliffs; that near the centre of this lake there is a small conical island, with a hole in its summit from which something projects that looks like a ladder; and that this is the hole through which they came up. Beyond the bounding cliffs four mountain peaks, often referred to in the sacred songs, are said to rise. The Navahoes fear to visit the shores of this lake; but climb the surrounding hills and view the waters from afar. The place is called *H*ad*z*inaí and Ni*h*oyost*s*ád*z*e, names which may be freely translated, Place of Emergence or, Land Where They Came Up. The description would answer fairly for Crater Lake in Oregon; but the Navahoes place their natal lake in the San Juan Mountains. Efforts have been made, without success, to determine which of the many lakes in the San Juan Mountains contains the Ni*h*oyast*s*ád*z*e. See "Navaho Legends,"[3] page 219.

7. The tobacco of commerce is never used by the Navahoes for filling sacred cigarettes or for other sacred purposes; for these they employ some species of *Nicotiana*, or true tobacco, indigenous to the southwest. According to their myths, songs, and plant-lore they are acquainted with four native species of *Nicotiana*, two of which have been identified, viz., *N. attenuata* and *N. palmeri*. The former, called dsï'*l*naẓo, or mountain tobacco, grows sparsely but widely in all the mountains of the Navaho country at altitudes of 7000 feet or more. The latter, called *d*epénạẓo, or sheep tobacco, has been found by the author in one locality only—in the Chelly Cañon, at the foot of a high preci-

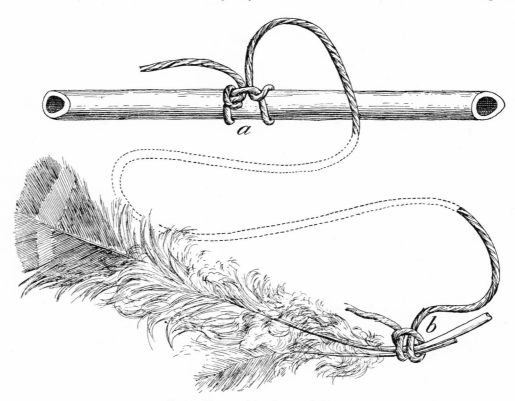

Fig. 19. Knots used in tying sacred objects.

pice in which were the ruins of a great cliff-house. It grew abundantly and might have been a vestige of ancient cultivation. The two other kinds, called glóina*t*o, or weasel tobacco, and kósna*t*o, or cloud tobacco, by the Navahoes, have not been identified. *N. attenuata* is the species used mostly in the ceremony of the night chant.

8. At the time this was written it was hoped that names might be found for the simple knots or hitches used by the Navaho medicine-men in making their kethawns; but all efforts to find terms have failed. They are not described or figured in any of the dictionaries or encyclopædias consulted. Specimens were sent to the Naval Academy at Annapolis in the hope that some "ancient mariner" there might help us; but no one was found who could name them. They are illustrated in fig. 19. Let us call *a* the Navaho knot and *b* the holy hitch.

9. The prayer of a Navaho shaman. (In American Anthropologist, vol. ii, no. 1, pp. 1–19. Washington, January, 1889.)

10. Tiéholtsodi is a god (or demon, according to the point of view) of terrestrial waters. Although commonly named in the singular, the Navahoes seem to believe in many divinities of this class. The chief dwelling of the god, or, perhaps we should say the dwelling of the chief god, is in the Atlantic Ocean. In the first world, he was chief of the great water of the east, and so he is in this, the fifth, world. But the myths indicate that a Tiéholtsodi is supposed to dwell in every permanent spring and every permanent river. He has his counterpart in the U*n*kté*h*i of the Dakotas and the water-gods of other Indian tribes. He is described as much like an otter in appearance, with a fine fur; but with horns like a buffalo. A picture of him is said to be made in a dry-painting of the ceremony of *hozóni hatál*; but the author has not seen it. He is one of the oldest of the gods. He existed before the Sun or the Moon deities, before Estsánatlehi, the war-gods, or First Man. To recover his young, which were stolen by Coyote, he caused the deluge which drove the people from the fourth world to this world and he threatened this world with flood until the stolen children were restored to him. A satisfactory analysis of his name has not been procured.

11. In addition to these, there are foods described in the myths which are still sometimes prepared; these are: 1. *H*anikaí, a dish of meat and corn boiled together. 2. Naněská*d*i or naněs *tád*i, round corn-cake, with a hole in the middle, made of a stiff dough and baked on hot coals. 3. Yï*t*elkaí, a fine white meal made of corn which is first boiled, then husked, and then ground. 4. Nïst*s*áiakan.

12. The Mountain Chant: a Navaho ceremony, by Dr. Washington Matthews, U. S. A. (In fifth annual report of the Bureau of Ethnology, pp. 379–467, Washington, 1887.)

13. Navaho houses, by Cosmos Mindeleff. (In seventeenth annual report of the Bureau of American Ethnology, part 2, pp. 475–517, Washington, 1898.)

14. For reasons given elsewhere (pars. 16–17) the rainbow is considered a female deity or goddess. The Navahoes say there are five colors in the rainbow and some aver that each color is a different individual. According to this theory there are five rainbow goddesses. They say the bows are covered with feathers which give the colors. In the dry-paintings, the rainbow is usually depicted with a head at one end, and legs and feet at the other. The head is always square to show that it is a female. Three colors only have been seen in the body of the bow, which is red and blue, bordered with white. In the sweat-house decoration depicted in plate II, fig. B, a rainbow symbol is shown with a head at each end, indicating that each separate band of color represents a separate goddess. In the decoration depicted in plate II, fig. A, the symbol is shown with five tail feathers of a chicken-hawk at one end, and five of a magpie at the other. In one of the dry-paintings of the mountain chant the rainbow is depicted as terminating at one end with five eagle plumes, at the other with five magpie plumes, and decorated near its middle with plumes of the bluebird and the red-shafted woodpecker. (See "The Mountain Chant," [12] p. 540.)

15. Hyĭná bĭltsós, breath feather or life feather, is a feather obtained from a living bird. The term is especially applied to the small downy feathers of the golden eagle, which are supposed to possess many virtues and are used for many sacred purposes. The eagle breath feather is one of the smaller contour feathers of the bird, having very little dark color at the tip and being mostly white. Unless the hyporachis is well developed the feather is not used. To procure a good supply of these feathers, the Pueblo Indians capture young eagles in the nest and rear them in captivity. The Navahoes often purchase their feathers from the Pueblos: but they also catch the adult birds in traps, pluck them, and set them free, in the manner witnessed by the author, among the Indians of the North, thirty years ago.

16. The International Folk-Lore Congress of the World's Columbian Exposition, Chicago, July, 1893, etc. Chicago, 1898, pp. 246 and 247.

17. Perhaps yucca should have been described under the head of medicines; but it is doubtful if remedial properties are assigned to it, even mythically. It is used as a detergent. The Navahoes say that the gods are cleanly—averse to foul sights and repulsive odors. Hence the patient must be clean, who expects a visit from succoring gods, and at times, as on the fourth night, when the vigil of the gods is kept, the shaman and his assistants must be clean, also. The following four kinds of yucca are mentioned in the myths and grow in the Navaho land: 1st, tsási or haskán, *Yucca baccata* (Torrey); 2d, tsasitsóz or slender yucca, *Yucca glauca* (Nuttall), *Yucca angustifolia* (Pursh); 3d, yébĭtsasi, or yucca of the gods, probably *Yucca radiosa* (Trelease), *Yucca elata* (Engelmann); 4th, tsasibĭté, or horned yucca, which seems to be but a stunted form or dwarf variety of *Yucca baccata*, never seen in bloom or in fruit by the author. Tsási is used as a generic name. All kinds are employed in the rites, sometimes indifferently, at other times only certain species may be used. All have, in their leaves, long tough fibres which are useful in the arts and are much employed in the rites, in making objects where strings or thread are required. All have saponine in their roots; but the root of *Yucca baccata* seems richest in this substance. The roots are called tálawus, or foam, by the Navahoes and amole by Mexicans and Americans; these names are sometimes applied to the entire plant. To prepare the yucca bath, the root is well contused, soaked and thoroughly mixed in water; by whirling twigs in the solution a lather is raised. In this book, the solution is called suds. One species, *Yucca baccata*, has an edible fruit, called haskán, from hos, thorny, and kan, sweet. This name is sometimes applied to the whole plant. The fruit is eaten raw and made into a tough dense paste or jelly both by Navaho and Pueblo Indians. The first and second kinds grow abundantly in the Navaho country; the third and fourth kinds are rarer.

18. The often-used terms yúdi and yúdi althasaí are here commonly translated, goods and goods of all kinds. The late Mr. A. M. Stephen translated them "soft-goods" in contradistinction to ĭnklĭ'z or "hard-goods" (see note 19) with which they are often named, in contrast or connection, in song, prayer, and story. His translation has merits and is sometimes adopted in this work. The terms, it would seem, were originally applied to furs, dressed skins, and textiles; but of late years, their significance has been extended so as to include most articles purchasable in a trader's store.

19. Ĭnklĭ'z, or ĭntlĭ'z, as an adjective, means hard and brittle, as a noun it denotes hard and brittle substances. Ĭnklĭ'z althasaí means hard and brittle things of all kinds. These terms particularly refer to shells, turquoise, colored stones, and cannel-coal, used for ornamental purposes. The late Mr. Stephen translated these expressions "hard-goods" (see note 18). In this work they are commonly rendered by the English words, jewels, and jewels of all kinds.

20. Navaho gambling songs. (In American Anthropologist, vol. ii, no. 1, pp. 1–19, Washington, January, 1889.)

21. In the winter of 1883–4 while at Fort Wingate, New Mexico, I made arrangements to attend a ceremony of the night chant at a point some 14 miles from the post. When the time came for me to depart, I was detained by professional duties. A member of the Regimental Band of the

13th Infantry, Sergeant Christian Barthelmess, who took a deep and intelligent interest in ethno-
graphic studies, expressed a desire to go.   I obtained for him a short leave, gave him a mount, and
arranged with the Indians for a kindly reception for him.   He arrived at the medicine-lodge on the
ninth day of the ceremony, saw the outdoor rites of the afternoon and the outdoor dance at night.
He observed well, and wrote an excellent account of what he saw, which was published in a German
paper of Chicago, *Der Westen*, in January, 1884.

22.   The word *tó'biaźi* is often heard in the Navaho songs.   It means literally, little water, or
child-water ; but in this work it is translated child-rain.   When a heavy drop of rain falls into a
pool, a reactionary splash rises at the point of impact.   The Navahoes liken this to an act of
impregnation (or believe it to be such perhaps).   The descending water is regarded as the male
element ; the pool, as the female element ; the ascending splash as the offspring, which is therefore
called child-rain.   We must carefully distinguish this name from that of the god *To'badźïstsíni* or
Child of the Water.

23.   *Thá'tsini* was, according to the Navaho Origin Legend,[3] the fourteenth gens which came
to form the Navaho nation.   It derives its name from a place called *Thá'tsi* which lies west of the
location of the old Navaho settlement on the San Juan.   Some translate this Red Water, others
say (as noted in the Origin Legend) that it means " Among the Red (Waters or Banks)."

24.   *Bïtáhatïni* means literally, His Imagination, His Visions ; but it is here freely translated
the Visionary.   One informant sometimes pronounced the name Bélahatïni.   It is a common as
well as a proper noun.   It is said of one who claims to have mysterious visions or hear mysterious
voices—a mystic, a medium.

25.   This word is said to mean the edge of an adobe wall, the edge of an arroyo, the top of a
perpendicular bank.   It has also been recorded Pïstá.

26.   Tsï'ni means " they say."   Some Navaho story tellers place this word after almost every
sentence until the listener is weary of it.   Tsïné is simply a variant of tsï'ni used for melodious
repetition.

27.   Igangishaltéle, He Picks on the Back, designates the crow, which is said to pick out the
spinal marrow between the vertebral joints.   Atékedasïtahi, He Sits between the Horns, designates
the magpie.   These are poetic or sacred names.   The ordinary term for magpie is a'á'i and that for
crow is kágí ; both of which are onomatopes.

28.   This is a purely pagan expression, yet it has an interesting resemblance to something which
a profane Christian might say under similar circumstances : " What, the Devil, has happened to the
deer ? "   The following is the text of the exclamation : Tsï'ndi *thá*'go ni pi*n* *d*azlín ?

29.   *Hatáłi* Natlói, from whom this song was obtained, said it was a good song to sing before
you rise in the morning if you intend to travel alone that day.   He is accustomed to sing it on such
occasions and then to pray, believing that if he does so, all will be well with him during the day.
He prays that all may be beautiful or happy before, behind, above, below, and all around him, that
day.   He does not pray thus every morning, but there are some Navahoes who do.   They usually
pray more when traveling than when staying at home.   If a man has bad or portentous dreams, a
shaman and assistants sing and pray for him four nights.   On the fourth night, the biklé songs are
sung and the singers go home.

30.   Ni'yĕ'lni or nihyĕ'lni is an owl.   Dr. Chas. W. Richmond of the National Museum, having
examined a wing-feather, pronounced the bird *Bubo virginianus pallescens*, or western great horned
owl.   Tsïd'ïltói, or the shooting bird, is also described as an owl.

31.   The necessity of paying shamans for their instructions, as well as for their treatment, is
often inculcated in the myths.

32.   Tsé'ïntyel, or Broad Rock, is a high perpendicular cliff, near the junction of Monument

Creek with Chelly Creek in the Chelly Cañon.   It rises more than 1000 feet above the floor of the cañon on the south side.   In plate V, fig. C, it is shown to the right of the picture behind one of the monuments, a bird flying over it.   There are ruins in its neighborhood.

33.   The Navaho name for this tale is, *Sĭ́néoƚe Paẖáni Hatáƚ*, the Story and Song of *Sĭ́néoƚe*. The latter word is said to mean, It whirls with me.   This is the pronunciation and definition of *Hatáƚ*i Natlói and others.   Noting from another informant, the name was recorded as Tsĭ́néoƚe and translated Whirling Wood (Logs, Sticks).   The lake or whirlpool where the whirling logs are said to be is called *Tó'nihiliŋ*, or Waters that Flow Around.

34.   The story of Natĭ́něstẖani, He Who Teaches Himself, the Self Taught, is told in "Navaho Legends."[3]   Like the hero of this story, he is said to have floated down the San Juan River in a hollow log.

35.   The three kinds of wood used for these plugs have some mythic relation, not fully investigated, to three ceremonies of the Navaho shamans.   To the klédze *hatáƚ*, belongs the cedar ; to the atsózi *hatáƚ*, the cliff-rose ; to the yói *hatáƚ*, the cottonwood.   These ceremonies are associated and much alike.   A priest of one ceremony may borrow material from a priest of another.

36.   In former days, when the Navahoes wished to cross the San Juan they made such a sacrifice as this to the waters, above the place where they intended to cross.   Then they thought they could cross safely.   If a man is nearly drowned and is ill as a result, or if he dreams of drowning, such sacrifices are made to the water ; but no cigarettes are made.

37.   The things he hoped mostly to learn were these : 1.   *Sĭ́néoƚe yikáƚ*, or picture of the whirling logs.   2.   *Táikĭsi yikáƚ*, farm picture, called also natánbe yikáƚ, or picture with the corn. 3.   *Tẖatládze Dsahadoldzábe yikáƚ*, or picture with the Fringe Mouths of the Water.   4.   A song for the trance or spasm which seizes the patient in the lodge.   5.   A prayer for the same.   6.   The Songs of the Įndiá' or Plumed Wands.

38.   In this, as in most other rite-myths, the youngest brother in a family is represented as the one who learns the songs and becomes the shaman, although he may not have been the discoverer or originator of the rites.   It is the custom now among the Navahoes to make the youngest son the *hatáƚ*i, no matter what ceremony is selected for his study.   They say he is the most intellectual member of the family and has the best memory.   This is not a compulsory law; but a general custom.   If an elder brother wishes to become a chanter, no one can prevent him.   Nakiĕstsái means a purulent secretion on the eyelids ; every youngest brother is thus called.

39.   This is described as a hogback near the modern town of Fruitland in New Mexico.

40.   This name denotes a broad flat place sloping down to the river.

41.   Could you make it rain that way now ?   *Hatáƚ*i Natlói was asked.   He replied, " Yes.   If we got the true mixture of all kinds of water, threw it four times upward, and sang the proper songs, rain would surely fall " [Here he sang the Rain Songs, not very musical].   "We do not sing these songs when we treat a patient.   If we did, it would rain all the time during the ceremony.   If it snows for five or six consecutive days and we get tired of it we do this : we get an earthern pot ; heat spruce leaves ; put them around it ; put the pot on the fire ; collect a large double-handful of snow from each of the four quarters ; melt it in the pot, and scatter the water to the four quarters of the world, blowing audibly after it."   The narrator said he had often tried this and never failed.

42.   The author possesses, of this dry-painting, a rude diagram from which the following description is made.   There is a bowl of water in the centre and the anthropomorphic rainbow in the periphery on three sides—south, west, and north.   Within this there are 16 divine figures in four groups of four figures each, with their feet toward the centre.   One group is east, another south, another west, and another north of the central bowl.   Each group stands on the sunbeam raft—a line of blue and a line of red, bordered with white—and consists, going sunwise, of a *H*astséyalᵗi, a yébaad, or goddess, a Dsahadoldzá, and a second goddess.   Four stalks of corn extend from the

water to the rainbow—a black stalk in the northeast, a white stalk in the southeast, a blue stalk in the southwest, and a yellow stalk in the northwest. Each cornstalk has three white roots. When the rest of the picture is finished, four footprints are drawn in meal, leading from the southeast edge to the centre of the picture : four plumed wands (black) are set up to the north and four (blue) to the south of the picture All the elements of this painting, except the sunbeam rafts, may be seen in the colored illustrations of this book. In general appearance the painting resembles somewhat that shown in plate VI.

43. This picture is called alké*t*a naáz*t*a yiká*l* or al*g*án *t*att*é*tdz*e yiká*l*, names which are said to signify, those-above-one-another picture. It has on three sides the anthropomorphic rainbow within which are 28 divine figures disposed in four rows, of seven each, their heads directed to the east. The first row, that farthest west, consists of *H*ast*s*éyal*t*i (in the north) and six yébaka, all dancing toward the north, on a black cloud (black line or band). The second row consists of *T*ó'ne*n*ïli (in the north) and six yébaad, all dancing toward the south, on a blue cloud (blue line or band). The third row is like the first, and the fourth row, that farthest east, is like the second ; but the dancing-ground for these two rows is called mist instead of cloud. This picture has some general resemblance to that shown in plate VII ; the most notable difference being that the former has four rows of dancers and the latter but two. The author is in possession of a diagram of this dry-painting. *H*a*t*á*l*i Natlói, from whom most of the above information was derived, says that he has made, or caused to be made, this picture but three times in his whole professional career.

44. Names for the forgotten picture are : naak*h*aí tláni yiká*l*, picture of many naak*h*aí dancers; yiká*l* tláni, many pictures, and naki*d*á*t*a *t*ahaz*t*h*á*ni yiká*l*, picture of dancers in twelve rows.

45. Some shamans say that the corn grew on the shores of the lake, and the picture seems to indicate this idea.

46. This is like the picture of the whirling logs, shown in plate VI, but it has four additional symbols radiating from the centre ; a symbol of tobacco in the southeast (west of the white corn), one of bean in the southwest, one of squash in the northwest, and one of wa, or bee-weed (*Cleome pungens*), in the northeast.

47. In many of the myths it is represented that crops grown in the gardens of the gods, or by men from seed obtained from the gods, grow, ripen, and increase with fabulous rapidity.

48. Na*t*án bikï'*t* *t*oi*h*ás*t*a, no sleep over the corn, or, freely translated, vigil of the corn.

49. A*t*é*th*aiĕni, Between Horns Dead, the magpie, I*g*á*ng*ïsiĕni, On Back Dead, the crow. Comparing this with note 27, it will be seen that the poetic or religious names, while nearly similar in meaning, differ in form in the two myths. The suffix ĕni or ni is often by the Navahoes added to the names of the dead; it is equivalent to our expression " late."

50. The ke*t*án yal*t*í', or talking kethawn, is made of willow. It consists of two parts each about four inches long. One is black and represents a god or *H*ast*s*ébaka. The other is blue and represents a goddess or *H*ast*s*ébaad. They are bound together with a string on which is a bead of white shell. A picture of this object is given in " The Mountain Chant," [12] fig. 59. Perhaps there are other forms of talking kethawns.

51. Here we have a definite statement that there are four war-gods ; that *L*éyaneyani and Tsówenatlehi are distinct myths. See par. 76.

52. The following brief description of these kethawns has been recorded : Each is a span long ; all are painted white ; two are sprinkled with specular iron ore ; one of each pair represents the male, the other the female ; one has, attached to it, a cotton string a natural yard in length. This string secures to the body of the kethawn three feathers of the bluebird and three feathers of the yellow warbler (one from tip of wing, one from base of wing, one from tail). Beads are strung on the string and to its distal end a turkey feather and an eagle feather are attached.

53. "A disease exists in Zuñi, which Mr. Cushing, freely translating the Zuñi name, used to call the 'warps.' It consists of a gradually increasing, symmetrical, antero-posterior curvature of the spine, which, when it reaches completion, after years of progress, brings the knees in close proximity to the chest and renders walking impossible. The patient is obliged to go around on short crutches and is reduced to a helpless condition, his only useful occupation being the knitting of stockings. The disease is not accompanied by abscesses or sinuses, and the general health of the afflicted person is not seriously impaired. It is said that on the first appearance of the malady, if the patient will permit himself to be tied night and day to a straight board, he may avoid the worst consequences ; but either this is not an infallible remedy, or there are some who have not the fortitude to submit to it, for the writer has seen at least half a dozen sufferers in the pueblo of Zuñi, all adults and mostly males." The above remarks are from a work by the author entitled, " Human Bones of the Hemenway Collection" (Memoirs of the National Academy of Sciences, vol. vi, p. 172). In the same connection we describe diseased vertebræ excavated by the Hemenway Southwestern Archæological Expedition in Arizona and New Mexico, that probably belonged to patients who suffered with " warps." This disease is said to exist among the Navahoes ; but it must be rare— the author has never met with an example of it among them.

54. Songs of sequence of the Navajos. (In Journal of American Folk-Lore, vol. vii, no. xxvi., pp. 185–194, Boston and New York, July–September, 1894.)

55. Ni'na*h*okád*dd*ïne', contracted into Na*h*okád*dd*ïne' and Ninokád*d*ïne', means People Standing on the Ground and is here translated People on the Earth. By this term, it is thought, the Navahoes designate the whole Indian race, as distinct from whites, Chinese, and other foreign races, and, in the myths, as distinguished from divinities. The word *D*ïné' is applied to the whole human race (although it is also the name proper of the Navahoes), and is sometimes used even in speaking of gods. The Hidatsa Indians of North Dakota had a term of similar significance (Amáka No*h*páka, People on the Earth) to especially designate the Indian race ; it included all tribes. If such a term has been found in other Indian languages, we are not aware of it. Dr. Albert S. Gatschet tells me he knows of none.

56. The Navahoes no longer make pipes and rarely use them,—the cigarette is their favorite,— but the pipe was once seen employed in the rites, and there are many traditions that pipes were formerly used and made by the Navahoes. Old broken terra-cotta pipes are sometimes picked up in the Navaho land. This place where pipes were made is said to be somewhere near Washington Pass.

57. Tsónsïla is the name of two high wooded buttes, about 25 miles north of Fort Defiance, in Arizona, near its eastern boundary line. Washington Pass separates them. The name, which signifies Stars in a Row, and has been translated Twin Stars, is of mythic origin. In recent government maps they are called Sonsala Buttes.

58. Very little has been found out about the god *H* astséel*t*od i. He seems to be a Navaho Mercury. One informant compared him to the orderly standing before the door at headquarters in Fort Wingate, and said that he stood in waiting to bear the messages of the other gods. The meaning of the name has not been determined.

59. Friezes, dadoes, and other interior wall decorations are often found in the ruined cliff-dwellings of the southwest. In Zuñi, it has become common, of late years, to paint friezes on the outsides of the buildings. This was not done 20 years ago.

60. It is thought unlucky among the Navahoes, now, to point at a rainbow with any digit but the thumb. If you point with one of the fingers, they say you will get a felon on it.

61. This was a mode of expressing surprise common to many Indian tribes of North America. The Navahoes use sign language only to a very limited extent.

62. Frequently in the myths, we find evidence of a relationship between the bighorn and mist

or moisture.   The Gánaskĭ*d*i or Bighorn Gods seem to be gods of the mist.   The following was told by a medicine-man : " In these days, when the Navahoes are hunting and the weather is too dry, if they kill a Rocky Mountain sheep, they cut out the tripe, clear it of its contents, and slap the moist interior surface against a stone.   This act in summer brings rain, and in winter, snow."

63.   T*s*úskai or T*s*ó*ĭ*skai, as the Navahoes call it, is a prominent conical hill, rising 8,800 feet above sea level in northwestern New Mexico about 26 miles north of Defiance Station, on the Atlantic and Pacific Railroad.   It is called Chusca Knoll, Chusca Peak, and Choiskai Peak by geographers.   It rises abruptly four hundred feet or more above the level of the neighboring ridge. It is visible at a great distance from the south and forms a prominent landmark.   The Navahoes limit the name T*s*úskai to this knoll ; but the Mexicans and the Americans apply the name in different forms to the whole mountain mass from which the knoll rises.   The name contains the words for spruce (t*s*o) and white (kai) but it has not been accurately translated.   According to the myth of the mountain chant, the holy dwellers of T*s*úskai are the Maidens Who Become Bears ; but this myth describes divinities of another sort.

64.   T*s*áapani signifies a Bat (buckskin-wing).   It is a name of a prominent pinnacle in the Chelly Cañon near the mouth of Monument Creek.

65.   This is an act of divination on the part of the gods.   *H*ast*s*éyal*t*i, although not informed of the purpose of the other gods, suspects it and endeavors to thwart it by putting his bow and arrows last on the trail and making them of the most inferior quality ; but his precautions have precisely the opposite effect to what he intended they should have.

66.   Navaho ethics do not require a very strict adherence to truth.   The myths indicate that under certain circumstances, falsehood is not only permissible but commendable, as it is, perhaps, with all races of men.   But this myth shows us that a solemn pledge is regarded as very sacred. The mother of the stricken twins is represented as submitting to much torture and willingly facing a most painful death rather than break her pledge, and the father, although apparently he has no personal suffering to fear, conceals his paternity as long as possible.

67.   The writer has heard ethnologists aver that the custom of shaking hands was unknown to the American Indians, previous to the Columbian discovery and that white men introduced it. These scholars would say that the incident here recorded is a growth in the myth.   The author is not one of those who entertain this idea ; he thinks there is evidence that the habit was prehistoric in America.   The ordinary Navaho greeting, a*h*aláni, seems to be derived from *h*ála, the hand.

68.   This is now the name of a ruin on the opposite side of the valley from the eastern Moki villages.   It was occupied within historic times.   By many whites the name is spelled and pronounced Tallyhogan or Tallahogan ; but the author has noted it differently.   The common translation is Singing House and we have seen the speculation advanced, that it was so called because there was a Catholic mission there once and the priests sang in it (as if the heathens did not sing enough). Navahoes, whom the author has questioned, say that *Th*ála*h*ogan means a House on a Promontory or Headland, if we may be allowed to apply the term promontory to a bluff or mesa that juts into a lower plain instead of a sea.   This is the Awátobi of the Moki Indians.

69.   The Navaho expression is here translated literally.   It is worthy of study as being the equivalent of the vulgar English imprecation, " Go to Hell ! "   We know of no better equivalent for t*s*ï′ndi than devil.

70.   This is one of several passages in the myth which indicate that among the Mokis, as among the Navahoes, the women have much influence and power.

71.   In all this description of the misfortune of the Mokis, we have but an exaggerated account, with mythic accessories, of the real difficulties experienced by Indian farmers in the arid region of the southwest.

72.   Here as in many other places we have forcibly taught the propriety of paying the shaman well for his services.

73. *H*astsétso signifies Great *H*astsé (God or Genius, see par. 24.)   Kli'stso or *L*ï'stso means Great Serpent.   The one seems to be a thunder god ; the other, a lightning god.   Lightning, atsï'niklï*s*, is regarded as a celestial serpent.   The insect *D*óntso is one which stridulates at the approach of a storm, hence his association with these gods.

74. This is but one of many accounts, in the Navaho myths, of men changed in appearance and beautified by means of magic rites.   In the myth of the mountain chant it is the Butterfly Goddess who appropriately makes the transformation.

75. This picture was once seen by the author, painted on the floor of the medicine-lodge ; but the sketches and description were lost.   It consisted of four rows of figures chiefly representations of the god *H*astséhog*an*.

76. The suffix *d*o seems usually to indicate desire.   It is commonly translated in this work by the English potential auxiliary, may ; thus, nasá*d*o is rendered, may I walk   But in some cases the context makes this translation of such doubtful propriety that in former works we have often rendered, in the indicative, words ending in *d*o, thus, nasá*d*o, I walk.

77. Plates VI, VII, and VIII are from paintings by Mr. Delancy W. Gill of Washington, copied under the supervision of the author from rude drawings by the latter.   They have often been submitted to shamans for observation and comment, to meet with invariable approval.   The blue and red colors in the plates are somewhat more brilliant than the corresponding colors of the original dry-paintings ; but the general effect is much alike in both.   Pictures of the same subjects, differing somewhat from these in detail, have previously appeared in the following work :— "Ceremonial of Hasjelti Dailjis and mythicals and paintings of the Navajo Indians," by James Stevenson.   (In eighth annual report of the Bureau of Ethnology, pp. 229–285, Washington, 1891).

INDEX

Plates

PLATE I.

A. — Preparations for making kethawns of the third day. See pars. 175, 374–382.

B. — Medicine-lodge in the morning after the completion of the ceremony. See par. 238.

C. — Ordinary Navaho sudatory. See par. 245.

D. — Arbor as seen from the door of the medicine-lodge. See par. 242.

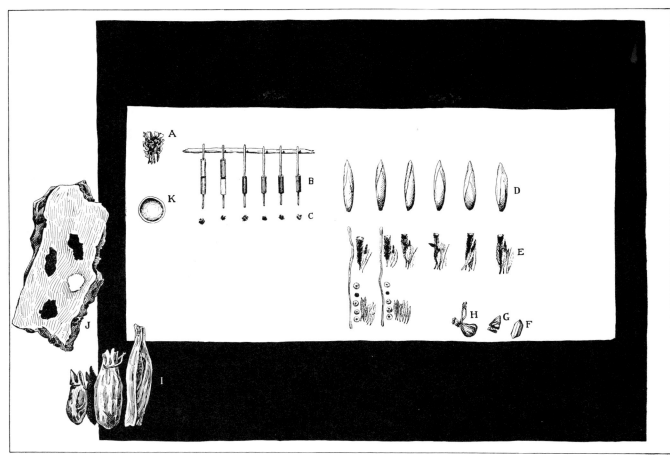

Fig. A

Fig. B

Fig. C

Fig. D

PLATE II.

A. — Vertical view of sweat-house, showing decorations on first and third days of sudorific treatment.

B. — Same as A, showing variant of decorations.

C. —- First dry-painting.

D. — Second dry-painting.

E. — Wooden kethawns of the ketan ĺáni, one male and one female of each color, two views of each.

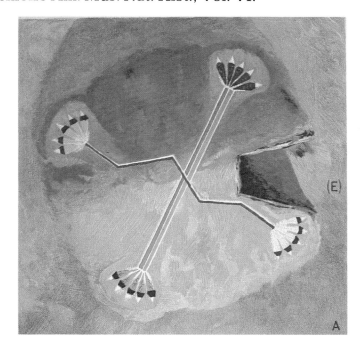

(E)

A

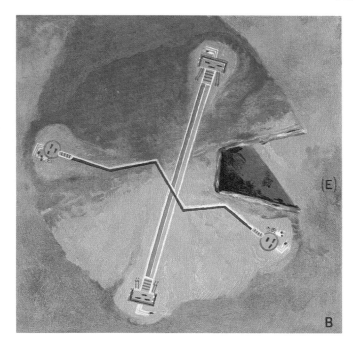

(E)

B

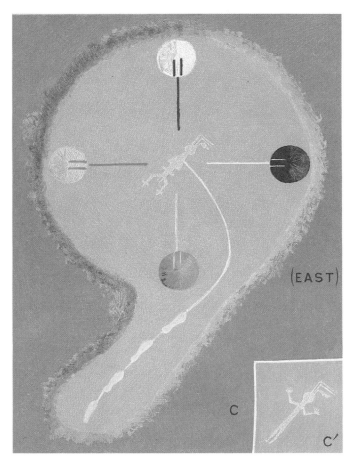

(EAST)

C

C′

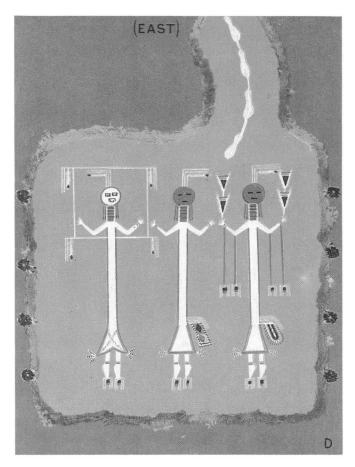

(EAST)

D

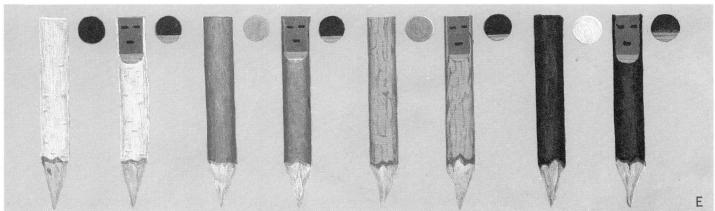

E

PLATE III.

PLATE IV.

A. — One of the eight plumed wands, female. See pars. 279–284.
B. — Talisman of the Yébïtsai, open. } See par. 285.
C. — Talisman of the Yébïtsai, closed. }
D. — Ceremonial basket, basket-drum. See pars. 286–291.
E. — Ceremonial basket, meal-basket. See pars. 286, 292.
F. — Yucca drumstick. See pars. 293–297.
G. — Yucca mask, incomplete. } See pars. 357–361.
H. — Yucca mask, complete. }

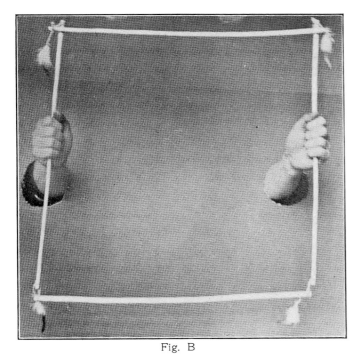

Fig. B

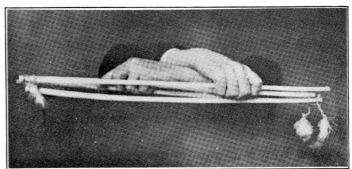

Fig. C

Fig. F

Fig. D

Fig. E

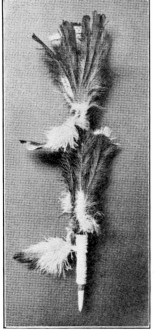

Fig. A

Fig. G

Fig. H

PLATE V.

A. — Ke*l*án *l*áni arranged in ceremonial basket. See pars. 172, 397–419.

B. — Batter for alkán or sweet bread, in a hole in the ground, lined with sheepskin. See par. 221.

C. — Kïninaékai or White House, a ruined cliff-dwelling in the Chelly Cañon. See par. 390.

D. — View in the Chelly Cañon ; the Monuments and Tsé'ïntyel or Broad Rock. See par. 905 and note 32.

Plate V

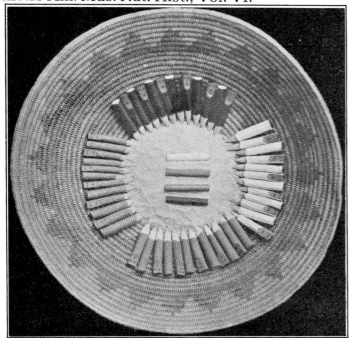

Fig. A

Fig. B

Fig. D

Fig. C

PLATE VI.

Dry-painting of the sixth day, *sĭlnéole* yikál, or picture of the whirling logs. See pars. 515–525.

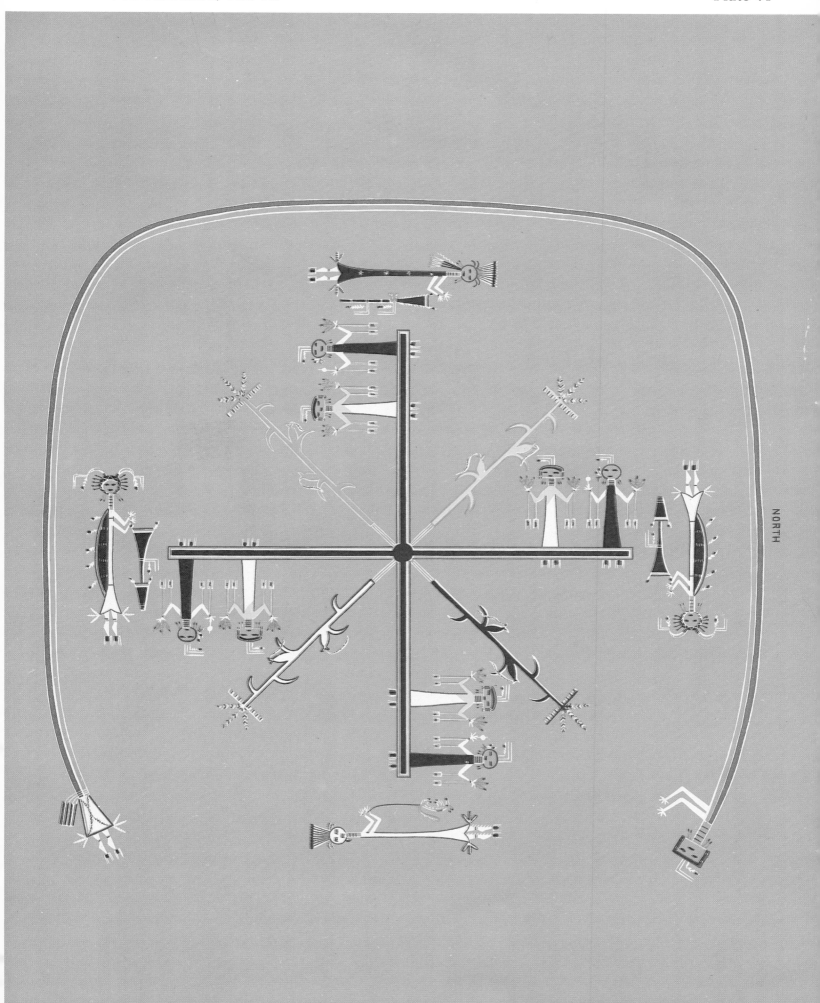

NORTH

PLATE VII.

Dry-painting of the seventh day, naak/ai yiká/, or picture of the naak/ai dance.   See pars. 553–554.

Plate VII

NORTH

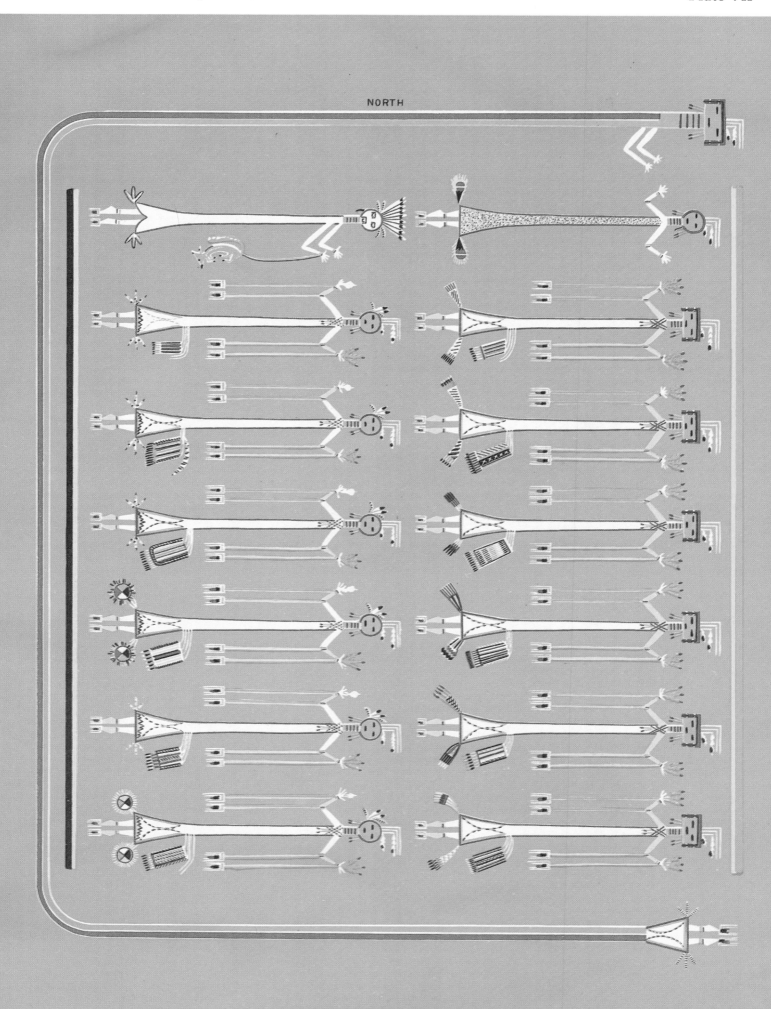

PLATE VIII.

Dry-painting of the eighth day, Dsaha*d*oldzábe yiká*l*, or picture with the Fringe Mouths. See pars. 567–572.

NORTH

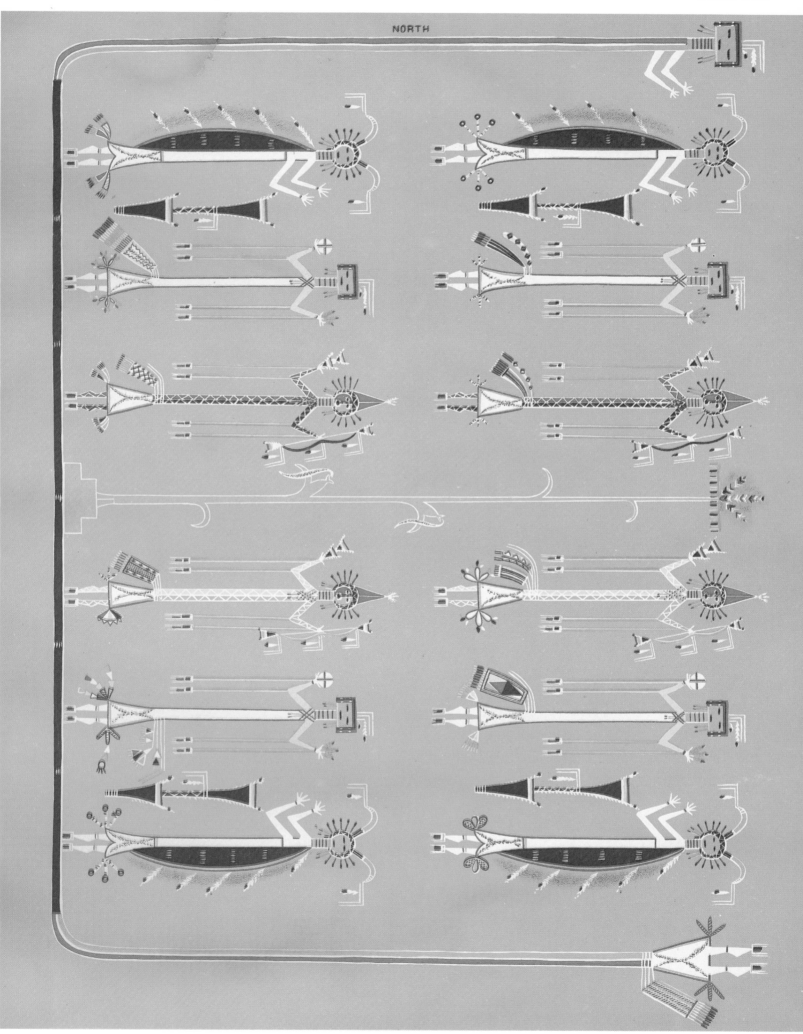

NORTH